Barcode in Back

International Perspectives of Festivals and Events: Paradigms of Analysis

International Perspectives of Festivals and Events: Paradigms of Analysis

Edited by
Jane Ali-Knight, Martin Robertson,
Alan Fyall and Adele Ladkin

AMSTERDAM • BOSTON • HEIDELBERG • LONDON • OXFORD • NEW YORK
PARIS • SAN DIEGO • SAN FRANCISCO • SINGAPORE • SYDNEY • TOKYO
Academic Press is an imprint of Elsevier

Academic Press is an imprint of Elsevier
525 B Street, Suite 1900, San Diego, California 92101-4495, USA
30 Corporate Drive, Suite 400, Burlington, MA 01803, USA
32 James town Road, London NW1 7BY, UK

First edition 2008

British Library Cataloguing-in-Publication Data
A catalogue record for this book is available from the British Library

Library of Congress Cataloging-in-Publication Data
A catalog record for this book is available from the Library of Congress

ISBN: 978-0-08-045100-8

For information on all Academic Press publications
visit our web site at www.books.elsevier.com

Typeset by Charon Tec Ltd., A Macmillan Company
(www.macmillansolutions.com)

Printed and bound in the Great Britain by MPG Books Ltd, Bodmin, Cornwall

08 09 10 11   10 9 8 7 6 5 4 3 2 1

Contents

Foreword

The nature of events, the nature of festivals and the nature of the event experience are changing far more rapidly than any of us in the industry could have imagined 10 years ago. The business of creating excellent arts events, of enabling high profile and rewarding sport events and the art of ensuring successful business events cross our lives in many exciting ways. Understanding this great dynamic has ensured that the City of Melbourne has become a major international player in the field of events and has a comprehensive event portfolio. For Melbourne to maintain its prominent position in the events industry amid increasing competition from other leading cities, we must draw upon knowledge in this field and stay abreast of changing market trends. Texts such as this play an important part in providing access to the growing body of knowledge that now exists in the events field and will help us maintain our competitive edge.

Brendan McClements
Chief Executive Officer
Victorian Major Events
Company Limited

About the Authors

Jane Ali-Knight is an affiliate of the Centre for Festival and Event Management at Napier University.

Responsible for the development of the Festival and Event Management programme at Napier University, Edinburgh, she is currently teaching and working in event tourism in the UAE. She has presented at major international and national conferences and has published in the areas of wine tourism, tourism, festival and event marketing and management. She is on the editorial boards of the *Journal of Vacation Marketing*, *International Journal of Event Management Research* and the *World Journal of Managing Events*, and has also been a Special Edition Editor for *Event Management*.

Graham Brown is Professor of Tourism Management at the University of South Australia. He gained his PhD from Texas A&M University. An enduring interest in the management of festivals and events has included studies that range from an examination of a clown festival in Bournemouth, England and a wine festival in the Okanagan Valley, Canada, to an event to celebrate a solar eclipse in outback Australia. Mega-events have not escaped his attention and he has published widely on the relationship between tourism and the Olympic Games with a particular focus on the role of corporate hospitality.

Thanh-Huong Bui is a PhD student at Department of Tourism, Leisure, Hotel and Sport Management at Griffith University, Queensland, Australia. Her tourism related expertise has been the result of 12 years industry experience as well as teaching and policy consulting. She is a former lecturer of Faculty of Management and Tourism – Hanoi University. Her PhD research interests cover anthropology of tourism, tourism development in Southeast Asia, particularly in Vietnam and youth tourism.

Misuk Byeon is a candidate for the PhD degree at the Department of Tourism, University of Otago New Zealand.

She has completed both a Postgraduate Diploma in Tourism and a Masters of Tourism at the University of Otago. Prior to academia, Misuk has acted as an interpreter at two major international sporting events, the 1986 Asian Games and the 1988 Seoul Olympic Games after she gained a BA (Thai Language) at HanKuk University of Foreign Studies in South Korea. She also worked as an Operation Manager for the Travel Company in Thailand for nearly seven years.

Misuk's research interests are mega-event impacts and management, travel behaviour, destination marketing and management, and hospitality management and marketing.

Neil Carr (PhD, University of Exeter) is a Senior Lecturer in Tourism at the University of Otago. His research focuses on leisure and tourist behaviour. In particular, Neil's research is focused on young people, university students, children, families, and non-humans (particularly dogs) and their owners. In addition, Neil has undertaken research into visitor safety and education, and gender differences and gendered identities within the pleasure environment. Neil has published over 35 peer-reviewed papers in a variety of academic journals and edited books and is on the editorial boards of three journals, including the *Annals of Leisure Research*.

Krzysztof Celuch joined the meetings industry as a tour leader for a number of DMC's in 2000 following a short career as an event coordinator in the SPA centre.

In 2004, he joined *MICE Poland* magazine as a journalist and over a period of three years, published more that 50 articles about the meetings industry. Following five years as a student he joined Meeting Professionals International and The Society of Incentive and Travel Executives. In February 2006, he got a scholarship from the Women's Leadership Initiative and decided to start his PhD studies in Warsaw University.

Krzysztof has spoken at numerous events including SITE's ESNEP conference in Warsaw, SITE's seminar in EIBTM Barcelona and Future Leaders Forum in Frankfurt, Pattaya and Warsaw. He is a chairman of MPI POLAND CLUB Steering Committee. He currently works with the Warsaw Convention Bureau as a Project Manager. He is also a lecturer in business tourism in the University of Economics and Computer Science based in Warsaw. He is also the organiser of the IMEX/MPI Future Leaders Forum in Warsaw.

Each year he launches annual Warsaw Meetings Industry Report on current and future developments in the conference meetings industry in Warsaw.

In 2007 he was nominated as one of *The Meeting Professional* magazine's '30 people under 30 age currently making an impact on the global meetings community'.

Shirley Chappel is an adjunct lecturer in the School of Management at the University of South Australia. She lectures in tourism. Her current research interest is in the ways in which tourism and events have been used to tell Australia's story and to reflect its debates about identity. She is also interested in literary tourism, particularly in the use of Australian fiction to interpret the Australian landscape.

Rob Davidson is a Senior Lecturer in Business Travel and Tourism at the University of Westminster in London. He joined the University in 1998, after spending nine years in France teaching at two universities (Lille and Montpellier) and at the ESSEC-Cornell Institute of Management in Paris. Prior to that, he spent five years as Education and Training Manager with *VisitBritain* in London. His main areas of expertise are conference and business travel, and he has written widely on these themes. His latest book was published in 2006: *Marketing Destinations and Venues for Conferences, Conventions and Business Events*, co-written with Tony Rogers of the British Association of Conference Destinations. In addition, he regularly writes articles for the professional business tourism press, including *Conference News*. Rob also runs his own *consultancy* business, and has carried out research for a number of major conference organisations in the United Kingdom and overseas.

Ros Derrett OAM is an academic at Southern Cross University (SCU), Australia. She lectures in planning, marketing, special interest tourism and event management. She has worked extensively in education, community development and arts administration in Australia and overseas.

Ros' interests and research activities have been in the areas of regional cultural and tourism development, identifying opportunities for collaborative events, enterprises and projects, with effective management strategies and community consultation. She has developed and managed imaginative collaborative multidisciplinary projects and business enterprises. Her doctoral research investigated community resilience through the nature and role of regional community cultural events.

Ros is the Head of SCU's Office of Regional Engagement committed to partnerships that enhance the region's economic prosperity, socio-cultural well-being and environmental sustainability.

Dr Geoff Dickson is an Associate Director of the New Zealand Tourism Research Institute where he leads the event tourism research programme area. He also leads AUT University's undergraduate and postgraduate sport management programmes. Prior to his appointment at AUT, he spent seven years at Central Queensland University. He has a PHD from the School of Marketing and Management at Griffith University (Australia).

Dr Jörgen Elbe is currently working as a Senior Lecturer in Business Administration at Dalarna University, Sweden, where he is teaching marketing. He received a PhD in Business Studies at Uppsala University in 2002 and his thesis is on destination marketing and development. He is actively engaged in the development of the tourism programmes, both on undergraduate and masters level, at Dalarna University, and he is also involved in several international exchanges within the field of tourism and marketing, including several countries in Europe as well as China. His research interests include events, destination marketing and tourism export.

Professor Malcolm Foley is Head of Learning, Teaching and Quality in the Caledonian Business School at Glasgow Caledonian University. With over 20 years of experience Malcolm is an expert in festivals and events development having worked for various national government organisations in Singapore, Indonesia, South Africa and South Korea. Malcolm has researched and published extensively on subjects as broad ranging as consumption, globalisation, culture, tourism, events and sport. In particular his work on Dark Tourism has won him international acclaim.

Dr Warwick Frost is a Senior Lecture in Tourism, Events and Heritage at Monash University in Australia. His background is in music and community events. He was the Convenor of the 150th Anniversary of the Australian Gold Rushes (2001), which won the Tourism Victoria Award for Best New Tourism Product. His research interests are in events, rural tourism, heritage, film-induced tourism and national parks. He is co-editor (with C. Michael Hall) of *Tourism and National Parks: International Perspectives on Development, Histories and Change* which will be published by Routledge in 2008.

Alan Fyall is Reader in Tourism Management in the International Centre for Tourism & Hospitality Research and Deputy Dean Research & Enterprise in the School of Services Management at Bournemouth University, UK. Alan has published widely with his areas of expertise spanning the management of attractions, heritage tourism and destination management. Alan has co-edited Managing Visitor Attractions: New Directions and Managing World Heritage Sites published by Elsevier Butterworth Heinemann, while he has co-authored Tourism Marketing: A Collaborative Approach and the third and fourth editions of Tourism Principles and Practice published by Channel View and Pearson Education respectively. Alan has managed a number of projects on the determination of suitable structures for emerging Destination Management Organisations in the UK while he has also conducted work in the Caribbean and Southern Africa for the Commonwealth Secretariat which delivered a strategic framework for future interventions by the Secretariat in the tourism sector. In addition, Alan has undertaken projects in most countries within the European Union, South

East Asia, India, the USA and Australia while he has served as an adviser to the EU on a tourism development project in Turkmenistan, Central Asia. Alan is currently serving as an adviser to the Commonwealth Tourism Centre based in Kuala Lumpur, Malaysia.

C. Michael Hall is a Professor of Marketing at the University of Canterbury, Christchurch, New Zealand and Docent, Department of Geography, University of Oulu, Finland. As Co-editor of Current Issues in Tourism, he has published widely in the areas of tourism, regional development, events and environmental history.

Dr Matthew Harvey is a lecturer in the School of Law at Victoria University, Melbourne, Australia. His PhD examined the impact of the European Union on national and international identities. His research and teaching interests include tourism law and legal issues relating to wine branding, appellation and marketing.

Lee Jolliffe is an Associate Professor in the Faculty of Business, University of New Brunswick Saint John, Canada and a Visiting Professor at Hanoi University. With an academic background in museum studies she has developed research interests in various aspects of cultural heritage tourism including the relationship of tea and coffee heritage and experiences to tourism. In 2007 she edited the book, Tea and Tourism: Tourists, Traditions and Transformations, published by Channel View and is currently working on a volume on Coffee and Tourism. Lee is on the editorial boards of Annals of Tourism Research; Journal of Heritage Tourism; Tourism – An International Journal and the International Journal of Tourism Policy.

Dr Ian Jones is Associate Dean for Sport and Leisure, and Acting Director of the Centre for Event and Sport Research (CESR), based in the School of Services Management at Bournemouth University. His research interests have continued to focus upon the relationships between sporting identities, and the concept of 'serious leisure'. His main teaching areas lie in the areas of sport sociology and research methods for sport and leisure. He is co-author of *Research Methods for Sport Studies* and co-editor of both *Leisure Cultures: Investigations in Media, Technology and Sport*, and *Serious Leisure: Extensions and Applications*. Ian is also a member of the Editorial Advisory Boards for the *Journal of Sport & Tourism* and the *Journal of Hospitality, Leisure, Sport and Tourism Education*.

Professor Adele Ladkin is Professor of Tourism Employment and Associate Dean of Tourism and Hospitality within the International Centre for Tourism and Hospitality Research, School of Services Management, Bournemouth University. She graduated with a BA in Geography from the University of Leicester, and worked in travel sales before undertaking an MSc in Tourism Management at the University of Surrey. Her PhD was gained at the University of Surrey in the area of human resources management in tourism and hospitality.

Her research interests and publications are in the areas of events and conventions, tourism education, career analysis and labour mobility in tourism and hospitality, and hospitality leadership. She has worked on a variety of research projects of national and international significance for both private and public sector organisations in these areas. Her current research in the convention field is focused on career development and human resource issues, with a particular interest in work history research methods. Professor Ladkin is Editor in Chief for the *International Journal of Tourism Research*.

Dr Janne J. Liburd is an Associate Professor and Director of Research, Centre for Tourism, Culture and Innovation at the University of Southern Denmark. She is a cultural anthropologist and her research interests are in the field of sustainable tourism development. She has published on national park development, heritage tourism, cruise tourism, tourism innovation, tourism crisis communication, Corporate Social Responsibility, NGOs and democratic accountability in the Eastern Caribbean. Dr Liburd has conducted a number of research projects relating to competence development for tourism practitioners and tourism educators. Dr Liburd is the chair of the *B.E.S.T. Education Network.*

Jane Lovell is a Senior Lecturer and Programme Director of the Events Management Undergraduate Programme at Canterbury Christ Church University. She worked at the Royal Opera House in Covent Garden for 10 years and went on to become the Tourism Development Officer for Canterbury City Council; responsible for the tourism strategy for Canterbury, Whitstable and Herne Bay, and managing events such as a city-wide outdoor sculpture show 'Blok' and the French-English Cathédrales en Lumière. Her PhD is entitled 'Cities of Imagination' and investigates the authenticity and experience of historic cities.

Dr David McGillivray is a Senior Lecturer in the Division of Cultural Business, Glasgow Caledonian University. His doctoral thesis applied a Foucauldian conceptual framework to the context of work–leisure relations. His recent research investigations have focused on the events-led urban entrepreneurial strategies of developed and emerging global cities. He has also recently published on the sports fan experience of the Germany 2006 World Cup Fan Parks, applying a Foucauldian critical lens to consider this emerging events-related phenomenon. Commissioned research work includes an evaluation of the design and delivery of cultural entitlements in a Scottish rural environment.

Dr Gayle McPherson is the Head of the Division of Cultural Business and a Senior Lecturer in Cultural Policy at Glasgow Caledonian University. She leads a team with interests in the consumption and production of festivals and events, both on a global scale and in enhancing community interests and in using culture to develop the social economy. She has a particular interest in the social and cultural impacts and benefits of events on local communities. Commissioned research work includes the use of culture, as a planning tool, in deprived communities to develop social economy. She co-wrote the Culture, Ceremonies and Education element of the successful Commonwealth Games bid Glasgow 2014 and was the cultural advisor for over a year.

Professor Simon Milne is the Director of the NZTRI. His research interests centre on regional development, the impact of new technologies on the tourism industry both with a view of improving the sustainability of tourism development in small resource dependent communities and large urban areas. Dr Milne has worked for several international agencies as a consultant (UNDP, UNESCAP, EU, CORFO, CIDA) and has conducted research in the Caribbean (Grenada, Cuba, Tobago), Canada, Vietnam, the Philippines, the South Pacific islands, Kenya, Russia and New Zealand.

Michael Morgan is a Senior Lecturer in the School of Services Management at Bournemouth University in Great Britain. He is the author of *Marketing for Leisure and Tourism* (Prentice Hall, 1996) and a number of journal articles and book chapters on destination marketing and elite sports competitions. His current research interests are in the area of consumer or participant experiences of leisure and tourism.

Thy-Hang Nguyen is a graduate of the Faculty of Management and Tourism (FMT), Hanoi University where she is currently an Assistant Teacher. Her graduation thesis focused on the relationship of coffee and tourism in Vietnam. She is also the coordinator for the University of California at Berkeley student abroad term in Hanoi.

Alexandros Paraskevas is a Senior Lecturer in Strategic Management in the Department of Hospitality Leisure and Tourism Management of the Business School at Oxford Brookes University. His research area is crisis/disaster management and business continuity in the hospitality and tourism sector. His doctoral research focuses on organisational crisis signal detection from a complexity theory perspective. Alexandros is an advisor of the Global Security and Crisis Management Council of the International Hotel and Restaurant Association (IHRA).

Martin Robertson is Lecturer in Events Management in the School of Hospitality, Marketing and Tourism, Faculty of Business and Law, Victoria University, Melbourne Australia. He has extensive public and private sector experience in the tourism and hospitality sectors (UK, Spain and Australia). Martin's research output is in the area of sport events and festivals, with particular focus on the areas of brand narrative, and socio-cultural and economic evaluation. In 2007 he co-edited special double issues of the journals *Event Management – an international journal and Managing Leisure – an international journal*. He edited the text *Sporting Events and Event Tourism: Impact, Plans and Opportunities* (2006) and co-edited the text books *Events and Festivals – Current Trends and Issues* (2008); *Festival and Event Management – An International Arts and Culture Perspective* (2004), and *Managing Tourism in Cities: Policy, Process and Practice* (1998).

Deborah Sadd is a PhD scholar in the School of Services Management at Bournemouth University, researching the urban regeneration legacies associated with the hosting of mega-events and in particular leveraging the legacy for London 2012. She is using both Sydney and Barcelona as case studies to develop a model of best practice for London 2012. Deborah completed a Tourism Management and Planning Masters degree in September 2004 with distinction. The research for her Masters was undertaken in Weymouth and Portland, Dorset, prior to the successful 2012 Olympic Bid. This research project is ongoing. She also completed in 2006 a Masters in Event Management. She teaches on the BA Events Management and MSc Events Management programmes as well as undertaking guest lectures within the Sports Management programme. Her research interests include social impacts of events, urban regeneration opportunities from events, legacy planning and in particular the opportunities to be gained from the hosting of London 2012 not just for the communities hosting the games in London, but also for the host community of Weymouth, the nearest Olympic venue to Bournemouth.

Richard Shipway is a Senior Lecturer in Sport Studies in the Centre for Event and Sport Research (CESR) at Bournemouth University. His areas of research interest include sport tourism, the impact and legacies of sporting events, Olympic studies (specifically social impacts, Olympic tourism and multiculturalism) and ethnographic studies in sport. Recent work includes studies of the social impacts of both Olympic tourism and sport tourism, including an analysis of residents' perceptions of the development of Europe's first artificial surf reef in Bournemouth, and a longitudinal Olympic project assessing host community reactions to major sporting events in Weymouth and Portland, host destination for the sailing events of the 2012 Games. Richard has also published on the experiences of endurance athletes as sport tourists. In 2007, Richard was awarded the prestigious Winston Churchill Memorial Trust Fellowship to undertake a community based Olympic sport project in Australia.

Dr Andrew Smith is a Senior Lecturer in Tourism within the School of Architecture and the Built Environment at the University of Westminster. Andrew's research mainly focuses on cities, in particular the tourism and image effects of flagship urban projects. More recently, he has published work on the relationship between events and urban regeneration. He completed a PhD thesis on a related theme in 2002, and subsequently has published research in journals such as *Urban Studies*, *Annals of Tourism Research* and *Tourism Geographies*. Andrew was involved in evaluating the SRB programme associated with Manchester's 2002 Commonwealth Games and he recently won an award for his paper on the value of 'sports-city zones' as tourism resources for urban areas. His teaching responsibilities include leading a new MA module in Events Tourism.

Chris Stone PhD MTS FHEA is a tourism expert and Senior Lecturer in Tourism Management in the Department of Food and Tourism Management at Manchester Metropolitan University. Before joining the institution, he devised and managed the first undergraduate and foundation degree programmes at the University of Sunderland, building on industry experience gained in a previous position managing consultancy projects serving the British tourism, leisure and environment sectors. A qualified university educator, he has a professional interest in quality issues in higher education, and acts as external examiner for tourism programmes at Bournemouth and Liverpool Hope Universities. Chris was appointed as EU TEMPUS Academic Expert in 2003, and reappointed in 2007 (for the 'Seventh Framework Programme', FP7) to serve until 2013.

Dr Marion Stuart-Hoyle started her career in teaching at a further education institution delivering a Higher National Diploma in Travel and Tourism Management and has been a principal lecturer in Tourism Studies at Canterbury Christ Church University since 1995. Her doctoral research focused on the development of Tourism as a subject in higher education. Her current teaching interests include Tourism Marketing and Heritage Tourism and her research focuses on teaching and learning strategies that take a blended learning approach and heritage tourism.

Professor Rhodri Thomas is ITT Professor of Tourism and Events Policy, UK Centre for Events Management, Leeds Metropolitan University. His research interests relate broadly to public policy issues and tourism, especially in relation to festivals, SMEs and economic development. He has recently acted as 'specialist expert' for the European Commission and OECD, and as International Evaluator for the National Research Foundation for South Africa.

Ms Fiona Wheeler is a PhD student and Research Assistant in the Monash University Tourism Research Unit. She holds a Masters in Tourism Management from Hong Kong Polytechnic University, which she gained while living in Asia for five years (1999–2004). Fiona's PhD research draws on multidisciplinary perspectives relating to branding, place, region, heritage and identity in order to examine the relationship between regional destination master branding and the nature and identity of individual destinations at the sub-regional and local levels.

Leanne White is a lecturer in the School of Hospitality, Tourism and Marketing at Victoria University in Melbourne, Australia. She has taught Marketing, Public Relations, Communications and Australian Studies at universities since 1988. Leanne has also worked in the areas of public relations, research and policy in government and higher education. Her research interests include advertising, national identity, commercial nationalism, Australian popular culture and Olympic movement. Leanne's doctoral thesis examined manifestations of official nationalism and commercial nationalism at the Sydney 2000 Olympic Games.

Dr Emma H. Wood is based within the UK Centre for Events Management, Leeds Metropolitan University. She has considerable experience of marketing research within a range of industries and has worked in the United Kingdom, South East Asia and Australia. She has been involved in numerous major research projects that include leading the first national survey of small firms in the events sector and a comprehensive survey of local government use of events for destination marketing. Her consultancy work is specialised in the area of public sector events and has involved a number of social and economic impact studies for local government as well as audience development research and studies of event marketing communication effectiveness. Her academic and consultancy research work is regularly disseminated at national and international conferences, and through academic journals. She is joint editor of the *Journal of Policy Research in Tourism, Leisure and Events* and also sits on the editorial board of two industry-related periodicals. Emma's co-authored book, *Innovative Marketing Communications for the Events Industry*, was published in 2006 by Elsevier.

Richard Wright is a PhD candidate and tutor in the University of Otago's Department of Tourism in Dunedin, New Zealand. Having obtained 1st class Honours from the University of Brighton, he spent several years as a Tourism Officer for his home town of Cambridge. After relocating to New Zealand, his subsequent postgraduate research has largely focused on special interest/niche markets including Film and Sport Tourism. In 2004, he investigated the impact of '*The Lord of the Rings*' tourism in several rural South Island sites and, in 2005, his Masters explored Sport Event Tourism at a regional level, comparing the approaches adopted by Region Tourism Organisations for the British and Irish Lions Tour. His current PhD research focuses on the inter-relationship between sport and tourism, particularly in terms of human behaviour, attachment to place and identity formation. Richard recently had his first article published within a special edition of the *Journal of International Tourism*. He has given or co-produced presentations at conferences in both New Zealand and the United Kingdom.

List of Contributors

Jane Ali-Knight
Napier University, UK.
Phone: +44(0)131 455 4340
E-mail: j.ali-knight@napier.ac.uk

Graham Brown
University of South Australia, Australia.
Phone: +61 8 830 20313
E-mail: Graham.Brown@unisa.edu.au

Thanh Huong Bui
Griffith University, Australia
E-mail: huong_bui@yahoo.com

Misuk Byeon
University of Otago, New Zealand.
Phone: 643479 7693
E-mail: mbyeon@business.otago.ac.hz

Neil Carr
University of Otago, New Zealand.
Phone: +64 3 479 5048
E-mail: ncarr@business.otago.ac.nz

Krzysztof Celuch
University of Economics and Computer
Science, Poland
Phone: +48 22 4572 300
E-mail: krzysztof.celuch@wsei.pl

Shirley Chappel
University of South Australia, Australia.
Phone: +61 8 830 20632
E-mail: shirley.chappel@unisa.edu.au

Rob Davidson
University of Westminister, UK
Phone: +44(0)20 7911 5171
E-mail: davidsr@westminster.ac.uk

Ros Derrett
Southern Cross University, Australia.
Phone: +61 2 66203150
E-mail: Ros.derrett@scu.edu.au

Geoff Dickson
AUT University, New Zealand,
Phone: +64 9 921 9999
E-mail: geoff.dickson@aut.ac.nz

Jörgen Elbe
Dalarna University, Sweden.
Phone: +46 23 77 89 31
E-mail: jel@du.se

Malcolm Foley
Glasgow Caledonian University, UK.
Phone: +44(0)141 331 3260
E-mail: m.t.foley@gcal.ac.uk

Warwick Frost
Monash University, Australia.
Phone: +61 3 9904 7042
E-mail: warwick.frost@buseco.monash.edu.au

Alan Fyall
Bournemouth University, UK.
Phone: : +44 (0) 1202 965496
E-mail: afyall@bournemouth.ac.uk

C. Michael Hall
University of Canterbury, New Zealand.
Phone: +64 3 364 2987 ext. 8612
E-mail: michael.hall@canterbury.ac.nz

Matthew Harvey
Victoria University, Australia
Phone: +613 9919 1838
E-mail: matt.harvey@vu.edu.au

Lee Jolliffe
University of New Brunswick, Canada.
E-mail: ljolliff@unbsj.ca

Ian Jones
Bournemouth University, UK.
Phone: +44 (0) 1202 965164;
E-mail: jonesi@bournemouth.ac.uk

Adele Ladkin
Bournemouth University, UK.
Phone: +44 (0) 1202 965584
E-mail: aladkin@bournemouth.ac.uk

Janne J. Liburd
University of Southern Denmark, Denmark.
Phone: (+45) 6550 1576
E-mail: liburd@sitkom.sdu.dk

Jane Lovell
Canterbury Christchurch, New Zealand.
Phone: 01227 783080
E-mail: jane.lovell@canterbury.ac.uk

David McGillivray
Glasgow Caledonian University, UK.
Phone: +44(0)141 331 8464
E-mail: dmcg@gcal.ac.uk

Gayle McPherson
Glasgow Caledonian University, UK.
Phone: +44(0)141 331 8480
E-mail: g.mcpherson@gcal.ac.uk

Simon Milne
AUT University, New Zealand
Phone: +64 9 921 9999
E-mail: simon.milne@aut.ac.nz

Michael Morgan
Bournemouth University, UK.
Phone: +44 (0) 1202 965174
E-mail: mmorgan@bournemouth.ac.uk

Hang Thy Nguyen
Hanoi University, Vietnam.

Alexandros Paraskevas
Oxford Brookes University, UK.
Phone: +44(0)1865 483835
E-mail: aparaskevas@brooks.ac.uk

Martin Robertson
Victoria University, Australia
Phone: +61 3 9919 4037
E-mail: martin.robertson@vu.edu.au

Deborah Sadd
Bournemouth University, UK.
Phone: +44 (0) 1202 966966
E-mail: dsadd@bournemouth.ac.uk

Richard Shipway
Bournemouth University, UK.
Phone: +44 (0) 1202 965692
E-mail: rshipway@bournemouth.ac.uk

Andrew Smith
University of Westminster, UK.
Phone: +44 (0) 20 7911 5000 ext. 3390
E-mail: smithan@wmin.ac.uk

Chris Stone
Manchester Metropolitan University, UK.
Phone: +44(0)161 247 2745
E-mail: chris.stone@mmu.ac.uk

Marion Stuart-Hoyle
Canterbury Christchurch, New Zealand.
Phone: 01227 782844.

Rhodri Thomas
Leeds Metropolitan University, UK.
Phone: +44(0)113 283 3462
E-mail: r.thomas@leedsmet.ac.uk

Fiona Wheeler
Monash University, Australia.
Phone: +61 3 990 47189
E-mail: Fiona.Wheeler@buseco.monash.edu.au

Leanne White
Victoria University, Australia.
Phone: +61 3 9919 1448
E-mail: leannek.white@vu.edu.au

Emma H. Wood
Leeds Metropolitan University, UK.
Phone: +44(0)113 283 3963
E-mail: e.wood@leedsmet.ac.uk

Richard Wright
University of Otago, New Zealand.
Phone: +64 3 479 5866
E-mail: rwright@business.otago.ac.nz

Introduction

The paradigms of analysis within the pages of this book have as their root a conference co-organised in 2007 by the School of Services Management, Bournemouth University and the Centre for Festival and Event Management, Napier University Business School. While the conference, 'Event Tourism: Enhancing Destinations and the Visitor Economy' brought forward journal publications particular to the conference themes, the range of research concepts, research practice and practical example evidenced around this indicated a need for a more expansive research text. It is from this environment that the book has emerged.

The interrelated nature of festivals and events, the fact that they are cultural, business, economic and emotional occurrences makes thematic distinction a great challenge. We, the editors, have nevertheless divided the work into four core subject themes, each with an introduction by one of the editors:

- Part one, Destination, Image and Development;
- Part two, Community and Identity;
- Part three, Audience and Participant Experience, and
- Part four, Managing the Event.

Through reading these articles the thematic division of the book will become clear. Equally we anticipate many other areas of investigation, interpretation and inference will emerge for the reader from the particular focus given to the subject by the respective author. This is as it should be. While student numbers for the subject area of festivals and events are growing, publication routes are emerging and the event sector grows so too the call for research synthesis is more evident.

As a relatively new research area so too there is a call for ensuring that academic rigour is applied to the analysis of festivals and events and their affect. This is all the more the case when there is a proliferation of research interest in, and evaluative skills being applied to, the social and cultural effects of festivals and events. The other micro and macro economic and business management requirements of events have not disappeared in the meantime. Academic and professional legitimacy for the subject area can only be maintained if quality is evident through all areas of analysis. Thus, we believe International Perspectives of Festivals and Events: Paradigms of Analysis is a distillation of the potential to offer strong components in a multi-disciplined whole.

The editors
Jane Ali-Knight
Martin Robertson
Alan Fyall
Adele Ladkin

PART 1

DESTINATION, IMAGE AND DEVELOPMENT

Martin Robertson

This first section offers five chapters each addressing the role of festivals in forming or at least play-ing a significant role in the definition of destination place. The title of this section, 'Destination, Image and Development' reflects the different areas covered by the respective authors.

In their individual chapters Smith and Saad address an important but yet less documented area of investigation: how do large events affect the viability, visibility and opportunity for developing areas outside the central hub of event activity? In Chapter 1 Smith assesses the function, actual and possible, for major events in promoting areas on the fringe of a city. The objectives of the research undertaken by Smith are threefold: first, to identify how peripheral urban areas can maximise the promotional prospect of major events; second, to evaluate the relationship between the media and these areas and third, an assessment of the potential role of major events as mechanism for promot-ing and improving the image of peripheral areas. Mediating on the interrelationship of the 2007 Tour de France starting stage, *Grand Depart*, London, and the area of Deptford in South East London – a 19th century Dockyard town, which has gone through a prolonged period of downturn in the latter half of the 20th century, the chapter highlights the challenges of attempting multiple (spatial) own-erships of major events. Through a combination of secondary research, semi-structured interviews with key stakeholders and review of related media materials, the work evaluates the success in accu-mulating promotional leverage and opportunities for co-branding association.

Chapter 2 by Saad inquires as to the degree to which the coastal towns of Weymouth and Portland have gained or are managing development in order to gain from Weymouth's hosting of the sailing events for the 2012 Olympics Games. In first evaluating the position of a once very well-renowned coastal resort in the south east of England which has embarked on a series of developments to regain prominence, Saad reflects on the ambiguity of the image and market position of Weymouth. Building on an extensive literature review of the growth, form and function of the events as town and city development tools, Saad assesses the current event product range, economic state, politi-cal readiness as well as the results of a questionnaire distributed to 1000 members of the resident population in Weymouth and Portland to determine desired as well suggest prudent use of the oppor-tunity afforded by their hosting of the Games.

The issues surrounding a destination and the effective and long-term strategic use of its event are inspected again in Chapter 3 by Liburd. Consideration is given to the successes, opportunities and limitations of events as drivers of destination themes which can serve to unify tourism providers. Here the appraisal is borne of reflection on existing reports, application of surveys, analysis of printed and electronic media as well as interviews related to Denmark's Hans Christian Andersen bicentenary event – the first occurrence of such a year long themed event. By comparing the original objectives of the event with the outcomes, an evaluation is made of the event product development affect and, most particularly, how effective the event was in animating international markets. Liburd's analysis espouses the positive results of collaboration between the tourist board, VisitDenmark, some DMOs and the principle public relation organisation in making the visitor experience successful. However Liburd also laments that the potential for more tactical collaborative thematic product development was undone by a continuation of a long-standing animosity between the culture and tourism sectors in Copenhagen. This resulted in many elements of the event not resonating with the predominant expectation by international visitors of experiences related to the Danish fairy tale author. The chapter concludes that there are still significant challenges in creating the links between these sectors to ensure long-term success.

In Chapter 4, Foley, McPherson and McGillivray, in their analysis of Singapore, query attempts to change the image of a place through events. This stimulating work utilises a mixed methods case study approach. From interviews regards events and festival policy in Singapore with leaders of statutory and non-statutory bodies affiliated with, respectively, tourism, sport, culture and enterprise for the country and city the findings have then been reviewed through analysis of strategy documentation. This approach first provides a critical synopsis of the political and cultural context in which Singapore attempts a brand extension, wherein its image foremost as a business (event) destination attempts transmutation into one in which Singapore is a 'vibrant cultural hub'. The work then goes on to gauge the mixture of traditional cultural events and manufactured sporting events of international standing as elements of global 'place' competition. The work concludes that the brand redefinition sought through events is inseparable from the overarching mixture of tradition and modernity that Singapore has long sought in its notion of Singapore as New Asia. The conclusion also warns that the aspiration to be the Event and Entertainment Capital of Asia may be too reliant on demonstrations of image and not enough on logical involvement.

One theme common to all these chapters is the need for collaborative endeavour to ensure long-term success for destinations that host major events. In this sections' final chapter, Chapter 5, Byeon addresses the limited extent to which stakeholders were included in the co-hosted 2002 FIFA World Cup. A longitudinal investigation of the role of the Korean hotel industry in the run up to, during and the period after the 2002 FIFA Football World Cup (held in and shared by Korea and Japan), clearly indicates the very limited extent to which this sector was included in the developmental aspirations of this mega-event. Moreover the finding suggests that the sharing of the advantage was not fairly distributed and favoured the deluxe hotels. As an area of very limited research elsewhere this analysis of the impacts upon and the perceptions of the hotel industry affected by the hosting of a mega-event is a very interesting one. Impact studies were executed before and after the event in order to more readily measure the hotel staff's perception of the benefits and disbenefits of the event, i.e. its affect on them, their socio-cultural environment, their work, the blight of the hotel, tourism and economic growth. The work concludes that the perceived benefits of the World Cup were far lower after the event than before, although economic benefit was still most clearly felt after the event in the deluxe class hotels.

Chapter 1

Using Major Events to Promote Peripheral Urban Areas: Deptford and the 2007 Tour de France

Andrew Smith

Introduction

Events are now established methods for promoting destinations, supplementing their traditional role as forms of exhibition and performance (Roche, 2000). This article assesses the value of major events as promotional tools for peripheral urban areas. This does not mean suburban areas (city outskirts), 'exurbs' (the urban–rural fringe) or 'edge cities' (economically self-contained satellites), but areas on the fringe of city centres. These are often disadvantaged, either because they were once industrial areas, because public transport provision is limited, and/or because these are neglected zones between city centres and affluent suburbs. Therefore, the term peripheral is used here to refer to both spatial and socio-economic marginalisation. As Phelps and Parsons (2003) argue, functioning urban peripheries are not only important for the people and businesses located there: they affect the viability of city centres. Peripheral areas are rarely in a position to stage major events themselves, so the specific focus here is how the promotional benefits of events can be directed towards them. The staging of the 'Grand Depart' – the initial stages of the 2007 Tour de France (TDF) – in London provides an illustrative case of an event where attempts were made to disseminate positive effects more widely. Although the event was hosted primarily to encourage cycling in London, efforts were made to generate spending in, and publicity for, peripheral areas along the course. The event was also staged as part of the strategy to position London as an events city, and to prepare it for its role as host of the 2012 Olympic Games. Therefore, this case study also highlights wider issues regarding the benefits and frailties of relying on events to deliver promotional goals.

Using this case study this chapter aims to address the following objectives:

1. To identify how peripheral urban areas can maximise the promotional opportunities arising from major events.
2. To evaluate how urban authorities can liaise with media agencies to optimise promotional exposure before, during and after events.
3. To assess the role of major events as a mechanism for promoting tourism to peripheral areas.

International Perspectives of Festivals and Events
Copyright © 2009 by Elsevier Ltd.
ISBN: 978-0-08-045100-8

These objectives will be pursued via specific reference to the interrelationship between one peripheral area along the TDF route (Deptford) and the event.

Events and Tourism Marketing

Although cities can pursue 'immediate' event leveraging designed to maximise spending, utilise local supply chains and build new markets, they also need to adopt a longer-term perspective. According to Chalip (2004), long-term event leveraging is all about developing images to assist place branding and a city's market position. Throughout history, events have been used to promote cities and towns. But in the contemporary era, this has become a more strategic and sophisticated activity. A lucrative market in 'footloose' events is the inevitable result, with cities prepared to pay large sums to secure the rights to stage high profile franchises. However, many cities still act opportunistically rather than strategically in deploying event initiatives. With respect to event tourism strategies in major Australian cities, Stokes' (2007, p. 8) research reveals that these 'often emerged on a project-by-project basis, that is for each event that was staged, rather than as part of an overall strategy'. Many cities assume that events will automatically generate positive publicity, when research has shown that events can actually deliver rather innocuous, or even negative, media coverage. One conclusion common to several studies is that destinations need to be more discerning about which events to stage (Smith, 2007). This is because 'the destination's image will be affected by the image of events that it hosts, and the particular effect will depend upon which dimensions of destination image are compatible with the event' (Chalip et al., 2003, p. 228). In other words, destinations need to think about what aspects of their image they want to develop, and stage events that can assist with these objectives. This requires destinations to research how they are perceived and seek events that can further emphasise positive associations or counteract negative ones.

A better understanding of marketing, and related advancements in event promotion, has led some commentators and some cities to consider how events can be more effectively integrated with destination brands. This approach is complicated by the realisation that some events can be considered to be brands in themselves. Accordingly, attempts to promote destinations via events have been increasingly understood as co-branding exercises (Brown et al., 2002; Chalip et al., 2003). The TDF is an example of a strong event brand, and is considered by Chalip and Costa (2005, p. 237) to be one 'nurtured by and tied to the host destination'. According to these authors, the close ties between the TDF and French tourism mean that the TDF is an example of a brand extension, rather than an alliance between two separate brands. But the alliance between London and the TDF in 2007 is a typical example of co-branding, where two well known, but separate, brands align themselves for mutual benefit. In these circumstances, the implicit intention is to transfer elements of the event brand to the destination brand and vice versa. Researchers have attempted to explain what factors allow this transfer to happen successfully. Within a sponsorship context, Gwinner (1997) identifies three moderating variables. The first of these is the degree of similarity between the event and the sponsor. According to Gwinner, effective similarities can either be functional (an oil firm sponsoring a car race) or perceived (a young, dynamic firm sponsoring a young, dynamic event). This is reaffirmed by Chalip and Costa (2005) within a tourism context. The authors state that transfer is more likely to occur if the event and destination are well matched. If this principle is applied to London's Grand Depart, promotional efforts could be hindered by the apparent incongruity of the TDF being staged by an English destination. As well as potentially restricting the transfer between co-brands, the need for congruence between the event image and the destination image may restrict the potential of events as vehicles for image change (Brown et al., 2002; Chalip and Costa, 2005). For example, a destination worried about its overly industrial image may decide to stage an event more associated with an established tourist destination, such as a yachting regatta. But due to the lack of 'similarity' between the brands, it would be difficult to secure a satisfactory transfer of associations. There may be ways of nurturing image change by aligning events that may seem dissimilar. To surmount the incongruity that may result from new associations, Chalip and Costa (2005) recommend highlighting attributes or benefits that the event and the destination share. The implication for London's Grand Depart was that organisers needed to find an aspect of the TDF brand and London's brand where there was congruence and emphasise this in associated promotions.

The second of Gwinner's (1997) factors (the level and exclusivity of sponsorship) is very much related to event/sponsor brand synergy, rather than the event/destination equivalent. However, it can be applied to the 2007 Grand Depart. London and Kent are the main 'sponsors', but places hosting sprints and climbs are also closely associated with the event, alongside others featured en route. This creates a hierarchy of destination 'brands' associated with the event. And Gwinner's ideas imply that the plethora of destination brands associated with the TDF will temper successful transfer. Gwinner's (1997) third factor relates to the frequency a sponsored event occurs, as more regular events allow a firmer relationship to be established between co-brands. Again, the relevance of this to destinations is reaffirmed by Chalip and Costa (2005, p. 231) who argue that 'a single event – even one with a high profile – has only a passing effect on the destination's brand'. Whilst this may be true, for many footloose events – including the TDF's Grand Depart – the host destination is deliberately rotated every year. This obviously restricts the reaffirmation of brand alliances. Again, this problem may not be insurmountable. Previous event host cities have used commemorative occasions, affiliated events and extended promotions to perpetuate event associations.

The success of event co-branding also relies on visible links between events and destinations. And there are no guarantees that a host city will be featured extensively. Research into the Women's 'Final Four' basketball event in the United States revealed that in the 11 hours and 45 minutes of televised coverage, visuals of the host city appeared for less than 3.5 minutes (Green et al., 2003). Similarly disappointing effects were recorded by researchers who quantified TV coverage of Sheffield generated by the 2002 World Professional Snooker Championships. During 100 hours of coverage, the city was only mentioned 123 times. Many of these mentions were incidental and the authors concluded; 'it would be difficult to argue that such mentions contribute towards positive images' (Shibli and Coleman, 2005, p. 21). This has led some commentators to suggest that host destinations should negotiate a minimum level of coverage with media companies, or include contractual stipulations that would guarantee the use of certain visuals, commentaries or camera angles (Chalip et al., 2003). It is logical that if destinations are paying for events to use them as promotional tools, then they should try to secure some control over the extent and direction of messages delivered. This was something attempted by Australian tourism officials before the 2000 Olympic Games. According to Brown et al. (2002, p. 177), by working with the media, the Australian Tourism Commission aimed to 'make the Olympics a two-week documentary on all aspects of Australian life'. But if this practice is adopted widely, then one of the main advantages of events over more traditional marketing communication – perceived credibility – will be undermined (Smith, 2001). Furthermore, the integrity of events and broadcasters may be compromised, which could ultimately diminish the true meaning of events. As will be discussed in the next section, this is less of an issue with the TDF where the host destination is constantly on view anyway, and where media and tourism objectives have always been prioritised.

The TDF: A Tourism and Media Event?

The TDF is an interesting case study of the promotional value of major events through which to address the objectives of this article. The event is perhaps the world's most watched (free) spectator event and has long established connections to tourism. Promotional opportunities arise for the scores of towns that the TDF passes through each year, particularly as it commands extended televised coverage for three weeks every summer. The event is inextricably linked to the media, not least because it was conceived by *L'Auto* magazine journalists who staged the first race in 1903. Jean Marie Ooghe, producer of France Télévisions coverage, emphasised recently that he aims to show not only the TDF, but also a tour of France as a country (Marchetti, 2003). This showcasing tradition can only be understood via reference to the frailties of the race as a spectator and media event. The length of each stage, the geographical extent of the race and the associated brevity of the experience for the static viewer, has encouraged journalists to embellish coverage with vivid descriptions of the landscape and heritage of destinations en route (Wille, 2003). New methods used to follow the race, via cameras mounted on motorbikes or helicopters, have assisted these embellishments, rather than making them redundant. Indeed, new camera technology allowing the race to be filmed clearly, stably and at distance, from above, is deployed as much to show dramatic scenery as it is to show the intricacies of the race. The race has never been embarrassed to acknowledge this promotional dimension. One of the main income streams for the race has always been payments by local councils wishing to stage the start or the finish of a stage. Jean Marie LeBlanc, Race Director 1994–2006, estimated that this provides 10% of the race's income, although this is down from 20% 10 years ago (cited in Marchetti, 2003).

In July 2007, part of the TDF was staged in London for the first time. Whilst it may seem contradictory to stage the TDF outside France, this is a long tradition. In the past the Tour has made frequent forays into Belgium, Germany and Switzerland, as well as two previous visits to the UK's south coast. Recently, organisers have invited bids from cities outside France to stage Le Grand Depart, and London was deemed to be an attractive option due to its status as a world city. Interestingly, the idea of staging certain events outside their logical territory has become increasingly common. During the 2007 Rugby World Cup in France some games took place in Cardiff (Wales) and Edinburgh (Scotland). In a similarly incongruous vein, the PGA European Golf Tour now has events in Asia. Even events considered to be geographically fixed are likely to be increasingly mobile, to allow organisers to maximise their income. Like the Grand Depart's visit to London, these relocations are motivated by the desire of the event organisers to widen interest, and more importantly, to generate large fees from host cities. Indeed, it is reported that London paid the TDF organisers £1.5 million to stage the Grand Depart.

Method

The research undertaken aimed to enhance understanding of how events could be used to promote peripheral urban areas. As the TDF prologue on Saturday 7 July was staged entirely in central London, this meant focusing on Stage 1 of the 2007 TDF, staged on a 203 km course from London to

Canterbury the day after. After leaving central London, the race passed through some disadvantaged parts of the capital's metropolitan area including the London Boroughs of Southwark, Lewisham and Greenwich in South East London. Due to the lack of co-operation from other compatible areas and its suitability for the study, one particular area on the route – Deptford – was selected as the main case study. The intention was to complement analysis of this localised case study with a review of initiatives at the central event management level to see if and how an integrated approach was developed. Accordingly, a combination of primary and secondary research was undertaken. Semi-structured interviews were conducted with key stakeholders to discuss their contributions to, attitudes towards and experiences of, the TDF event (see Figure 1.1). These included interviews with key representatives from the lead event organisers (Transport for London), as well as discussions with the organisation responsible for tourism in the capital who were supporting the event (Visit London). Meetings and interviews were also conducted with those responsible for producing the UK TV coverage (Sunset + Vine). In Deptford, interviews were conducted with individuals who organised local events (Deptford's Town Centre Manager; hereafter DTCM), and promoted them (a PR Consultant employed by Lewisham Council; hereafter PRC). To give some indication of the envisaged objectives of event initiatives, as well as how effective they were, some interviews were carried out before the event (Visit London, Sunset + Vine), whilst others were undertaken in its immediate aftermath (TfL, PRC). As the main focus was peripheral urban areas, DTCM was interviewed both before and after the event. A list of interviewees and the abbreviations used to identify them is given in Figure 1.1. A semi-structured topic guide relevant to the person being interviewed was produced prior to each interview which was recorded and then transcribed. The flexibility of the topic guides meant that issues raised by one stakeholder could be discussed with another. Interviews lasted between 30 minutes and 1 hour 30 minutes. This produced nearly 100 pages of transcripts which were analysed using basic qualitative data analysis procedures as suggested by Dey (1993).

The primary research was supplemented with a review of media materials. National newspaper and television coverage of the event was collected and reviewed. The aim was to collect materials related to

Wednesday 20 June 2007: Deptford Town Centre Manager (DTCM)

Friday 22 June 2007: BV, Sunset + Vine

Friday 6 July 2007: KK, Visit London

Saturday 7 / Sunday 8 July 2007 Tour de France/MIDF Weekend

Tuesday 10 July 2007: Transport for London
     PTfL (Programmes Manager)
     MTfL (Marketing Manager)
     GTfL (Technical Manager)
     TTfL (Stakeholder Manager)

Tuesday 17 July 2007: Post event visit to Sunset + Vine, London

Wednesday 18 July 2007: PR Consultant (PRC)

Monday 13 August 2007: Deptford Town Centre Manager (DTCM)

Figure 1.1: List of interviewees and associated abbreviations.

Deptford's association with the race that had been consumed by potential (domestic) tourists. Television coverage of the event was collected with the assistance of production staff from Sunset + Vine.

Vive La Deptford: the TDF Comes to London's Periphery

Deptford is an area in South East London with a rich maritime history. In the 16th century, King Henry VIII moved the British Naval Fleet there, which led to it becoming an important port area. Shipbuilding and the dockworks subsequently moved further downstream, leaving Deptford to flounder as a rather dilapidated and peripheral part of the capital. The area suffered from high unemployment and social problems in the latter part of the 20th century, but there have been recent signs of a revival. Much effort has been made to regenerate the area and it has benefited from improved transport links: Deptford is now linked to Canary Wharf via a rapid rail transit system and it continues to enjoy good mainline rail links to central London. In 2005 its high street topped a list of the London's most diverse and vibrant high streets due to the unusually large proportion of independent shops located there. Recent regeneration efforts have capitalised on the area's emerging reputation as a centre for creative industries. This strategy is linked to the presence of prestigious creative institutions located nearby. These include Goldsmith's College, The Trinity School of Music and the Laban Dance Centre. The latter was opened in 2003 in a building designed by famous 'st-architects', Herzog and de Meuron. However, the notable absence of a bombastic design mean that it is perhaps unfair to include this as an example of the flagship regeneration so typical of other recent urban development strategies (Smith, 2005).

Deptford is located on the border of three London Boroughs, although its centre is formally part of the Borough of Lewisham. This means that it is both peripheral to London's centre and peripheral to local centres of governance. The Borough of Lewisham is remarkably undeveloped as a tourism location, despite its relatively close proximity to central London. It currently offers little accommodation provision, and hosts one attraction of note: the Horniman Museum. Deptford is in the far north of the Borough, close to Maritime Greenwich, an area which is a popular tourism destination. A Town Centre Manager is employed within the Economic Development team of the Borough Council to promote the ongoing vitality of the town centre. This individual is also responsible for tourism in the area, with the support of the Borough's Tourism Development Officer. The combination of these roles makes sense as most of Deptford's 'tourism' comprises day visits to central shops, restaurants and cultural venues. The TDF became part of DTCM's responsibility, in conjunction with the Borough's Cycling Officer and other members of the Economic Development team. A consultant was also hired to organise to assist with Public Relations (PR).

Once the TDF route had been confirmed, representatives from Lewisham Council were left to decide how they might best use the opportunity afforded by the race's passage through Deptford: a rather strange phase between the ceremonial start and the real start in Greenwich (see Figure 1.2). The most important decision taken was to move the annual 'Made in Deptford Festival' (hereafter MIDF) to the weekend of the race. According to the DTCM, there was complete consensus regarding the decision to move the Festival from May to July. As DTCM explained:

> Last year after the festival, we decided that because we knew the TDF was coming through, it was too big an opportunity to pass up. Also the weather was miserable last year during the festival, so we thought July – that sounds better.

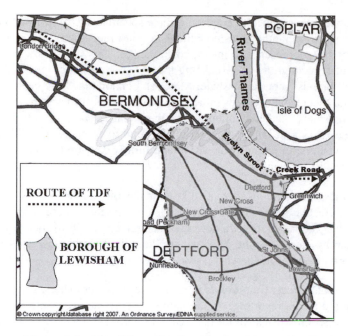

Figure 1.2: Map illustrating Deptford and route of TDF.

The rescheduling of the festival coincides with Chalip's (2004) and O'Brien's (2007) ideas about extending visitor's stay via augmenting a major event with other subsidiary events. As DTCM explained, the value of moving the festival was:

> Having potentially lots of people who haven't been to Deptford before coming to watch the Tour de France and having that as an opportunity to say while you're here stick around and explore, there are all these great things on offer.

Deptford's plan for the weekend of 7/8 July was to use the TDF as the centrepiece of a rescheduled weekend-long community festival (the MIDF) which was itself made up of 'hundreds of events' (DTCM). Some of these were specifically designed to link in with the TDF. For example, a French market and cycle demonstrations were staged on sites adjoining the route. At the main arts venue, visitors were offered the opportunity to watch the rest of the race via specially constructed screens. Other events were put on that were totally unrelated to the TDF. These included a fashion show, talent show, beauty pageant, business exhibitions, plus various plays and street performances. The overall aims were to publicise Deptford as a day out destination, to increase revenues for local businesses, and as the MIDF primarily exists to advance community cohesion, to bring the area closer together.

Leveraging Promotion: Key Issues that Emerged from the Research

The TDF was primarily conceived to assist London with its own branding objectives. These envisaged benefits were explained by KK of Visit London who claimed that the Tour was an ideal partner brand for London, because it helped to emphasise three specific aspects of London's branding: sustainability (via cycling associations), cosmopolitanism (via French and other international connections) and connectivity (via presence of international media). This shows how organisers were able to overcome the initial incongruity of associating the TDF and London, by emphasising three specific traits that both 'brands' supposedly share. Although London may have been able to link up well with the TDF brand, this chapter focuses on a more difficult task: to lever promotional benefits for Deptford. Efforts to achieve the latter commenced approximately six months before the event, when the first press release was sent out by the consultant hired to promote the MIDF. Her main aims were to attract day visitors, to promote the MIDF and further develop the image Deptford is trying to emphasise. As the PRC explained:

> [The] Key messages were an alternative London day out, a maritime past, an innovative present, creative future. Three themes; history, culture and creativity if you like. So it was really a chance to get a new audience seeing Deptford for the first time – leading them by the pull of the TDF and sneaking the Made in Deptford Festival in the back for the people who had never ever looked at it before.

Levering promotional effects from events involves two different tactics: showcasing the destination via event inspired media reporting; or alternatively, using the event in advertising and promotions (Chalip, 2004). As only one advert was taken out to promote Deptford's TDF/MIDF weekend, the first of these tactics was the one primarily deployed in this case. Deptford's promotional efforts involved contacting media organisations and trying to get them to feature the TDF/MIDF weekend. The focus was mainly local newspapers and magazines, plus local radio and TV. Efforts were also made to ensure that MIDF events were included in listings, or on websites hosted by event partners. Commendably, the promotional efforts seem to have been devoid of hyperbole and hype. As PRC explains, the objective was to:

> Get local people on board and get London seeing Deptford and then after that move more national with it. You can't sell something that's not there because they will never come back again. It's in its infancy still. If you're trying nationally to get things, you've got to make sure it's worth their while. It is worth someone's while to come from another part of London but it needs more before it can be a justification for someone to come from Manchester.

The PRC adopted the entirely logical argument that there was no point telling national media that the various augmentations of the MIDF/TDF were 'must-see', when many of them were clearly low-key events for the benefit of the local community. The PRC's approach had been influenced by experiences two years ago when the result of inviting the national press to Deptford was a less than complimentary article in *The Guardian* entitled: 'Dredging up Deptford'. As the PRC recognised, even though Deptford was now hosting the TDF; 'You can't go from "Dredging up Deptford" to glamour in one go'.

Co-branding Deptford and the TDF

Applying Chalip and Costa's (2005) principle of capitalising on small, shared co-associations, those responsible for Deptford's promotion did manage to make some coherent connections between the area and certain dimensions of the TDF brand. As can be seen from Table 1.1, these included imaginative links to the artist Toulouse Lautrec and various specialist cycling attributes. Other co-branding was a little less subtle and more tenuous, comprising thankless attempts to transfer event associations with French sophistication to Deptford. The PRC felt: 'It was quite fun to say "Ooh la la! Deptford" for the Tour de France, which was the line I went with.' This slogan was included on the official MIDF promotional materials which were dominated by a generic cycling image and 'tri-colour' livery to reinforce the TDF connections (see Figure 1.3).

Like other areas who were not main sponsors, Deptford was unable to use the official TDF logo. As DTCM stated 'They're very protective of the logo; we weren't even able to put it on our post-cards for advertising so we had a designer do something to allude to the Tour.' As TTfL explained, only destinations which were primary partners were allowed to use the official logo (to protect the interests of other TDF sponsors). MTfL claimed that TfL had assisted local Boroughs to counter this inevitably protective stance:

> We came up with ideas and went to them with ideas of how it could work. We went with graphic ideas of what could be used and marketing campaigns that could work and ideas about promotions that could work. We provided the solution rather than just providing the problem and I think that was key.

This resulted in some imaginative solutions, including the one adopted by Deptford (Figure 1.3). Branding restrictions aimed at protecting the rights of sponsors were not limited to pre-race publicity. Officially, Boroughs were not allowed to adorn the route with banners and restrictions

Table 1.1: Connections between the TDF and Deptford made by those responsible for promoting the area.

'We found a link with Toulouse Lautrec who'd come to Lewisham in 1895 to sketch some bicycles at the Catford Track and we got a little story about that.' (PRC)
'We've also had cycle magazines doing write ups saying the best places to watch, and they say Deptford is the place.' (PRC)
'The Tour de France has been really beneficial, we have gotten more attention already for MIDF than we do usually because of this different angle to it. That ties in quite well so a lot of people are quite interested in it. Special interest stories have been done on Witcomb Cycle Shop which has been here since 1940 as it's the last cycle shop in all London that still designs and builds bicycles from scratch. It's a father and son team: Ernie Witcomb just turned 85 and his son is in his 60s. It's this fantastic little business down on Tanner's Hill you can see it's right down in there. So we've got the Guardian to do a little feature on them. It's tied into the Tour de France because they have designed bicycles for past races of the Tour and they have some of those, which will be on exhibit for the whole race and for the MIDF. Those kinds of things have really helped a lot.' (DTCM)
'We've got an old institution pub the Dog and Bell, which repeatedly wins South East London pub of the year award and has a die hard following among cyclists because it's on the Thames Path and there is cycle parking out front. Those are some links we are able to build up a bit more and to say "You've probably ridden through the area but you should come here for the festival."' (DTCM)

Figure 1.3: Logo used by Deptford to associate MIDF with the TDF.

were placed on items that could be sold in the immediate vicinity of the race route. This meant that Deptford had difficulty getting permission to stage its French market – an initiative designed to help co-brand the race and the local area. Via this initiative, and others, Deptford made a concerted effort to 'dress' its part of the route – even if it meant contravening some of these restrictions. DTCM felt that 'we worked really well together to try and promote the area and say, "Welcome to Deptford" … we had "Welcome to Deptford" banners though technically we weren't supposed to have banners along the route'. Perversely, this 'illicit' localised co-branding was appreciated by race organisers, who realised the value of initiatives that joined up 'French and British life' in presenting a coherent and meaningful image, both of individual destinations and the event as a whole (MTfL).

Despite the restrictions imposed, the promotional efforts of central event partners and local areas were integrated and reinforced one another. This integration existed on an institutional, as well as a thematic level. For a peripheral area like Deptford, one of the most positive promotional effects levered by the TDF was that it was able to use the services of larger and more professional press offices associated with event partners. This assistance was appreciated by the PRC:

> DTCM had put me in contact with also Visit London and Totally London. We concentrated on them as they have their own press officers. It made sense to use as many PR people who were working alongside us as possible. We did get good attention from them.

As TTfL explained, the relationship between central and local press relations was a reciprocal one:

> We always say to them [the Boroughs], 'we know a lot about the [London Evening] Standard and a bit about the nationals. We're trying to learn about the local newspapers.

You guys know so much more than us, you've got your own in house papers that go to every doorstep in the borough. You got your own websites and you have won contacts in your local media. Help us to help you by us using them together'.

The Cynicism of National Newspaper Coverage

If the destination image benefits of a major event rely on co-branding, which in turn relies on audiences perceiving similarities between the two brands, then Deptford's association with the TDF would seem to offer something of a challenge. The apparent incongruity was something that the national newspaper coverage seemed keen to capitalise upon. This coverage comprised two clear phases: the weeks leading up to the race and a series of immediate post-race reflections. In the pre-race coverage, the only specific mentions of Deptford (other than merely listing it as part of the route) were in The Independent and The Observer. The Independent article (also syndicated nationally), by travel writer Simon Calder, was dominated by a rather dismissive attitude. Alongside labelling the area 'despondent Deptford', the writer made continual references to the bleakness of the initial part of the route compared to its subsequent journey through Kent. Indeed, Calder suggested that when race day arrives, riders may 'suspect that the organisers have a grudge against them'. The later Observer article was written from a similar perspective – a writer sampling the route that the professionals would subsequently follow. It also adopts a similar tone to Calder's piece, this time unfavourably comparing the part of the route near Deptford to the more glamorous race vistas in central London: 'We loop around the capital's classic sights – under Admiralty Arch, past Big Ben, the London Eye, Tower Bridge, then err Deptford, Plumstead and Woolwich.' The writer continues in this vein, and includes the comment: 'Its not exactly postcard stuff and you can't really imagine crowds of flag waving fans along the dusty dual carriageways.' This was refuted by the large crowds that did line the entire route on race day. However, the article also contained a slightly more positive angle, which did fit in with Deptford's marketing message; 'but it's fascinating to see this other side of London'.

Pre-race satirical negativity was repeated in the immediate post-race newspaper coverage, although in diluted form due to the manifestation of large crowds and public support. Again this satire was largely based on the perceived discontinuity between Deptford and the TDF. Three national newspaper articles mentioned Deptford in their race reports beyond simply listing it as part of the route. All used Deptford to inject some form of humour into their pieces. *The Guardian's* Sean Ingle suggested that the race was such a spectacle that 'even the boozers at The Harp in Deptford looked up from their Sunday-morning settlers to see what all the fuss was about'. Giles Smith's article in the *Times* poked fun at Deptford's peripherality. It cited the live ITV commentary which suggested that peloton had reached 'the middle of nowhere'. According to Smith, this 'was a bit rough on the people of Deptford, through which the Tour happened to be passing at the time'. In a syndicated piece that appeared in *The Herald* (Scotland) and other regional papers, James Toney highlighted the difficulties squaring some of the destinations on the Stage 1 route with the destinations normally associated with the TDF: 'Maybe Deptford, Dartford and Gillingham don't have quite the same romance as the Alpe d'Huez and the Col du Portet d'Aspet but organisers did their best to give some Gallic flavour to the route.' This final clause suggests co-branding efforts were appreciated. And it also recognises that it was often the least glamorous locations that made the biggest effort to make the most of the TDF – something also acknowledged by GTfL in a post-race interview. Overall, the coverage obtained was a little disappointing. Although Deptford gained a surprising number of mentions in the national press, the cynicism of this coverage reaffirmed negative stereotypes.

Intervening in TV Coverage

Alongside traditional PR, several commentators suggest that event hosts need to maximise promotional opportunities by liaising with TV companies to ensure coverage of their destination during an event (Brown et al., 2002; Chalip et al., 2003). With respect to international events like the TDF, this is not particularly easy, as the television pictures are disseminated by one company, with editing and commentary added by host broadcasters. Local areas have little bargaining power, as they have no say over who gets the media rights to cover the event. Even when financial contributions are made by individual destinations, this is no guarantee of coverage. As BV highlighted, when the Tour last came to England in 1994 'Basingstoke paid quite a reasonable amount of money, as much as £1 million and the French director came over and decided to pick up his coverage just outside Basingstoke'. Deptford could have persuaded TV companies to mention certain local features as the race went by, or to produce a feature on the area. However, it is unlikely that producers would have ceded to such requests. Staff at Sunset + Vine, the producers of the UK coverage, stated that they received emails from local authorities and other organisations, but that their requests were usually ignored. Worthy enquiries tend to get hidden underneath a deluge of other requests. This means that the usual way of attracting coverage is not by contacting the producers of domestic coverage but by commanding the attention of the official broadcaster's TV cameras. Accordingly, rudimentary promotional banners and signs are usually used. The difficulties faced by local areas wishing to influence event media coverage are exacerbated by firmly established practices within the media. This is certainly true of the TDF, which is followed every year by a very slick, but very predictable, media circus. This makes attempts to encourage different angles even more difficult.

An Obsession with Icons

A recurring theme in the interviews was the media's obsession with iconic landmarks. As BV suggests, the main thing TV companies covering the TDF are looking for is spectacular scenery and this was a major incentive to bring the race to London. Although helping to reinforce London's symbolic identity, the obsessive use of iconic images by the media during TDF coverage caused some problems – centrally and locally. According to KK, during events such as the TDF, Visit London has great difficulty persuading international media companies to avoid simply focusing on the city's main iconic sites. Locally, this was even more of a concern, as TV companies tend to ignore Boroughs without the requisite icons. This became apparent during the TV coverage of the TDF through South East London, where helicopter shots of 'The Gherkin', City Hall, Tower Bridge, the University of Greenwich, the Millennium Dome and the Thames Barrier constantly interrupted the live race feed, even though the riders were not actually passing these icons at the time. As these were the official pictures, they would be used by every international broadcaster choosing to show the early part of the 'race'. Fortunately for places like Deptford, other media are understandably less obsessed with icons. The PRC identified: 'I had more chance with Radio as they couldn't have visuals anyway so they were much happier with the alternative angle. It's not that I didn't try [to get TV coverage for Deptford] but I was competing with London landmarks.'

The iconic obsession was not merely a result of the preferences of TV companies, but reflected the motives and interests of the organisers. The people at TfL responsible for the route readily confessed their pre-occupation with central London icons. However, TTfL suggested that their attempt to depict central London via these images was accompanied by an attempt to provide a genuinely honest representation of London by showing how the central city merged into its own periphery. TTfL explained how they tried to create some continuity between Saturday's time trial in London, and Sunday's stage from London to Canterbury:

> It would have looked strange to have a prologue in the middle of the city to have all of those iconic structures and then you start in Greenwich. For a major city like London it wants to be seen as not just W1 [the centre], but other parts that have a lot for people to look at and a variety of cultures; it's a very diverse city. Having the prologue in the centre of the town and moving from the centre out – there's a genuine transition between central London and suburbia.

Unfortunately, actual coverage is governed by TV producers, not destination representatives, and their priorities became clear as the coverage of Stage 1 began. Riders were shown in central London and on Tower Bridge, but then, rather than showing the riders progressing though peripheral London, extended helicopter views of The City, Tower Bridge and City Hall were presented. As the peloton progressed through Bermondsey and Surrey Quays (see Figure 1.2), some shots of the riders (mainly from overhead) were shown, but again these were interspersed with iconic images that exhibited iconic sites in and around Greenwich, including the Royal Naval College and the Millennium Dome. The riders had not reached these sites yet, but they were given precedence over live coverage of the 'race'. As the riders approached Deptford, they were shown from overhead coming down Evelyn Street (see Figure 1.2) and then the editors cut to a ground level shot at the end of Deptford High Street to capture the large cheers that went up as the peloton passed. Almost immediately, the live coverage then switched to an extended helicopter view of the Thames Barrier, despite this structure being c.5 km away. When the coverage came back to the peloton, it was crossing Deptford Creek into Greenwich.

In the United Kingdom, live coverage was shown on a digital/satellite channel (ITV4). On the main commercial terrestrial channel (ITV1) at the time the riders came through South East London, the producers were busy reviewing the previous day's action, and introducing Sunday's race. Coverage only switched to the live race as they passed the meridian in Greenwich. The omission of large parts of South East London, including Deptford, continued in the highlights package shown later on ITV1 that evening. This programme showed the riders on Tower Bridge, then cut to the race once it had left Greenwich. The net outcome of this was that Deptford and other peripheral parts of inner South East London were largely absent from UK TV coverage of the event. This reaffirms Green et al.'s (2003) fears about the visibility of event–destination connections. Pictures of peripheral South East London were shown intermittently on the live international feed, but the extended vistas of central London and spectacular sites located in Greenwich left little opportunity to represent or discuss local features. The only places on this part of the route worthy of a caption were deemed to be 'La Cité', 'L'Université de Greenwich', 'le Dôme de Millénium' and 'Le Barrage Thames'. Everywhere else remained unidentified, and, therefore, seemingly unworthy of discussion.

Events Clutter

In the interviews it became apparent that one of the major challenges faced by those promoting London's Grand Depart, was the clutter of other events that were being staged at the same time. This included national events, other events being staged in London, and even other local events that seemingly affected Deptford's efforts to promote the TDF weekend. For UK or London-wide tourism organisations, this was a very positive thing. But for those trying to promote a one-off event like the TDF it was an obstacle. Although most summer weekends are busy, the weekend of 7/8 July 2007 was particularly so. As KK stated: 'There are a lot of things around the Tour, like Wimbledon and the Live Earth concert and Justin Timberlake over the weekend. There are plenty of other things going on at the same time.' According to PRC, Deptford's promotional efforts were directly affected by these national and London events:

> I was chuffed to bits that ITV [local], LBC [radio] and BBC [London] came to Deptford because we were competing not only with the Tour de France and other areas of the Tour but there was Wimbledon, a global warming concert [Live Earth], the Grand Prix, and trillions of things. For us to get what we did I was delighted as it could have been so much worse. I feel we got our fair share considering.

For Deptford it was not simply a case of competing with events outside the Borough of Lewisham – other Borough events also caused problems. Moving the MIDF to coincide with the TDF had meant that it was very close to another annual community event in Lewisham, and this limited the promotional support it received from Lewisham Council. This was explained by the DTCM:

> The Council has a long standing event called 'People's Day' which is the weekend after the Tour de France and Made in Deptford Festival and it's been a bit of a battle internally and a struggle to get the press office to promote this [TDF].

Publicity for the MIDF was also adversely affected by the unavailability of the Council outdoor advertising space because of 'People's Day'. This affected awareness of the event in other parts of Lewisham Borough. DTCM felt that without the influence of the TDF, MIDF would have been lost in this clutter of events. But she also felt that the number of events in July meant that it was more difficult to get the full attention of Visit London and Visit Britain, who are more proactive when they are short of events to promote. The clutter of events and the difficulties this poses is one reason that the organisers are considering rescheduling the 2008 MIDF.

Budgetary Considerations

Other obstacles to the successful leverage of promotional benefits from the event inevitably included budgetary constraints. The PRC hired by Deptford bemoaned the rather restricted amount of money available to lever coverage. This clearly narrowed the scope of Deptford's ambitions. PRC claimed that if her budget had allowed, she would have tried to encourage French journalists to write about the area as a London day out. The tight budget and heavy workloads of all involved may also be another reason to question the simultaneous staging of the MIDF and the TDF. As these events are effectively managed and promoted by a handful of people, combining them may create some opportunities, but it also restricts the amount of time available to organise them and promote them properly. As the PRC admits, 'Had I had more time I could have brought in some cyclists, got French coverage out of it and really connected the area with France.' This may have assisted efforts to co-brand Deptford and the TDF.

Conclusions

The case study of event leverage presented here is a complex one. Deptford rescheduled an event (MIDF), to coincide with a major event (London's Grand Depart) that was coincidentally routed through its streets. That major event was itself part of a three-week mega-event (the TDF) primarily staged in France. To complicate matters further, the part of the event staged in Deptford was not actually a formal part of the race, but a preliminary phase before the official start. This took place early on Sunday morning, hardly a time conducive for the media and tourists targeted. But despite, and because, of these complexities the case does illustrate a number of important points about events and peripheral areas. It shows that major events are not only of benefit to those areas where venues and activities are concentrated. Indeed, Deptford's experiences show that even when a minor part of an event is allocated to a peripheral area, promotional benefits can accrue. The imaginative ways that Deptford generated benefits from its minor TDF role shows that event associations are not fixed, but are to some extent malleable. Even areas with tenuous links to events can use them as promotional opportunities. One of the ways this can be done is by tying a major event into a network of other local events. This can generate extra participation, publicity and funding for those events, and lever wider image benefits for host destinations.

It should be noted that the modest and tentative outcomes reported here have been achieved by a budget that in marketing/PR terms is miniscule. The costs were essentially the (part-time) employment of two key members of staff, the Town Centre Manger and a hired PRC. Even these costs were offset by extra sponsorship that TDF associations helped to secure. Admittedly, there were other local costs associated with the TDF – an event paid for by publicly funded organisations. It should also be pointed out that there were some disbenefits associated with the leverage strategy adopted by Deptford. Moving the MIDF reduced the amount of time the DTCM had to promote it, and subjected it to greater competition from other events. The association with the TDF also exposed Deptford and the MIDF to negative publicity surrounding the event in general. At the London level this included cynicism regarding the safety of cycling around the city's streets and, at the wider level, suspicions about the use of performance enhancing drugs. Nevertheless, the extent of the positive outcomes resulting from TDF associations means that the decision to reschedule the MIDF was vindicated. Both the TDF and MIDF benefited as a result, securing greater promotional opportunities than would otherwise have been possible. This promotion was mainly the result of specific efforts to lever publicity and exposure, rather than relying on the event to generate media coverage automatically.

The TDF did assist Deptford's promotion, as it gained valuable coverage on local TV and radio. This was gained via effective liaison between DTCM/the PRC and media agencies. But national newspaper and television coverage was disappointing. This was an inevitable consequence of competition from other events staged at the same time and the media's obsession with icons. As PRC concluded: 'At the end of the day, there were so many things on that weekend and TV cameras wanted Parliament in the background, [so] you can't get them to come to Deptford.' Disappointing newspaper coverage was also the result of cynical journalists keen to point out the discontinuity between Deptford and the TDF. But the extensive and positive local media coverage levered means the MIDF is certainly better known as a result. This coverage has helped to develop Deptford's image as day visit destination for Londoners, but cannot be expected to deliver wider tourism effects. Therefore, in the short term, tourism effects are likely to be restricted to day visits from other parts of London. Whilst this was the realistic objective of the PRC, she admitted that if more money had been made available then she would have tried to encourage French visitors to come to Deptford. This is perhaps not unrealistic. KK of Visit London identified that many European repeat visitors are beginning to seek out more unusual parts of London and Deptford's proximity to Greenwich may prove to be a related advantage. Therefore, the modest tourism outcomes will be viewed by pessimists as commendable realism, but as a missed opportunity by those with a more optimistic outlook.

Although authors suggest destinations need to intervene in event media coverage (Chalip et al., 2003), the case study analysed here suggests this is very difficult. Unless an official arrangement between a TV company and a destination is in place, producers and editors are unlikely to listen to ideas for angles, or vistas, let alone produce specific features. This restricts opportunities for peripheral areas. But Deptford did gain some useful local media coverage via imaginative associations with the TDF brand. This shows that almost any destination can benefit from an event brand if common aspects of each are emphasised. The TDF case also illustrated that local imagination and central support is needed to find ways of bypassing event branding restrictions. Most major events restrict use of official logos, but the event brand can still be alluded to in promotional material and this is vital if peripheral areas and an event are to be visibly aligned. Finally, destinations need to be aware that even if TV producers can be persuaded to focus on destination attributes, not merely events themselves, then they are likely to focus on iconic structures.

This chapter has raised some interesting issues that deserve further attention from researchers. These include the event networks that surround many major events, the effects of multiple destinations claiming 'ownership' of an event, the difficulties caused by restricted access to event logos and the territorial dissemination of event benefits. More work is also required to understand if and how sport events and cultural events can be usefully combined. The case discussed should provide some useful lessons for other peripheral areas seeking to benefit from events that they are unable to stage themselves. By hosting parts of certain events; smaller affiliated events or simply by exploiting event themes, destinations can lever promotional benefits. As these initiatives do not necessarily require expensive new venues, they can make a useful contribution to the sustainable development of peripheral urban areas.

References

Brown, G., Chalip, L., Jago, L. and Mules, T. (2002) The Sydney Olympics and Brand Australia. In Morgan, N., Pritchard, A. and Pride, R. (eds.), *Destination Branding: Creating the Unique Destination Proposition*. Oxford: Butterworth-Heinemann, pp. 163–185.

Chalip, L. (2004) Beyond impact: A generalised model for host community event leverage. In Ritchie, B. and Adair, S. (eds.), *Sports Tourism: Interrelationships, Impacts and Issues*. Clevedon: Channel View, pp. 226–252.

Chalip, L. and Costa, C. (2005) Sport event tourism and the destination brand: Towards a general theory. *Sport in Society*, 8(2), 218–237.

Chalip, L., Green, B. and Hill, B. (2003) Effects of sport event media on destination image and intention to visit. *Journal of Sport Management*, 17, 214–234.

Dey, I. (1993) *Qualitative Data Analysis*. London: Routledge.

Green, B., Costa, C. and Fitzgerald, M. (2003) Marketing the host city: Analyzing exposure generated by a sport event. *International Journal of Sports Marketing and Sponsorship*, 4(4), 335–352.

Gwinner, K. (1997) A model of image creation and image transfer in event sponsorship. *International Marketing Review*, 13(3), 145–158.

Marchetti, D. (2003) The changing organisation of the Tour de France and its media coverage – an interview with Jean Marie Leblanc. *International Journal of the History of Sport*, 20(2), 33–56.

O'Brien, D. (2007) Points of leverage: Maximising host community benefit from a regional surfing festival. *European Sport Management Quarterly*, 7(2), 141–165.

Phelps, N. and Parsons, N. (2003) Edge urban geographies: Notes from the margins of Europe's capital cities. *Urban Studies*, 40(9), 1725–1749.

Roche, M. (2000) *Mega Events and Modernity: Olympics and Expos in the Growth of Global Culture*. London: Routledge.

Shibli, S. and Coleman, R. (2005) Economic impact and place marketing evaluation: A case study of the World Snooker Championship. *International Journal of Event Management Research*, 1(1), 13–29.

Smith, A. (2001) Sport-based regeneration strategies. In Henry, I. and Gratton, C. (eds.), *Sport in the City: The Role of Sport in Economic and Social Regeneration*. London: Routledge, pp. 127–148.

Smith, A. (2005) Conceptualizing image change: The reimaging of Barcelona. *Tourism Geographies*, 7(4), 398–423.

Smith, A. (2007) Large-scale events and sustainable urban regeneration: Key principles for host cities. *Journal of Urban Regeneration and Renewal*, 22(3/4), 79–93.

Stokes, R. (2008) Tourism strategy making: Insights to the events tourism domain. *Tourism Management*, 29, 252–262.

Wille, F. (2003) The Tour de France as an agent of change in media production. *International Journal of the History of Sport*, 20(2), 128–146.

Chapter 2

Weymouth's Once in a Lifetime Opportunity

Deborah Sadd

Introduction

On the 6 July 2005 much changed for the towns of Weymouth and Portland, Dorset as they heard that in seven years time they would be hosting the sailing for the successful London 2012 Olympic Bid. Two years later on, and whilst the Weymouth and Portland National Sailing Academy (WPNSA) has swung into action with its preparations, the town of Weymouth itself in some respects appears to be unsure of it's future direction. At the time of the bid the road issue was still uppermost in the minds of the residents; however that issue has potentially been resolved with the Government announcing the decision to build the relief road in time for the 2012 Games which will alter significantly the arrival of visitors into the town from Dorchester, until now a potential traffic nightmare for both visitors and residents alike with long delays and traffic bottlenecks. Yet, within the town itself, little has changed. Many plans are being suggested about developments including the new Pavilion Peninsula and also the redevelopment of the waterfront esplanade, but it would appear that the town is slightly indecisive as to where it wants to position itself with regard to attracting visitors and income to the town.

Weymouth needs to decide on its strategy for the future, by adopting a concerted approach to attract certain segments of the market and invest sensibly in these areas, rather than trying to spread itself too thinly across all market sectors. The role of a good events portfolio could be a major contributor to a successful marketing strategy. From research undertaken in 2004 (Sadd, 2004), it is evident that the locals are keen for the 'season' to be all year around and they recognise the importance of events in the town and how, historically, they have been a great source of celebration, ranging from the military parades to the hosting of the tall ships for an unprecedented three times. This chapter will explain the historical underpinning of Weymouth's present situation and will make suggestions for possible events based strategies to maximise the potential benefits to be gained from being Olympic Hosts in 2012.

International Perspectives of Festivals and Events
Copyright © 2009 by Elsevier Ltd.
All rights of reproduction in any form reserved.
ISBN: 978-0-08-045100-8

Weymouth's Historical Background

Weymouth is a medium sized resort on the south coast of England, 160 miles from London and with a population of about 60,000. Weymouth purports to be 'The First Resort' of the United Kingdom as over 200 years ago King George III and his family holidayed there. Weymouth Bay has long been called 'England's Bay of Naples' and is renowned for having the best sunshine record in England. In January 2003 it held the record for the sunniest January since records began. The winter climate is mild and Weymouth often beats its close neighbour Bournemouth in the temperature stakes. The history of the town is closely linked to the sea with ships setting sail to fight the Spanish Armada and to fight in WWII. Weymouth, Massachusetts is so named after the emigrants set sail from Weymouth, United Kingdom.

It has sandy beaches and shallow offshore waters, with a sheltered harbour measuring over 2500 acres containing reputably some of the best sailing waters in the world (Princess Royal, opening ceremony of new sailing centre, 2005) and a large area of flat land with waterside access. Traditionally Weymouth has celebrated its maritime heritage through its nationally and internationally renowned military parades, and more recently with the hosting of the Tall Ships races attracting over 125,000 people to the town on one day. These events have not only gained the town a good reputation for putting on such large-scale celebrations, but also the locals welcome the opportunity to celebrate the maritime heritage through using the natural facilities of the beach and harbour. They would welcome more opportunity to undertake more events of this type.

Weymouth's Current Position

Weymouth in relation to Butler's life cycle (Butler, 1980) would appear to be in the stagnation stage, as like many English resorts, it has suffered a decline in the number of tourists visiting (Figure 2.1).

Figure 2.1: Weymouth Seafront and Beach and Portland Borough Council.
Source: Picture courtesy of Weymouth Seafront and Beach and Portland Borough Council.

In 1992 it was awarded the last of the Tourism Development Action Programmes in order to use strategic thinking amongst key organisations to try to overcome the decline; however the process was not successful (Agarwal, 2002). It has been hit by many factors including the loss of the local naval base, the loss of a major distribution centre for the UK retailer New Look (although recent press announcements indicate this company may return to the area) and alternative cheaper holidays available both overseas and within the United Kingdom. The accommodation sector is in need of an overhaul and other than the sea life centre there are limited wet weather facilities. The main attraction for visitors is the beach and harbour, although the use of the water itself is somewhat limited.

A closer examination of Butler's resort life cycle model highlights the need to ensure that the organisation of events should be directly linked to an overall resort development strategy, as many events are not wholly dependent on the tourist market alone (Sadd and Jackson, 2006). Indeed, many destinations are constantly evolving and events can be used to add differentiation to the product, lengthen stay and encourage repeat business (Ali-Knight and Robertson, 2004). Events can play a crucial role through their uniqueness, the types of experience they offer and also their ability to smooth out the extremes in seasonality seen in seaside resorts with the development of facilities such as conferences during what are known as the shoulder months, those that border the more traditional summer months. Getz (2000) questions the life cycle and saturation issues involved in hosting these events. He believes that with the rapid expansion seen within the events sector over the past few decades, it is perhaps opportune to debate whether this rate of expansion can continue, or whether they will enter a period of decline '*or a golden age of permanent maturity*' (Getz, 2000, p. 175). He believes that no single factor has been responsible for this rapid growth, rather a combination of the global growth in population, disposable incomes, increased leisure time and mobility. He also argues that there is a strategic emphasis associated with event portfolios through mandates to promote tourism destinations. Urban consumers particularly enjoy events held in rural communities and resorts, with events becoming more entertainment orientated, but the danger can be of too many events in some areas. Jones (1993, in Gartner and Lime, 2000) reported that whilst around 9000 festivals are held in the United Kingdom each year, at least half are running at a loss. In conclusion, Getz (2000) identified that should a destination's popularity decline, then so will some of its attractions and events. It is also true that if it is the other way around then the destination may well suffer as a consequence, as many events are not designed for the tourist market specifically, so the evolution of the destination may not follow the same path.

Traditional British Seaside Resorts

Many traditional seaside resorts are considering ways of restructuring (Agarwal, 2002), with regeneration featuring highly. Yet many resorts are using conferences, entertainment and the possibility of casino developments as their catalysts whilst there is huge scope to use sporting events as main attractions. For example, Eastbourne successfully hosts the Lawn Tennis Association's Women's International Championships, a warm up for Wimbledon and they also have the four-day International Seafront Air show. Weymouth and Portland have the opportunity to capitalise on the media attention the hosting of the sailing events for London 2012 will bring to the area, even though they will be some 160 miles from the main focus of attention. The 'place distinctiveness' of the resort is vitally important and should be recognised and appreciated (Agarwal, 2002) with the unique sailing water adjacent to the World Heritage Coastline and the world class developments being undertaken in the area to complement the use of the water facilities. Urry (1997 in Shaw and Williams) believes that cultural change in seaside resorts, which is often attributed to external forces, is more due to cultural shifts and changes in beliefs, values and identities. No amount of money invested in accommodation or types of entertainments can overcome the shifts in values that people hold towards the facilities seaside resorts offer. Therefore, it is imperative to look at the cultural offerings and Weymouth has now invested, through the local college, in a Cultural Officer for the town. In addition, a Public Art Commissioning Plan for Weymouth and Portland 2012 Cultural Olympiad is underway already. Young (2007) agrees in that traditional 'attractors' such as cinemas and multiplexes are no longer sufficient and that new differentiated 'attractors' are required to bring in visitors and locals alike. These include visitor attractions, cultural and arts venues, arenas, conference centres and learning centres. The key reasons for developing this area are to raise profile and create brand awareness, to create footfall and increase dwell time, to improve quality of life and raise values (Young, 2007). Smith (2004) also argues for the opportunities for cultural regeneration through events, already seen in many European cities (e.g. Barcelona).

Present Redevelopments

There is a Royal Yachting Association (RYA) 'centre of excellence' in the WPNSA, redeveloped with a £6 million grant from the Sport England Fund, English Institute for Sport, the South West of England Regional Development Agency (SWRDA) and the RYA. This grant was given not only in preparation of the Olympic bid, but also to increase and improve the facilities to host more annual world class events irrespective of the bid outcome. The council that is jointly responsible for Weymouth and Portland has recognised the need to strengthen its staffing infrastructure and has recently appointed a new economic development officer who also has the responsibility for regeneration of the town, a role that was never recognised previously. As a result of this new appointment, and also in recognition of the need to upgrade facilities in preparation of the hosting of the games, a wholesale redevelopment of the seafront is taking place. Included in these plans are the restorations of the three major statues along the seafront promenade, the strengthening of the esplanade itself, the restoration of the Victorian shelters, along with new bars and cafes, new lifeguard and tourist offices. In order to carry out many of the proposed alterations and improvements to the buildings along the seafront, permission is necessary from various preservation trusts. However with this comes the opportunity to apply for grants and funding to carry out these works. These projects include the restoration of the Victorian curved facades to certain buildings, the restoration of balconies and windows and the general repair of many of the classic features. However, as previously mentioned, despite the intention to regenerate the seafront with this large restoration project, there is no strategy in relation to the type of tourist the town wishes to attract. It can be argued that the developments are as much for the local population as any visitors, however as the town relies on its tourist trade it must therefore decide the future of its tourism business. The resort has traditionally relied on being a family destination, but has suffered in the last 30 years from cheaper forms of holiday both domestically and internationally. Weymouth does not benefit from an all year around resort profile, therefore international recognition and a chance to revamp its image within the international media will greatly enhance the town and its surrounding areas both in prestige as well as economic benefits.

The Waterfront Revitalisation project, also known as the Pavilion Peninsula, relates to a new development taking place in urban space besides the harbour and will also include gentrification through economic reinvestment, residential rehabilitation and commercial redevelopments, yet possibly displacing relatively poorer social classes through the more affluent urban 'gentry' moving in.

Growth in Events Business

More and more towns and cities are using events as a means of delivering on a range of objectives, including increasing tourists visits and spend, regeneration strategies to increase community pride and regional economic initiatives (Ali-Knight and Robertson, 2004; Bowdin et al., 2001; Hall, 1992). Events have long played an important role in society and special events have a role in the development of the tourism industry, especially as they have the potential to attract visitors globally. Sadd (2004) amalgamating previous work from Hall (1992) and Getz (1997), believe there are eight reasons for the growth seen in the mega-event business:

1. Positive imaging – putting the region, city and community on the map (Monclus, 2003), very important for a town such as Weymouth, but also seen in the example of Barcelona and the hosting of the 1992 Olympics (Auld and McArthur, 2003; Chalkley and Essex, 1999; Law, 1993; Stamakis et al., 2003).
2. One city or destination seeking to emulate the success of another (Madden, 2002; Searle, 2002; Toohey and Veal, 2000; Waitt, 2001).
3. Economic development potential as seen by government (Auld and McArthur, 2003; Crompton and McKay, 1997; Hall, 1992; Hughes, 1993; Jeong, 1999; Matheison and Wall, 1989).
4. Segmentation and specialisation within the tourism market (Chalip, 2002; Crompton and McKay, 1997; Morse, 2001; Shackley, 2000).
5. Availability of government grants for sports, art and culture (Hall, 1992; Gunn, 1994; Persson, 2002).
6. Attracting of investment by the use of profile and image (Burgan and Mules, 1992; Shone and Parry, 2001; WTO, 1997).
7. Promotion of civic pride and the desire to overcome adverse circumstances (Chalkley and Essex, 1999; Law, 1993).
8. The changing nature of leisure activity in western society (Boniface and Cooper, 1994; Cooper et al., 2000; Crompton and McKay, 1997; Faulkner et al., 2000; Pearce and Butler, 1999).

Source: Sadd and Jackson (2006).

According to Hall (1992), mega-events, otherwise referred to as special or hallmark events, are major fairs, festivals, expositions and cultural and sporting events which are held on either a regular or one-off basis. He further writes that these events have become a key tool in the tourism marketing strategies at international, national and regional levels through their primary function of providing tourism opportunities. These events are also extremely significant as '*they may leave behind legacies which will impact on the host community far more widely than the immediate period in which the event actually took place*' (Hall, 1992, p. 1). Gunn, (1988, p. 259 in Hall, 1992) argues, '*Probably the fastest growing form of visitor activity is festivals and events*'. Law (1993, p. 97) agrees that they are '*large events of world importance and high profile which have a major impact on the image of the host city*'. Examples of impacts include: large-scale public expenditure, improved infrastructure, the redevelopment of urban areas and increased world profile. In contrast, Hall (1992, p. 1) argues that the study of mega-events '*is fraught with definitional, methodological and theoretical problems which reflect the many research directions that exist within the study of tourism*'. Moreover, Armstrong (1986, in Hall, 2000) recognises that the hosting of international events promotes esteem, allowing local people to display their skills, cultural attitudes and civic pride. Other writers (Ritchie, 1984; Hall and Selwood, 1987 all in Hall, 1992) believe that the primary function of the hallmark tourist event is to allow the host community the opportunity to have a prominent role in the tourism market for a short, well-defined period of time. The event is distinguished from other attractions as it is not continuous or a seasonal phenomenon.

Current Major Events in Weymouth and Portland

The Veterans Awareness Week incorporating the Annual Military and Veterans Festival (Figure 2.2) is held in June every year and is endorsed by the Ministry of Defence as one of the official UK Regional 'Veterans Day' Flagship events.

> Veterans will be able to discover and receive the support available through the various agencies and charity organisations; and visitors to the events will be able to appreciate and support the important role played by the veterans and the service associations. With many uniquely nostalgic, social and commemorative experiences, Weymouth & Portland is the ideal destination for one of Britain's largest Veterans Festivals (Weymouth and Portland Borough Council).

Sailing Academy

This year the sailing club has already hosted some major sailing events very successfully including the following events: J24 Spring Cup, Dart 18 National Championships, European Championships,

Figure 2.2: Pictures from the Veterans Day Celebrations.
Source: Courtesy of Weymouth and Portland Borough Council.

RYA Olympic Training Camp, European Championships, Laser National Championships, National Championships, RYA Youth and Masters Windsurfing Championships, Skandia Sail for Gold Regatta and RYA South Zone Championships. The intention of the sailing centre was to attract world class sailing events to the area, irrespective of whether the 2012 bid was successful, and this it has achieved because of the natural and man-made facilities on offer. The centre provides high-performance training both ashore and afloat including disabled access and inclusion, in addition to supporting the local community and economy by encouraging supporting facilities and businesses (estimated impact of academy resulting in £35.9 million increase in demand on local firms and 150 full-time equivalent jobs) (Tweed, 2004).

In April 2007, a '500 for £5' event was held enabling local children to have access to sampling sailing. The normal cost should have been £25 per head but with funding from The Chesil Trust of £20 per head far more local children were able to take part. Further funding was also secured to allow a further 350 children to have the same experience, and more sessions are planned for the future. The children got the chance to learn about knots, rigging boats and how sails work, as well as getting to the water and meeting Olympic Sailors of the future who were at an Olympic Squad training Camp at the centre at the same time (Figure 2.3).

The WPNSA are particularly proud of their 'green credentials' and include the environmental programme whereby at certain times of the year, notably in the winter, sailors have to abide by exclusion zones due to birds 'over wintering' on the outskirts of the sailing waters. All new dredging in relation to new developments at the centre are mindful of the shelter afforded to certain breeds of protected worm that populate the area as well as Portland Sea Lavender and scaly crickets. In addition to the precautions the WPNSA instigate themselves, they are monitored by bird watchers and environmentalists.

Figure 2.3: Children enjoy sailing for a fiver.
Source: Courtesy of Sail Laser and The Chesil Trust – photo courtesy WPSNA, 2007.

The Royal Yachting Association (2004), whilst originally formed to harmonise racing conditions and to represent the views of all water users and has now evolved into policy making that affects all boat users and includes the 'Boating for Life' publication. This document sets out the environmental strategy for sustainable boating until 2009, and figures strongly in the developments around the Weymouth and Portland Harbours. Amongst the recommendations are the allowing for boating interests and landscape planning to 'live in harmony'; have RYA representatives on management and advisory groups to support the sustainable use of the coast for recreational boating; protect important recreational anchorages; and recognise the importance of the local boating industry. The RYA's influence was crucial in persuading Powergen not to proceed with their plans to place wind turbines on the outer harbour wall, as the RYA was concerned about the effect the turbines would have on the high-performance racing as well as on boating in general (http:www.rya.org.uk).

As sport tourism continues to grow in popularity with concerted efforts in the South West region of the United Kingdom to develop this segment of the market, the Weymouth and Portland area must pursue these opportunities using the natural features of the area. Sports tourism facilitates with the opportunity to utilise natural resources, often encouraging a longer tourism 'season'. South West tourism use the words 'adventure', 'lifestyle' and 'extreme' in their promotional material. Events associated with this market have the ability to be the catalyst for social and physical regeneration, a fact pertinent to Weymouth. Higham (2005) believes that sport plays an important and increasingly important role in the development of tourism destinations and also in the life cycles of older tourism destinations. Communities benefit from the hosting of water based events as they develop community cohesiveness as well as civic pride, and indeed the reason the Olympics are coming to the area of Weymouth and Portland is because of the sea.

Economic Prosperity

A report compiled by Dorset County Council in 2003 (Gray, 2003) recognised that the economy and labour market for the Weymouth and Portland area is service sector orientated, with a large proportion of small firms of lower than average productivity and low GDP per head. The area also has a slightly lower than average level of economic activity with a higher proportion of people having low or no qualifications pertinent to being service orientated, and whilst there is an above average unemployment figure, this is due to the seasonal nature of large sectors of the market. In February 2006 a further paper was published from the International Centre for Tourism and Hospitality Research, Bournemouth University (Fletcher, 2006) highlighting the Olympic effects in Weymouth and Portland, and the South West region as a whole of the consequences of the 2012 sailing event. The author concluded that there was a shortage of information relating to the economic impacts of the Olympics, despite the longevity of the event. Yet, from the data that is available there is a huge variety and complexity in terms of how the event was run (public versus private money), and also how the data itself was collected. The report compared the Weymouth anticipated economic effects to that of the Special Olympic World Winter Games held in 2001, in Anchorage, Alaska. These games had 4500 volunteers and 8500 residents attending the events. The Games brought $22 million into the economy, spending generated of $12 million and a total impact of $32 million in sales. The annual average equivalent of 400 new jobs was created and 98% of residents said the Games improved their quality of life (Fletcher, 2006). In summary, the Bournemouth University report highlighted that to truly evaluate the economic impacts, a long-term study of at least 6–10 years is crucial and at this stage there are many unknown variables. However, looking at the experience from other mega-events, the pre-games impacts result in an increased profile, increased levels of investment and participation rates. The anticipated cumulative impact of increased visitor spend could be as much as £9.6 million over 6 years with £19.2 million recorded over a 12-year period. Regionally, the tourism expenditure could rise by as much as £180 million with the equivalent of 4900 full-time equivalent jobs created. Increased demand for the sailing facilities, through the increased media coverage, could inject £24 million annually into the economy from an average 10% increase in demand for sailing. Whilst the officials and athletes will be housed in floating temporary hotels during the Games there will still be some visitors staying locally and day visitor spend to anticipate giving a projected total expenditure during the Olympic Games as between £5.8 and £9.5 million. Countering all these figures, there will be some displacement effects such as that of investment funds, business activity diverted elsewhere, visitor spending elsewhere and even locals, opting to spend there time elsewhere (Royal Wedding Effect), although research from Sydney showed that this effect was not as pronounced as predicted (DCC, 2005). There may also be the danger that tourists who would normally visit the sites in question, may stay away whilst the events are taking place, due to concerns overcrowding and price inflation. A phenomenon called the 'London' effect after the Royal Wedding in 1981 or the 'Los Angeles' effect after the 1984 Olympic Games (Zwolak, 1987 in Hall, 1992 and Getz, 1991). This was seen in Athens where accommodation prices fell in some cases by as much as 40%.

To these figures must also be added the estimations for the Paralympics Games, with a total expenditure of between £480,000 and £850,000, with media coverage adding a further £150,000 to the level of local spending. Additional opportunities could arise form any run-up/test events held before the Games in addition to the possibility of any training camps.

Organisers of events need analysis of economic impacts in order to evaluate the benefits for the local economy, assess projected levels of attendance and finally to provide information for the public domain (the local community), on the merits of the event, especially if it is considered a potentially contentious issue. Negative economic impacts include opportunity costs, over-dependence on tourism, higher inflation and fluctuating land values, seasonality and external costs. These impacts include high leakages from developing countries whereby tourism income is taken out of the country back to the tourism developers' home nation. Land speculation was seen in Australia during the America's Cup Defence (Hall, 1992). Low returns on investment because of seasonal fluctuations in demand and over-dependence have been lodged as major criticisms of the tourist industry in general (Standeven and DeKnop, 1999; Turco et al., 2002). Smaller events in smaller towns will have a larger impact per business, yet the visitors might not stay as long because there is less to see and do; this is described as the 'Zone of Influence' by Andersson et al., 1999 and Hall (1992, 2000). The concentration of mega-event activities has several advantages but because of the type of some of the activities, especially in the variety of sporting events at the Olympics, it is not always possible. The advantages of concentrating the facilities include lower travel costs, more efficient use of transport and venues, better management of visitors and as a consequence fewer negative impacts on the environment and community (Hall, 2000). Conversely, the dispersal of events could prevent congestion. It is the nature of the event that determines how much dispersal is acceptable or geographically necessary, for example the location of suitable sailing facilities (www.athenshousing.com/olympicshistory/olympicsports/sailing.html).

Other Impacts

Whilst many different writers discuss the economic impacts of hosting Olympic mega-events (Andersson et al., 1999; Brown et al., 2002; Burgan and Mules, 1992; Fayos-Sola, 1998;

Humphreys and Plummer, 1995; Kang and Perdue, 1994; Kasimati, 2003; Madden, 2002; Morse, 2001; Ritchie, 1984), only a few study the non-economic impacts and include Hiller (1998, 2000), Lenskyj (1992, 1994, 1996, 2002) and Shone and Parry (2001, p. 66) who state that the benefits of hosting mega-events include opportunities *'to create better social interaction, help to develop community cohesion, increase cultural and social understanding and improve the communities identity and confidence in itself'*. Shaw and Williams (2000) write that changes brought about by 'guest–host' encounters run through both social and cultural dimensions and should be viewed separately, yet Mathieson and Wall (1989) argue that it is extremely difficult to do this as they interact. Few studies measure the social impacts of tourism, the most widely used framework for describing the effects of tourists on a host society being 'Doxey's Index of Irritation' developed in 1976. This index represents the changing attitudes of the host population to tourists along a linear scale with increasing levels of irritation as the volume of tourists grows. The stages of progression begin with euphoria as tourism develops, to apathy, irritation and finally antagonism in the face of increasing development. The sequence is determined both by numbers and compatibility of each group, related to culture, economic status, race and nationality (Turner and Ash, 1975 in both Mathieson and Wall, 1989 and Shaw and Williams, 2000). Doxey's scheme, useful in exploring the reactions of residents, is limited in that it does not allow for the inclusion of visitor management schemes, which may reduce visitor pressure, or cases where local communities become involved in tourism planning. Haywood (1988) encourages responsible and responsive planning of tourism in the community. Though his suggestion was written over 19 years ago, it is still relevant in today's planning processes. He advocates citizen involvement through a more participatory approach, not the abandonment of centralised government tourism planning but more tourism planning at the community level. Many of his suggestions appear in the South West Tourism document 'Towards 2015' (the regional body responsible for the South West of England and their strategic plan for the future).

In addition, sports tourism developments can have negative impacts on local communities, especially the trend of building new facilities on the outskirts of towns. Sheldon and Abenoja (2001) argue that through evaluating the attitudes of residents towards tourism and involving them in developments is a vital step towards creating sustainability. Wahab and Pigram (1997) agree and comment that whilst tourism faces many challenges for both tourist and host communities, tourism must respond to changes in the global environment and in societies' structures through acknowledging the need for sustainable development. Hovinen (2002) also argues that the potential for significant decline exists if the opportunity to promote sustainable tourism through strategic planning is missed. Agarwal (2002) believes that a 'restructuring' with a greater appreciation of place distinctiveness is the solution to overcoming resort decline. Smith (2004) argues that cultural regeneration has superseded the need for sustainability in seaside regeneration.

Carrying Capacity

The impact of tourism and mega-events should include the concept of carrying capacity. This relates to the point beyond which further levels of visitation or development would lead to unacceptable deterioration in the physical environment and of visitors' enjoyment (Archer and Cooper; Williams and Gill both in Theobald, 2005; O'Reilly, 1986). Carrying capacity plays a pivotal role by intervening in the relationship between visitor and resources. The character of the resource, that is its natural features, is equally important and the resort/area must decide its physical limits and robustness to continued tourism development (Mathieson and Wall, 1982; O'Reilly, 1986).

Impacts on Coastlines

In western countries and particularly in the United Kingdom, it is the fragile coastlines that have received maximum environmental damage (Matheison and Wall, 1982; Shaw and Williams, 2000) from tourists and through the development of ports, refineries, marinas, sporting facilities and power generators. Much of the damage has been caused through inadequate planning with not enough consideration being given to complex ecostructures, whereby flora and fauna disappear due to drainage and excavation. The effects arising from sightseeing include disruption to zonations, destructions to habitats, erosion of dunes and interference with breeding habitats of wildlife (Matheison and Wall, 1982), in addition to problems with litter, sewage disposal, fires and erosion. Other impacts include the architectural pollution of developments, for example the Costa del Sol in Spain (Pearce, 1978 in Matheison and Wall, 1982); the overloading of infrastructure, the segregation of local residents and traffic congestion. Along some parts of the Mediterranean coastline, locals have been barred from enjoying natural facilities, as almost half the coastline has been acquired through development for the sole use of hotel guests (Archer and Cooper, 1999 in Theobald, 1999). Widner and Underwood (2004) have carried out research on the patterns of boating traffic in Sydney harbour before, during and after the 2000 Olympic Games to measure the environmental impacts (Widner and Underwood, 2004).

Tourism Planning and Urban Regeneration

Mega-events have become increasingly popular as tourist attractions, contributing to the opportunity for urban regeneration, for example in Manchester and Cardiff (Law, 1993). Law (1993, p. 93) focuses on the potential of sport and leisure to promote tourism and especially in regenerating city centres and inner areas. He writes '*sport and tourism may also increase civic pride, community spirit and collective self image*' and he continues, '*The role of sport and tourism in urban regeneration in Britain has only recently begun to be considered*'. Gunn (1994) believes that for successful tourism planning there needs to be three levels: continuous national tourism planning, regional strategic planning and local tourism planning. He believes that all three levels need to be integrated and a strategic vision adopted advocating an orderly and structured planning process, combining objectives' determination with research and synthesis. A feasibility study looks at the viability of accomplishing the event, identifying possible sources of income. It also gathers information regarding the community and special interest groups, and if used effectively, helps to develop good relations within the community and overcome any objections to the event taking place (Farmer et al. in Turco et al., 2002). Similarly Getz (1997) writes that whilst a feasibility study will assess the affordability and profitability of an event, it should also be used to evaluate the desirability and suitability. He believes that any event being staged should play a role in the destination's tourism plan and that sound planning should accompany the pursuit of events rather than the irrationality that is often seen. Table 2.1 shows strategies aimed at communities and destinations contemplating a bid for a mega-event or in the process of planning an event.

Table 2.1: Strategies for optimising the tourism impacts of mega-events.

Plan for the long term	Specifically plan for pre- and post-event impacts as well as the event itself. Have a clear vision for the future and focus on the intended legacies of the event. Clear guidelines and responsibilities of organisers and reporting channels, by planning the organisational and marketing evolution necessary to ensure long-term benefits for all.
Optimise facility development and use of existing facilities	The development of new facilities represents one of the largest costs and entails great risks of oversupply with limited use after the event. The use of cruise ships to supply temporary accommodation where feasible is a popular option as is turning accommodation facilities into low cost affordable housing or university accommodation as seen in Atlanta (Toohey and Veal, 2000).
Plan for sustained awareness and image-making efforts	Combat negative publicity, as seen in the British Press and their criticisms of the London 2012 bid (Wooldridge, I. (2004). *Daily Mail*, May 22nd). Involve the press from the planning and feasibility stages right through to the after event summaries and looking to the future. Smith (1989, in Getz, 1991, p.253) notes, '*it is the media, backed by word-of-mouth which generates and controls the hype*'. Getz (1991) also writes that although travel and sports writers have their own specialised readership, it is news reporters who have the largest audiences and therefore the biggest influence. In return the television distribution rights for the coverage of the Olympics will cost US \$800 million for the 2006 winter games and US \$1700 million for the 2008 summer games (Persson, 2002).
Tourist facilitation	Making the stay of the visitors as comfortable as possible. The ease of purchasing tickets must be considered on a global scale with the utmost precision to combat 'black market' tickets being sold at inflated prices. Similarly, the ease of entry for all nationals across international borders must be considered and the provision of information in as many languages as possible. The host population must be willing and helpful to all visitors.
Target marketing	The possibility of attracting higher yield, quality visitors must be considered as opposed to the mass market, large volumes. Residents however, should not be excluded.
Combat displacement effects	In order to avoid visitors staying away through fear of overcrowding, price inflations, crime and terrorism, a concentrated programme of information and an image-making campaign must be initiated as soon as possible. Residents must be persuaded that the event is so unique that they should forego their other trips.
Dispersal of benefits	If possible spread the events over a large area to avoid congestion. However, depending on the event it may be more prudent to concentrate facilities to reduce costs and to make it a more pleasant experience for the visitor.
Maximising tourism benefits	Encourage visitors to stay longer by organising pre-and post-event celebrations. Use high-quality souvenirs to encourage visitors to buy more items and use local suppliers to increase the multiplier effect. Include in the event planning entertainment opportunities, yet do not over-supply permanent facilities.

Source: author (2008) adapted from Andersson et al. (1999).

Community Participation in Tourism Planning

Tourism is of considerable economic significance for the borough through job opportunities, accommodation, catering and leisure, tourism expenditure including retail and transport sectors (www.weymouth.gov.uk). The awarding of the heritage site status to the Jurassic Coastline in 2002 upon which Weymouth is situated has positioned the area on the international tourist destination map and should be a huge opportunity to develop the area as a key tourism and education destination. Haywood (1988) believes all tourism planning should involve a 'broader, more participatory approach' involving the local community with local governments in particular, recognising the importance of consulting the local citizens affected by tourism through public consultation. Local residents become part of the tourist product and whilst benefits are often perceived only in economic terms, there are other opportunities:

- Opportunity to improve management of the tourism life cycle.
- Clear understanding of those community elements that impact upon the tourism.
- Better anticipation of the internal and external challenges to tourism.
- Chance to overcome or lessen negative impacts.
- Opportunity to include everyone involved in the tourism product.

At present the community in Weymouth and Portland is marginally involved in a two-way exchange of information and ideas through the Citizen's Panel and other forms of consultation available through open meeting formats. The business community is felt by some residents to have a more influential voice within the Weymouth and Portland area. In 2004 when the research discussed in this chapter was carried out, none of the respondents was aware of the Community Plan 'Our Community, Our Future', which was at the time a new initiative for Weymouth. Some residents felt that the council places the wishes and needs of the tourists above those of the local residents. The Portland residents do not seem to enjoy being classified alongside Weymouth, which they regard as a 'bucket and spade' tourist destination. They believe the potential sailing event to be Portland based and seem to resent the press implications that it is Weymouth that is to host the events. Weymouth residents on the other hand recognise that new sailing facilities are being built at Osprey Quay, but would welcome the opportunity to play host to the event in 2012. The publication of 'Your Place, Our Future', the development of the Weymouth and Portland Community Plan 2007–2016, has been produced by the Weymouth and Portland Partnership with 'Themes of Action' identified to improve the quality of life for those who live in the boroughs being, health and well being, environment, housing, safer, stronger communities, learning culture and the arts and business success (Weymouth and Portland Partnership, 2007). At this stage the whole process is in the consultative stage with on-going community involvement, a clear improvement on past consultation. In addition, The Local Government Framework published in 2004, sets out the portfolio of documentation defining the proposed planning strategy for Weymouth and Portland Borough.

Weymouth's Place Distinctiveness

Local distinctiveness as identified in a 2003 report from the English Tourist Board and Tourism Management Institute includes the natural features, man-made features and heritage, culture and traditions of the area including events, festivals, history and arts. All of the above constitute a powerful tourism marketing tool by differentiating the resort from the competitors, affording product development opportunities, awareness of the ecosystem and providing themes for promotional campaigns. However, the important fact here is to decide on the destination positioning it itself in relation to its marketing and in the use of imagery (Day, Skidmore and Koller, 2001). In 2005, the marketing and communications department of Weymouth and Portland Borough Council produced a range of publicity material catering across a whole spectrum of visitors from retired couple to singles, families to young persons, teenagers to young professional, therefore trying to cater to everyone.

Weymouth Population Research Results

Research was carried out via a questionnaire distributed to 1000 members of the Citizen's Panel with the full cooperation of the Council. A response rate of 43% was recorded within the initial timeframes and 63% when the deadline was extended. The data was analysed using SPSS(v11) and some of the key findings in relation to the questions asked were the following.

What Types of Events Do You Wish to See?

- Beach concerts
- Tall ships
- Conferences
- Water sport events
- Open air and classical music events
- More use of the pavilion
- Wet weather entertainment facilities

By cross tabulating the response to more events with a break down of age groups, the results show that all age groups are open to all types of events, not just the young and middle aged. Interestingly, 65.4% of the 55+ age group welcomed more events (Figure 2.4).

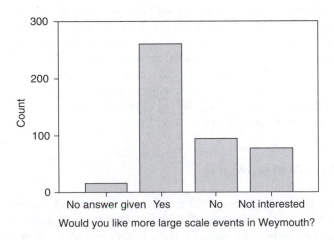

Figure 2.4: Public interest in large-scale events in the Weymouth and Portland areas.

How Important Are Festivals and Events to the Area?

The importance of festivals and events is described in Figure 2.5.

Reasons Why Visitors Come to Weymouth

The most popular reason is the beach and weather with 95.1% of respondents rating it at least important (3) and above (maximum 6). The harbour and bay was next with 90.6%, surrounding countryside was third followed by sailing facilities in fourth place. Festivals and events were considered at least important to 78.3% of respondents (Figure 2.6).

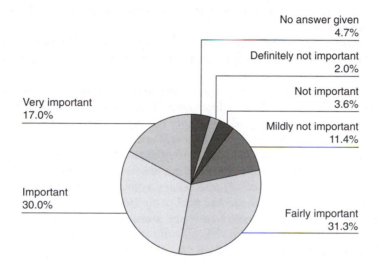

Figure 2.5: Importance of festivals and events.

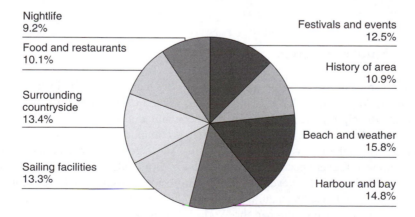

Figure 2.6: Reasons why visitors come to Weymouth.

What Would You Like to Change About Weymouth?

This open ended question was posed to all members of the panel and below is a selection of responses:

- Weymouth sets its sights too low; a beautiful bay filled with popcorn sellers, an empty bandstand, Georgian buildings carved up or neglected, yesterdays' 'entertainers' in the pavilion, no special attractions for children apart from Punch & Judy show, no attempt to appeal to any but the lowest common denominator mass market. A refusal to feature Portland and capitalise on its 'difference'.
- *If we want tourists we much provide facilities for them as well as amusement, for example sensible road systems and open toilets.*
- We have no 4 star accommodation for competitors or top brass. Local societies are against any structural or environmental improvements to the town. A typical example of local planning is the underpass on the seafront.
- *We need to learn from the success of the 'Tall Ships', both locals and tourists enjoyed the event. Roads being shut with park and ride gave a real happy atmosphere. The festival events on the beach were excellent too.*
- If Weymouth had a real plan it could transform the town. I believe it could become a serious option for people to consider as a holiday first choice. It has to fix its appearance.
- *The infrastructure of the town really needs sorting out before any major sailing events come to town. The present situation will give the town a bad name.*
- I think the Tourism Department have done well over the past 5/10 years to develop new ideas, but to be successful as a resort more events and more out of season facilities are needed.
- *We have some of the best waters around for water sports and yet the powers that we just look for sailing, why not power boat racing as we had back in the 1990s and ski racing.*
- Weymouth in summer is tacky; I would like to see a classier image. More needs to be done to attract 'high class' visitors to Weymouth. The majority at the moment are 'inner city' grockels on beach holidays and hen/stag nights that just want to get drunk. The town needs more culture, music and theatre.
- *Water sports are all year events that should be encouraged, whilst keeping a high level of summer trade.*

Weymouth's Future Direction

Residents have expressed a wish to see the town move 'up market'. All the interview respondents from 2004 believe Weymouth to have great potential, yet the council must act quickly to encourage developments to help rejuvenate the town. The economic consequences for the town alone will justify rejuvenation. The development 'boutique' style accommodation, an innovation in accommodation standards, where the rooms are of 4 star quality but there are no restaurant or bar facilities, could encourage fewer, higher spending clientele, who in turn could encourage more upmarket restaurants and shops to the area. However, the majority of residents were keen to see more events held in the area and especially to use the natural facilities of the bay and harbour. Only two questionnaire responses and one interviewee mentioned the World Heritage Site of the Jurassic Coastline yet, the Weymouth and Portland National Sailing Academy (WPNSA) have placed great emphasis on this site's proximity to the sailing centre and used its potential backdrop as one reason for holding the Olympic Sailing in the area. The residents to not feel that the impacts of hosting events in the area will place any greater infrastructure pressures than already seen in the town and the construction of the relief road will mitigate the congestion. The majority of residents welcome the positive opportunities, although many look forward to daytime events for families in preference to evening events.

In conclusion Weymouth could adopt the following strategies:

- Have a clear vision of the future and focus on the intended legacies of the Olympics event, through using events in the pre- and post-games periods as well as the Games itself.
- Use the media, whether local journalists, sports writer or TV producers to generate interest in the area and its outstanding natural features through publicity for proposed events and festivals celebrating the local cultural and landscape.
- Engage the local population as hosts during the Games by involving them early on through events specifically aimed at celebrating Weymouth and Portland's role in the 2012 Olympic Games.
- Encourage visitors to stay longer and explore more of the area through the strategic planning of the portfolio of events and festivals.

This chapter has explained the position within which Weymouth and Portland, Dorset, United Kingdom currently find themselves as host to the sailing competition of the 2012 Olympic Games. It highlights the fact that the area needs regeneration and rejuvenation and how the use of an events portfolio could play a major role within this strategy. The research carried out, a small section of which was used to highlight some of the suggestions, will be an on-going project as the Games approach and it will be interesting to see how successful any event initiative become.

References

Agarwal, S. (2002) Restructuring seaside tourism – the resort lifecycle. *Annals of Tourism Research*, 29(1), 25–55.

Ali-Knight, J. and Robertson, M. (2004) Introduction to arts, culture and leisure. In Yeoman, I. et al. (eds.), *Festival and Events Management*. Oxford: Elsevier Butterworth-Heinemann.

Andersson, T. D., Persson, C., Sahlberg, B. and Strom, L-I. (1999) *The Impact of Mega-Events*. Ostersund, Sweden: European Tourism Research Institute.

Auld, T. and McArthur, S. (2003) Does event-driven tourism provide economic benefits? A case study from the Manawatu region of New Zealand. *Tourism Economics*, 9(2), 191–201.

Boniface, B. G. and Cooper, C. P. (1994) *The Geography of Travel and Tourism*. London: Heinemann.

Bowdin, G., McDonnell, I., Allen, J. and O'Toole, W. (2001) *Event Management*. Oxford: Butterworth-Heinemann.

Brown, M. D., Var, T. and Lee, S. (2002) Messina Hof Wine and Jazz Festival: An economic impact analysis. *Tourism Economics*, 8(3), 273–279.

Burgan, B. and Mules, T. (1992) Economic impact of sporting events. *Annals of Tourism Research*, 19(4), 700–710.

Butler, R. W. (1980) The concept of the tourism areas life cycle of evolution: Implications for management resources. *Canadian Geographer*, 24(1), 5–12.

Chalip, L. (2002) Using the Olympics to optimise tourism benefits (online), www.blues.uab.es/olympisstudies/lessons/f17.html

Chalkley, B. and Essex, S. (1999) Urban development through hosting international events: A history of the Olympic Games. *Planning Perspectives*, 14, 369–394.

Cooper, C., Fletcher, J., Gilbert, D., Shepherd, R. and Wanhill, S. (2000) *Tourism, Principles and Practice* (2nd Edition). Harlow: Longman.

Crompton, J. L. and McKay, S. L. (1997) Motives of visitors attending festival events. *Annals of Tourism Research*, 24(2), 425–439.

Day, J., Skidmore, S. and Koller, T. (2001) Image selection in destination positioning: A new approach. *Journal of Vacation Marketing*, 8(2), 177–186.

Dorset County Council (2006) *Economic Impacts for Dorset of hosting the Sailing in 2012*, Dorchester, DCC.

Faulkner, B., Moscardo, G. and Laws, E. (eds) (2000) *Tourism in the 21st Century*. London: Continuum.

Fayos-Sola, E. (1998) The impact of mega-events. *Annals of Tourism Research*, 25(1), 241–245.

Fletcher, J. (2006) Olympic Effects in Weymouth–Portland and the South West Region 2012. Paper prepared for the South West Regional Development Agency Economists Panel, Bournemouth University, UK.

Gartner, W. C. and Lime, D. W. (eds) (2000) *Trends in Outdoor Recreation, Leisure and Tourism*. Oxon, UK: CAB International.

Getz, D. (1991) *Festivals, Special Events and Tourism*. New York: Van Nostrand Reinhold.

Getz, D. (1997) *Event Management and Event Tourism*. New York: Cognizant Communication Corporation.

Getz, D. (2000) Festivals and special events: Life cycle and saturation issues. In Gartner, W. and Lime, D. (eds.), *Trends in Outdoor Leisure and Tourism*, UK: CAB International.

Gray, A. (2003) *Weymouth and Portland – A Profile of the Economy and the Labour Market*. UK: Dorset County Council.

Gunn, C. (1994) *Tourism Planning*. USA: Taylor & Francis.

Hall, C. M. (1992) *Hallmark Tourist Events: Impacts, Management and Planning*. London: Belhaven Press.

Hall, C. M. (2000) *Tourism Planning: Policies, Processes and Relationships*. London: Prentice Hall.

Haywood, K. M. (1988) Responsible and responsive tourism planning in the community. *Tourism Management*, 9(2), 105–118.

Higham, J. (eds) (2005) *Sports Tourism Destinations: Issues, Opportunities and Analysis*. Oxford: Butterworth Heinemann.

Hiller, H. (1998) Assessing the impact of mega-events: A linkage model. *Current Issues in Tourism*, 1(1), 47–57.

Hiller, H. (2000) Mega-events, urban boosterism and growth strategies: An analysis of the objectives and legitimations of the Cape Town 2004 Olympic bid. *International Journal of Urban and Regional Research*, 24(2), 449–458.

Hovinen, G. R. (2002) Revisiting the destination lifecycle model. *Annals of Tourism Research*, 29(1), 209–230.

HRH The Princess Royal (2005) *Opening Ceremony Speech*. Dorset, UK: WPSNA.

Hughes, H. L. (1993) Olympic tourism and urban regeneration. *Festival Management and Event Tourism*, 1, 157–162.

Humphreys, J. M. and Plummer, M. K. (1995) The economic impact of hosting the 1996 Summer Olympics, www.selig.uga.edu/forecast/olympic/OLYMTEXT.htm.

Jeong, G.-H. (1999) Residents' perceptions of the long-term impacts of the Seoul Olympics to the Chamsil area development in a tourism perspective. In *The Impacts of Mega-Events*, Ostersund, Sweden: European Tourism Research Institute.

Kang, Y-S. and Perdue, R. (1994) Long-term impact of a mega-event on international tourism to the host country: A conceptual model and the case of the 1988 Seoul Olympics. In Theobald, W. F. (ed.), *Global Tourism (1999)*. Oxon, UK: Butterworth-Heinemann.

Kasimati, E. (2003) Economic aspects and the Summer Olympics: A review of related research. *International Journal of Tourism Research*, 5(6), 433–444.

Law, C. M. (1993) *Urban tourism: Attracting visitors to large cities*. London: Mansell.

Lenskyj H. L. (1992) More than Games: Community involvement in Toronto's bid for the 1996 Summer Olympics. In R. K. Barney and K. V. Meier (eds) *Critical Refelections on Olympic Ideology*. pp. 78–87. London, Ontario: Centre for Olympic Studies, University of Western Ontario.

Lenskyj H. L. (1994) Buying and Selling the Olympic Games: Citizen Particpation in the Sydney and Toronto Bids. In R. K. Barney and K. V. Meier (eds) *Critical Reflections on Olympic Ideology.* pp. 70–77. London, Ontario: Centre for Olympic Studies, University of Western Ontario.

Lenskyj H. L. (1996) When winners and losers: Toronto and Sydney Bids for the Olympic Games *Journal of Sport and Social Issues.* 20(4), 392–410.

Lenskyj, H. L. (2002) *The Best Olympics Ever? Social Impacts of Sydney 2000.* New York: New York State University Press.

Madden, J. (2002) The economic consequences of the Sydney Olympics: The CREA/Arthur study. *Current Issues in Tourism*, 5(1), 7–21.

Mathieson, A. and Wall, G. (1982) *Tourism: Economic, Physical and Social Impacts.* UK: Longman.

Monclus, F. J. (2003) The Barcelona Model: An original formula? From 'reconstruction' to strategic urban projects. *Planning Perspectives*, 18(4), 399–421.

Morse, J. (2001) The Sydney 2000 Olympic Games; how the Australia Tourist Commission leveraged the Games for tourism. *Journal of Vacation Marketing*, 7(2), 101–107.

O'Reilly, O. M. (1986) Tourism carrying capacity: Concepts and issues. *Tourism Management*, 7(4), 254–258.

Pearce, D. G. and Butler, R. W. (1999) *Contemporary Issues in Tourism Development.* London: Routledge.

Persson, C. (2002) The Olympic site decision. *Tourism Management*, 23(1), 27–36.

Ritchie, J. R. B. (1984) Assessing the impacts of hallmark events: Conceptual and research issues. *Journal of Travel Research*, 23(1), 2–11.

Royal Yachting Association (2004) *Boating for Life Southampton.* UK: RYA.

Sadd, D. J. (2004) *The impacts of ega-events at satellite venues: A case study of Weymouth and Portland as a possible Olympic Sailing venue.* Unpublished Masters Dissertation, Bournemouth University Bournemouth, UK.

Sadd, D. J. and Jackson, C. J. (2006) Planning for resort regeneration: The Role of the Olympic 2012 Bid for Weymouth and Portland Dorset, UK. LSA Publication, *Festivals and Events: Beyond Economic Impacts* Vol. 1. Sporting Events and Event Tourism: Impacts, Plans and Opportunities, Brighton, UK: LSA.

Searle, G. (2002) Uncertain legacy: Sydney's Olympic stadiums. *European Planning Studies*, 10(7), 846–860.

Shackley, M. (ed) (2000), *Visitor Management – case studues from World Heritage Sites.* UK: Butterworth-Heinemann.

Shaw, G. and Williams, A. M. (2000) *Critical Issues in Tourism – A Geographical Perspective* (2nd Edition). Oxford, UK: Blackwell.

Sheldon, P. J. and Abenoja, T. (2001) Resident attitudes in mature destination; the case of Waikiki. *Tourism Management*, 22(5), 435–443.

Shone, A. and Parry, B. (2001) *Successful Event Management – A Practical Handbook.* London: Thomson.

Smith, M. K. (2004) Seeing a new side to seasides: Culturally regenerating the English seaside town. *International Journal of Tourism Research*, 6(1), 17–28.

Stamakis, H., Gargalianos, D., Afthinos, Y. and Nassis, P. (2003) Venue contingency planning for Sydney 2000 Olympic Games. *Facilities*, 21(5/6), 115–125.

Standeven, J. and DeKnop, P. (1999) *Sport Tourism.* USA: Human Kinetics.

Theobald, W. F. (2005) *Global Tourism.* Oxford: Butterworth-Heinemann.

Toohey, K. and Veal, A. J. (2000) *The Olympic Games.* Oxon, UK: CAB International.

Turco, D. M., Riley, R. and Swart, K. (2002) *Sport Tourism.* West Virginia, USA: Fitness Information Technology Inc.

Tweed, J. (2004) *Sailing for the World* presentation given to Bournemouth, Dorset and Poole Economic Partnership. Portland, UK: Weymouth and Portland National Sailing Academy.

Wahab, S. and Pigram, J. J. (1997) *Tourism, Development and Growth: The Challenges of Sustainability.* London: Routledge.

Waitt, G. (2001) The Olympic spirit and civic boosterism: The Sydney 2000 Olympics. *Tourism Geographies*, 3(3), 249–278.

Weymouth and Portland Partnership (2007) *Your Place, Our Future*. Consultation documentation. Weymouth, Dorset, UK: WPP.

Widner, W. M. and Underwood, A. J. (2004) Factors affecting traffic and anchoring patterns of recreational boats in Sydney Harbour, Australia. *Landscape and Urban Planning*, 66(3), 173–183.

Wooldridge, I. (2004) Sorry Barbara, but a London Games just isn't worth it. *Daily Mail*, 22nd May.

WTO (1997) *Towards new forms of Public-Private Sector Partnerships*. Spain: WTO.

Young, S. (2007) Putting the mix into mixed use. *Locum Destination Review*, Issue 17.

www.ospreyquay.com/news.

www.rya.org.uk.

www.southwestrda.org.uk.

www.wpsa.org.uk.

www.weymouth.here-on-the.net.

www.weymouth.gov.uk.

Chapter 3

Tourism and the Hans Christian Andersen Bicentenary Event in Denmark

Janne J. Liburd

Introduction

Events have always enjoyed a special role in the celebration and demarcation of local and national cultures. More recently, with contemporary increases in leisure time and discretionary spending, governments and tourism organisations have adopted events as strategic means to international marketing and the promotion of a particular image. Events have also become an increasingly important aspect of a destination's tourism product, acting as an additional tool through which places can enhance specified tourism objectives. In order for events to be successfully associated with the tourism goals of the host destination, they must be carefully planned and managed to ensure that objectives are met. In connection with the commemoration of the Danish fairy tale writer, Hans Christian Andersen's bicentenary in 2005, the *Hans Christian Andersen 2005 Foundation* designated tourism as a special area for attention to attract more visitors to Denmark and further international awareness. The yearlong celebration became the first nationwide event since the Danish Government in 2003 identified events as a contributing factor to making certain parts of the country more attractive as a tourist destination while striving to create new prospects for Danish citizens. The 2005 Andersen celebration was targeted towards international tourists and local interest groups alike to also provide the latter with new socio-cultural opportunities to generate economic growth and cultivate theme related interests.

By comparing the original objectives, of which some were modified during the yearlong celebration to the achieved results, this chapter will assess the role of international tourism in the 2005 Hans Christian Andersen event in Denmark. First, the process of awareness raising will be outlined. This is followed by an analysis of the economic effects, focusing specifically on areas of product development and media exposure. Analysing next the collaborative approach between the culture and tourism sectors an intangible and contextualised aspect to event evaluation is presented. Clearly, a local, recurring festival with a limited thematic appeal will produce social, cultural, economic and

International Perspectives of Festivals and Events
Copyright © 2009 by Elsevier Ltd.
ISBN: 978-0-08-045100-8

environmental impacts that differ noticeably from a unique, nationwide event with international, cultural and artistic relevance, such as the Hans Christian Andersen bicentennial celebrations. Finally, the conclusion will summarise important learning experiences and problems encountered towards raising the level of professionalism in the growing Danish event industry. Event evaluation and dissemination of lessons learned are particularly important when considering the role of tourism in the implementation of a common, long-term event strategy, which is often the result of work carried out several years in advance.

Methodology

The analysis builds on an independent evaluation of secondary data in the form of reports, visitor surveys, economic analyses and PR material for printed and electronic media. One in-depth interview was conducted with a member of the Hans Christian Andersen 2005 Board of Directors and Event Manager at VisitDenmark. Several semi-structured telephone interviews were carried out, among others, with the Acting Director of the Secretariat of the Hans Christian Andersen 2005 Foundation and the Head of Events, a former employee at the Odense City Museums. The following limitations in the forthcoming analysis should be noted. First, the majority of statistics is secondary data and not designed by the author. Therefore, only select socio-economic objectives and collaborative efforts between the culture and business sectors will be evaluated. It is generally recommended that the range of evaluation activities to ultimately determine cost effectiveness, economic, social, cultural and environmental impacts and visitor satisfaction levels adopt a holistic approach (Presbury and Edwards, 2004). The strength of a holistic approach is that it views social, cultural, environmental and economic impacts as part of the whole and therefore interrelated. Secondly, adding to the complexity of holistic event evaluation, the Hans Christian Andersen bicentenary was held in multiple locations and over the course of an entire year. Thirdly, event evaluation is a process or cycle. Imputing and analysing data based on observation, feedback and surveys should feed back into the management process and lead to more efficient planning and improved event outcomes (Allen et al., 2005, p. 449). The present evaluation was undertaken in the autumn of 2006 and consequently, it has not added to the improvement of results before or during the Hans Christian Andersen 2005 event. Fourthly, the analysis draws on the anthropological method of participant observation among the Danish tourism industry, organisations and individual actors, which particularly has informed the discussion of intangible impacts. Finally, the author's multi-disciplinary experiences from teaching event management at university level are also explained in this chapter.

Findings: Creating Awareness

In December 2002 the Danish Tourist Board (now VisitDenmark) set up a tourism task force with representatives from the regional DMOs (destination marketing organisations), the Foundation FynTour and Wonderful Copenhagen, Odense Visitor's Bureau (now VisitOdense), VisitDenmark, the Hans Christian Andersen 2005 Foundation, Have PR & Communication, Destination Odense and at a later stage Odense City Museums. Immediately, this tourism task force produced a paper on international tourism marketing strategies for the celebration of the Andersen bicentenary (Blicher-Hansen, 2002). The document framed the group's plan of action and event activities that are described in further detail below. The paper also formed the basis for a special grant of 10 million Danish kroner (equivalent to 1.35 million euros) for international tourism marketing from the Danish Ministry of Economic and Business Affairs. The grant was not a part of the overall Hans Christian Andersen 2005 Foundation's sizeable budget of 220 million Danish kroner, or approximately 30 million euros. Administered by VisitDenmark, the grant could not be allocated to offset existing costs or already budgeted activities. Instead, the money should further new initiatives and create additional focus on select international markets. Feasibly, activities were to support the overall strategy plan of the Hans Christian Andersen 2005 Foundation. The overall strategy identifies three distinct objectives for tourism, which accordingly deserves closer attention:

1. Development of tourism products
2. Cultural activities and attractions leading to tourism
3. International tourism marketing.

As the first two areas (1) and (2) are interrelated, they will be addressed together in the following. It does not mean, however, that all Andersen related artistic and cultural activities appeal to international tourists. Neither does it imply that the activities equal the artistic products. Events, in this perspective, take on a functionalist view in which culture is made tangible to consumers. The event is used to facilitate or tell about the artistic product that is made available to the public – whether international tourists or local residents – as an experience (Have, 2006). Whereas many of the cultural activities and attractions were not developed with an international dimension at heart still, they may have contributed positively to the quality of the experience for the tourists who visited Denmark for other reasons than the Hans Christian Andersen celebrations.

Notable projects that contributed to attract international visitors are listed in Table 3.1.

From the list of projects in Table 3.1 only the last three have no permanency and did not continue after the year 2005. Supposedly, this has a positive implication on the value of the celebration and

Table 3.1: Tourism related projects.

A Tivoli Fairy tale

The projects under the auspices of the *Odense City Museums*, including the modernisation of the *Hans Christian Andersen Museum*, activities in the *Funen Village* and the set up of *The Annex* of Hans Christian Andersen's old attic room in Vingaardsstraede, Copenhagen

Andersen Was Here, tracing places described in Andersen's fairy tales around Denmark

The celebration of the birthday of the *Little Mermaid* by the statue in the harbour in Copenhagen

The addition of the *Eilschou Almshouses* in the Old Town in Aarhus

The performances by the *Hans Christian Andersen Parade* in Odense

The Christmas Market in Odense

The fairy tale theme of the *Annual Flower Festival* in Odense

The Little Mermaid Musical at the harbour in Copenhagen

The Golden Days' project, *In the Footsteps of Hans Christian Andersen* in Copenhagen

The International Parade in Copenhagen

---

image creation of Hans Christian Andersen's Denmark abroad, to which I will return below. One of the cultural projects expected to have an immediate positive impact on international tourist arrivals was the exhibition *The Greatest Fairy Tale* at the Rosenborg Castle. Unfortunately, it never material-ised as intended because the opening date of the exhibition was postponed more than once from the original date in May until the middle of October 2005. By then the peak of the Danish tourist sea-son had passed. In another project, international tourism and education were successfully linked as *edutainment*. The school project *The Flying Trunk* was targeted at primary school pupils 10–11 years of age in Belgium, Holland, Luxemburg, Great Britain and Ireland. A popular part of the project was a writing competition where the winning prizes were trips to Denmark. The competition obtained substantial Danish and international press coverage, according to VisitDenmark (2006), which in other words was free publicity of Denmark as a tourist destination. VisitDenmark's primary task is to promote Denmark abroad. Consequently, comprehensive documentation conducted by third party analysts is available. International tourism marketing focused on 11 select markets from 2003 to 2005: Sweden, Belgium, Holland, Luxemburg, Great Britain, Ireland, Italy, the United States, Germany, China, Spain and Japan. The specific marketing strategy targeting the areas of sale, MICE (Meetings, Incentives, Conferences and Exhibitions) planners and travel writers is well documented. Another, which deserves closer attention due to its overall impact, is the collaborative link intended between the main Danish tourism product areas (Coastal holiday, Active holiday, City break, MICE), the DMOs and their local industry associates to embrace the Andersen related marketing activities. The marketing strategy specifically emphasises the importance of 'the development of a range of suitable tools and concepts' including a sort of quality control, and 'motivation of Danish tourism businesses to develop products (and use) the same tools from the Toolbox' (Blicher-Hansen, 2002, p. 7). These tools include a press kit, photo materials and photo database, Video News Releases (VNR), a special logo to complement the official logo of the Foundation (to be used only in con-nection with activities supported by the Foundation), mobile exhibition units, web services and a so-called Hans Christian Andersen Agent Manual. The motivational aspects and creation of the Agent Manual will be discussed in further detail below. Quite impressively, the new Andersen Internet portal (www.visitdenmark.com/hca2005) was available in the 10 languages spoken in the above-mentioned markets and customised to cater to their specific target groups. The portal included a news page and information on tourist related events, a list of appointed *Hans Christian Andersen Ambassadors*, links to organisers and related homepages. In addition, a section of the national tour-ism portal (www.danskturisme.dk) was produced for the domestic tourism industry offering a range of tools and various types of event information (photo materials, logos, summaries of events, con-tact information). Accordingly, individual businesses, organisations and entrepreneurs that make up the majority of the Danish tourism industry were able to use Hans Christian Andersen as the main theme for re-thinking marketing activities where relevant.

Economic Effects

Based on the broad range of activities and projects mentioned above, the revised plans of action spec-ify the expected outcomes for international arrivals and bed nights (Hans Christian Andersen 2005 Foundation, 2004a, b). In 2004, an increase in the number of international bed nights of 465,000 equal-ling 2% was expected. In the running evaluations of the marketing activities in 2005, the projected number of international bed nights were conservatively reduced to less than half, 200,000, with a directly related total tourist turnover of 100–150 million Danish kroner, or 13.3–20 million euros. The drastic reduction in the projected economic impact was not accounted for. Only, a regional break down was provided. The objectives for Copenhagen and the island of Funen were maintained at 75,000 and 30,000 additional bed nights, respectively. This corresponds with a projected increase in international arrivals by 2.5%, whereas arrivals for the rest of the country were significantly reduced, which will be further discussed in the context of collaboration below.

Main Economic Effects

The following documentation of the obtained results and main economic effects on Danish tourism from the Hans Christian Andersen celebrations builds on analysis performed by Observer Danmark A/S that was part of an independent analysis of VisitDenmark's own marketing activities in 2005. The derived advertisement values were balanced by VisitDenmark and not audited by Observer. The analysis draws on VisitDenmark's (2006) report to the Danish Ministry of Economic and Business Affairs concerning the additional grant of 10 million Danish kroner for international marketing as well as data from Statistic Denmark in the annual 2005 statement of the *Economic and Employment Related Importance of Tourism*. The 2005 analysis contained a separate investigation into the effects of the Hans Christian Andersen event on international tourism in Denmark. A representative spot test was carried out nationwide among 3303 foreign tourists staying at hotels or in holiday cottages. Performed as a face-to-face interview, the survey focuses on the extent of international tourists' awareness of the celebrations and whether the event had been a contributing factor in their choice of holiday destination. The key findings are summarised in Table 3.2.

In particular, tourists from Denmark's near markets, Germany, Sweden, Norway and Holland expressed awareness of the celebrations; 79.25% of the hotel guests from those near markets and 67% of the tourists staying in holiday cottages had heard about the celebrations prior to their visits to Denmark. In total, 69% of international tourists staying in hotels and 59% of the international visitors staying in holiday cottages were aware of the bicentennial event. Based on those numbers, the national economic effects of international tourism during the Hans Christian Andersen event can be estimated to 1.2 billion Danish kroner, or 160 million euros. Just below 6% of the foreign tourists indicated that the celebrations were a contributing reason for their choice of Denmark as holiday destination in 2005. About 1% indicated that the celebrations were their main reason for travelling to Denmark. The latter group of tourists represents an estimated increased turnover of 107 million Danish kroner, or 14 million euros. A significant proportion of this can be considered 'new' money infused into the destination, having indirect and induced impacts on the economy (Burns and Mules, 1986).

The two main areas for the celebrations, the island of Funen where Hans Christian Andersen was born and the capital of Copenhagen, experienced a particularly significant growth in the number of bed nights of 10.5% and 12%, respectively, against the conservative estimate of 2.5%. The growth in the number of foreign bed nights in the rest of the country surpassed expectations slightly with an increase of 3.1%. Although the rise can be seen as a plausible indication of the positive economic impact that the event might have had on international tourism in Denmark during the yearlong event, caution needs to be exercised.

'The techniques chosen to assess the economic impact of events have often grossly overstated the impact by including expenditure that would have occurred irrespective of the event taking place.

Table 3.2: Main results of the quantitative analysis.

	Main results
Knowledge	69% of foreign hotel visitors and 59% of foreign tourists staying in holiday cottages in 2005 had heard about the celebrations prior to their visits.
Motivation for traveling	6% of foreign hotel visitors and tourists staying in holiday cottages indicated the celebrations as a directly contributing cause for their choice of holiday destination. 1% of the hotel visitors indicated the celebrations as the main cause. Less than 1% of the tourists staying in holiday cottages said so.
Economy	The turnover from the tourists who indicated the celebrations as the main cause is estimated at 107 million Danish krone. If the tourists indicating the celebrations as a contributing cause are included, the turnover is estimated at 1.179 billion Danish krone.
Press and TV	33–39% of all articles in the foreign press dealt with the 2005 celebrations.* Similarly, for 2004 the estimate is 18%. The advertisement value 2005 is reckoned to be 109.3 million Danish krone. About 500 million foreign TV viewers watched the VNR broadcast on the celebrations, giving an estimated advertisement value of 57,378,736 Danish krone.
Bed nights	Copenhagen and Funen saw a growth in the number of foreign bed nights of 10.5% and 12%, respectively. The growth in the rest of the country was 3.1%.

Source: Adapted from VisitDenmark (2006) and Observer (2006).
*The difference is due to a discrepancy between Observer's 2005 report (p. 6) and VisitDenmark's report for the Danish Ministry of Economic and Business Affairs (VisitDenmark (2006, p. 2).

Excessive multipliers have also been used in many studies to further inflate the overall results' (Jago and Dwyer, 2006, p. 1).

Consequently only 'new money' or 'inscope' expenditure should be used to assess the economic impacts of events due to the indirect and induced effects on the economy, where multipliers are used to determine the contribution to value added and to employment (Burns and Mules, 1986).

Media Exposure

An important benefit to events can derive from media exposure of a destination before, during and after the event. While media exposure in the foreign press and on television is intangible in nature and thus difficult to quantify, media impacts were documented by Observer's (2006) analysis of VisitDenmark's own marketing efforts. In total, 1619 articles were produced of which 33% in the foreign press paid specific attention to the celebrations in 2005; for 2004 the number was 18%. The advertisement value for 2005 is estimated by VisitDenmark at 109.3 million Danish kroner, or 14.5 million euros. In addition, the capital's DMO, Wonderful Copenhagen, produced 13 VNRs that were displayed on news channels, the Internet and as parts of thematic broadcasts in cultural programmes (Wonderful Copenhagen 2005). These VNRs were estimated to have reached potentially 557,291,946 viewers worldwide, excluding the United States and China. The VNRs were shown there as well, but for financial reasons surveys were not performed in those markets. According to Wonderful

Copenhagen, the converted advertisement value for the 13 VNRs were assessed at 57,378,736 Danish kroner, equivalent to 7659 million euros. Disregarding the cost of production, the free publicity for Denmark as a tourist destination are imputed as advertising expenditure saved. Drawing on key competences the range of international marketing activities was an outcome of effective collaboration between VisitDenmark, the involved DMOs and notably Have PR & Communication. The latter was in charge of all media communication for the Hans Christian Andersen 2005 Foundation. Have PR & Communication was also responsible for the main press strategy of the Foundation, special adaptation of artistic and cultural media included, whereas the DMOs and VisitDenmark's marketing offices worked closely together with the international travel press.

It should be noted that the multiplier effect used in assessment of advertisement value is prone to a degree of subjectivity involved in the estimation process and costs saved, just as unfavourable media exposure make adequate assessment difficult (Dwyer et al., 2000). Moreover, evaluating event impacts should not be reduced to simple reflections concerning a satisfactory return of investment in international tourism marketing and arrival statistics, the value of which are roughly represented in the numbers above. The key input to economic impact assessment is the amount of 'new' expenditure generated from tourists, residents, organisers, delegates, sponsors, media and others (e.g. exhibitors) attending the event. A more stringent approach to the economic dimensions of event evaluation is needed to ensure that events maximise their contribution to the host region (Jago and Dwyer, 2006) and moreover, that cultural and social aspects are included in a holistic evaluation. This is particularly important concerning international artistic and cultural events like the celebrations of Hans Christian Andersen due to the scale, timeframe and numerous contexts involved. Such comprehensive undertaking, which is beyond the scope of this chapter, calls for specific data collection and qualitative interviews with relevant stakeholders, visitors and local residents before, during and after the event.

Intangible Impacts

There are always intangible impacts associated with events, notably in socio-cultural areas, which are often addressed in the framework of destination costs and benefits during and after an event (Dwyer et al. 2005). Events do not operate in a vacuum. In the following, a contextual understanding of the socio-cultural milieu in which the Hans Christian Andersen 2005 event was staged will be provided. First, focus will be on organisational collaboration between what can roughly be divided into a culture and a tourism sector. Also, the ownership of the event among Danish tourism businesses will be addressed. Finally, reflections on the potentially added value, when cultural expressions become experiences through the mediation of the event, will point to future challenges and opportunities for the nascent event industry.

Assessing the collaboration between the culture and tourism industry it is important to note that the Danish tourism industry, VisitDenmark and its DMOs do not enjoy a long-standing tradition of collaboration. Conventionally, the Danish DMOs market specific geographical areas. Local partnerships are made within the destination between tourism related businesses, municipalities and visitor bureaus. Strategic links are made to the four product areas or so-called Alliance groups: Coastal Tourism, City Break, Active vacation and MICE. Established in 2002 the four Alliance groups are voluntary, cross-sectoral initiatives that are coordinated by VisitDenmark. The Alliance groups launch specific marketing and development activities that are predominantly based on industry networks rather than the typical place-bound, destination approach (Simonsen, 2006, p. 95). Still, there are only a few examples of successful attempts to favourably link the Danish business and cultural sectors (Figure 3.1) as advocated by the Danish Government (2003), let alone adopting international perspectives in the process.

In other words, the Danish tourism industry and its organisations ventured into virgin territory in the yearlong celebration of Andersen. Focusing on some of the organisational and socio-cultural impacts it will be argued that the existing division between the majority of tourism enterprises and the organisations in Copenhagen were magnified in the process.

According to the tourism task force's marketing strategy, the two regional DMOs, FynTour and Wonderful Copenhagen, were to develop the aforementioned Hans Christian Andersen Agent Manual. Nonetheless, the prioritised Manual was never produced. Whether this is a manifestation of internal organisation problems or a lack of collaborative practice between the respective DMOs should be further probed. Demonstrated elsewhere (Liburd, 2007), a qualitative approach is particularly useful towards an in-depth understanding of the webs of interacting cultures at stake in order to facilitate collaboration between colleagues who are also competitors. Moreover, a recent structural analysis of tourism in Denmark concludes that the sector lacks a shared identity and suffers from low self-esteem, which negatively impacts on collaboration in areas of distribution, marketing, competence development and innovation at local, regional and national levels (Simonsen, 2007, p. 106). Records from interviews confirm that there was a mutual lack of knowledge and respect between the culture and tourism sectors in Denmark. Whereas both sectors are comprised of highly diverse micro-enterprises, the culture sector do not necessarily see itself as part of a bigger entertainment potential, neither in a national nor international context. Artists often enjoy dubious status and recognition, a phenomenon well known to the service sector. Employment patterns are random and insecure and yet they are pivotal to the success of the many Danish summer events and festivals.

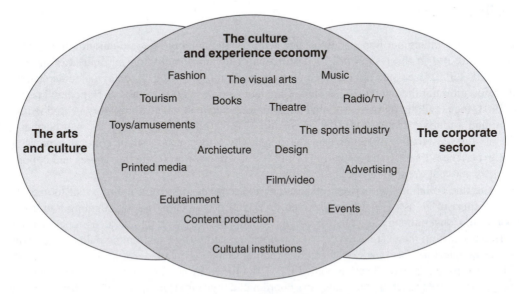

Figure 3.1: The culture and experience economy.
Source: Danish Government (2003, p. 8).

Singling out the music industry for illustrative purposes, many musicians associate negative impacts with the commoditisation of culture in tourism (Have, 2006). If an artist chooses to commercialise a cultural production, entering the globally competitive marketplace may prove overwhelming particularly if support from either a local, regional or national tourism organisations is not available. In the context of the Andersen celebrations, this meant that many cultural events were not planned with timely considerations for public announcements before the show. Consequently, international tourism operators, Danish DMOs and the Alliance groups were not aware of thematically relevant cultural events. Since the timeframe for the production of tour programmes and guide materials are often several years, the creation of the Hans Christian Andersen Agent Manual, as initially envisaged by the tourism task force, appears to be a very challenging, if not impossible task.

The distinctive aspect of cultural experiences is that they provide a unique value to the individual consumer or tourist. Often appealing to both mind and heart, cultural experiences are actively used in identity creation and may positively impact status and social recognition (Liburd, 2005). Originating from quality, attitude, sensuality, aesthetics, authenticity, context and history, cultural creativity thus contributes to the creation of unique experiences that may change perceptions of the world and self. In other words, culture borne experiences are about collaborative links and transformations – among consumers and providers, businesses, organisations and public authorities. When facilitated in the form of events, advertisement and linkages to other products and services can subsequently be realised. If customers identify with the theme of the experience these linkages may become even more lucrative (Jantzen and Jensen, 2006). First, however, businesses must take a certain degree of ownership of the event in order to implement and capitalise on the linkages made. Mindful that the celebration would be held in multiple locations nationwide, the so-called 'Toolbox' contained a variety of motivating instruments to simultaneously assure uniform marketing and exercise a degree of quality control (Blicher-Hansen, 2002, p. 7). However, the intended collaboration between the tourism businesses and the main organisers in Copenhagen proved inadequate. Long-standing animosities between its organisations in Copenhagen and the rest of the country were prevalent in the lack of event ownership. In this perspective, a negative focus by the national media on a sizeable budget deficit in connection with the event opening show became yet another reason to distinguish 'Us' from 'Them'. The opening show featuring Tina Turner singing 'Simply the best' at the national football stadium in Copenhagen did not resonate with a commonly held modest image of the Danish fairy tale writer. More fundamentally, the majority of micro- and small tourism enterprises consistently market a single, often well-defined product and they frequently lack the capacity to make new investments and to develop the part of the business that can enter into a dialogue with relevant organisations, such as VisitDenmark.

In sum, the Danish tourism industry did not identify with the Hans Christian Andersen bicentennial nor did the sector embrace some of the values so popular abroad. This has likely caused the tourism task force to diminish expected arrivals and the economic impact on tourism. The culture and tourism sectors lacked collaboration and the competences needed to create experience related transformations, which were magnified in the context of the event. This also illustrates that events do not operate in a vacuum, which calls for in-depth understandings of the socio-cultural contexts in order to create desirable linkages and transformations. This is particularly important when *content production* has become a critical, competitive parameter in the new experience economy (Pine and Gilmore, 1999). An example from one of the participating museums is helpful. The three-tiered obligation of Danish public museums and cultural institutions are to educate, research and preserve cultural heritage. At the same time, these institutions must adapt to an international competitive situation in which experiences have become a quality parameter. According to the former Director of Odense City Museums:

> The visitors' encounter with Hans Christian Andersen's original pen must be staged so that a magic room for the experience of the real and authentic is created. At the same time, the visitor is hopefully motivated to learn more, ideally inspiring another visit (personal communication).

The example is illustrative in its recognition of experiential transformations that are facilitated through cultural creativity and intangible elements. Indeed, intense artistic, cultural experiences educate, entertain and challenge our understanding of culture. For instance, how are art, culture and cultural heritage to be chosen, represented and reinvented? How can authentic experiences of certain places and products be a part of the global commercialisation without loosing its significance in the process?

Unfortunately, there is no evidence of knowledge management and dissemination of lessons learned during the event, which can also be attributed to the lack of collaboration within the tourism sector. Only the tourism task force and the Hans Christian Andersen 2005 Foundation have produced regular progress reports that were not disclosed to the tourism and culture sectors. In an event held in multiple locations over an entire year it seems even more pressing that uniform processes of accountable communication, including monitoring, data collection and reporting are adopted. Applying a holistic approach to event evaluation that include both tangible and intangible impacts would be an important step forward for the emerging Danish event industry, which furthermore permits comparison with international events held in other contexts.

Conclusion

This chapter has assessed the role of tourism in the 2005 Hans Christian Andersen event in Denmark, which was held in multiple locations under the auspices of a single theme over the course of an entire year. With the overarching aim of attracting more international tourists to Denmark, the approach taken by the tourism task force appeared to be both visionary and appropriate. In the past, tourism was frequently introduced as a counterpart to already existing business activities, a less important add-on, whereby international momentum was often lost and the risk of shortsighted solutions was markedly raised. This was not the case with the 2005 Andersen event. Through the systematisation of Hans Christian Andersen related experiences and a common Internet portal, information on Hans Christian Andersen's life and works were made available to the Danish and international public. The permanent impact of Hans Christian Andersen related attractions, notably the *Andersen Was Here* and projects under the auspices of the Odense City Museums are expected to create added experience related value that extend beyond measurable statements for the 2005 celebrations. Although the applied measurable economic impact methods were subject to critique, funds earmarked by the Danish Ministry of Economic and Business Affairs for new tourism initiatives and international marketing gained the intended international exposure. Focusing predominantly on return of investments, arrival statistics and marketing values are useful to obtain political and economic support, especially seen in the context of the government's 2003 growth strategy. It was argued next that event evaluation that focuses on simplistic economic returns fails to account for socio-cultural effects. Indeed, it is questionable whether the Andersen event became a fundamental component of the destinations' tourism development strategy as intended. The objective to motivate Danish tourism to take ownership and use the celebrations to create new, thematically related products and marketing strategies was a limited success. Significant challenges still exist in making the necessary links between the culture and tourism sectors to be able to create added value for the individual as well as society at large. The Andersen event exposed the need for tourism organisations to enter into equitable dialogue with representatives from the artistic and cultural sectors, and vice versa, so that the intended synergies can be based on mutual understanding and respect for professional competencies. It is equally important that running evaluations of economic, cultural, social and environmental effects are documented through objective and internationally compatible measurements. The event evaluation tool *Encore* (*Sustainable Tourism Cooperative Research Centre*) represents a promising option, which was only made commercially available in 2006.

The implementation and lessons learned from the Hans Christian Andersen event have set the base line for a professional beginning for the Danish event industry. To be successful, future event managers must embrace the collaborative challenges that are at the core of the Danish tourism and culture sectors. Prioritising knowledge management and dissemination between relevant public institutions and private businesses, and learning from international examples are of pivotal importance, particularly in the context of meaningful content production in the 21st century culture and experience economy.

References

Allen, J., O'Toole, W., McDonnell, I. and Harris, R. (2005) *Festival and Special Event Management* (3rd Edition), Milton, QLD, Australia: John Wiley & Sons.

Blicher-Hansen, L. (2002) *Notat. Strategy for international turisme markedsføring af HCA 2005.* Copenhagen, Denmark: Danmarks Turistråd.

Burns, J. P. A. and Mules, T. J. (1986) An Economic Evaluation of the Adelaide Grand Prix. In Syme, G. J., Shaw, B. J., Fenton, P. M. and Mueller, W. S. (eds.), *The Planning and Evaluation of Hallmark Events.* Avebury, England: Aldershot, pp. 172–185.

Danish Government (2003) *Denmark in the Culture and Experience Economy. Five New Steps.* Copenhagen, Denmark: Schultz Grafisk.

Dwyer, L., Mellor, R., Mistilis, N. and Mules, T. (2000) A framework for assessing 'tangible' and 'intangible' impacts of events and conventions. *Event Management*, 6(3), 175–191.

Dwyer, L., Forsyth, P. and Spurr, R. (2005) Estimating the impacts of special events on an economy. *Journal of Travel Research*, 43, 335–351.

Hans Christian Andersen 2005 Foundation (2004a) *Handlingsplan*, Version 6, marts. Copenhagen, Denmark: Status på turismeområdet (in Danish only).

Hans Christian Andersen 2005 Foundation (2004b) *Handlingsplan*, Version 7, May. Copenhagen, Denmark: Status på turismeområdet (in Danish only).

Have, C. (2006) Synlighed er eksistens. Eller synlighed bliver eksistens i de kommende år. In Jantzen, I. and Jensen, (eds.), *Oplevelser: Koblinger og Transformationer.* Aalborg, Denmark: Ålborg University Press, pp. 131–144, (in Danish only).

Jago, L. and Dwyer, L. (2006) *Economic Evaluations of Special Events. A Practitioner's Guide.* Altona, Victoria, Australia: Common Ground Publishing and Sustainable Tourism Centre for Cooperative Research.

Jantzen, C. and Jensen, J. F. (eds.) (2006) *Oplevelser: Koblinger og Transformationer.* Aalborg, Denmark: Ålborg University Press, (in Danish only).

Liburd, J. J. (2005) Sustainable Tourism and Innovation in Mobile Tourism Services. *Tourism Review International*, 9(1), 107–118.

Liburd, J. J. (2007) Sustainable tourism, cultural practice and competence development for hotels and inns in Denmark. *Tourism Recreation Research*, 32(1), 41–48.

Observer Danmark A/S (2006) *Gulliver. Danmark i de internationale medier*. Copenhagen, Denmark (in Danish only).

Pine, B. J. II. and Gilmore, J. H. (1999) *The Experience Economy: Work is Theatre and Every Business a Stage*. Boston, USA: Harvard Business School Press.

Presbury, R. and Edwards, D. (2004) *BEST Teaching Module – Sustainable Festivals, Meetings and Event Management*. Sydney, Australia: University of Western Sydney.

Simonsen, P. S. (2006) Turisme erhvervets struktur og aktører. In Sørensen, A. (eds.), *Grundbog i Turisme*. Frydenlund, Copenhagen: 85–107.

Simonsen, P. S. (2007) Turisme erhvervets struktur og aktører. In Sørensen, A. (eds.), *Grundbog i Turisme*. Copenhagen, Denmark: Frydenlund, pp. 186–200, (in Danish only).

VisitDenmark (2006) *HCA 2005 International Turismemarkedsføring. Evaluering og afrapportering vedrørende Økonomi- og Erhvervsministeriets særbevilling til den internationale markedsføring af HCA 2005*. Copenhagen, Denmark (in Danish only).

Wonderful Copenhagen. *Hans Christian Andersen Anniversary 2005*. Celebration Video Cavalcade DVD. Wonderful Copenhagen. Copenhagen, Denmark.

Chapter 4

Establishing Singapore as the Events and Entertainment Capital of Asia: Strategic Brand Diversification

M. Foley, G. McPherson and D. McGillivray

Introduction

Contained within Singapore Tourism Board's (STB) vision for tourism 2015 is the stated intention to establish Singapore as the 'Events and Entertainment Capital of Asia'. This strategy is part of wider economic development agency attempts to diversify Singapore's brand beyond its well established reputation as a leading business destination. The city wants to capture the attention of global tourism markets by redefining itself as a vibrant cultural hub with an events and entertainment offering to rival some of the world's most attractive cities. This strategy can be viewed as a response to the intensification of global place wars for attention which have increased the pressure on destinations the world over to create unique attractions to entice valuable mobile capital. This chapter provides a critical overview of the global context for inter-urban place wars before focusing on the value of an events-led strategy in delivering competitive advantage for Singapore. Methodologically, it draws on elite interviews with leading Singaporean cultural policy makers, observations at local, national and international events and documentary analysis of the recent strategic environment for Singapore tourism. We contend that the city branding and place-making strategies employed by the Singaporean state apparatus are designed to create cultural strategies which ensure the gentrification of space and place necessary for the reception of global tourism inflows. In essence, we suggest that Singapore has used its events-led strategies to extend its internal processes of cultural planning, regeneration and development at the same time as securing a global position in the increasingly competitive events (and place) bidding wars.

Animating Cities: Events and Festivals and Symbolic Image

A significant body of literature borrowing from the cross-disciplinary areas of political economy, political science, geography, sociology, social policy and cultural studies has considered the role of

International Perspectives of Festivals and Events
Copyright © 2009 by Elsevier Ltd.
All rights of reproduction in any form reserved.
ISBN: 978-0-08-045100-8

events (or culture)-led strategies in establishing competitive advantage for cities within the global economy. Hall (2006), reflecting on the growth of sports mega-events, argues that neoliberal entrepreneurial growth strategies are now regularly played out by cities around the world. In Zukin's (1995) words, culture is increasingly the 'business of cities', an 'instrument in the entrepreneurial strategies of local governments and business alliances' (p. 12). In urban environments across Europe, the Americas and Asia, public and private growth coalitions come together to utilise events and festivals as a means of gaining competitive advantage in increasingly aggressive place wars (Haider, 1992; Short and Kim, 1999; Yeoh and Chang, 2001) with other aspiring global cities. These place wars are driven by the need to create a favourable image to tourism, migration and business marketplaces. Increasingly, sporting and other cultural festivals and events represent particularly attractive communication vehicles for cities as they interact with the globalised media complex and vie for the attention of policy makers, consumers and investors, alike. In the competition for attention (Goldhaber, 1997), places seek out means of differentiation and distinction; unique qualities which can attract valuable mobile capital to advance their economic standing. The decision to engage in city event branding of this sort is almost always politically motivated, rather than cultural or even economic. Today, cities are under pressure to be seen to be bidding for sporting mega-events or to create large scale festivals so that they maintain position in the rankings of top global cities (Shoval, 2002).

However, exploiting the cultural cache of festivals and events is not the only (or even the most popular) means for cities to secure attention. Richards and Wilson (2004) suggest that branding the built urban environment with signature or iconic buildings and cultural quarters is perhaps the most frequently used means of altering perceptions of a locale. Yet, regenerative strategies based on the transformation of the builtscape (Chang and Huang, 2005) suffer from the threat of homogeneity and serial monotony (Harvey, 1989) which has afflicted other destinations. Moreover, in the fast-paced global economy, an over-reliance on inflexible, physical spaces of regeneration can leave destinations vulnerable to changing architectural fashions and ambitious competitors. In contrast, events and festivals 'provide a means of adding flexibility to fixed structures, supplying a source of spectacle which adds to the image value of a landmark' (Richards and Wilson, 2004, pp. 1931–1932), or of a destination. Events are an attractive proposition for policy makers because they animate objects, they enliven the physical environment and, in their uniquely media-friendly form, they transcend geographical boundaries. Using Chang and Huang's (2005) terminology, the creation of 'eventscapes' also allows places to produce new symbolic (often contrived) meanings, catering for 'new lifestyle needs' (p. 276). For example, reflecting on the regeneration of the Singapore River, they argue that a process of 'creative destruction' has taken place whereby the neoliberal ideological policy of the city has transformed the environment into 'an image of leisure and entertainment at the waterfront, at the expense of landscapes of past economic and social ills' (p. 279).

Investing in, and creating, festivals and events is doubly attractive to semi-peripheral cities and states (Whitson and Horne, 2006) as they can use these spectacles to establish themselves on the world map. These events can also give others the impression that a city has an achievement and entrepreneurial orientation, informing potential suitors (e.g. investors) that political leaders are enterprising (Whitson and Horne, 2006). Festivals and events permit semi-peripheral, or regional powers, to showcase their offerings through the global media to a watching audience, influencing perceptions of place identity – both externally (to the possessors of circulating capital) and internally (to members of the host population).

The strategies discussed thus far only bear fruit because cities now operate in a fluid symbolic realm, where image enhancement carries a value; where the hosting of unique events helps cities express their 'personalities' and advertise their position on the global stage (Essex and Chalkley, 1998). Sporting and cultural events also fit with the dominant logic of consumption, providing a 'point of identification' (Richards and Wilson, 2004, p. 1932) for consumers in a crowded marketplace. In discussing place images and their relationship with events, Richards and Wilson argue that 'events have become a particular valuable form of cultural currency' (p. 1933) creating a favourable impression of the city or nation as a destination worth visiting. The proliferation of cultural and sporting festivals can be associated with, and supports, similar trends towards a cosmopolitan ethic which defines a neighbourhood or city as vibrant. When contrived or manufactured events are hosted, the façade of the city is invariably dressed is such a way as to communicate specific impressions to target audiences. Events are invariably located in gentrified spaces (or in places which are undergoing gentrification processes) and help choreograph forms of cultural consumption which fit with how the city wishes to be perceived, and with the values of those people it wishes to attract (principally the incoming visitor).

The visual representation of cities is particularly valuable in the dominant symbolic realm of inter-urban place marketing competition. Festivals and events provide city marketers with a plethora of suitable vibrant, colourful and multicultural images which are easily packaged for global circulation. Sydney has its Mardi Gras, Rio exploits the Carnival and London uses Notting Hill Carnival to represent the city in a suitably cosmopolitan way. The process often involves recreating a sanitised historical narrative (Chang and Huang, 2005), one that the governing agencies can utilise to secure the consent of the host population and which is also, crucially, exploitable as a tourism resource. Internationally renowned festivals, such as Notting Hill Carnival, were often created to address the threat posed by social unrest and riots and were targeted towards a particular ethnic minority group. Today, however, these events are invariably used as a clever marketing tool for civic leaders to showcase their destinations' cultural diversity. Political decision makers in cities such as Rio and New Orleans have continually reinvented their festivals by globalising local celebrations and selling them as unique attractions via global media networks.

Behind many city event-led strategies sit entrepreneurial governments seeking to attract circulating capital (Schimmel, 2006) which brings the 'footloose consumption' (Short and Kim, 1999, p. 39) of tourists and conventions to their destinations. In the 1980s and early 1990s, US downtowns were transformed into packaged landscapes (Boyer, 1992) with cultures of consumption being defined by spectacularised urban space (Hannigan, 1998; Harvey, 1989). This format for urban growth is now replicated across the world, with cultural consumption at its core. In developing major festival and events strategies, cities tend to work to a common denominator in respect of the markets being courted. These tend to be high spending tourists, middle-class professionals and potential investors. However, the beneficiaries of these event-led strategies are not always those people to whom the city leaders are democratically accountable. It is to the politics of event-led growth that we now turn.

The Politics of Growth: Events and Private Capital

Of course, in the competition for favourable city status there are invariably winners and losers. As Hall (2006) contends, pursuing a major events strategy may well produce lucrative short term gains for private interests (e.g. construction firms, advertisers or sponsors), but this can bring more negative long term consequences for other public stakeholders. This view is supported by the work of Smith (2002), MacLeod (2002) and others who consider the changing urban policy landscape to be defined by a dominant neoliberal logic in central and local government towards urban entrepreneuri-alism subsidised by the public purse, which leaves some stakeholders disempowered from decision-making processes and from the promulgated economic rewards.

As control over content and promotion is handed over to multinational conglomerates – the driv-ing force for many large scale events – cities and nations also risk alienating the citizens who are identified as the main beneficiaries. Once sponsors have a stake in an event, the presentation of place for target market consumption is more difficult to manage and control. Hall (2006) identifies the problem as being about a perceived democratic deficit, whereby local citizens are disempowered from their rights in the furtherance of a large scale events policy. Alongside Whitson and Horne (2006), Zukin (1995) and Richards and Wilson (2004), Hall (2006) asserts that the dominant dis-course of capital accumulation provides an 'ideological justification for place-competitive re-imaging strategies' (p. 64), and a 'competitiveness hegemony' (p. 64), which places the logic of capital central to policy discussions and decisions. Gray (2007) labels this the commodification of cultural policy, where decisions on investment in forms of cultural expression are made with economic logic in mind.

In pursuing an events-led regeneration strategy as a means of escaping 'routine identities' (Richards and Wilson, 2004, p. 1932), cities also face the threat of reinforcing sameness and cultural uniformity, in creating a 'homogenised uniqueness'. Furthermore, in following a strategy of creating international (or global) events for touristic consumption, the sharp contrast between the host popu-lation and the affluent tourist tribes (Schimmel, 2006) being targeted by city governments may also be thrown into view. For example, Judd (1999), commenting on the fallout from an overemphasis on attracting tourist dollars in the United States, warns that the islands of affluence created often hide the real material deprivation and cultural exclusion faced by some host residents.

Cultural and sporting events have also been employed as a means of addressing the tensions asso-ciated with multiculturalism (Zukin, 1995) expressed in the promotion of 'local' ethnic uniqueness (Chang, 1999). Yet, this again can be understood as an intentional policy response to the threat posed by global (read standardised) culture, using cultural diversity as an instrumental tool to attain non-cul-tural aims and objectives (Gray, 2007). The symbolic realm (Zukin, 1995) – a realm of images, signs and spaces in cities – permits the creation of collective identity forms, albeit one frequently mediated by the relationship between 'cultural symbols and entrepreneurial capital' (Zukin, 1995, p. 3).

In implementing an events-led strategy with the discourse of enterprise at its core, debate over the appropriate use of contested public space is also brought to the fore. The loss of public space free from the logic of consumption is an issue which has attracted the attention of academic com-mentators and anti-globalisation prophets in recent years (see Klein, 2001; Zukin, 1995). They argue that civic spaces are now colonised by private capital (e.g. sponsors), often at the bequest of the public authorities. There are a number of problems associated with this development when con-sidered in relation to festivals and events and their projected tourism returns. First, as invented or contrived cultural events and festivities colonise civic space (e.g. squares, main avenues) the out-come can be the production of intensely regulated, or gated, communities identified by the presence of security barriers, security guards and the ubiquity of CCTV cameras. Regulatory control over licences, traffic management, environmental pollution and the like ensure that the civic authorities and their (growth) coalition partners can easily manage the cultural offering to produce 'safe' spaces for tourist consumption. However, this can leave the impression of a public culture controlled and contained, managed and directed for the benefit of the footloose consumer. The implications of what Gray (2007) calls an acceptance of a commodified conception of public policy is that collective space is re-conceptualised as consumable space. In focusing on the Singaporean context for events and festivals over the last decade, the empirical component of this chapter will now review critically the implications of the nation's drive towards the title of 'Events and Entertainment Capital of Asia'.

Research Context: Singapore

Since gaining independence from the United Kingdom in 1965, the Singaporean government's main aim has been to maintain stability in the areas of economic and environmental development. At the same time, the government has also continued with its drive to reinforce a discourse of national identity through the development of cultural policies based on the promotion of Singapore's shared values. Politically, whilst the city-state is a democracy, the People's Action Party (PAP) has been the only ruling power since it took over the reigns from the colonial governor. Singapore does have a representative democracy and has official United Nations' recognition as a parliamentary republic. Despite being small in physical size, Singapore has a high population density of approximately 4.5 million people which in the 2000 Census encompassed a multi-ethnic mix of Chinese 76.8%, Malay 13.9%, Indian 7.9% and others 1.4% (www.singstat.com, 2007).

As a post-colonial power, Singapore has invested heavily in creating a sense of national identity, often using the vehicle of cultural events as a means of integrating the diverse multi-ethnic population along the lines of shared Singaporean values (e.g. National Day celebrations). Indeed, in Singapore, the debate over the need for a strong sense of national identity started at independence from British colonial rule (Kong, 1999). This movement strengthened in the 1980s and 1990s as part of a larger nation building initiative. The PAP's authoritarian regime (Tamney, 1996), at least in the first three decades of independent rule, promoted a discourse of national survival and the protection of Asian values in the face of the challenge posed by perceived Western decadence. However, as Singapore rapidly industrialised, the focus of government policy shifted from 'protection' and the cultivation of shared national values, to the promotion and encouragement of inward investment in entrepreneurial growth strategies. The success of this strategy is illustrated by Singapore's position as the most economically successful country in South East Asia (Ooi, 2002). Singapore's rapid industrialisation in the 1970s and 1980s was based on the authoritarian regimes' tight regulation and exploitation of shared national values of hard work and nation before community. However, as strong economic returns were amassed, the attention of government and citizens alike turned from necessity to luxury; from work to leisure and consumption. Through the 1990s and into the new millennium, the government has had to re-evaluate its authoritarian approach as its working population reflect upon the sacrifices made in the name of economic growth. In policy terms the government has created heritage spaces and other 'places to play' (Judd, 1999) whilst, at the same time, maintaining a 'hegemonic' control over their population.

However, in recent years, Singapore has also sought to exploit its popularity as a travel destination, even in the face of the SARS (severe acute respiratory syndrome) crisis early in the new millennium. Despite this crisis, tourism has evolved into one of its largest industries, with around 9.7 million tourist visits in 2006. The Singaporean government has set a target of at least 17 million visitor arrivals by 2015. The Orchard Road district is the central retail hub in Singapore but, until recently, the city has suffered from a relatively low attractions base. However, this has been addressed by the tourism authorities and the Urban Redevelopment Authority over the past few years. These agencies have been involved in the development of two integrated resorts at Marina South and Sentosa Island, alongside the Singapore Flyer, the Gardens by the Bay, the Singapore River development and the construction of the Double Helix Bridge connecting tourist attractions in and around the packaged landscape of Marina Bay. Whilst the 'builtscapes' (Chang and Huang, 2005) have been markedly enhanced, this has gone hand-in-hand with the development of the accompanying 'eventscapes' (Chang and Huang, 2005). The Great Singapore Sales, Singapore Food Festival, the Singapore River Hong Bao Festival, the Singapore Arts Festival and the Chingay Parade represent opportunities to promote Singapore to regional and international markets. Add to this sporting events, like the Singapore Masters, the Singapore Marathon and the F1 Grand Prix (due to visit Singapore in 2008 for the first time), and it is clear that Singapore is following a well-trodden path towards the use of events and other cultural forms as valuable commodities worth packaging and selling to the rest of Asia and, increasingly, to wider tourism markets.

In many respects, Singapore has invested in its creative and cultural offering as much out of necessity as of choice. This need is driven by the fact that there are scant natural resources in this island nation, due to its small land mass and high population density. Unlike Korea and Taiwan, Singapore does not have ship building or agricultural activities on which to generate economic growth. However, the ruling party seized the opportunity to use 'cultural maintenance' to both exercise power over the people and form new markets (Miller and Yudice, 2002). From the late 1990s onwards, the Singaporean state, through its vehicles of economic development (the Ministry of Trade and Industry and the Singaporean Tourism Board), has pursued an ambitious strategy to attract global tourism spend by re-branding Singapore as more than a business travel destination. In recent campaigns, Singapore has been labelled a 'global arts city', 'uniquely Singapore', an 'eventful city' and, most recently, the 'Events and Entertainment Capital of Asia'. It is the final label, the Events and Entertainment Capital of Asia that will occupy our attention in the remainder of this chapter.

Methodology

In the furtherance of this study on the event and festival strategies being utilised in the promotion of Singapore as a tourist destination, a mixed methods case study approach was employed as it 'allows an investigation to retain the holistic and meaningful characteristics of real-life events' (Yin, 1994, p. 3). Yin (1994) argues that the benefit of employing a case study approach in the contextual situation of the studied phenomena is integrated into the mode of enquiry, thereby permitting the relationship between context and phenomena to be delineated.

The research strategy underpinning this chapter took two main forms. The substantive phase of fieldwork was gathered by members of the research team during a field trip to Singapore in February 2004. Elite semi-structured interviews were conducted with representatives from statutory and non-statutory bodies drawn from the tourist sector, from cultural institutions and from enterprise organisations. Interviews were held with individuals from the National Arts Council (2), National Heritage Board (1), Singapore Tourism Board (1), Singapore Sports Council (1) and the International Festival and Events Association (1). The research team intentionally selected interviewees who were in a position to make meaningful comment on strategic issues pertaining to events and festival policy in Singapore, whether in the arts or in sport. Each interviewee was asked questions around key themes concerning the rationale for investment in festivals and events and the policy outcomes sought. Themes included:

- The perception of events and festivities in the tourism product of Singapore now and in the future.
- The strategy to make Singapore the Events and Entertainment Capital of Asia.

- The sensitivity of multi-racial diversity issues in promoting events and festivals to tourist audiences.
- Placing Singapore on a global map and the importance of local cultural heritage in that positioning.
- The role of sports and arts events in making Singapore into a global player for the events sector.
- The marketing of Singapore as the bridge between the East and the West for international events.
- The role of local events in forming Singaporean cultural identity and the promotion of this globally.

Given the three-year time lag since the completion of the elite interviews, an extensive desk-based research phase was also undertaken in 2007 to provide an update on the Singaporean context and to investigate the policy rationale behind a significant intensification in Singapore's pursuit of an events-led strategy since 2004. Documentary analysis was carried out on a number of strategy documents pertaining to economic and tourism policy and on press coverage relating to several of Singapore's renowned cultural and sporting events. The documentary analysis eschewed content analysis techniques in favour of discourse analysis. The former is a quantitative and scientific approach which focuses on the 'direct, deterministic and unilinear link' within documents, 'from sender to communication to recipient' (Jupp and Norris, 1993, p. 38). However, in evaluating the contents of government policy and strategy, it is more meaningful to consider the status of 'official' documents as socially constructed entities. That withstanding, documents are subject to multiple interpretations both temporally and spatially. For this chapter, a more qualitative, discourse analysis of strategy and policy documents was undertaken, taking into consideration the distinctive political and economic context of Singapore at the time of their publication. When considered alongside the views of the elite interviewees – the 'local interactional context' (Flick, 1999, p. 198) – a more thorough evaluation of strategic rhetoric and local realities can be accessed.

Singapore: The Events and Entertainment Capital of Asia

Leisure and tourism markets represent key strands in STB's strategy to create a unique Destination Singapore brand identity that complements its well established reputation as a leading business destination. The STB has a professed aspiration to establish Singapore as the 'Events and Entertainment Capital of Asia' (STB, 2007), attracting 'a big variety of the world's best events year round for visitors to enjoy'. Working in tandem with the principal economic development agency, the Ministry for Trade and Industry (MITA), the STB provides public subsidy and expert support to incentivise cultural and sporting festivals and events to attract tourist expenditure.

This approach is in line with the city's long term goal of competing on a global level, and in presenting itself as safe Asia (Foley et al., 2007) offering sanitised, hyper Asian experiences alongside dominant Western ideologies of consumption. Events and festivals have become a key plank of the city's global strategy to communicate, or present, an alternative Singaporean identity to the rest of the world. Chang and Huang (2005) suggest that the Singaporean authorities are pursuing a strategy of 'forgetting to remember', a 'strategic undertaking that streamlines the past in ways that are coherent to the present and profitable for the future' (p. 267). Chang and Yeoh (1999) also suggest that Singapore's cultural landscapes are repackaged as marketable commodities. In the case of Singapore's events-led strategy, the 'profitable future' is build around increasing tourism spend and in creating favourable impressions of Singapore as a distinctive destination to visit – a destination which is progressive and sophisticated, yet still an expression of the Asian soul (e.g. the New Asia marketing campaign). That it is a strategic undertaking that is evidenced in the level of government support which some showcase events receive, whether that be in the arts and cultural area or in relation to large sports events. In many cities government support is forthcoming because of the projected international tourism returns accruable from events, but in recent years Singapore has deliberately altered its strategy to limit the number of events it invests in. As the Singapore Director of the International Festivals and Events Association (IFEA) acknowledges:

> Our strategy is now to improve on developing quality in world class activities that have got tourism appeal (Wong, 4 February 2004, interview).

In developing events with tourism appeal, the place marketers encourage the promotion of activities which Ooi (2002) argues falsify time and place; events without a past but with an exploitable future. These events overlook some elements of the rich cultural heritage of the city, in favour of marketable commodities. The promotion of what Chang and Yeoh (1999) call inauthentic products is apparent in Singapore's recent successful attempt to attract one of the world's most lucrative transportable sporting events the F1 Grand Prix to its streets in 2008. This event promises to be the first ever night race, designed specifically to exploit television audiences in Asia, Europe and the United States. The Singapore government expects tourism revenues of £33 million from the event (MTI, 2007); however, the direct economic benefits are only a small part of the overall strategic rationale for hosting the event in Singapore's recently redeveloped marina area. The principal strategic driver is to re-position Singapore as a leisure and tourism destination in the minds of existing and new markets.

In the intensely competitive Asian region, Singapore is adopting a strategy of urban entrepreneurialism, competitiveness and growth (Hall, 2006). Driven by its agencies of economic development, the Singaporean state has engaged in a place-competitive re-imaging strategy intended to produce a 'vibrant global city that is abuzz with high quality entertainment and events' (MITA, 2007). To further emphasise the strategic importance of this flagship event to the city, the STB has made a commitment to fund 60% of the costs from a Tourism Development Fund, complementing private investments. This represents an example of public and private growth coalitions working in tandem to showcase an area's unique facilities and attractions, as a means of gaining valuable coverage in the global media complex.

Singapore's events-related investment is not, however, restricted to the realm of mediasport events. The arts and cultural field is also following what Gray (2007) calls a commodified conception of public policy, the instrumental use of culture for non-cultural outcomes in its adoption of flagship arts events (e.g. Singapore Arts Festival) to promote Singapore to a watching global audience. As the Director of Programme Development at the National Arts Council suggests:

> Our mission is to develop Singapore into a global arts city. So that's the way we are and so creating these events will help to put us on the world map … that sense of positioning ourselves and how we make strategic positioning of Singapore … how we can use the arts to give Singapore an identity and an image which I think reflects us (Lee, 4 February 2004, interview).

Much of the strategic rhetoric in Singaporean policy is concerned with creating distinction within an increasingly competitive global marketplace, capitalising on a (constructed) shared heritage, unravelled cultural diversity and outstanding infrastructural hardware. As the Director of Special Projects at the STB indicates:

> We would use events as a main hook, a main magnet – we have to differentiate our-selves ... so what we look for as strategy for Singapore is events. It is events which actually leaven what you call the bread. The bread could be baking with shopping, with a lot of lifestyle activities, but it is events which have a fantastic pulling power (Khor, 6 February 2004, interview).

Singapore is certainly using 'unique' events to attract attention from key markets as a means of increasing its levels of tourist visitation towards its 2012 target of doubling visitor arrivals to 15 million a year (Tourism Working Group Report, 2005). The government's investment in attracting large scale regional and international sports events (e.g. Singapore Open Golf, Lexus Cup Golf, Singapore Masters Golf, AVIVA Singapore Open Badminton, Singapore Marathon) has recently been supported by the construction of the Singapore Sports Hub, the 'hardware' (Wong, 4 February 2004, interview), which is described as 'A unique cluster development of integrated world-class sports facilities within the city ... it will play a critical role in accelerating the development of the sports industry' (Singapore Sports Council, 2007). Singapore clearly wishes to enhance its level of status and prestige, giving visitors a reason to identify with the city. As the STB Chief Executive, Lim Neo Chian, illustrates with respect to the Grand Prix, Singapore wants to position itself as a place to 'be in and be seen in' (STB press release, 2007). This further reinforces Richards and Wilson's (2004) view of the cultural currency of events in creating a favourable impression of the city or nation as a desirable destination. In referring to the importance of the Chingay festival in promoting Singapore to external markets, the Director of IFEA emphasises the:

> Marketing value of this event being broadcast in Portugal, for example, and the eye-balls that see Singapore as a happening and aspirational place – it is imprinted on this individual's mind – one day I would like to go to Singapore (Wong, 4 February 2004, interview).

Using hallmark or special events to manage impressions of a destination can further enhance the existing product offering, whether cultural, sporting or business. Returning to the Singapore Grand Prix, the STB believes that its presence in Singapore will create 'positive energy', unrivalled 'expo-sure' and an opportunity to showcase the city's physical, cultural, sporting, artistic and historical landmarks. Events provide an unparalleled immediacy of message which makes them attractive to place marketers:

> Branding brings in immediate returns in terms of media attention, global media atten-tion. So we are very conscious of the branding potential of ourselves as an eventful city. But now we are going to be more strategic and discriminating in picking up the ones (events) that will attract different markets (Khor, 6 February 2004, interview).

What is apparent in this strategy is that the government agencies are now discriminating between those events which have local value and meaning and those which will bring exposure to new audi-ences and lucrative broadcasting revenues. At this time, the agencies responsible for economic development are concentrating on exploiting the potential of the latter, sometimes at the expense of events with significant national (and regional) appeal:

> You have ... events like table tennis and badminton which we are actually quite good at, in Asian culture we are quite good at. We have opportunities to win Gold medals at Olympics or Asian Games, but from the commercial infrastructure perspectives it is limited because the sports are not really sexy – there isn't enough appeal (Khoo, 4 February 2004, interview).

In this example, decisions over the support for specific sports events are made on the basis of commercial appeal and not national participation targets. This reflects the dominance of neoliberal entrepreneurial strategies and their impact on other public stakeholders within the Singaporean context. The Singapore Sports Council interviewee (Khoo, 4 February, interview) indicated a tension between the needs of the sports development agenda and the economic imperatives underpinning the international events strategy. The logic of capital certainly informs sport and arts policy in Singapore, but with low levels of expressed discontent a feature of Singaporean society, the outcomes of the policy drive are perhaps less noticeable than in other cities (e.g. Toronto).

Another noticeable feature of Singapore's event-led strategy is the way in which the promotion of indigenous cultural events (e.g. Chingay, River Hong Bao Festival and Taipusam Festival) comes together with world-class sporting spectaculars to symbolise the notion of a 'New Asia' brand, where 'East meets West, Asian heritage blends with modernity and sophistication, and old world charm combined with new world vision' (MITA, 2002). Chang and Huang (2005) argue that the creation of the New Asia brand in Singapore is tied up with re-fashioning the built environment (e.g. the river), the staging of events and activities (e.g. the F1 Grand Prix) and the establishment of public art installations. They also see this move as reflecting wider state attempts to create new memories and identities for Singapore – memories befitting its aspiration to acquire and sustain global city status through Destination Singapore. Returning to MITA's version of the New Asia Brand, the F1 Grand Prix epitomises the 'West', 'modernity' and the 'new world vision'. The street circuit is designed specifically to open up key landmarks to media view, animating the city's wider cultural heritage attractions to the watching world. In the Singapore context, like elsewhere, events operate as brand vehicles employed to communicate visual and audio messages via the symbolic realm of inter-urban place marketing competition.

However, despite Singapore's apparent success in attracting the attention of the world's arts and sporting glitterati in the form of the Singapore Arts Festival and the F1 Grand Prix, there are clear dangers associated with a rapid rise to prominence. Given the earlier discussion of the dangers of serial monotony and homogenised uniqueness, it is important to subject Singapore's events-led strategy to further critical scrutiny on the basis of its ongoing sustainability. In interviews with key policy makers, it was apparent that there is some concern associated with a shift away from a mainly local or regional events policy, driven by the demands of national unity towards a more abstract, place branding strategy. Chang and Yeoh (1999) warn of the creation of inauthenticity and the Sports Council representative reinforces this view in the following commentary:

> I think the first priority is to understand that events must be local first before you go outside. If you have a 50,000 seater and you can only fill it with 5,000 people even though it has got massive international appeal you are really losing out because international appeal takes time to build. I think for Singapore, six to eight major events probably is just right for us and you can underpin that with a whole group of different events that can bring the vibrancy of a community (Khoo, 4 February 2004, interview).

This response was also repeated in interviews with the cultural agencies and with representatives of the STB. However, whilst the global place wars continue apace, it is unlikely that Singapore's agents of economic development will alter their internationalisation strategies in the face of the inevitable global forces which require cities around the world to engage in interdependent transnational relationships with other aspiring contenders. Singapore is often described as a 'hub' for a variety of business and travel processes, but it is now striving to exploit its events and entertainment offering to gain recognition as a tourism destination in its own right rather than as a stopover on the journey to Australia.

Conclusion

Since gaining independence from the United Kingdom in 1965, the Singaporean government has undertaken a series of national unity projects designed to secure the active consent of its population around the values of hard work and thrift. However, with its rapid industrial and subsequent post-industrial growth, Singapore has had to embrace the challenge of securing the valuable mobile capital of investors and tourists in the face of increasingly competitive global place wars. Since the turn of the new millennium, Singapore has invested heavily in an events-led strategy designed to secure its position as the Events and Entertainment Capital of Asia. In its use of sporting and cultural events to re-brand itself as a vibrant destination, Singapore has sought to animate its existing attractions and landscapes to communicate positive cosmopolitan credentials to regional and international audiences. As part of this strategy, Singapore has invested significant public funds to support infrastructural developments and bids for internationally recognised sporting events which bring immediate symbolic returns, in terms of the communication of managed images through the global media complex. The forthcoming Singapore F1 Grand Prix is the vehicle on which Singapore hopes to build an international reputation as a leisure and entertainment hub – one worth visiting as a destination in its own right. The brand identity transmitted in the interface between traditional cultural events and manufactured sporting spectacles is inseparable from the notion of Singapore as New Asia – a city in which tradition and modernity sit as one alongside multi-ethnic diversity and globally recognisable products and services. The old and the new, the authentic and the contrived are immutable features of the Singaporean events offering. However, should the balance of power shift too far towards a reliance on disconnected and de-territorialised media events, then Singapore may be relying on an aspirational Event and Entertainment Capital of Asia brand built more on the pursuance of symbolic identity than on material logic.

References

Association of South East Nations Tourism Statistics 2001–2006, http://www.aseansec.org/5167.htm

Boyer, M. C. (1992) Cities for sale: Merchandising history at South Street Seaport. In Sorkin, M. (ed.), *Variations on a Theme Park: The New American City and the End of Public Space*. New York: Hill & Wang.

Chang, T. C. (1999) Local uniqueness in the global village: Heritage tourism in Singapore. *Professional Geographer*, 51(1), 91–103.

Chang, T. C. and Huang, S. (2005) Recreating place, replacing memory: Creative destruction at the Singapore River. *Asia Pacific Viewpoint*, 46(3), 267–280.

Chang, T. C. and Yeoh, B. S. A. (1999) 'New Asia – Singapore': Communicating local cultures through global tourism. *Geoforum*, 30, 101–115.

Essex, S. and Chalkley, B. (1998) Olympic Games: Catalyst of urban change. *Leisure Studies*, 17(3), 187–206.

Flick, U. (1999) *An Introduction to Qualitative Research*. London: Sage.

Foley, M., McPherson, G. and Matheson, C. (2007) Cultural identity and festivity: Generating Singapore through citizenship and enterprise in events activity. In Aitchison, C. and Pritchard, A. (eds.), *Festivals and Events: Culture and Identity in Leisure, Sport and Tourism*. Brighton: LSA Publication No. 94.

Goldhaber, M. H. (1997) The attention economy and the net. *First Monday*, 2(4).

Gray, C. (2007) Commodification and instrumentality in cultural policy. *International Journal of Cultural Policy*, 13(2), 203–215.

Haider, D. (1992) Place wars: New realities of the 1990s. *Economic Development Quarterly*, 6(2), 127–134.

Hall, C. M. (2006) Urban entrepreneurship, corporate interests, and sports mega-events: The thin policies of competitiveness within the hard outcomes of neo-liberalism. *The Sociological Review*, 54(2), 59–70.

Hannigan, J. (1998) *Fantasy City: Pleasure and Profit in the Postmodern Metropolis*. London: Routledge.

Harvey, D. (1989) From managerialism to entrepreneurialism: The transformation in urban governance in late capitalism. *Geografiska Annaler*, 71(1), 3–17.

Judd, D. R. (1999) Constructing the tourist bubble. In Judd, D. R. and Fainstein, S. S. (eds.), *The Tourist City*. New Haven: Yale University Press.

Jupp, V. and Norris, C. (1993) Traditions in documentary analysis. In Hammersley, M. (ed.), *Social Research: Philosophy, Politics and Practice*. London: Sage.

Klein, N. (2001) *No Logo*. London: Flamingo.

Kong, L. (1999) The invention of heritage: Popular music in Singapore. *Asian Studies Review*, 23(1), 1–24.

MacLeod, G. (2002) From urban entrepreneurialism to a 'Revanchist City'? On the spatial injustices of Glasgow's renaissance. *Antipode*, 34(3), 602–624.

Media Development Authority, Singapore, www.mda.gov.sg/wms.www/aboutus.aspx

Miller, T. and Yudice, G. (2002) *Cultural Policy*. London: Sage Publications.

Ministry of Trade and Industry (MTI) Singapore (2007) Opening Remarks by MOS Iswaran on the Formula 1 Grand Prix Singapore (press release) http://app.mti.gov.sg/default.asp?id=605

MITA (2002) Imagination A New Agenda for A Creative and Connected Nation. Investing in Singapore's Cultural Capital. Ministry for Information and the Arts, Signapore.

Ooi, C-S. (2002) *Cultural Tourism and Tourism Cultures*. Copenhagen: Copenhagen Business School Press.

Richards, G. and Wilson, J. (2004) The impact of cultural events on city image: Rotterdam, cultural capital of Europe 2001. *Urban Studies*, 41(10), 1931–1951.

Schimmel, K. (2006) Deep play: Sports mega events and urban social conditions in the USA. *Sociological Review*, 54(2), 160–174.

Short, J. R. and Kim, Y.-H. (1999) *Globalization and the City*. Harlow: Pearson Prentice Hall.

Shoval, N. (2002) A new phase in the competition for the Olympic gold: The London and New York bids for the 2012 Games. *Journal of Urban Affairs*, 24(5), 583–599.

Singapore Tourism web site, (2007) http://app.stb.gov.sg/asp/str/str06.asp

Singapore Tourism web site, http://www.newasia-singapore.com

Singapore Sports Council (2007) Three Consortiums Short-listed for Singapore Sports Hub Project http://www.ssc.gov.sg/publish/corporate/news/media_release/2006_media_releases

Singapore Tourist Board (2007) http://app.stb.gov.sg/asp/new/new03a.asp?id=7603

SingStat Web Site, http://www.singstat.gov.sg/stats/themes/people/hist/popn.html

Smith, N. (2002) New globalism, new urbanism: Gentrification as global urban strategy. *Antipode*, 34(3), 427–450.

Tourism Working Group (2005) Report of the Tourism Working Group Singapore. Economic Review Committee, Ministry of Trade and Industry, Singapore.

Tamney, J. B. (1996) *The Struggle Over Singapore's Soul*. Berlin: Walter de Gruyter.

Whitson, D. and Horne, J. (2006) Underestimated costs and overestimated benefits? Comparing the outcomes of sports mega-events in Canada and Japan. *Sociological Review*, 54(2), 71–89.

Yeoh, B. S. A. and Chang, T. C. (2001) Globalising Singapore: Debating transnational flows in the city. *Urban Studies*, 38(7), 1025–1044.

Yin, R. K. (1994) *Case Study Research: Design and Methods Newbury Park*. California: Sage.

Zukin, S. (1995) *The Cultures of Cities*. Oxford: Blackwell.

Chapter 5

The South Korean Hotel Sector's Perspectives on the 'Pre-' and 'Post-event' Impacts of the Co-hosted 2002 Football World Cup

Misuk Byeon, Neil Carr and C. Michael Hall

Introduction

It has been claimed that mega-events, such as the 1986 Asian Games and 1988 Seoul Olympics (Ahn and Ahmed, 1994; Ahn and McGahey, 1997; Chon and Shin, 1990; Hall, 1997a; Kang and Perdue, 1994; Kim and Song, 1998; Kwon, 1990; Lee and Kwon, 1995; Lee et al., 1996) and the Daejeon Exposition (Expo) (Kim and Uysal, 1998; Lee and Kwon, 1995) have been a critical component in South Korea's tourism expansion, contributing not only to increased international market awareness and visitor numbers but also to the development of tourist infrastructures (Hall, 1997a; Kang and Perdue, 1994; Kim and Uysal, 1998). Furthermore, Ministry of Culture and Tourism MCT, 2003) have claimed that the 2002 Football World Cup and the 2002 Busan Asian Games also boosted South Koreans' self-confidence and pride, and helped further develop tour products and infrastructures. For example, in 1965 South Korea had only 37 hotels with 1837 rooms (Hall, 1997a; Ministry of Transport (MOT) and Korea National Tourism Corporation (KNTC) (=former Korea National Tourism Organisation (KNTO)), 1980) compared to 127 hotels with 19,296 rooms in 1981. At the time of the 1988 Olympics 265 hotels accounted for a total of 33,189 rooms (Chon and Shin, 1990). In the year of the World Cup, there were 526 hotels, which provided 55,579 rooms. This number had increased by 6.7% for hotels and 4.8% for rooms from the year 2001 (when there were 493 hotels and 53,017 rooms in South Korea). By 2005, this figure had increased to 558 hotels with a total of 58,950 rooms (MCT and KNTO, 2006). The increased interest in South Korea from foreign tourists, and greater leisure time and disposable income for South Koreans has also corresponded with this growth in accommodation (Chon and Shin, 1990; Hall, 1997a; MCT, 2003).

Despite the example of apparent significance of mega-events on the South Korea's case it is only since the 1980s that substantial attention has been paid to their management, marketing, planning and impacts on host societies (e.g. Getz 1998; Hall, 1992, 1996, 2001; Hiller, 1998; Page and Hall, 2003; Ritchie and Aitken, 1984, 1985; Ritchie and Lyons, 1990; Ritchie and Smith, 1991). Furthermore, there has been a tendency to focus on assessing the economic impacts of events in an extemporal context with relatively little attention having been given to the event as part of a broader

International Perspectives of Festivals and Events
ISBN: 978-0-08-045100-8

longitudinal process (Crompton and McKay, 1994; Crompton et al., 2001; Delpy and Li, 1998; Hall, 1992; Hiller, 1998; Mitchell and Wall, 1986; Marsh, 1984). Political/administrative impacts as well as the social/cultural and psychological/perceptual impacts of events are among the least studied of the six potential impacts identified in the literature (Hall, 1992; Shultis et al., 1996).

The study of hallmark events has generally assumed a positivistic, non-critical approach to their subject matter which the majority of tourism research has been done (Hall, 1989). As time passes, there seems to be global critiques on the mega-event impacts (Gibson, 1998; Preuss, 1998; Wall, 1988) which the same as the growth of tourism has prompted perspective observers to raise many questions concerning the social and environmental desirability of encouraging further expansion (Mathieson and Wall, 1982).

Unlike Olympic Games there has been relatively little attention paid to the impacts of the Football World Cup (Preuss, 2007). Nevertheless, the need for such research has been long recognised. As Ritchie (1984, p. 11) noted in his seminal work on the impact of hallmark events, there is a need for 'more definitive and more comprehensive … [approaches] to the assessment of the impact of hallmark events' that are employed in most situations.

Despite the economic, political and tourist significance of the event, limited research (Hall, 1992; Ritchie and Aitken, 1984) has been undertaken on the pre-/post-event impacts. Only a few scholars have examined the longitudinal mega-events impacts, (e.g. Kim and Petrick, 2005; Kim et al., 2006; Ritchie and Aitken, 1984, 1985; Ritchie and Lyon, 1987, 1990; Ritchie and Smith, 1991). From a tourism perspective, the impacts of mega-events on the long-term success of the host destination have been unclear. Therefore, a call for a longitudinal examination of the range of impacts provides a better understanding of the impacts of mega-events, like the Football World Cup (Ritchie and Lyons 1990).

In spite of the event and its consequences are considered in terms of short and long term their effects on the host community, a significant ingredient in the desire of many cities to promote themselves has been a scarcity of research into different perceptions between the host city (HC) and non-host city (NHC) (Hall, 1992; Ritchie, 1984), specifically, in the hotel section as this research points out. In this respect, this study attempts to examine the South Korean hotel sector's perspectives on the positive and negative impacts of the pre- and post-2002 Football World Cup on their hotel.

Although focused on the perceptions of the hotel industry, such research may also help to provide a greater understanding of the potential longer-term impacts of hosting mega-events (Jeong and Faulkner, 1996). Projected events in an area would be a valuable indicator for hotel management in forecasting accommodation demand for the area in the future (Kim and Uysal, 1998). This study makes a contribution to the hotel sector's perception of the co-hosted Football World Cup events literature by examining the longitudinal pre- and post-event impacts.

Based on the gaps in the current understanding of the impact of events on host societies the aims of the research on which this chapter is based were to compare pre-/post-event perspectives of the Football World Cup 2002 in two areas:

1. Pre-/post-perspectives held by the South Korean hotel sector relating to their individual hotels.
2. Possible differences in pre-/post-perspectives between hotels in HCs and NHCs.

The Significance of Mega-Events

Mega-events, otherwise referred to as hallmark or special events, are major fairs, festivals, EXPOs, cultural and sporting events (Hall, 1992, 1997b; Ritchie, 1984; Roche, 1992). Such events are some of the most important image builders of modern-day tourism (Hall, 1992; Roche, 1992). Within the mega-events, sport events represent one of the fastest growing niche markets for tourism (Getz, 2003; Gratton and Taylor, 2000; Hinch and Higham, 2004; Jago et al., 2003). This is due to the growing interest of participants in sports, which in turn provides the potential to increase tourism opportunities (Hinch and Higham 2004). Sport events can attract participants, spectators and tourists (Chalip et al., 2003; Getz, 1991; Hall, 1992; Hinch and Higham, 2004; Ritchie, 1984). Sport events are extremely significant not just for their immediate tourism component and attract media attention but also because they may have long lasting benefits and costs based on tourism/commercial, physical, economic, socio-cultural, psychological and political impacts on the host community and country (Deccio and Baloglu, 2002; Hall, 1992; Kang and Perdue, 1994; Ritchie, 1984).

The most commonly catalogued physical impacts of mega-events are the new facilities constructed as a result of the event, as well as the improvement of local infrastructures which might not have been politically or financially feasible without the event (Ritchie, 1984). Events have also been recognised for their role in highlighting the international profile and increased awareness of the host country or region (Deccio and Baloglu, 2002; Jeong and Faulkner, 1996; Ritchie and Smith, 1991), and improving the host community's quality of life (Deccio and Baloglu, 2002; Goeldner and Long, 1987). Hall (1989) indicated that a mega-event has the power to strengthen regional values and traditions and even lead to cultural understanding among visitors and residents. Increased long- and short-term employment opportunities are one of the perceived benefits of holding a mega-event (Deccio and Balcoglu, 2002; Hall, 1989; Jeong and Faulkner, 1996; Ritchie and Lyons, 1990).

Negative impacts created by a major event may include price inflation, which directly impacts to non-mega-event tourists due to higher room prices. It also increases tax burdens, and mismanagement of public funds by organisers in host communities (Ritchie and Aitken, 1984). Specifically on the issue of housing, local tenants have to live with the mega-event prices which are relevant to the Seoul case of post-Olympics in Seoul (McKay and Plumb, 2001). Traffic congestion, increased crime, overcrowding and environmental damage are also potential negative impacts (Deccio and Balcoglu, 2002; Hall, 1992; Mihalik and Cummings 1995; Ritchie, 1984). In addition, employment opportunities could be limited due to the short-term nature/season of the mega-event (Burgan and Mules, 1992; Wang and Gitelson, 1988). In other words, events generally produce positive impacts for some, and negative effects for others (Getz, 2004; Hall, 1992).

The World Cup

The Federation Internationale de Football Association (FIFA) World Cup is the largest single sporting event in the world (FIFA, 1999a) and an extremely expensive event to host (Preuss, 2007). The Football World Cup has an extremely high international and national profile and is keenly sought after by nations and cities (Hall, 1992). The 2002 Football World Cup, jointly hosted by South Korea and Japan, was perceived to be an important mega-event for both countries (FIFA, 1996b) due to its potential to boost the host country's economy by direct and indirect effects. At the same time, the World Cup had the potential to enhance the national image of South Korea and Japan as tourist destinations (Hall, 1992; Ritchie, 1984; MCT, 2003).

More hotels (especially low- or medium-priced hotels) were constructed in South Korea while the country prepared for the World Cup (Seoul Metropolitan Government, 2002). More than 232,000 foreign soccer fans visited South Korea during the games (Hotel and Restaurant, 2002a; KNTO,

2002). The receipts from tourism in South Korea in June 2002, the World Cup period, amounted to US$460 million (MCT, 2003).

Methodology

The hotel sector was chosen as the sample population for this study for five reasons. Firstly, the hotel sector is one of the largest sectors of the South Korean tourism and hospitality industry in terms of capital investment and tourist expenditure (Kim and Uysal, 1998). Secondly, hotels provide the largest number of jobs, generate the greatest multiplier effect outside the industry and are major foreign currency earners (Kim and Uysal, 1998). Thirdly, in order to bid for the 2002 FIFA World Cup, one of FIFA's requirements of the host country to have compliance with under FIFA's stipulation was secure accommodation for the FIFA's family and delegation (Lee, 2000; WCOIA, 1995). Fourthly, it has been claimed that the hotel sector is the most affected by events due to the direct impact of event related visitor arrivals and the resulting demand for short-term accommodation (Dwyer et al., 2006; McKay and Plumb, 2001). Finally, little research has been specifically undertaken on the perspectives of the hotel sector on the hosting of mega-events (Shultis et al., 1996; Byeon, 2002; Byeon and Hall, 2003; Byeon, 2008).

The data for the pre-/post-event impacts study were obtained through a questionnaire using closed question techniques. The questionnaire was first draughted in English and then translated into Korean by the researcher, who is Korean. The questionnaire was designed to identify the Korean hotel industry's perspective on the positive and negative aspects of the Football World Cup 2002 on their individual hotel. A five-point Likert scale ranging from 'strongly disagree' (1) to 'strongly agree' (5) was used to rate 24 impact variables of the 2002 Football World Cup for the pre-event impacts study. However, when present results, percentage of 'strongly agree' and 'agree' were combined as 'agree' and 'strongly disagree' and 'disagree' were joined as 'disagree'. Alreck and Settle (1995, 2004) noted that scales are used to obtain responses which will be comparable to one another and may be regarded as both efficient and practical. Twenty-four impact variables were generated from a combination of several sources of information including Ritchie's (1984) article concerning the analysis of the impact of hallmark events, Hall's (1992) hallmark tourist events book and a review of the Seoul Olympics by Jeong (1987, 1992). Table 5.1 presents 24 pre-event impact study's variables. To make a comparison between the two points in time, including total 24 impact variables of the pre-event impacts study and adding 3 more impact variables which derived from limitation of pre-event impacts study were used to rate. Thus, a total of 27 impact variables were used in the post-event impacts study (see Table 5.2).

The pre-event impacts survey was administered to the entire hotel industry (as of 19 April 2000) in South Korea. Korean hotels are divided into five classes and they are divided by facilities. The quality of the hotel is symbolised by a Rose of Sharon and exhibited by a bronze shield in the lobby. They are deluxe 1st class (=super deluxe, 5 Rose of Sharon), deluxe 2nd class (=deluxe, 5 Rose of Sharon), first class (4 Rose of Sharon), second class (3 Rose of Sharon), third class (2 Rose of Sharon) (KNTO, 2000). Since the hotel classes are divided by facilities, Chi-Square test conducted to see there is any relationship between the hotel class and hotel room numbers' variables. The results revealed a significant relationship between the two variables in both the pre- and post-event studies.

Even though the entire population was sampled both in the pre-/post-event studies, the two points in time results are predominantly those of first class hotels because factors other than equal

Table 5.1: Results of the pre-event study.

R	Variables	Mean	1		2		3		4		5		Total		Missing	
			F	%	F	%	F	%	F	%	F	%	F	%	F	%
1	Increases international guests during the event	3.79	14	5.1	31	11.2	44	15.9	97	35.0	91	32.9	277	100	0	0
2	Increases revenue	3.53	13	4.7	29	10.5	83	30.0	91	32.9	54	19.5	270	97.5	7	2.5
3	Increases in your hotel staff's pride	3.38	15	5.4	37	13.4	95	34.3	89	32.1	41	14.8	277	100	0	0
4	Increases international guests before the event	3.33	19	6.9	54	19.5	55	19.9	109	39.4	37	13.4	274	98.9	3	1.1
5	Increases domestic guests during the event	3.25	21	7.6	60	21.7	69	24.9	82	29.6	45	16.2	277	100	0	0
6	Improves/creates congress, conference and exhibition facilities	3.24	38	13.7	28	10.1	74	26.7	103	37.2	34	12.3	277	100	0	0
7	Creates/increases additional employment	3.22	26	9.4	49	17.7	68	24.5	97	35.0	32	11.6	272	98.2	5	1.8
8	Stimulates conferences before, during and after event	3.21	31	11.2	40	14.4	74	26.7	96	34.7	31	11.2	272	98.2	5	1.8
9	Benefits outweigh any disadvantages associated with event	3.09	26	9.4	52	18.8	92	33.2	74	26.7	27	9.7	271	97.8	6	2.2
10	Increases international guests after the event	3.04	23	8.3	65	23.5	86	31.0	79	28.5	21	7.6	274	98.9	3	1.1
11	Creates/develops recreation facilities	3.03	41	14.8	47	17.0	72	26.0	88	31.8	24	8.7	272	98.2	5	1.8
12	Increases domestic guests before the event	3.02	22	7.9	80	28.9	73	26.4	72	26.0	29	10.5	276	99.6	1	0.4
13	Improved relations with sports associations and/or organisations	2.96	27	9.7	56	20.2	105	37.9	70	25.3	15	5.4	273	98.6	4	1.4
14	Promotes investment opportunities	2.95	39	14.1	62	22.4	76	27.4	69	24.9	28	10.1	274	98.9	3	1.1
15	Increases your hotel room prices	2.83	48	17.3	48	17.3	94	33.9	67	24.2	15	5.4	272	98.2	5	1.8
16	Increases room numbers	2.82	71	25.6	45	16.2	53	19.1	75	27.1	31	11.2	275	99.3	2	0.7
17	Increases domestic guests after the event	2.72	33	11.9	79	28.5	107	38.6	44	15.9	12	4.3	275	99.3	2	0.7
18	Overcrowding in your hotel facilities	2.68	45	16.2	68	24.5	100	36.1	53	19.1	8	2.9	274	98.9	3	1.1
19	Lack of parking lots	2.67	63	22.7	58	20.9	76	27.4	60	21.7	17	6.1	274	98.9	3	1.1
20	Underutilised hotel facilities after the event has ended	2.50	61	22.0	74	26.7	89	32.1	33	11.9	14	5.1	271	97.8	6	2.2
21	Reduces hotel tax	2.46	69	24.9	69	24.9	82	29.6	38	13.7	12	4.3	270	97.5	7	2.5
22	Increases in negative hotel staff interactions due to overcrowding and overdemanding guests	1.89	113	40.8	97	35.0	54	19.5	8	2.9	4	1.4	276	99.6	1	0.4
23	Increases crime around your hotel	1.89	111	40.1	85	30.7	54	19.5	11	4.0	2	0.7	263	94.9	14	5.1
24	Increases prostitution around your hotel	1.78	135	48.7	86	31.0	37	13.4	16	5.8	2	0.7	276	99.6	1	0.4

Note: Scale indicates 1 = strongly disagree, 2 = disagree, 3 = neutral, 4 = agree, 5 = strongly agree, R = rank, F = frequency, % = per cent.

Table 5.2: Results of the post-event study.

R	Variables	Mean	1		2		3		4		5		Missing	
			F	%	F	%	F	%	F	%	F	%	F	%
1	Increased international guests during the event	2.84	71	24.1	45	15.3	62	21.1	86	29.3	27	9.2	3	1.0
2	Increased your hotel staff's pride	2.81	60	20.4	48	16.3	93	31.6	69	23.5	22	7.5	2	0.7
3	Increased the revenue of your hotel	2.80	60	20.4	60	20.4	77	26.2	66	22.4	28	9.5	3	1.0
4	Benefits outweighed any disadvantages associated with event	2.48	70	23.8	76	25.9	89	30.3	46	15.6	9	3.1	4	1.4
5	Increased international guests before the event	2.46	84	28.6	63	21.4	80	27.2	53	18.0	10	3.4	4	1.4
6	Increased hotel's publicity associated with FIFA World Cup	2.43	86	29.3	67	22.8	79	26.9	42	14.3	16	5.4	4	1.4
7	Improved your relations with sports associations and/or organisations	2.33	103	35.0	59	20.1	79	26.9	36	12.2	16	5.4	1	0.3
8	Increased your hotel room prices	2.30	105	35.7	63	21.4	60	20.4	46	15.6	13	4.4	7	2.4
9	Increased investment opportunities	2.26	99	33.7	80	27.2	61	20.7	42	14.3	10	3.4	2	0.7
10	Increased domestic guests during the event	2.17	102	34.7	87	29.6	60	20.4	35	11.9	7	2.4	3	1.0
11	Reduced hotel tax in your hotel	2.13	116	39.5	73	24.8	55	18.7	37	12.6	8	2.7	5	1.7
12	Improved/built conference, meeting and exhibition facilities in your hotel	2.11	115	39.1	75	25.5	62	21.1	28	9.5	10	3.4	4	1.4
13	Increased international guests after the event	2.10	108	36.7	84	28.6	69	23.5	28	9.5	4	1.4	1	0.3
14	Underutilised hotel facilities after the event	2.04	110	37.4	82	27.9	71	24.1	17	5.8	5	1.7	9	3.1
15	Increased domestic guests before the event	2.02	103	35.0	101	34.4	64	21.8	20	6.8	2	0.7	4	1.4
16	Increased domestic guests after the event	2.01	104	35.4	98	33.3	71	24.1	15	5.1	2	0.7	4	1.4
17	Stimulated conferences, meetings and exhibitions during the event	1.97	121	41.2	93	31.6	47	16.0	20	6.8	8	2.7	5	1.7
18	Stimulated conferences, meetings and exhibitions before the event	1.91	122	41.5	92	31.3	53	18.0	14	4.8	5	1.7	8	2.7
19	Created/increased additional employment in your hotel	1.87	129	43.9	90	30.6	60	20.4	9	3.1	4	1.4	2	0.7
20	Insufficient parking lots in your hotel	1.86	140	47.6	81	27.6	42	14.3	18	6.1	7	2.4	6	2.0
21	Created/developed recreation facilities in your hotel	1.85	139	47.3	78	26.5	47	16.0	19	6.5	4	1.4	7	2.4
22	Stimulated conferences, meetings and exhibitions after the event	1.85	125	42.5	87	29.6	58	19.7	10	3.4	2	0.7	12	4.1
23	Increased total hotel room numbers in your hotel	1.69	169	57.5	58	19.7	37	12.6	15	5.1	5	1.7	10	3.4
24	Overcrowding of your hotel facilities	1.64	160	54.4	82	27.9	42	14.3	5	1.7	1	0.3	4	1.4
25	Increased negative hotel staff/guest interactions	1.44	194	66.0	71	24.1	20	6.8	4	1.4	1	0.3	4	1.4
26	Increased prostitution around your hotel	1.40	210	71.4	59	20.1	11	3.7	8	2.7	3	1.0	3	1.0
27	Increased crime around your hotel	1.38	205	69.7	66	22.4	15	5.1	2	0.7	2	0.7	4	1.4

Note: Scale indicates 1 = strongly disagree, 2 = disagree, 3 = neutral, 4 = agree, 5 = strongly agree, R = rank, F = frequency, % = per cent.

probability of being chosen in each sample may be present. Moreover, 79.8% ($n = 221$) were found to be non-deluxe (first, second and third class) and 20.2% ($n = 56$) were deluxe (deluxe 1st and 2nd class) in the pre-event study and 73.5% ($n = 216$) were revealed to be non-deluxe and 26.5% ($n = 78$) were deluxe hotels in the post-event study. Therefore, in the post-event study deluxe hotels were more represented and non-deluxe hotels were less revealing than the pre-event impacts study, both studies' results would more likely reflect the non-deluxe hotels perspectives of the 2002 Football World Cup.

The population was identified from the 1999 and 2000 Korea Hotel Directory (KHD) and Korea Hotel Association (KHA). The total defined hotel population for the pre-event impacts study was 461. However, after confirming hotel details with each hotel (hotel address and name of the general manager (GM) and/or managing director (MD) with information given by 1999 KHD before distribution of the questionnaire to all hotels for the actual survey, the entire hotel industry population differed from the actual number of questionnaires distributed because of changes to the membership base and member's circumstances. Therefore, from the entire Korean hotel population of 461, the actual distributed questionnaire population in the pre-event study was 431 hotels (see Table 5.3).

Since the pre-event impacts study, Korean hotel numbers have grown continuously. As shown in Table 5.3, at the time of the post-event survey there were 530 hotels in South Korea (according to KHD as of 22 March 2004). The same procedure was followed as in the pre-event study to confirm hotel details, a total of 468 hotels were approached for the post-event impacts study.

The survey was mailed to potential respondents and a reply-paid envelope was included, as is standard practise with this distribution method. The mail-out distribution method for the survey was employed as it is one of the most productive methods when attempting to gather information from large and geographically dispersed population (Alreck and Settle, 1995, 2004). Moreover, the mail-out method gives advantages to respondents in terms of time convenience to fill out the questionnaire (Buckingham and Saunders, 2004).

An initial covering letter providing an introduction to the research and a questionnaire with a stamped reply envelope attached was sent to a specific MD and/or GM by name between 25 January and 18 May 2000 (pilot test period, 25 January to 10 February 2000, included) for the pre-event impacts study. Pilot testing was required so that the survey could be modified slightly in content and in structure, and to ensure that mail surveying would do the job reliably (Alreck and Settle, 1995, 2004). Thus, the questionnaire was pilot tested on 15 hotels in South Korea. Since a high response rate was expected from pilot testing, mainly deluxe 1st and 2nd class and first class hotels in 10 HCs were randomly chosen for the pilot test. The results of this research did indeed confirm that deluxe 1st and 2nd class and first class hotels presented high response rates compared with the other hotel classes. The pilot test recorded a 60% ($n = 9$) result, so no amendments were found to be necessary. While conducting the actual survey a few more questionnaires were returned from the pilot survey.

Table 5.3: Response rates.

	Respondents	Actual no. of questionnaires distributed	No. of members of KHA
The post-event	294 (62.8%)	468	530 (as of 22 March 2004)
The pre-event	277 (64.3%)	431	461 (as of 19 April 2000)

Note: No: Number; KHA: Korea Hotel Association.

Thus, the final pilot test response rate was 93% ($n = 14$). By the nature of research conducted on the entire South Korean hotel industry, pilot test respondents were included in this study.

GMs are viewed as holding the key executive position in the hotel industry (Ladkin, 1999). They are considered the most knowledgeable and responsible person within the hotel. By sending it to specified personnel it was an attempt to increase the response rate and also hoped that all surveys would be answered by an equivalent person in all hotels. If a hotel did not have a GM position, questionnaires were addressed to the MD or the manager who is equivalent to GM position within the hotel. With the same administration as pre-event impacts study, the post-event impacts survey was conducted between 31 March and 10 September 2004.

Non-respondents were identified from the initial questionnaire distribution list and telephone follow-up calls were made in order to increase the response rate both the pre- and post-event impacts study. During the telephone follow-ups, it was found that some hotels had misplaced or did not receive the questionnaire. Therefore, the questionnaire was sent again during the two time periods survey to those who still wanted to participate in the survey. Fax and email were also used both for the second distribution of questionnaires and their return to save delivering time while conducting the pre- and post-event impacts survey. As presented in Table 5.3, in total 277 (64.3%) and 294 (62.8%) replies were received for the pre- and post-event impacts surveys, respectively. From these results, even if this sample population approximates the overall distribution of hotel population in South Korea, it is clear that hotel samples are skewed towards the Seoul area because of the distribution of hotels in South Korea and may therefore be biased.

Frequency counts and percentages for all the responses and mean scores were used to identify significant hotel industry perspectives of the 2002 Football World. Cross-tabulation using the Pearson Chi-Square was performed to identify the association between the two variables and their relationship simultaneously on the contingency table. t-test was undertaken to examine the significant differences between the two time periods mean scores. The following discussion addresses findings related to the two research aims.

Results and Discussion

Overall Pre-event Impacts

Profile of respondents   Table 5.4 summarises the demographic profile of the study respondents. Of the respondents 69.7% were GMs and 24.2% had worked for 16–20 years in the hotel industry. In terms of the characteristics of the respondents' hotels, 42.2% were rated as first class hotels (see Table 5.5) and 22.4% were located in Seoul; 55.2% of respondents were located in cities hosting World Cup games.

Table 5.4: Respondents profile.

	General manager %	**Male %**	**Length of work**
The post-event	64.6	95.9	21–25 years (21.4%)
The pre-event	69.7	97.5	16–20 years (24.2%)

Divided by classification Chi-Square test showed that the majority of the deluxe 1st and 2nd hotels have over 151 rooms in the South Korea hotel industry. Hotels with between 51 and 100 rooms were mostly first class. The majority of third class hotels only had between 1 and 50 rooms. This result indicates that deluxe 1st and 2nd class hotels have more rooms than first, second and third class hotels (Pearson Chi-Square value (PCSV): 240.000; significant level (SL): 0.000). The post-event study also reveals the same results (PCSV: 250.738; SL: 0.000).

Respondents who were located in HCs have a greater number of deluxe 1st class (=super deluxe) (7.8%), deluxe 2nd class (=deluxe) (18.3%) and third class (13.7%) hotels than NHCs (4.8%, 8.3% and 8.1%, respectively). Therefore, deluxe (1st and 2nd) class and HCs have more capacity to cater for guests demand in rooms than non-deluxe hotels and NHCs during mega-event periods.

Different perspectives between HCs and NHCs Chi-Square tests conducted on HCs and NHCs and individual hotel variables indicated that there were significant differences between perspectives on HCs and NHCs. As illustrated in Table 5.6, eight variables were perceived as significantly different between HCs and NHCs on the individual hotel. HCs registered higher agreement for both positive and negative impact variables than NHCs on their hotels. However, interesting notes that Chi-Square test conducted on Seoul and non-Seoul and variables found that 12 variables were perceived as markedly different between Seoul and non-Seoul (refer to Table 5.6). Hotels located in Seoul revealed higher agreement for both positive and negative impact variables than hotels located in non-Seoul and even hotels located in HCs and NHCs.

Moreover, two Chi-Square tests between Seoul and Busan/non-Seoul and Busan and variables (10 variables had significant relationships), and between Seoul, Gyeonggi and Incheon/non-Seoul, Gyeonggi and Incheon and variables (12 variables had significant relationships) also found that there

Table 5.5: Comparison by hotel grade of respondents, actual number of questionnaires distributed and number of KHA ($n = 294$).

| | Post-event research (2004) | | | | | | Pre-event research (2000) | | | | | |
| | Respondents | | Actual number of distribution | | Number of members of KHA | | Respondents | | Actual number of distribution | | Number of members of KHA | |
Classification	F	%	F	%	F	%	F	%	F	%	F	%
Deluxe 1st class	28	9.5	43	9.2	43	8.1	18	6.5	29	6.7	29	6.3
Deluxe 2nd class	50	17.0	56	12.0	64	12.1	38	13.7	48	11.1	50	10.9
First class	134	45.6	175	37.4	192	36.2	117	42.2	177	41.1	188	40.8
Second class	60	20.4	112	23.9	131	24.7	73	26.4	109	25.3	120	26.0
Third class	22	7.5	69	14.7	80	15.1	31	11.2	61	14.2	67	14.5
Undecided grade	N/A	N/A	13	2.8	20	3.8	N/A	N/A	7	1.6	7	1.5
Total	294	100.0	468	100.0	530	100.0	277	100.0	431	100.0	461	100.0

Note: Deluxe 1st class = super deluxe, deluxe 2nd class = deluxe hotel; F = frequency.

Table 5.6: Results of Chi-Square tests of pre- and post-event periods.

Variables	Host/non Pre	Host/non Post	Seoul/non Pre	Seoul/non Post	Seoul and Busan/non Pre	Seoul and Busan/non Post	Seoul, G, I/non Pre	Seoul, G, I/non Post	Seoul, G, I and B/non Pre	Seoul, G, I and B/non Post	Busan/non Pre	Busan/non Post
Increased the revenues of your hotel	26.263 0.000 0.298	36.500 0.000 0.334	17.117 0.002 0.244	14.914 0.005 0.222	15.016 0.005 0.230	13.064 0.011 0.207	15.817 0.003 0.235		15.027 0.005 0.230	14.912 0.005 0.221		13.836 0.008 0.214
Increased your hotel room prices	25.708 0.000 0.294	19.380 0.001 0.252	56.104 0.000 0.414		30.450 0.000 0.317	15.986 0.003 0.230	47.882 0.000 0.387	18.364 0.001 0.245	29.855 0.000 0.314	19.961 0.001 0.255		
Creates/increases additional employment in your hotel			10.873 0.028 0.196		16.563 0.002 0.240							
Increased investment opportunities		17.654 0.001 0.239	15.882 0.003 0.234		10.208 0.037 0.190	11.404 0.022 0.194	15.300 0.004 0.230			10.144 0.038 0.183		
Reduced hotel tax in your hotel		10.013 0.040 0.183										
Benefits outweighed any disadvantages associated with event		12.831 0.012 0.206										
Increased domestic guests before the event		13.901 0.008 0.214										
Increased domestic guests during the event		19.729 0.001 0.252										14.985 0.005 0.222

	C1	C2	C3	C4	C5	C6	C7	C8	C9	C10	C11
Increased domestic guests after the event		13.517 0.009 0.211									
Increased international guests before the event		44.635 0.000 0.365		10.878 0.028 0.190		21.916 0.000 0.265		12.803 0.012 0.206		26.448 0.000 0.289	13.045 0.011 0.208
Increased international guests during the event	27.130 0.000 0.299	48.817 0.000 0.379	16.682 0.002 0.238		14.514 0.006 0.223	11.021 0.026 0.191	17.500 0.002 0.244		19.729 0.001 0.258	11.204 0.024 0.193	
Increased international guests after the event		28.780 0.000 0.299	16.168 0.003 0.236		12.907 0.012 0.212	13.767 0.008 0.212	20.898 0.000 0.266		16.765 0.002 0.240	13.924 0.008 0.213	9.883 0.042 0.187
Stimulates conferences, meetings and exhibitions before, during, and after ent		25.814 0.000 0.288					11.308 0.023 0.200				
Stimulated conferences, meetings and exhibitions before the event		31.132 0.000 0.312						10.898 0.028 0.191		11.336 0.023 0.194	
Stimulated conferences, meetings and exhibitions during the event											
Increased hotel's publicity associated with FIFA World Cup		36.846 0.000 0.336		12.024 0.017 0.200		15.859 0.003 0.228		11.975 0.018 0.199		15.590 0.004 0.226	
Increases room numbers			12.091 0.017 0.205			13.441 0.009 0.216					

(Continued)

Table 5.6: Continued.

Variables	Host/non		Seoul/non		Seoul and Busan/non		Seoul, G, I/non		Seoul, G, I and B/non		Busan/non	
	Pre	Post	Pre	Post	Pre	Post	Pre	Post	Pre	Post	Pre	Post
Improved/built conferences, meeting and exhibition facilities in your hotel	16.335	12.453	20.768		17.753		15.888		13.242			
	0.003	0.014	0.000		0.001		0.003		0.010			
	0.236	0.203	0.264		0.245		0.233		0.214			
Created/developed recreation facilities in your hotel	13.261	13.723	24.212		15.554		15.205		10.679			
	0.010	0.008	0.000		0.004		0.004		0.030			
	0.216	0.214	0.286		0.233		0.230		0.194			
Insufficient parking lots in your hotel	10.237	14.062										
	0.037	0.007										
	0.190	0.216										
Improved your relations with sports associations		22.095				12.087						
		0.000				0.017						
		0.265				0.199						
Overcrowding in your hotel facilities	25.746		31.292		20.511		23.549		17.367			
	0.000		0.000		0.000		0.000		0.002			
	0.293		0.320		0.264		0.281		0.244			
Increased your hotel staff's pride	11.862	33.999	13.080		12.818	9.953				9.659		
	0.018	0.000	0.011		0.012	0.041				0.047		
	0.203	0.323	0.212		0.210	0.182				0.179		

Note: Figure in the above table denote: 1st row = PCSV, 2nd row = SL, 3rd row = contingency coefficient value; Pre: = the pre-event, Post = the post-event; Seoul, G, I/ Non = Seoul, Gyeonggi, Incheon/Non-Seoul, non-Gyeonggi, non-Incheon; Seoul, G, I and B/Non = Seoul, Gyeonggi, Incheon and Busan/Non-Seoul, non-Gyeonggi, non-Incheon and non-Busan; For the pre-event 'stimulated conferences, meetings and exhibitions of before, during and after event' examined into only one variable. However, 'stimulated conferences, meetings and exhibitions before, during and after event' are examined individually in the post-event study.

were significant relationships (see Table 5.6). Surprisingly, most of the above significant relationship results again received a higher level of agreement for positive and negative impacts than results of significant relationships between HCs/NHCs and variables. This implies that respondents perceive that Seoul and Busan would get more benefits and costs than the other HCs. Additionally, Seoul, Gyeonggi and Incheon would get more benefits and costs than the other HCs.

Overall Post-event Impacts

Profile of respondents   As presented in Table 5.4, GM respondents represented 64.6% for the post-event study. Amongst respondents, unlike the pre-event study results, 21.4% had between 21 and 25 years length of work in the hotel industry. Of the respondents 95.9% were males; 45.6% were rated as first class hotels. 52.7% of respondents were located in HCs, and 21.1% of hotels were from located in Seoul. Since the questionnaires were personalised by sending them to named GM/MD, GMs were highly represented amongst the respondents of both the pre- and post-event study. Male respondents were the predominance (97.5% and 95.9%) in the two time periods result (refer to Table 5.4).

Different perspectives between HCs and NHCs   As shown in Table 5.6 in contrast to the pre-event study results, 19 out of 27 variables were perceived as significantly different between HCs and NHCs on their hotel. NHCs registered higher disagreement for both positive and negative impact variables than HCs, on their hotels. This result confirmed the proposition that hosted events are beneficial to the HCs (e.g. Hall, 1989, 1992). This result also indicates that benefits and costs generated from hosting the sports event could be differentiated by the degree of direct (e.g. HCs) or indirect (e.g. NHCs) involvement in the event. The 'direct involvement group' has significantly more agreement perceptions towards positive and negative impacts than the non-involvement group and the findings of Jeong's (1992) study and this longitudinal study result support this notion.

Hotels which benefited from the event experienced increased revenues and increased numbers of international guests during the event. Hotels in Busan showed the highest agreement that revenue had increased during the event, with 59.2% of hotels experiencing this, a significantly higher percentage than hotels not in Busan (PCSV: 13.836;SL: 0.008). In addition, in HCs, 45.4% of hotels considered that they had experienced increased revenue and in the group that consists of Seoul, Gyeonggi, Incheon and Busan, 46.4% agreed that there was increased revenue due to the event.

Unlikely the pre-event study results, only three variables are significantly different between hotels located in Seoul and non-Seoul (see Table 5.6). Not unsurprisingly, hotels located in non-Seoul (46.3%) showed higher agreement for 'increased your hotel room prices' variable (PCSV: 14.914;SL: 0.005) than hotels located in Seoul (35%), HCs (27.5%) and NHCs (13.0%) (PCSV:19.380;SL: 0.001). Interesting note that hotels located in Seoul, Gyeonggi and Incheon (35.7%) (where are Seoul metropolitan areas) showed the high level of agreement on 'increased their hotel room prices' (PCSV: 18.364;SL: 0.001).

It is interesting to note that prior to the games, respondents believed that Seoul would receive more benefits and incur more costs than other HCs. This prior to the World Cup's result might be influenced by 1988 Seoul Olympics' actual impacts outcome which Seoul gained great benefit because usually Olympics are held in one city. Likewise, traditionally Seoul already has the most international visitors compared to other HCs (84.7% of visitors visited Seoul, followed by Busan (17.8%) and Jeju Island (8.2%) while visiting South Korea) (KNTO, 2001). However, after the actual tournament outcomes, the hotel sector perceived that each HCs' actual benefits from the World Cup were significantly different amongst cities. It is because of the characteristic of Football World Cup which was hosted in 10 cities.

Even though the entire population was sampled both in the pre-/post-event study, the two points in time results are predominantly those of first class hotels because factors other than equal probability of being chosen in each sample may be present. Moreover, 79.8% ($n = 221$) were found to be non-deluxe (first, second and third class) and 20.2% ($n = 56$) were deluxe (deluxe 1st and 2nd class) in the pre-event study and 73.5% ($n = 216$) were revealed to be non-deluxe and 26.5% ($n = 78$) were deluxe hotels in the post-event study. Even though, in the post-event study deluxe hotels were more represented and non-deluxe hotels were less revealed than the pre-event impacts study, both study's results would more likely reflect the non-deluxe hotels perspectives of the 2002 Football World Cup.

Comparison of Pre and post-event Impact Perception

The pre-event impacts   Table 5.1 shows the impact variable results of the pre-event study. From the perspective of individual hotels, the highest ranking benefit was in terms of tourism and commercial impacts, namely that the World Cup would increase international guests during the hosting of the event (mean = 3.79) (see Figure 5.1). Economic impact such as 'increases revenues' was the second

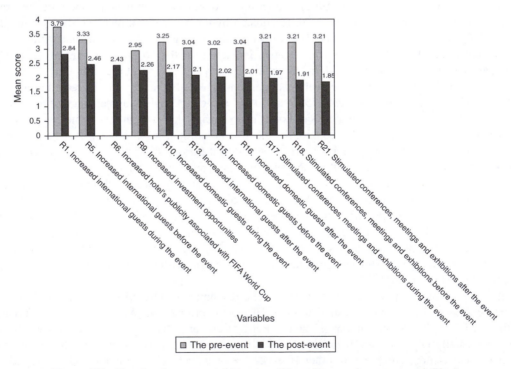

Figure 5.1: Tourism/commercial impacts.(*Note*: R = rank among variables).

highest expected benefit (mean = 3.33) followed by psychological impact 'increases in your hotel staff's pride' was the third highest expected benefit (mean = 3.38) (refer to Figures 5.2 and 5.3). As shown in Figures 5.4 and 5.5, 'Overcrowding in your hotel facilities' (mean = 2.68) was perceived as the highest cost followed by 'lack of parking lots' (mean = 2.67). 'Increases crime' and 'increases prostitution' received a high level of disagreement at their hotel (mean = 1.89 and mean = 1.78, respectively).

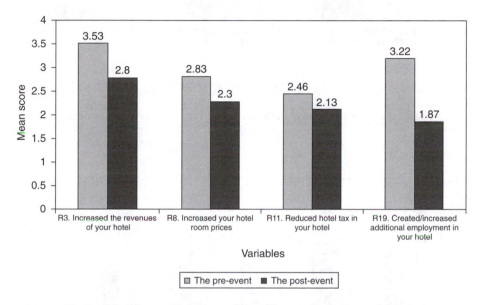

Figure 5.2: Economic impacts.(*Note*: R = rank among variables).

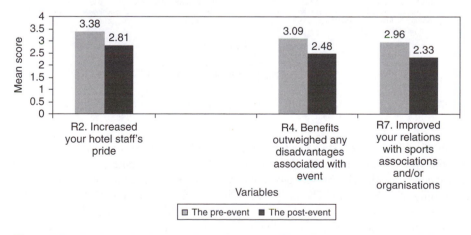

Figure 5.3: Psychological and political impacts. (*Note*: R = rank among variables).

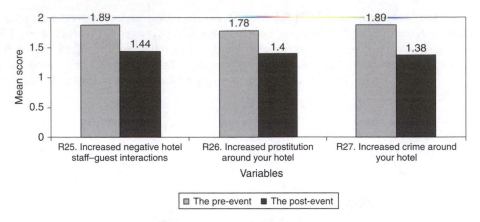

Figure 5.4: Socio-cultural impacts. (*Note*: R = rank among variables).

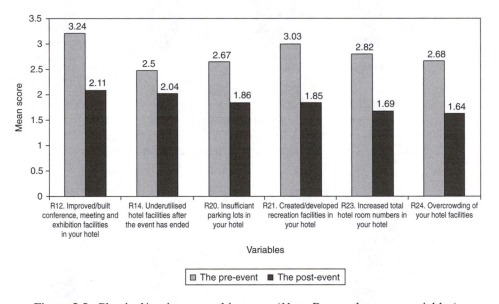

Figure 5.5: Physical/environmental impacts. (*Note*: R = rank among variables).

The result of a Chi-Square test showed that 70.9% of deluxe (deluxe 1st and 2nd class) hotels perceived that the World Cup would increase revenue in relation to their hotel. While 55.9% and 45.1% of first and second class hotels showed agreement with 'increases revenue' in relation to their hotels respectively, only 35.5% of third class hotels showed positive agreement (PCSV: 39.461; SL: 0.000) (see Table 5.7). As shown in Table 5.8, 85.7% of deluxe (deluxe 1st and 2nd class) hotels agreed that the World Cup would increase international guests during the event (PCSV: 20.703; SL: 0.000). These results reflect Chon and Shin's (1990) note that deluxe class hotels that cater mostly to

Table 5.7: Percentage of hotels from four different classes agreeing that revenue increased in the two time periods.

Classification	The post-event %	The pre-event %
Deluxe class (deluxe 1st and 2nd)	52.6	70.9
First class	25.0	55.9
Second class	25.4	45.1
Third class	22.7	35.5

Note: Recoded into deluxe (deluxe 1st and 2nd) and first, second and third class hotels.Chi-Square test results of the pre-event: PCSV = 39.461, SL = 0.000, contingency coefficient value = 0.357. Chi-Square test results of the post-event: PCSV = 25.682, SL = 0.012, contingency coefficient value = 0.285.

Table 5.8: Percentage of hotels from four different classes agreeing that international guest numbers increased in the two time periods.

Classification	The post-event %	The pre-event %
Deluxe class (deluxe 1st and 2nd)	59.0	85.7
First class	34.1	62.4
Second class	26.9	
Third class	27.2	

Note: The pre-event study – recoded into deluxe (deluxe 1st and 2nd) and non-deluxe (first, second and third class). Chi-Square test results of the pre-event: PCSV = 20.703, SL = 0.000, contingency coefficient value = 0.264. Chi-Square test results of the post-event: PCSV = 25.656, SL = 0.012, contingency coefficient value = 0.285.

international visitors experience the highest occupancy rates in general. Moreover, FIFA's accommodation request to the host country for FIFA's family and press are mainly for super deluxe, deluxe and first class hotels (Lee, 2000; WCOIA, 1995). Deluxe (deluxe1st and 2nd class) hotels showed higher agreement (51.9%) on 'increase hotel room prices' than first (30.7%), second (17.2%) and third (19.4%) class (PCSV: 32.395;SL: 0.001;62.5% of deluxe (deluxe 1st and 2nd class) hotels agreed that the World Cup would increase their hotel staff's pride (PCSV: 10.980; SL: 0.027).

The post-event impacts   Table 5.2 presents the overall variable results of the post-event study. Respondents revealed the outcomes of actual experiences of the games that the 2002 World Cup increased international guests during the event (mean = 2.84) which received the highest mean score (refer to Figure 5.1). As presented in Figures 5.2 and 5.3 and Tables 5.1 and 5.2, inconsistent with the pre-event study results, the second highest gained benefit from the World Cup was 'increased their hotel staff's pride' (mean = 2.81) followed by 'increased the revenue of your hotel (mean = 2.80). As shown in Figure 5.3, notably, 'benefits outweighed any disadvantages associated with event' variable (mean= 2.48) ranked higher in the post-event study (ranked 4) than the pre-event study (ranked 9, mean = 3.09). 'Improved your relations with sports associations and/or organisations' and 'increased your hotel room prices' variables also noticeably showed higher ranking in the post-event study (ranked 7th and 8th, respectively) than the pre-event study (ranked 13th and 15th, respectively) (see Figures 5.2 and 5.3, Tables 5.1 and 5.2). However, 'increased domestic guests during the event' markedly ranked lower after the games (ranked 10th, mean = 2.17) than prior to the games (ranked 5th, mean = 3.25) and generated high differences in mean score (1.07) between the two points in time (refer to Figure 5.1, Tables 5.1 and 5.2). The respondents experienced very low agreement on the 'created/increased additional employment in your hotel' (mean = 1.87). This variable created the largest gap mean score (1.35) between the two time periods. Whereas the 'reduced hotel tax in your hotel' generated the smallest gap mean score (0.33) between two points in time (the pre-event study mean: 2.46; the post-event study mean: 2.13) (see Figure 5.2., Tables 5.1 and 5.2). As illustrated in Figure 5.5, 'underutilised hotel facilities after the event has ended' (mean = 2.04) was experienced as the highest cost followed by 'insufficient parking lots in your hotel' (mean = 1.86). In contrast to some previous research on the negative impact of mega-events (Hall and Hodges, 1996; Olds, 1998) the likelihood that the World Cup 'increased prostitution' and 'increased crime' received a high level of disagreement again at their hotel (mean = 1.40 and mean = 1.38, respectively) (refer to Figure 5.4, Table 5.2).

Additionally, results of paired t-tests reported in Table 5.9 revealed that there were significant differences ($p < .05$) on 26 impact variables between the two points in time.

When compared with the pre-event study, only 52.6% of deluxe (deluxe 1st and 2nd class) hotels agreed that the World Cup increased revenue in relation to their hotel; 44% and 52.5% of first and second class hotels showed disagreement with 'increased revenue' of their hotel respectively, 50% of third class hotels showed negative agreement (only 25%, 25.4% and 22.7% of first, second and third class hotels, respectively, showed agreement on 'increased revenue') (PCSV;25.682, SL: 0.012).

The Chi-Square test showed there is a significant difference between the types of hotel in terms of how many agreed the World Cup would increase international guests during the event, 59% of deluxe (deluxe 1st and 2nd class) hotels agreed the World Cup increased international guests during the event. In comparison, 43.2%, 52.5% and 50% of first, second and third class hotels showed disagreement with 'increased international guests during the event' of their hotels respectively, just 34.1%, 26.9% and 27.2% of first, second and third class hotels agreed, respectively, on 'increased international guests during the event' (PCSV;25.656, SL: 0.012).

Deluxe (deluxe 1st and 2nd class) hotels (56.4%) agreed that the World Cup increased their hotel staff's pride. However, merely 21.2%, 23.3% and 22.7% of first, second and third class hotels agreed, respectively, that the World Cup increased their hotel staff's pride (PCSV;45.656, SL: 0.000).

Tourism/commercial impacts   Prior to the games, the respondents showed the highest positive agreement that hosting the 2002 World Cup would bring benefits of 'increases international guests during the event' to their hotels. This result might reflect findings of Byeon (2002) and Byeon and Hall's (2003) national levels the highest positive agreement on 'increases international visitors to Korea during the event' (ranked 1st and mean = 4.22) and high positive agreement of 'increases hotel occupancy rates' at a national level (ranked 3rd, mean = 4.16). Even though, judged by mean score, the hotel sector perceived that it did not receive benefit from the co-hosted 2002 World Cup. This consistent finding in both the pre- and post-event study supports previous literature that resulting events brings international visitors to the country (Hall, 1992; Ritchie, 1984) thus increased international guests to the hotel sector (Dwyer et al., 2006). However, there were also domestic guests displacement occurred during the event. This result indicates that domestic guests probably stayed away during the World Cup because of a possible perception that the event would be marked by inflated prices, crowds and difficulties in finding accommodation. Regular tourists can be displaced when events take up available accommodation (Getz, 2004).

Table 5.9: *t*-test results for comparisons of the hotel industry's perspectives on impacts at two points in time.

Impact variables	The pre-event	The post-event	*t*-value	*p*-value
Increases/increased the revenue of your hotel	3.53	2.78	7.357	.000
Increases/increased your hotel room prices	2.81	2.30	4.854	.000
Increases/increased additional employment in your hotel	3.21	1.89	14.429	.000
Increases/increased investment opportunities	2.94	2.27	6.422	.000
Reduces/reduced hotel tax in your hotel	2.45	2.15	2.957	.003
Benefits outweighs/outweighed any disadvantages associated with event	3.09	2.47	6.465	.000
Increases/increased domestic guests before the event	3.02	2.03	11.418	.000
Increases/increased domestic guests during the event	3.25	2.17	10.758	.000
Increases/increased domestic guests after the event	2.71	2.02	8.520	.000
Increases/increased international guests before the event	3.32	2.45	9.183	.000
Increases/increased international guests during the event	3.80	2.85	9.072	.000
Increases/increased international guests after the event	3.03	2.12	10.220	.000
Stimulates/stimulated international guests before the event	3.19	1.91	13.784	.000
Stimulates/stimulated international guests during the event	3.20	1.96	12.791	.000
Stimulates/stimulated international guests after the event	3.19	1.85	14.438	.000
Increases/increased hotel room numbers in your hotel	2.80	1.69	10.601	.000
Improves, build/improved, built conference, meetings and exhibition facilities in your hotel	3.23	2.12	10.871	.000
Creates, develops/created, developed recreation facilities in your hotel	3.02	1.89	11.515	.000
Insufficient parking lots in your hotel	2.66	1.87	8.095	.000
Underutilised hotel facilities after the event	2.50	2.03	5.190	.000
Increases/increased prostitution around your hotel	1.77	1.40	5.280	.000
Increases/increased crime around your hotel	1.89	1.39	7.476	.000
Increases/increased negative hotel staff–guest interactions	1.88	1.44	6.305	.000
Overcrowding of your hotel facilities	2.66	1.64	12.649	.000
Improves/improved your relations with sports associations and/or organisations	2.96	2.36	6.038	.000
Increases/increased your hotel staff's pride	3.37	2.84	5.271	.000

Note: For the pre-event 'stimulated conferences, meetings and exhibitions of before, during and after event' are examined into only one variable. However, 'stimulated conferences, meetings and exhibitions before, during and after event' are examined individually in the post-event study. Therefore, pared *t*-tested tests for both events are done by three variables in the post-event with the one variable of the pre-event.

However, Ohmann, et al. (2006) study found that displacement due to an increase of rents and house prices in preparation for mega-events, as demonstrated by Hall (2001) and Wilkinson (1994), was not the case in Munich in 2006 Football World Cup. From these results it could be said that perceived impacts of mega-events are differentiated from country to country.

Economic impacts   The pre-event study results indicate that hotel sector highly agreed that individual hotels would benefit economically during the World Cup which is an ambivalent response at the national and city/town level in the findings of Byeon (2002) and Byeon and Hall (2003). The pre-event perception is probably due to a direct correlation between 'increases international guests during the event' (1st ranked) and their accommodation expenditure. In addition, individual hotels do not have to contribute to the costs of staging such national event so therefore their income from the World Cup would be expected to be greater. However, lower ranking agreement on the 'increased the revenue of your hotel' in the post-event result than the pre-event study supported growing numbers of global critiques on the hosting event and justification for establishing large sports facilities (Hall, 1992; Hiller, 1989; Thorne and Munro-Clark, 1989). Kim et al. (2006) also found that the economic benefits were rather a big disappointment for local residents. Those two results may be reflected from outcomes of economic gains from hosted events and confirmed Dwyer et al. (2006) proposition that the actual net impact of events on economic activity are invariably much lower than conventionally estimated.

While deluxe 1st class hotels' occupancy rates decreased by 5.1%, revenue increased by 22% in June 2002 over the previous year due to increase hotel room prices (increased by 32.4% in June 2002 over the previous year) (Hotel and Restaurant, 2002a). During the June 1988 Football World Cup event in France, hotel occupancy rates were only 70% in Paris and visitor numbers had decreased 10% compared with the previous year due to the cancellation of other conferences and exhibitions (Kim, 1998). Moreover, during the Football World Cup event in Spain (1982) and in Italy (1990), visitor numbers also decreased 20% and 30%, respectively (ibid).

Likewise, in the year of 1988 Seoul, 1992 Barcelona, 1996 Atlanta and 2000 Sydney suffered a decline in average occupancies during the Olympic year, largely due to the increased level of room supply. While occupancy levels have fallen in all markets in the World Cup and Olympic year, all HC have experienced a substantial increase in average daily rate (ADR) during the mega-events years. The increased room rates have generally been sufficient to offset lower occupancies, as a result, those HCs have recorded an increase in hotel performance as measured by revenue per available room during the Olympic year (McKay and Plumb, 2001).

Given this fact and previous mega-events cases it is not surprising that the post-event result revealed higher ranking on 'increased your hotel room prices' than the pre-event study and generated small gap (difference) mean score (0.53) between the two points in time. A Chi-Square test result indicates that hotels located in non-Seoul area significantly increased room prices during the World Cup. This result, probably due to World Cup, was held in 10 HCs in South Korea thus increased in accommodation demand phenomenon in HCs other than Seoul. From this result it could be said that outcomes of mega-events are differentiated by the types of mega-events such as Olympic or Football World Cup event.

The largest gap mean score (1.35) between the two time periods on the 'created/increased additional employment in your hotel' implies that there was not an increased number of employees due to increased demand during the event. During a very short period of time, the increased demand associated with an event may be just met by existing labour working overtime (Dwyer et al., 2006).

The 'reduce hotel tax' (mean = 2.46) result in the pre-event study indicates that respondents disagree with this variable despite the government having implemented a series of measures since 1997, including financial and tax incentives, to stimulate the development of tourist hotels in order to expand accommodation for foreign visitors (MCT, 1999). The pre-event study finding might be explained by the probability that the availability of tax incentives from the government is limited to just a few hotels and that such incentives benefit hotels less than other industries who receive a greater level of tax incentive. However, the smallest gap mean score (0.33) between two points in time on the 'reduced hotel tax in your hotel' indicated that the hotel sector received benefit in reducing hotel tax due to the hosted World Cup. From this result it could be said that perceived impacts of mega-events are differentiated by the government policy.

Socio-cultural impacts   Not unsurprisingly, the hotel sector highly disagreed in two time periods that the World Cup 'increases crime and prostitution around hotel areas'. This is consistent with Jeong's (1987, 1992) findings and indicate that unlike other countries or destinations, event related crime and prostitution is perceived as being less likely to happen in South Korea because of the fact that South Korea has strict anti-prostitution laws (Jeong, 1992). The crime rate fell 11.6% during the World Cup (Kim, 2002). Likewise, social problems were hardly noticed during the World Cup when prostitution and crime were much less than residents expected in the findings of Kim et al. (2006). The large majority of respondents also refuted the statement that the co-hosting of the 2006 Football World Cup resulted in a general increase in crime and prostitution (Ohmann et al., 2006).

Physical/environmental impacts   After the games were over, 'underutilized hotels after the event' appeared to be the greatest concern of the hosted World Cup. This result implies that there needs diversification of market segmentation to increase occupancy rates and marketing of hotels.

Psychological impacts   The 2002 Football World Cup boosted up South Korean pride (MCT, 2003) since the winning of hosting over other locations and the winning of events themselves (Hall, 1989). South Korea's victory against Spain in the quarterfinals of the World Cup on 22 June was the happiest day for Koreans (Lee, 2002). Although, Labrie (1988) argued that psychological impacts cannot be measured accurately, respondents perceived that World Cup brought pride to hotel staff which revealed higher ranking than prior to the games. Benefits were realised markedly on staff who are working in deluxe hotels. In other words, the results explained that staff from deluxe hotels experienced a greater level of pride about being Korean than staff who worked in non-deluxe hotels. This was might be because staff from deluxe hotels experienced a greater degree of involvement with international guests.

Political impacts   Even though 'benefits outweighed any disadvantages associated with event' variable did not receive a higher mean rating than the other top three ranking significant variables, after the games reality result produced higher ranking than the prior games may indicate that, based on actual experience, hosting events are beneficial in overall. Moreover, when comparing Byeon (2002) with Jeong and Faulkner's (1996) study, the 'benefits outweigh any disadvantage associated with event' at the city/town level variable result shows that Jeong and Faulkner (1996) received a higher mean (3.27) than Byeon (2002) study (3.15). This result explained that perceived impacts from hosting the mega-event could be differentiated by sample population. These results also support the scholars' perception that while there are costs to having an event, these costs are outweighed by the benefits and thus cities and nations are willing to host the event (e.g. Hall, 1989, 1992; Sparrow, 1989). In addition, hosting the World Cup improved their hotels' relations with sports associations and/or organisations which can be utilized to bring further benefit to hotels in the future.

The pre-event research findings indicate that there were perceived benefits by the Korean hotel sector to co-hosting the 2002 Football World Cup. Therefore, the pre-event impacts study result may confirm the belief that the accommodation sector gains benefits from the mega-event.

The post-event impacts research results produced lower agreement on positive and negative impacts than the pre-event impacts research results. Judged by mean score, the post-games reality revealed that the Korean hotel sector did not feel that they received benefits from the co-hosted 2002 FIFA World Cup.

The pre-event impacts research results may have been influenced by the prospects that respondents could have had high expectations and were highly optimistic about the positive impacts from the 2002 World Cup. A lower mean for the post-event impacts result may be because the benefits of the event were not significant and were given more emphasis as a result of the respondent's experience of the Football World Cup 2002. The notion also confirmed with significant results the different perspectives between HCs and NHCs held by Korean hotel sectors relating to their individual hotels. Kim et al. (2006) also found that after the games residents realised that the benefits generated by the games were lower than they expected. These results may support Hill's (1996) proposition that bidding committees may over-estimate the advantages of holding games but games reality is not. Lower mean score results in the post-event study overall supports one academic group's proposition of critiques on the hosting event.

However, the reality of the 2002 World Cup was not affected by mismanagement, but by the impact of several external factors. Lee and Kwon (1998) also already note the panel of experts stated that international tourism demand during the World Cup Games would be highly dependent upon the promotion of the World Cup, capacity of hotel rooms and airline seats, interest in the World Cup by participating countries, and internal and external political circumstances. Since the 11 September terror in 2001, visitor numbers to South Korea already decreased which was a global phenomenon (e.g. in the Asia Pacific region international arrivals decreased by 7.4% in 2001) (MCT and KNTO, 2002; MINTeL International Group, 2002; WTTC, 2002). In addition after the World Cup in 2003 the tourism industry experienced a decrease in international arrivals due to severe acute respiratory syndrome (SARS) and the war in Iraq (MCT and KNTO, 2004). Global circumstances were not good for South Korea utilising co-hosted Football event to increase international visitors to South Korea before, during and after the World Cup. Specifically, during the World Cup periods in June 2002 a total of 403,466 visitors travelled to South Korea, a decrease of 12.4% over 2001 (460,330) (MCT and KNTO, 2002). A main cause of the decrease was the declining number of Japanese tourists by 45% who used to account for 46% of the total inbound travellers (MCT, 2003).

This after the reality of the games did not support the findings of Byeon (2002) and Byeon and Hall's (2003) high mean score (4.13 and ranked 4th out of 53 variables) of 'increases in inbound and outbound tourism between Korea and Japan during the event'. This is evidence that prior to the games the hotel sector mispredicted the impact of the hosted World Cup. There were many other causes for the decrease of inbound travellers. One of South Korea's major inbound markets, the USA, remains uncertain in the overall economic environment. The most numerous visitors to South Korea, Japan, were in the throes of yet another recession (MINTeL International Group, 2002). Moreover, because of the co-hosted World Cup with Japan, benefits may have been split and the inspiring performance of its soccer team held them watching at home. The rise of travel costs in

Korea including the hotel room prices also played a role to make them hesitate to come to South Korea (MCT, 2003). Chinese tourists to South Korea for the event were held back to generate a mere 60,000 decrease from the expected maximum 100,000 due to Chinese travel agents requiring excessive deposit money for returning home (scales from 5 million won up to 10 million won) and the poor performance of the Chinese soccer team (3 defeats in a row with no goals).

Making the problem worse was FIFA's official agent Byrom Inc. who was in charge of the international ticket sales and hotel rooms (MCT, 2003). Forcedly and/or voluntarily, Korean hotels signed an agreement with SEAMOS Marketing Ltd (World Cup Accommodation Bureau Korea, WCABK) while in preparation for the World Cup to secure hotel rooms for anticipated visitors that the agreement was unfair to each hotel (Hotel and Restaurant, 2002c). Agreement contents were hotel shall be reserved for the exclusive use of WCABK during the period from 27 May to 2 July 2002. Hotel shall not have the right to change the number of World Cup Rooms which is no less than 70% of each class of hotel room in hotel's entire inventory of guest rooms (Hotel and Restaurant, 2002b). Since the Byrom company could not sell hotel rooms, they cancelled and returned 70.7% (562,863 rooms of the total contract of 796,158 rooms) of blocked rooms to hotels by 30 April 2002. However, it was too late and too difficult to sell rooms to other visitors during the World Cup periods (Hotel and Restaurant, 2002c).

On the other hand, positive sites for hosting the World Cup was inbound travellers from European and Middle South American regions, where they show soccer fever, registered the record high of 55% and 386% increase, respectively. Such a remarkable increase has shown possible niche markets for the Korean tourism to further develop (MCT, 2003). Likewise, as deluxe hotels predicted before the games, they were perceived to have received more benefits than non-deluxe hotels. The hotel sectors which gained significant benefits were tourism/commercial, psychological and economic benefits in contrast to Kim et al. (2006) findings of societal and cultural benefits than economic gains for Koreans. From these results it could be said that perceived benefits are differentiated by level of each sample population (private sector, government or residents).

Conclusion

This study has examined the views of the hotel sector on the pre-/post-event impacts of the 2002 Football World Cup. The study provides perspectives on both hotel industry attitudes towards the impacts of two points in time a mega-event as well as the perceived impact of a World Cup in soccer. Both of these areas are under researched in the event literature. This longitudinal study revealed that the hotel sector's expectation of the benefits from the co-hosted World Cup was higher before the event but reality was not satisfied as they expected. However, deluxe (deluxe 1st and 2nd class) hotels and HCs received benefits from the hosted World Cup the results of which this longitudinal study answered the question of who gets benefit from the hosted sport event even though hotel sector's high expectation was not satisfied in the reality of the games.

Economic benefit was still ranked highly after the games that confirmed events bring benefit to the accommodation sector. Those deluxe hotels which received economic benefit was due to increased demand pumping up increased hotel room prices whilst remarking lower occupancy rate than previous years. Likewise, clearly, hosting a mega-event generated and increased international guest numbers whilst displacement occurred among domestic guests and possibly non-World Cup international guests.

Because of these two points in time results were predominantly by non-deluxe hotel (79.8%: pre-event, 73.5%:post-event), losers' perception dominated winners. Regardless of how events are used there will always be winners and losers in their implementation (Hall, 1989). Therefore, over-all results support critiques on the hosting mega-event that was not enough to justify spending over US$2 billion dollars constructing state-of-the art stadiums in South Korea. However, benefits out-weighed costs due to the hosted World Cup perceived by the hotel sector. A question remains.

On the other hand, it was a once in a lifetime experience which boosted Korean hotel staff's pride. The hosted World Cup has brought future connections with European market to South Korea which needs to be further developed. Events may be used as a tool for development and growth and for personal and institutional goals (Hall, 1989).

This longitudinal study has been made to provide some understanding of Football World Cup impacts and has shown that the hotel respondents' perspectives changed over the period of the study because of differences between the expectations and the realities of the hosted mega-events. The extent of sports events impact on a host community is by no means clear and far more research is needed.

To conclude this study's findings, this longitudinal study confirmed previous findings of Byeon (2002) and Byeon and Hall (2003). The significant benefit and cost impacts of hallmark events differ for each particular event, over time, for each host community (country or region), each level of host community (private sector, city/town and nation), each sample population (private sector, government or residents), for the involvement groups (direct or indirect) and government policy. Thus, from the largest of mega-events through to the smallest non-profit event, the perspective of many stakeholders must be considered. Different planning and policies are thus required to suit different hallmark events in order to maximise benefits and minimise or ameliorate costs and negative impacts. Therefore, on-going monitoring is also required to better manage impacts generated from hallmark events (Hall, 1992).

Implementation

As mega-events are political events (Hall, 1989), organisers need to understand dynamics of the impact of hosting the event which includes the unpredicted external factors. Therefore, a 'future' hosts of mega-event needs to be more realistic to the estimation of the event's outcomes. Expecting that the event would bring totally 'honey pot' into the destination would result in the disappoint-ments. Thus, the future host events need to bring all possibility of displacements into their consid-erations. Consequently, their historical tourism industry experienced needs to be included into the more precise planning of hosting the mega-event.

Since the event organisers had too much control in hotels due to over-anticipated lack of rooms, each hotel could not do much personal management during the World Cup. Future events organis-ers need to consider each hotels moderate autonomous management while preparing to host mega-events. Fifty per cent of rooms blocked by event organiser would be ideal. Since South Korean tourism is too much dependent on major visitor markets (Japan, USA and China), Korean tourism organisation need the dynamics of further tourism development and developing new markets (MCT and KNTO, 2002). Hotels are also needed for on-going development of well diversified market mix of leisure, convention/group, commercial and government/airline business to utilise already created hotel facilities and to increase occupancy rates and marketing of hotels.

Further Study

Because the survey was conducted solely with the Korean hotel industry, the results are valid only in this context, that is, a different sample population may have different perspectives on the impacts of the co-hosted the Football World Cup 2002. Further research in the area of different sample population perspectives on the co-hosted of the FIFA World Cup 2002 is needed. The perception of different types of lodging could also be measured. Since 2002 World Cup was co-hosted by South Korea and Japan, further research in the area of Japanese perspectives on the co-hosted of the FIFA World Cup 2002 is needed for comparison. Likewise, since the mega-event often has a long-term effect (Ritchie and Aitken 1985; Roche 1994; Mihalik and Cummings 1995), on-going long-term post-World Cup 2002 impacts need to be measured. Further research needs to examine with a more critical approach to broader process longitudinally.

Acknowledgements

Authors would like to thank Professor Stephen Boyd and Professor James Higham for advice in the initial stage of this study. Many thanks also to all those hotel managers and staff who took the time to complete these longitudinal study questionnaires.

References

Ahn, J.-Y. and Ahmed, Z. U. (1994) South Korea's emerging tourism industry. *Cornell Hotel and Restaurant Administration Quarterly*, 35(2), 84–89.

Ahn, J.-Y. and McGahey, S. (1997) South Korea: Interaction between inbound and outbound markets. In Go, F. M. and Jenkins, C. L. (eds.), *Tourism and Economic Development in Asia and Australia*. London: A Cassell Imprint, pp. 255–272.

Alreck, P. L. and Settle, R. B. (1995) *The Survey Research Handbook* (2nd edn.). Chicago: Irwin.

Alreck, P. L. and Settle, R. B. (2004) *The Survey Research Handbook* (3rd edn.). Boston: McGraw-Hill/Irwin.

Buckingham, A. and Saunders, P. (2004) *The Survey Methods Workbook: From Design to Analysis*. Cambridge: Polity Press.

Burgan, B. and Mules, T. (1992) Economic impact of sporting events. *Annals of Tourism Research*, 19(4), 700–710.

Byeon, M.-S. (2002) The Korean Hotel Sector's Perspectives on the Potential Impact of Co-hosting the Football World Cup 2002, Unpublished Master Thesis, University of Otago, Dunedin.

Byeon, M. (2008) 2002 Football World Cup: potential impacts, the South Korean Hotel Sector's perspectives. Saarbrücken: VDM Verlag, Dr. Müller, Aktiengesellschatt & Co. K.G.

Byeon, M.-S. and Hall, C. M. (2003) The Korean hotel sector's perspectives on the potential impact of co-hosting the 2002 FIFA World Cup. *Journal of Hospitality and Tourism*, 1(2), 11–34.

Chalip, L., Green, B. C. and Hill, B. (2003) Effects of sport event media on destination image and intention to visit. *Journal of Sport Management*, 17, 214–234.

Crompton, J. L., Lee, S. and Shuster, T. S. (2001) A guide for undertaking economic impact studies: The Springfest example. *Journal of Travel Research*, 40, 79–87.

Crompton, J. L. and McKay, S. (1994) Measurement the economic impact of festivals and events: Some myths, misapplications and ethical dilemmas. *Festival Management and Event Tourism*, 2, 33–43.

Chon, K. and Shin, H. (1990) Korea's Hotel and Tourism Industry. *Cornell Hotel and Restaurant Administration Quarterly*, 31(1), 69–73.

Deccio, C. and Balcoglu, S. (2002) Nonhost community resident reactions to the 2002 Winter Olympics: The Spillover impacts. *Journal of Travel Research*, 41(1), 46–56.

Delpy, L. and Li, M. (1998) The art and science of conducing economic impact studies. *Journal of Vacation Marketing*, 4(3), 230–254.

Dwyer, L., Forsyth, P. and Spur, R. (2006) Assessing the economic impacts of events: A computable general equilibrium approach. *Journal of Travel Research*, 45(August), 59–66.

Federation Internationale de Football Association (FIFA) (1999a). *Federation Internationale de Football Association: The World Cup,* http://www.fifa.com/fifa/handbook/fifa.html, accessed 18 August 1999.

Federation Internationale de Football Association (FIFA) (1999b) *Handbook: Media Information.* http://www.fifa2.com/scripts/runisa.dll?M2.65816:gp::67173+mrel/Display+07698+E, accessed 17 August 1999.

Getz, D. (1998). The impacts of mega events on tourism: Strategies and research issues for destinations. *1998 Australian Tourism and Hospitality Research Conference.* pp. 417-39. Canberra: Bureau of Tourism Research.

Getz, D. (1991) *Festivals, Special Events, and Tourism.* New York: Van Nostrand Reinhold.

Getz, D. (2003) Sport event tourism: Planning, development, and marketing. In Hudson, S. (ed.), *Sport and Adventure Tourism.* New York: The Haworth Hospitality Press, pp. 49–88.

Getz, D. (2004) Geographic perspectives on event tourism. In Lew, A. A., Hall, C. M. and Williams, M. (eds.), *A Companion to Tourism.* Oxford: Blackwell Publishing, pp. 410–422.

Gibson, H. (1998) Sport tourism: A critical analysis of research. *Sport Management Review*, 1(1), 45–76.

Goeldner, C.R. and Long, P.T. (1987) The role and impact of mega events and attractions on tourism development in *North America. Proceedings of the 37th Congress of AIEST*, 28, 119–131.

Gratton, C. and Taylor, P. (2000) *The Economics of Sport and Recreation.* New York: E & FN Spon.

Hall, C. M. (1989) The politics of hallmark events. In Syme, G. J., Shaw, B. J., Fenton, D. M. and Mueller, W. S. (eds.), *The Planning and Evaluation of Hallmark Events.* Aldershot: Avebury, pp. 219–241.

Hall, C. M. (1992) *Hallmark Tourist Events: Impacts, Management and Planning.* London: Belhaven Press.

Hall, C. M. (1996) Hallmark events and urban re-imaging strategies: Coercion, community and the Sydney 2000 Olympics. In Harrison, L. and Husbands, W. (eds.), *Practicing Responsible Tourism: International Case Studies in Tourism Planning, Policy and Development.* New York: John Wiley, pp. 366–379.

Hall, C. M. (1997a) *The Pacific Rim: Developments, Impacts and Markets* (2nd edition). Melbourne: Longman.

Hall, C. M. (1997b) Mega-events and their legacies. In Murphy, P. (ed.), *Quality Management in Urban Tourism.* Chichester: John Wiley and Sons Ltd, pp. 75–87.

Hall, C. M. (2001) Imaging, tourism and sports event fever: The Sydney Olympics and the need for a social charter for mega-events. In Gratton, C. and Henry, I. (eds.), *Sport in the City: The Role of Sport in Economic and Social Regeneration.* London: Routledge, pp. 166–183.

Hall, C. M. and Hodges, J. (1996) The party's great, but what about hangover? The housing and social impacts of mega-events with special reference to the 2000 Sydney Olympics. *Festival Management and Event Tourism*, 4, 13–20.

Hill, C. H. (1996) *Olympic Politics Athens to Atlanta 1896-1996* (2nd edn.). Manchester and New York: Manchester University Press.

Hiller, H. (1998) Assessing the impact of mega-events: A linkage model. *Current Issues in Tourism*, 1(1), 47–57.

Hiller, H. H. (1989) Impact and image: The convergence of urban factor in preparing for the 1988 Calgary Winter Olympics. In Syme, G. J., Shaw, B. J., Fetton, D. M. and Mueller, W. S. (eds.), *The Planning and Evaluation of Hallmark Events.* Aldershot: Avebury, pp. 119–131.

Hinch, T. and Higham, J. (2004) *Sport Tourism Development.* Clevedon: Channel View Publications.

Hotel and Restaurant (2002a) South Korean hotel industry, World Cup impact 'lower outcomes than expectation'. *Monthly Hotel and Restaurant*, September, 64–67, Issue.

Hotel and Restaurant (2002b) WCAB – South Korean hotel Agreement. *Monthly hotel and Restaurant*, August, 66–69, Issue.

Hotel and Restaurant (2002c) 'Special report': Hotel rooms agreement between WCABK and South Korean Hotel sector. *Monthly Hotel and Restaurant*, August, 64–65, Issue.

Jago, L., Chalip, L., Brown, G., Mules, T. and Ali, S. (2003) Building events into destination branding: Insights from experts. *Event Management*, 8, 3–14.

Jeong, G.-H. (1987), *Tourism Expectation on the Seoul Olympics: A Korean Perspective,* Unpublished Master Thesis, University of Wisconsin-Stout, Menomonie, WI.

Jeong, G.-H. (1992), *Perceived Post-Olympic Socio-cultural Impacts by Residents from a Tourism Perspective: A Case Study in Chamsil, Seoul, Korea,* Unpublished Doctor of Philosophy Thesis, University of Minnesota.

Jeong, G.-H. and Faulkner, B. (1996) Resident perceptions of mega-event impacts: The Taejon international exposition case. *Festival Management and Event Tourism*, 4(1), 3–11.

Kang, Y.-S. and Perdue, R. (1994) Long-term impact of a mega-event on international tourism to the host country: A conceptual model and the case of the 1988 Seoul Olympics. In Uysal, M. (ed.), *Global Tourist Behaviour*. New York: Haworth, pp. 205–225.

Kim, H.-J., Gursoy, D. and Lee, S.-B. (2006) The impact of the 2002 World Cup on South Korea: Comparisons of pre- and post-games. *Tourism Management*, 27(1), 86–96.

Kim, J-H. (1995), Major trends and challenges of the Korean tourism industry. In *World Tourism Organization, ASIA Tourism Towards New Horizons, WTO Asian Tourism Conference*, Islamabad, Pakistan, 10–15 January, pp. 77–82.

Kim, K.-I. (1998) Cancelled another event…decreased tourist numbers. *Chosun Daily Newspaper*, 10 July, 9.

Kim, M. (2002) World Cup boosted economy, confidence: Survey. *Korea Herald*, 9 July.

Kim, S. and Song, H. (1998) Analysis of inbound tourism demand in South Korea: A cointegration and error correction approach. *Tourism Analysis*, 3, 25–41.

Kim, Y. and Uysal, M. (1998) Time-dependent analysis for international hotel demand in Seoul. *Tourism Economics*, 4(3), 253–263.

Kim, S. and Petrick, J. (2005) Residents' perception on impacts of the FIFA 2002 World Cup: the case of case of Seoul as a host city. *Tourism Management*, 26(1), 25–38.

Korea National Tourism Organisation (KNTO) (2000) Visit Korea, http://www.knto.or.kr (assessed 5 May 2000).

Korea National Tourism Organisation (KNTO) (2001) Statistics, 2000 Survey of Overseas Tourists to Korea, http://www.knto.or.kr/.eng/07statustucs/0704.html (assessed 15 February 2002).

Korea National Tourism Organisation (KNTO) (2002) *A Report of Monthly Statistics of Tourism*. Seoul: KNTO.

Kwon, H.-J. (1990) The impact of 1988 Seoul International Olympics on inbound tourism in Korea. *Study on Tourism*, 14, 235–245.

Labrie, P. (1988) The long term tourism and economic impact of major sports events: Montreal and the 1976 Olympics – a love story In *Tourism Research: Expanding Boundaries, Travel and Tourism Research Association, Nineteenth Annual Conference*, Montreal, Quebec, Canada, 19–23 June, Bureau of Economic and Business Research, Graduate School of Business, University of Utah, Salt Lake City, pp. 103–105.

Ladkin, A. (1999) Hotel general managers: A review of prominent research themes. *International Journal of Tourism Research*, 1(3), 167–193.

Lee, C. (2002) Managing peak society under cool headed leadership. *The Korea Times*, 26 June.

Lee, C.-K. and Kwon, K.-S. (1995) Importance of secondary impact of foreign tourism receipts on South Korean economy. *Journal of Travel Research*, 34(2), 50–54.

Lee, C.-K. and Kwon, K.-S. (1998) International tourism demand for the 2002 World Cup Korea: A combined forecasting technique. *Pacific Tourism Review*, 2, 157–166.

Lee, C.-K., Var, T. and Blaine, T. W. (1996) Determinants of inbound tourist expenditure. *Annals of Tourism Research*, 23(3), 527–542.

Lee, K.-W. (2000) *An Estimation of Accommodation Demand for 2002 World Cup Games in Korea and Efficient Management Strategies of Medium and Low Priced Accommodation*. Seoul: Linepia Ltd.

Marsh, J. S. (1984) The economic impact of a small city annual sporting event: An initial case study of the Peterborough Church League Hockey Tournament. *Recreation Research Review*, 11, 48–55.

Mathieson, A. and Wall, G. (1982) *Tourism: Economic, Physical and Social impacts*. Harlow: Longman.

McKay, M. and Plumb, C. (2001) *Reaching Beyond the Gold: The Impact of the Olympic Games on Real Estate Markets*. Illinois: Jones Lang Lasalle.

Ministry of Culture and Tourism (MCT) and Korea National Tourism Organisation (KNTO) (2006) *Korea Annual Statistical Report on Tourism 2005*. Seoul: MCT and KNTO.

Mihalik, B.J. and Cummings, P. (1995) Host perceptions of the 1996 Atlanta Olympics: Support, attendance, benefits and liabilities. *Travel and Tourism Research Association 26th Annual Proceedings*, pp. 397–400.

Ministry of Culture and Tourism (MCT) (1999) *Korean Tourism: Annual Report 1997–1998*. Seoul: MCT.

Ministry of Culture and Tourism (MCT) (2003) *Korean Tourism: Annual Report 2001-2002*. Seoul: Daejongpio Ltd.

Ministry of Culture and Tourism (MCT) and Korea National Tourism Organisation (KNTO) (2002) *Korea Annual Statistical Report on Tourism 2001*. Seoul: MCT and KNTO.

Ministry of Culture and Tourism (MCT) and Korea National Tourism Organisation (KNTO) (2004) *Korea Annual Statistical Report on Tourism 2003*. Seoul: MCT and KNTO.

Ministry of Transportation (MOT) and Korea National Tourism Corporation (KNTC) (1980) *Korean Tourism Statistics 1979*. Seoul: MOT and KNTC.

Mitchell, C. and Wall, G. (1986) Impacts of cultural festivals on Ontario communities. *Recreation Research Review*, 13(1), 28–37.

MINTeL International Group (2002) The Asia Pacific Hotel Industry. *Travel and Tourism Analyst*, 4, 3–9.

Ohmann, S., Jones, I. and Wilkes, K. (2006) The perceived social impacts of the 2006 Football World Cup on Munich residents. *Journal of Sport & Tourism*, 11(2), 129–152.

Olds, K. (1998) Urban Mega-events, evictions and housing rights: The Canadian case. *Current Issues in Tourism*, 1(11), 2–45.

Page, S. J. and Hall, C. M. (2003) *Managing Urban Tourism*. Harlow: Prentice-Hall.

Preuss, H. (2007) FIFA World Cup 2006 and its legacy on tourism. In Conrady, R. and Buck, M. (eds.), *Trends and Issues in Global Tourism 2007*. Verlag: Springer, pp. 83–100.

Press, H. (1998) Problemizing Arguments of the Opponents of Olympic Games, R. Barney, K. Wamsley, S. Martyn, and G. MacDonald (eds), 'Global and cultural critique: problematizing the Olympic Games, Fourth International Symbosium Olympic Research, Ontario, The University of Western Ontario, pp. 197–219.

Ritchie, J. R. B. (1984) Assessing the impacts of hallmark events: Conceptual and research issues. *Journal of Travel Research*, 23(1), 2–11.

Ritchie, J. R. B. and Aiken, C. (1984) Assessing the impacts of the 1988 Olympic Winter Games: The research program and initial results. *Journal of Travel Research*, 22(3), 17–25.

Ritchie, J. R. B. and Aiken, C. (1985) Olympulse II – Evolving resident attitudes toward the 1988 Olympic Winter Games. *Journal of Travel Research*, 24(3), 28–33.

Ritchie, J. R. B. and Lyons, M. (1987) Olympulse III/Olympulse IV: A mid-term report on resident attitudes concerning the XV Olympic Winter Games. *Journal of Travel Research*, 26(1), 18–26.

Ritchie, J. R. B. and Lyons, M. (1990) Olympulse VI: A post-event assessment of resident reaction to the XV Olympic Winter Games. *Journal of Travel Research*, 28(3), 14–23.

Ritchie, J. R. B. and Smith, B. (1991) The impact of a mega-event on host region awareness: A longitudinal study. *Journal of Travel Research*, 30(3), 3–10.

Roche, M. (1992) Mega-events and micro-modernization: On the sociology of the new urban tourism. *British Journal of Sociology*, 43(4), 563–600.

Roche, M. (1994) Mega-events and urban policy. *Annals of Tourism Research*, 21(1), 1–19.

Seoul Metropolitan Government (2002) *A Report of Action Plan for 2002 FIFA World Cup Korea*. Seoul: Seoul Metropolitan Government.

Shultis, J., Johnston, M. E. and Twynam, G. (1996) Developing a longitudinal research program to measure impacts of a special event. *Festival Management and Event Tourism*, 4, 59–66.

Sparrow, M. (1989) A tourism planning model for hallmark events. In Syme, G. J., Shaw, B. J., Fenton, D. M. and Mueller, W. S. (eds.), *The Planning and Evaluation of Hallmark Events*. Aldershot: Avebury, pp. 250–262.

Thorne, R. and Munro-Clark, M. (1989) Hallmark events as an excuse for autocracy in urban planning: a case history. In Syme, G. J., Shaw, B. J., Fetton, D. M. and Mueller, W. S. (eds.), *The Planning and Evaluation of Hallmark Events*. Aldershot: Avebury, pp. 154–171.

Wall, G. (1988) Effects of hallmark events on cities. *Annals of Tourism Research*, 15(2), 280–281.

Wang, P. and Gitelson, R. (1988). Limitations with the economic benefits of short-term events. pp. 257-5 In *Tourism Research: Expanding Boundaries, Travel and Tourism Research Association, Nineteenth Annual Conference*, Montreal, Quebec, Canada, 19–23 June, Bureau of Economic and Business Research, Graduate School of Business, University of Utah, Salt Lake City.

Wilkinson, J. (1994) *Olympic Games: Past History and Present Expectation*. Sydney: NSW Parliamentary Library.

World Cup Organising Invite Association (WCOIA) (1995) *2002 FIFA World Cup: List of Requirements for the Organising National Association*. Seoul: WCOIA.

World Travel & Tourism Council (WTTC) (2002). Asia-Pacific Destinations Dominate Forecasts for Travel & Tourism (April 16) (assessed 24 September 2002).

PART 2

COMMUNITY AND IDENTITY

Alan Fyall

This second part of the book introduces five chapters that explore specifically dimensions of community and identity within the broader context of festivals and events. In Chapter 6, White explores the tensions between Australia's indigenous populations, namely Aboriginal and Torres Strait Islander Australians, and attempts made by organisers of major events, such as the Sydney 2000 Olympic Games, to be more sensitive and inclusive with regard to the country's heritage. The Sydney Olympiad is a very pertinent example in that from the very outset, the Sydney Olympic Committee for the Olympic Games (SOCOG) made a concerted effort to draw attention to aspects of Aboriginality and Aboriginal culture. Eight years before the landmark 'apology' made recently by the new Prime Minister in February 2008, something that the previous Government steadfastly refused to concede, the Sydney Games both started and closed with ceremonies that depicted strong elements of Aboriginal culture; ceremonies that were witnessed by 3.7 billion people in 220 countries around the world with many previously not aware of Australia's fractious past. Most significant, perhaps, in the eyes of the world, were the iconic 'reconciliatory' images of Aboriginal athlete Cathy Freeman standing under the Olympic cauldron against a backdrop of nature's contrasting elements – fire and water. The chapter explores in depth the design, rationale and implementation of the two ceremonies and examines in depth the extent to which each reflected Australia's indigenous past and the means by which harmony was restored to what remains still a relatively new nation.

Chapter 7 by Derrett, meanwhile, examines how festivals represent a human 'ecosystem' that fosters resilience in communities through the sharing of values, interests and traditions that are central to the host community. Derrett argues that such festivals represent an expression of identity at the local level and the internal life of the community. This interesting and insightful chapter explores the characteristics of community cultural festivals and identifies the necessary partnerships required to make such festivals work. The chapter begins with a critical overview of the role of festivals and the part they play in the cultural life of communities before exploring the collaborative partnerships recognised as necessary for community festivals to prosper. Four regional community cultural festivals are explored in depth with some common characteristics revealed and discussed. The chapter concludes that festivals add value to communities, 'creatively' embed culture and offer a delicate balance of local community content through authenticity, interest, quality and entertainment which collectively feed the content for the tourism experience.

In Chapter 8, Jolliffe, Huong and Hang, introduce the case study of the Buon Ma Thuot Coffee Festival and the means by which it engaged community participants, involved a broad range of stakeholders and influenced local thinking about the branding of the region as a coffee destination. This attempt to develop a 'niche' form of tourism is based on the fact that Vietnam is the second largest producer and exporter of the Robusta variety of coffee, first introduced by the French in the 19th century. The Vietnamese love of coffee, the distinct style in which they prepare their coffee and their all encompassing café culture collectively help build the credibility and strength of the branding approach and the high media profile given to it by the Vietnamese media. The paper concludes that although intended initially as a festival to promote and market the coffee brand, its success has contributed to it being widely regarded as a festival with a far broader tourism dimension than was ever imagined.

The theme of cultural identity is again explored in Chapter 9 where Brown and Chappel examine the Tasting Australia festival which is a biennial festival in Adelaide, Australia, and which attracts both Australian and international celebrities who share an interest in food and drink. Beginning in 1997, there is little doubt that this is an 'invented' tradition in that it was deemed by the tourism authorities at the time as an ideal means by which the state could differentiate itself and establish its position as a 'lifestyle' destination. More broadly, however, the chapter aims to show how Tasting Australia is in fact a manifestation of recent developments in South Australia's socio-cultural and economic life. The chapter begins with an analysis of the development of a food and drink culture in Australia before concluding with an examination of the extent to which the festival emerged from its humble origins rooted in local culture to become a festival of international significance.

Bringing Part 2 to a close, Chapter 10 by Wood and Thomas examines the impact of festivals and tourism in rural economies. Using three case studies, the Llangollen Food Festival, the North Wales International Music Festival and the Art on the Railings Festival, Chepstow, Monmouth, the authors seek to develop a clearer understanding of the type of festival which most benefits the local economy in terms of visitor expenditure and maximises the benefits to local people. The chapter delivers some interesting findings in that many local businesses did not feel that they benefited financially and that the direct economic returns were for the most part marginal for the events studied with very little being spent in the locale. A number of recommendations are proposed to enhance the benefits to be derived by local communities while the chapter accepts that although much academic attention is on specific economic benefits, far greater attention ought to be perhaps given to the benefits to be drawn from community cohesion to be derived from events. The chapter concludes by suggesting that policy makers need to consider a greater blend of events locally that will deliver benefits to the local economy in addition to enhancing greater levels of community cohesion.

Chapter 6

Indigenous Australia and the Sydney 2000 Olympic Games: Mediated Messages of Respect and Reconciliation

Leanne White

Introduction

After Australia's Bicentenary of European settlement in 1988 major event organisers realised they would need to be much more inclusive, particularly with regard to Aboriginal and Torres Strait Islander Australians, if they were to minimise criticism and avoid possible protest at future events of national and international significance such as the Sydney 2000 Olympic Games (also called the Sydney Games or the 2000 Games). While Aboriginal and Torres Strait Islander Australians protested widely on 26 January 1988 – the Bicentenary of white settlement in Australia – only about 500 protesters gathered in Sydney's Hyde Park on 15 September 2000 – the day of the Opening Ceremony of the Games. The demonstrators chanted 'Always was, always will be, Aboriginal land' and urged Prime Minister John Howard to issue a formal apology to the 'Stolen Generation' (Lenskyj, 2002, p. 208).

The Sydney Olympic Committee for the Olympic Games (SOCOG) had the advantage of being able to learn from the lessons of the past. Consequently, as will be discussed in this chapter, SOCOG made a concerted effort to highlight aspects of Aboriginality in the Olympic Games. The absolute centrality of Indigenous Australia to the nation's past, present and future could no longer be hidden. This chapter explores two key moments during the Sydney Games – the Opening Ceremony and the Closing Ceremony. These significant events played an enormous part in changing the way in which the story of Australia was told to the world at the 2000 Games.

Literature Review

It was Benedict Anderson (1991, p. 86) who contended that 'official nationalism' was the 'willed merger of nation and dynastic empire' and argued that the concept came about in response to popular

International Perspectives of Festivals and Events
Copyright © 2009 by Elsevier Ltd.
All rights of reproduction in any form reserved.
ISBN: 978-0-08-045100-8

nationalism that emerged in Europe from the 1820s. Anderson (1991, p. 159) argued that official nationalism emanated 'from the state' and has as its primary feature a focus on 'serving the interests of the state first and foremost'.

Richard White (1981, p. x) argued that national identity is an invention which is constantly being 'fractured, questioned and redefined'. He claimed that the issue is not whether definitions of Australia are accurate, but who is responsible for the production of these definitions and in whose interest do they serve? Anne-Marie Willis' (1993, p. 9) argument that 'visual imagery becomes enmeshed in processes of the construction of national identity' was also borne out by the examination of Indigenous Australian images surrounding the Sydney Games. The work of Willis provided a useful framework for the analysis of manufactured nationalism.

Methodology

The methodology used in this chapter combines the benefits of qualitative and quantitative research, thus providing a multi-angled framework for the research question to be approached. Combining different research methodologies was particularly appropriate for this chapter as content analysis was able to substantiate semiotics and structuralism. Consequently, the quantitative analysis can work to further validate the qualitative analysis and thus 'broaden, thicken, and deepen' the overall interpretation (Denzin, 1989, p. 247).

Semiotics was employed as it is a useful methodology for examining a wide range of texts – from postage stamps to large-scale cultural productions. John Fiske, Bob Hodge and Graeme Turner were some of the earlier researchers to examine signifiers of 'Australianness'. They argued that Australia can be signified by 'kangaroos, the flag, Alan Bond, the map, images of landscape, the Sydney Opera House, and so on' (Fiske et al., 1987, p. xi). Structuralism was also incorporated into the analysis of this chapter as it is a helpful methodology for examining how texts combine to form narratives and stories of a nation – or what Stuart Cunningham (1992, p. 83) refers to as the 'grammar of national imaging'. Structuralism was a useful tool for making sense of the larger narrative, that is, the bigger picture. This chapter examines compressed narratives such as Indigenous Australian signifiers in the Sydney Olympic Games Ceremonies, while also attempting to probe issues surrounding some of Australia's more grand and complex narratives such as those of Australia's Indigenous heritage and reconciliation. In structuralist theory, narratives are comprised of two parts – a story and a discourse. Tony Bennett (1993, p. 74) claims that 'nations exist through, and represent themselves in the form of, long continuous narratives'. This is worth keeping in mind when examining past, present or future images of the nation. Finally, content analysis is concerned with the frequency of content contained in a particular dataset. It is primarily concerned with studying what was actually evident in the text, rather than questions of quality or interpretation. Thus content analysis was integrated into this study as it provided a useful tool for examining the larger picture and producing a systematic overview.

The readings and interpretations of the Indigenous Australian signifiers examined in this chapter took place within an Australian context at a particular time in history. The research approach is partly one of reflection and reflexivity, while focusing on particular signs, scenes, narrative structures and meaning systems that may generate a wider resonance. The aim has been to study representations of Indigenous Australian signifiers at the Sydney Games while limiting personal biases as far as possible to ensure an unclouded examination.

Findings

This study has found that the use of particular Indigenous Australian images can serve the interests of those wanting to promote an official dogma of nationalism (such as the federal government or government departments and that sometimes this is via significant public events or advertising campaigns).

Sydney Games organisers learned many lessons from the 1988 Bicentenary. They had also successfully built on a number of social, cultural and political events concerning Indigenous Australia that had taken place between 1988 and 2000. These events included (but were not limited to) Prime Minister Paul Keating's powerful and apologetic Redfern speech (1992); the Mabo ruling (1992); the Wik decision (1996); and Coroboree (2000) when around 250,000 people marched across the highly symbolic meeting place of the Sydney Harbour Bridge in a show of support for reconciliation. This final event was particularly significant. Philip Morrissey (2001, p. 32) described the march as 'the largest protest vote in Australia's history'.

One can only hope that the powerful images of Australia's Indigenous community beamed to billions – particularly those evident in the Opening and Closing Ceremonies of the Sydney 2000 Olympic Games – may have played a part in forming a compelling foundation from which a more reconciled Australia might eventually emerge.

Discussion

With the Opening Ceremony of the Sydney 2000 Olympic Games, Australia staged the most watched television sporting event in history. The Ceremony was televised to a global television audience of 3.7 billion in 220 countries – a record for the most popular Olympic and sporting event in the world (Loland, 2004). The Sydney Games more generally were the most watched sporting event in the history of television, and 'nine out of every ten individuals on the planet with access to a television' watched the Games at some stage (Girginov and Parry, 2005, p. 238). The Olympic Games is regarded as the *spectacle par excellence* and the Opening Ceremony is often considered the most important event in the 16 days of Games telecast. Inclusive of the presentation of medals the budget for the Opening and Closing Ceremonies was $68.5 million or 3% of total Games operating expenditure (Girginov and Parry, 2005). In an Olympic Opening Ceremony central prominence is deliberately given to the national identity of the host country (Larson and Park, 1993). The Sydney Games was the second Olympics that Australia had hosted. The first was in Melbourne in 1956 when the event became fondly remembered as 'The Friendly Games' and the emphasis then was as much British (with design overthrows from London's Festival of Britain in 1951) as it was Australian. Australian athletes performed extremely well at the 1956 Olympics, and it was not until the Atlanta Games in 1996 that the Australian Olympic team achieved a higher tally of medals. In the 1956 Olympic Games 3184 athletes from 67 countries participated in 16 sports. For the Sydney Games, more than three times as many athletes – in excess of 10,300 people – from 199 countries took part in 28 types of sport.

The Sydney 2000 Olympic Games Opening Ceremony began with a stirring 'Welcome' sequence. This was followed by seven separate themes and individually choreographed segments. They were 'Deep Sea Dreaming', 'Awakening', 'Fire', 'Nature', 'Tin Symphony', 'Arrivals' and 'Eternity'. Underpinning and intersecting these segments was the overall theme of the natural elements – fire, earth and water. Following the seven segments the Sydney 2000 Marching Band took to the arena, followed by the parade of athletes, official speeches, the flag ceremony, the reading of the oath for athletes and officials, and concluding with the all-important lighting of the Olympic flame.

The Awakening sequence, orchestrated by Stephen Page of the Bangarra Dance Theatre, was particularly important in setting the tone of respect and reconciliation for the rest of the evening's performance – a tone which continued strongly throughout the 16 days of the Olympic Games and into the Closing Ceremony. The reconciliation message was designed, in part at least, to placate the prying eyes of the world. The cultural and social impact of the reconciliation message in Australia – while impossible to measure – cannot be underestimated. During this Awakening segment, Stadium Australia was symbolically cleansed by a traditional smoking ceremony with the burning of green eucalyptus leaves. Master of Ceremonies, Ric Birch, explained that the Awakening segment also marked the first time that 1,100 dancers from Australia's diverse Aboriginal clans had come together for one Songline. Organisers spent many months negotiating with tribal elders to make the event possible (Birch, 2004). The purpose of the smoking ceremony was for the participants and the audience to be 'bathed' in the smoke in order to cleanse, purify and drive away any evil spirits for a new beginning. The important ceremony takes place within a circle to keep the positive spirits enclosed before later being released and shared.

The main formation made by the dancers was an inner and outer circle and parallel lines leading to them. Fertility was the message being conveyed with the formation of a circle within a larger one. Circles – which represent the continuation of life, the celebration of life and the strong kinship of Aboriginal culture – often feature in Aboriginal art. Anne-Marie Willis (1993, p. 122) argues that 'Aboriginal art has taken on specific meanings within the official culture of Australia' and that it 'fulfils certain requirements of the mythology of nation: antiquity, spirituality, continuity, an expression of myths of creation and origin'. While the young 'Hero Girl' of the Opening Ceremony (Nikki Webster) symbolised Australia's future, Aboriginal Songman and elder (Djakapurra Munyarryun) represented Australia's proud and ancient indigenous past. Djakapurra calls together Indigenous clans to welcome the world to the Olympic Games. As Ric Birch (2004, p. 259) explained, Nikki Webster 'epitomised young Australia – frank, friendly and fearless, an innocent on the edge of greatness'. The older and wiser Songman led the young white girl through her fascinating journey of discovery on behalf of an Australian nation. The Hero Girl and the Songman linked all seven sequences of the Opening Ceremony with their journey from Deep Sea Dreaming to Eternity.

Some observers have criticised the meanings presented here by Nikki and Djakapurra. Helen Lenskyj (2002, p. 221) argued that the symbolism was too heavy-handed and was perceived as 'schmaltzy and tear-jerking'. Jan Kociumbas (2003) saw the Aboriginal culture presented 'as offering something more complex, ancient, sophisticated and unique than the old bush mythologies that formerly signalled Australian nationhood' (p. 127), but also argues that racial stereotypes were again reinforced as the elder was represented as part of a 'dying race, sadly but inevitably giving way to the young, innocent and more talented newcomers' (p. 132). Opening Ceremony organisers originally planned to have a small boy meet with Djakapurra in the vast outback (Birch, 2004) which would have avoided the sexual but not the racial implications of this highly overt binary opposition. However, it is unlikely that many viewers would have made these associations; the important (if empty) message of reconciliation between black and white Australia was loud and clear for the world to hear – even though it was only in the realm of the symbolic. One of the unintended but joyous consequences of the Aboriginal performance was that for hundreds of the women, the dancing continued on in the days following the Opening Ceremony.

In the Awakening segment the ancient spirits were ceremonially called upon to cleanse the stadium and make it ready for the sporting events which were to take place over the forthcoming fortnight.

A 32-metre banner of the Wandjina spirit that comes from the Kimberley region of Western Australia rose slowly from the earth. The well-known *Wandjina Spirit* painting by Charlie Numblar has come to be regarded as one of the symbols of hope for reconciliation between black and white Australia. John Stanton (1988, p. 26) explains that the Wandjina art tradition is a 'distinctive and relatively well-known style' of Aboriginal rock art. The Wandjina are 'a group of ancestral beings who came from the sky and sea and were associated with fertility. They controlled the elements and were responsible for the formation of the country's natural features' (Croft, 2001, p. 71). Ric Birch (2004, p. 261) explained, 'Traditionally, the Wandjina are involved with lightning and storms, so we used the appearance of the spirit to cue a thunderous lightning strike'. In an act signifying reconciliation, Djakapurra and Nikki later came together on the 'Bridge of Life', illuminated by the word 'Eternity'. Djakapurra then walked Nikki around the arena where all the performers from previous segments had now congregated. The coming together of Djakapurra and Nikki sent a powerful visual message of reconciliation. Stadium Australia was the physical space where the story of black and white Australia was presented to the world. This image encapsulated the key message of the Opening Ceremony – old Australia meets new Australia and common ground is found. Ric Birch (2004, p. 260) commented that 'the integrity and spiritual power of the ancient culture … struck a chord with all Australians'.

The Opening Ceremony was capped off with the image which was to be emblazoned on the front pages of many of the world's newspapers the next morning: the Aboriginal athlete Cathy Freeman standing under the Olympic cauldron against a backdrop of nature's contrasting elements – fire and water. After being handed the flame, Freeman held the torch aloft then proceeded to jog up the stairs of the Northern stand towards the imposing Olympic cauldron. With great spiritual significance Freeman carefully walked across the water, again held up the flame, then leaned down to light a ring of fire that then rose from the water. The lone athlete was then surrounded by a ring of fire which roared above her. The outline of the cauldron was revealed and water simultaneously cascaded down. Freeman held her torch up while remaining in the centre of the circle. She then stepped out from the surrounding water to face the sheer might of the fiery cauldron. Up until this point of the evening, everything ran smoothly. However, the cauldron initially became jammed and 'failed to proceed' to the top of the stand. It was later revealed that a safety switch was triggered due to the cascading water and the mechanism had to be manually adjusted before the cauldron could make its way to the top of the stand. As a result, Freeman stood perilously challenged by water and fire for a heart-stopping 220 seconds before the flaming cauldron suddenly lurched then began its shuddering ascent.

This significant moment of the Games was to become a central theme in commentaries on the nation's identity. The international news media focused on the issue of reconciliation as the dominant news story of the Games. This central story was very much personified by Cathy Freeman. The symbolism of Freeman's lighting of the cauldron at the Opening Ceremony of the Sydney Games was highly significant and emblematic. Wearing a pure white body suit and holding the Olympic torch, the champion black athlete performed the chief ceremonial act which marked the official opening of the Games. Choosing Cathy Freeman for this key moment was an important and symbolic choice for race, gender and nation. The choice of Cathy Freeman to light the cauldron was considered an inspired and highly appropriate one. Garrie Hutchinson (2002, p. 143) wrote, 'She was widely seen to have single-handedly become the symbol, the end-point, of the reconciliation process … it was definitely the most powerfully emotional moment for black and white relationships in Australian history'. Harry Gordon (2003, p. 186–187) further argues that 'the Freeman culmination … amounted to a quietly eloquent statement about the kind of nation Australia aspired to be. It underlined itself bodily as a significant moment in the nation's history'.

The Channel Seven commentators couldn't hold back their enthusiasm at the choice of Cathy Freeman to light the flame stating, 'It must rank as the greatest single event in the modern history of Australia', and 'What an inspired choice! Cathy Freeman – such a powerful statement' (McAvaney, 2000). Alan Tomlinson (2004, p. 154) argued that the choice of Freeman to light the flame had the effect of 'rounding off the ceremony's depiction of the history of Australia as an Aboriginal meta-narrative'. Marian Quartly states that Manning Clark would have referred to Freeman's lighting of the flame as an enlarging moment in history. Quartly argues that 'Cathy Freeman's still, waiting figure ringed with water and crowned with fire continues to resonate as a profound symbol of recon-ciliation and national regeneration (as yet unachieved)' (in Bail and Bagnall, 2005, p. 110).

The choice of Freeman to light the flame was widely considered the right choice and it served to emphasise the highly considerable indigenous themes throughout the Opening Ceremony. The indigenous theme continued on during the Games and into the Closing Ceremony in a way that was partly orchestrated and partly developed a life of its own due to the actions of particular individuals. As outlined earlier, in 1988 many Indigenous Australians and their supporters had protested against Australia's celebration of 200 years of white settlement with the slogans 'White Australia has a Black History' and '40,000 Years don't make a Bicentenary'. By the year 2000, Australia's Aboriginal com-munity were very much part of the overall story of their country. They were no longer marginalised and sidelined – rather perhaps appropriated.

The Closing Ceremony of the Sydney 2000 Olympic Games, televised on 1 October, was the second most watched event in Australia's history. As stated previously, the Opening Ceremony com-manded the largest television audience for an Australian event. The Closing Ceremony was designed to be a giant party where the less formal side of Australia could be shown to the world. Historian Harry Gordon (2003, p. 254) described the Closing Ceremony as a 'kaleidoscope of kitsch' in which the 'clichés were rampant'. The Games were now almost over and the general consensus was that Sydney had staged a successful Olympics.

As with the Opening Ceremony, representatives from Australia's Aboriginal and Torres Strait Islander community were also included in the Closing Ceremony. The first performance was a stir-ring rendition of the song *Island Home* by Christine Anu. Christine Anu was born in the Queensland city of Cairns and is of Torres Strait Islander descent. Like Peter Allen's *I Still Call Australia Home*, to which Qantas bought the rights in 1993, *Island Home* has become something of an unofficial national anthem. Performing with Anu were Indigenous Australian dancers with Aboriginal-style paintings of animals displayed on their backs.

To further promote harmony and friendship, Australian pop duo Savage Garden performed their hit song *Affirmation*. When band members Darren Hayes and Daniel Jones were first shown, what was immediately apparent was that lead singer Hayes was wearing a black sleeveless top that fea-tured the Aboriginal flag. While Savage Garden's official duty was to perform, there may have been some tension experienced by International Olympic Committee (IOC) officials with the unofficial message presented in the choice of clothing. The statement made was indeed significant given that the band had recently completed their successful 'Affirmation World Tour' during which the stirring song and accompanying music video had topped the music charts in a number of countries.

When the Australian bands Midnight Oil and Yothu Yindi performed at the Closing Ceremony, the political message was very clear. The mood of the Ceremony had changed thus from irreverence to inclusiveness to, finally, the unashamedly political. Midnight Oil's lead singer Peter Garrett had decided that if Prime Minister John Howard was not going to say sorry to Aboriginal Australians, his band would. Midnight Oil first performed in 1976 and throughout the 1970s, 1980s and 1990s,

Peter Garrett led the popular Australian band well known for their stance on anti-war, environmental and indigenous issues. As McKenzie Wark (1993, p. 113) explains, Garrett represents 'republicanism, egalitarianism, participatory democracy, the rights and needs of the little people'.

At the Closing Ceremony, Garrett and his band performed the 1987 hit *Beds are Burning* – an emotive song about Aboriginal land rights. The song is regarded as something of a reconciliation anthem (Dennis, 2000, p. 3) and was written by band members Rob Hirst, Jim Moginie and Peter Garrett. It is the first track on the *Diesel and Dust* album which sold three million copies worldwide. But it was what the band wore even more than the song, which made the strong political statement. Midnight Oil wore black outfits with the word 'Sorry' emblazoned in large white letters across the back and front of their top and pants. The careful placement of the important word 'Sorry' in four places on the outfits meant that the television cameras would not be able to avoid sending out their controversial message to the estimated four billion viewers tuned in around the world. The possibly contentious segment received 4 minutes and 40 seconds of global television coverage. It is significant that the organisers allowed Midnight Oil to sing the words 'It belongs to them, let's give it back' in front of such a huge audience.

Given the IOC ban on wearing clothes that project an overt political, religious or cultural message, Midnight Oil's statement was all the more powerful. The band got away with wearing the controversial outfits as they had them hidden under black overalls which they quickly ripped off seconds before going on stage. Very few people knew what Midnight Oil had in store. Peter Garrett had mentioned the idea of the 'Sorry' message to Yothu Yindi's lead singer Mandawuy Yunupingu. Apparently, Yunupingu 'gave the concept a double thumbs-up' (Dennis, 2000, p. 3). Garrett explained the statement he was attempting to make:

> We saw one of the essential themes of the Olympics – the Opening Ceremony, Cathy Freeman's victory – as recognition of the extraordinary culture of indigenous people. The only thing that hadn't been raised was the question of an apology, so we figured we would do it (Jones, 2000).

The cameras within Stadium Australia managed to capture images of an exceptionally anxious-looking Prime Minister who appeared decidedly uncomfortable as he watched the performance from the comfort of the open viewing area reserved for Olympic officials.

Peter Garrett was also one of the writers of the song which followed – *Treaty*. This further reinforced the overwhelming message of reconciliation. David Day (2001, p. 339) describes *Treaty* as a 'politically loaded song'. The Australian singer and song writer Paul Kelly also collaborated with Mandawuy Yunupingu and Garrett to produce the song. *Treaty* was written around the time of Australia's Bicentenary when Prime Minister Bob Hawke was talking about the increasing need for a treaty between indigenous and non-indigenous Australians. The song calls for a treaty so that the rights of Indigenous Australians can be documented and made clear to Australians and the international community. *Treaty* was the song that launched the international success of Yothu Yindi. The chorus is sung in the Aboriginal language Gumatj. Channel Seven commentator Garry Wilkinson (2000) provided a narrative link to the performance by commenting, 'Never afraid to make a statement. That statement by Midnight Oil is a fitting introduction to our next performance by Yothu Yindi. Timeless Indigenous Australian music'.

The clear message was that a bridge needed to be built between black and white Australia, and this point was reinforced with an inflatable yellow arched bridge featuring black and red light globes – the three colours of the Aboriginal flag. Yunupingu was impressed with the way the Opening Ceremony had presented indigenous issues. When asked if he watched it and what he thought he said, 'I did and gave it 9 out of 10. I was really proud that Cathy Freeman lit the Olympic flame. The Aboriginal performances really moved me and it was great to see indigenous culture being highlighted' (Remuzzi, 2000).

Conclusion

While the Sydney 2000 Games provided the prime platform for Aboriginal Australians to make an unambiguous political statement, similar protests on a smaller scale had been organised during Australia's Bicentenary in 1988 and at the Brisbane Commonwealth Games in 1982. As outlined earlier, SOCOG were acutely aware of this potentially divisive issue and worked conscientiously to include rather than exclude Australia's Indigenous community. Peter Sheehan has argued that the notional or actual rift between black and white Australia was the one grand narrative that the international media were keen to explore:

> It's because the great story of reconciliation in Australia, or lack of it, is the one mighty narrative that can actually travel around the world – can actually be told easily – can actually appear to be translated easily. It's the one mighty narrative we've got (Australian Broadcasting Corporation, 2001).

The Premier of New South Wales, Bob Carr, announced after the event that the Opening Ceremony had been Australia's greatest creative work (Veal and Lynch, 2001). Carr proudly stated, 'Sydney 2000 is one story nobody need fake. This was Australia on show as never before – an intelligent, friendly, contemporary society…' and the Sydney Games were '…the biggest and most exciting thing to happen in this nation during peacetime'. Richard Cashman (1999, p. 16) also argues that 'The Olympic Games have become the world's greatest peacetime event because it is an evolving and dynamic festival'. If the Sydney 2000 Games were Australia's greatest story, the Opening and Closing Ceremonies were considered the bookends (Webb, 2001).

References

Anderson, B. (1991) *Imagined Communities: Reflections on the Origins and Spread of Nationalism* (2nd edn), London: Verso.

Australian Broadcasting Corporation (2001) 'The Games' (episode 1), *Selling Australia* (television series), 14 August, Sydney.

Bail, K. and Bagnall, D. (eds.) (2005) The 125 moments that changed Australia. *The Bulletin*, 10 May, 123(6469). Sydney: Australian Consolidated Press Publishing, pp. 52–111.

Bennett, T. (1993) The shape of the past. In Turner, G. (ed.), *Nation, Culture, Text: Australian Cultural and Media Studies*. London: Routledge, pp. 72–90.

Birch, R. (2004) *Master of the Ceremonies: An Eventful Life*. Crows Nest: Allen and Unwin.

Cashman, R. (1999) The greatest peacetime event. In Cashman, R. and Hughes, A. (eds.), *Staging the Olympics: The Event and its Impact*. Sydney: University of New South Wales Press.

Croft, B. (2001) Visual art. In Singh, S., Andrew, D. et al. (eds.), *Aboriginal Australia and the Torres Strait Islands Guide to Indigenous Australia*. Footscray: Lonely Planet Publications, pp. 65–88.

Cunningham, S. (1992) *Framing Culture: Criticism and Policy in Australia*. Sydney: Allen and Unwin.

Day, D. (2001) *Claiming a Continent: A New History of Australia*. Sydney: Harper Collins.

Dennis, A. (2000) Oils wear hearts on their sleeves. *The Age* (Melbourne), 3 October, p. 3.

Denzin, N. (1989) *The Research Act: A Theoretical Introduction to Sociological Methods* (3rd edn), New Jersey: Prentice Hall.

Fiske, J., Hodge, B. and Turner, G. (1987) *Myths of Oz: Reading Australian Popular Culture*. Sydney: Allen and Unwin.

Girginov, V. and Parry, J. (2005) *The Olympic Games Explained: A Student Guide to the Evolution of the Modern Olympic Games*. London: Routledge.

Gordon, H. (2003) *The Time of Our Lives: Inside the Sydney Olympics*. St. Lucia: University of Queensland Press.

Hutchinson, G. (2002) *True Blue*. Viking, Camberwell: a suburb in Victoria, Australia.

Jones, C. (2000) 'Blue Rodeo performs while Oils protest', *Now* (Toronto), 5 October, http://www.nowtoronto.com/issues/2000-10-05/newsbriefs.html, viewed 17 June 2003.

Kociumbas, J. (2003) Performances: Indigenisation and postcolonial culture. In Teo, H. and White, R. (eds.), *Cultural History in Australia*. Sydney: University of New South Wales Press, pp. 127–141.

Larson, J. F. and Park, H. S. (1993) *Global Television and the Politics of the Seoul Olympics*. Boulder: Westview Press.

Lenskyj, H. J. (2002) *The Best Olympics Ever? Social Impacts of Sydney 2000*. Albany: State University of New York.

Loland, S. (2004) The vulnerability thesis and its consequences: A critique of specialization in Olympic Sport. In Bale, J. and Krogh Christensen, M. (eds.), *Post-Olympism? Questioning Sport in the Twenty-First Century*. New York: Berg, pp. 189–199.

McAvaney, B. (2000) *Sydney 2000 Opening Ceremony*, Channel Seven, 15 September.

Morrissey, P. (2001) History. In Singh, S., Andrew, D. et al. (eds.), *Aboriginal Australia and the Torres Strait Islands Guide to Indigenous Australia*. Footscray: Lonely Planet Publications, pp. 22–32.

Remuzzi, M. (2000) Australia Journal: Australian music with Mandawuy Yunupingu, lead singer of the band Yothu Yindi, *Washington Post*, 20 September, http://discuss.washingtonpost.com/wp-srv/zforum/00/yothu0920.htm, viewed 17 June 2003.

Stanton, J. E. (1988) From the sky, for the land, to the rock. In Thomas, D. (ed.), *Creating Australia: 200 Years of Art, 1788–1988*. Sydney: International Cultural Corporation of Australia, pp. 26–27.

Tomlinson, A. (2004) The disneyfication of the Olympics? Theme parks and freak-shows of the body. In Bale, J. and Krogh Christensen, M. (eds.), *Post-Olympism? Questioning Sport in the Twenty-First Century*. New York: Berg, pp. 147–163.

Veal, A. J. and Lynch, R. (2001) *Australian Leisure* (2nd edn), Frenchs Forest: Pearson Education Australia.

Wark, M. (1993) Homage to Catatonia: Culture, politics and midnight oil. In Frow, J. and Morris, M. (eds.), *Australian Cultural Studies: A Reader*. St Leonards: Allen and Unwin, pp. 105–116.

Webb, T. (2001) *The Collaborative Games: The Story Behind the Spectacle*. Annandale: Pluto Press Australia.

White, R. (1981) *Inventing Australia: Images and Identity 1688–1980*. Sydney: George Allen and Unwin.

Wilkinson, G. (2000) *Sydney 2000 Closing Ceremony*, Channel Seven, 1 October.

Willis, A. (1993) *Illusions of Identity: The Art of Nation*. Sydney: Hale and Ironmonger.

Chapter 7

How Festivals Nurture Resilience in Regional Communities

Ros Derrett

Introduction

This chapter examines how festivals represent a human ecosystem that fosters resilience in communities. The more one peels back the layers of interaction that occur within community festivals, the easier it is to appreciate how they nurture resilience through sharing the values, interests and traditions central to the host community. Such festivals are thus an expression of local identity and reflect the internal life of the community, not withstanding they are impacted and influenced by external forces.

Festivals seem to satisfy an instinct for community. Regardless of the transient nature of such experiences, their value is that they induce and sustain a shared sense of occasion and excitement. Festival preparation, production and promotion also allow for a connection of the local landscape to a community's daily living culture. Festivals provide a heightened experience of this connection that may not be interpreted the same way by all participants, but each recognises the significance of the shared event.

The chapter explores the characteristics of community cultural festivals, particularly in smaller regional communities (Table 7.1). It identifies the partnerships required to develop and deliver celebrations that are of interest not only to the locals but to visitors as well. It recognises that the process of preparing a festival provides clues to the future capacity of that community to meet challenges that might beset them. It could be argued that a robust festival culture is vital to minimising a community's vulnerability in times of stress. The skills and experience gained from sustained collaboration that is required for effective and attractive festivals prepares individuals and communities for more substantive activities.

Volunteer festival organisers, who are actively involved with numerous social networks in their community, feel obliged to commit their limited time and energy to celebratory projects like festivals. Their involvement requires them to choose how they can formally and informally best collaborate with and lead like-minded folk to deliver a festival that authentically represents the best interests of other residents.

International Perspectives of Festivals and Events
Copyright © 2009 by Elsevier Ltd.
All rights of reproduction in any form reserved.
ISBN: 978-0-08-045100-8

Table 7.1: Festival characteristics.

Domain	Characteristics
Festive spirit	Reflection of values and belonging through ritual, revelry, scale, fantasy, magic.
Satisfaction of basic needs	Physical, interpersonal, social and psychological needs.
Uniqueness	Distinctive features of programme, image making, promotions, site, scale, food and beverage, outside normal experience.
Authenticity	Elements associated with local cultural attributes. The participation of community as hosts, staff, performers, suppliers.
Tradition	Events rooted in community, closely associated with reinforcing traditions and practices, can even be fabricated.
Flexibility	Events developed with minimal infrastructure, adapted to changing markets, provide umbrella for a variety of activities.
Hospitality	Willingness of community to host visitors and residents alike.
Tangibility	Experience of place through festival content and host community.
Theming	Theming can be the physical manifestation of elements like tradition, authenticity and festive spirit.
Symbolism	Elements of production can relate to cultural values, political or economic objects.
Affordability	Can provide affordable leisure, social or cultural experiences for hosts and guests.
Convenience	Access to spontaneous leisure and social opportunities.

Source: Getz (1991, p. 326).

Festivals in Literature

Festivals have played a significant part in the cultural life of communities. It seems groups of people have understood the capacity of such gatherings to lift spirits, transfer knowledge and enhance neighbourliness. Festivals emerge from the local lived culture and allow residents and visitors to be involved with their creation. Williams (1965, p. 57) suggests that by participating in festivals we find a particular sense of life, a particular community of experience that hardly needs explanation. Festivals, as a social phenomenon, permit encounters with authentic expressions of culture.

The publicity festivals and events can generate for a community not only have a cumulative impact on the location as a tourist destination but also feed into the image and identity of the community and assist with creating an appealing and consolidated sense of community. The festival is about people having a good time and rarely requires massive infrastructure as it is generally organised around existing resources. These planned events offer the potential, too, to foster local organisational development, leadership and networking, all of which are critical underpinnings of community-based tourism development.

Festivals and events are seen to build social capital and in community development terms showcase the strengths of a community at play and to demonstrate its capacity to cope with external stresses and disturbance as a result of social, political and environmental change (Adger, 2000). The connectivity, pleasure and leisure festivals offer residents and visitors provide experience that can assist host communities deal with unexpected change. Festivals demonstrate how individual and cooperative strengths can be harnessed and deliver outcomes that can be replicated in the future to meet diversecommunity needs.

Organising a major festival takes a lot of individual and collective effort. To get the job done the organisers have to be able to give a lot of time personally and be able to call in a lot of favours and/or inspire volunteerism. Celebration can bind a community and it can also be the instrument that keeps community a fresh and constantly renewing experience, an elixir that keeps community relevant and responsive to the needs of the times. Annual festivals create a community of witness that marks the passage of time, notes the changing of the guard as new power relations arise and old ones change. Kanter (1995) suggests in organisational terms that communities need to have both *magnets* and *glue.* Magnets broaden community horizons, attract and expand skills and attract external resources. Leaders, festival spirit and experience can be the glue that bring people together through social cohesion, with joint plans and agreed strategic goals.

The attributes of the nature and roles exemplified by festivals recognised in the literature and in case studies presented in this chapter include those identified by Getz (1991, p. 326). Those involved in designing and delivering community festivals would recognise a spectrum of engagement in Getz's typology.

Festival Partners

Community festivals are collaborative phenomena and partnerships are recognised as essential for their sustainability. Most festivals take advantage of trusting relationships between multiple enterprises that generally exist independently of one another, yet for a festival are mutually interdependent. This places substantial responsibility on each of the players involved in the collaboration. A process of evolution and change can be observed in each festival. Individuals drive them. Agencies looking to exploit new opportunities like festivals wish to satisfy their own constituency, while appealing to shared wider community aspirations.

Key partners in community festival making include local government, strategic alliances with regional and government agencies, the local business community, special interest groups in destination communities, local media, individual community champions, festival organisers, residents and visitors. The emphasis and level of participation by each partner in each community varies. The interaction is influenced by the individuals involved, the organisational structures in place, traditions inherent in each community's socio-cultural exchange, the history of public engagement by public authorities and the appeal of the region to potential visitors (Figure 7.1).

Getz et al. (2007) highlight the importance of networking with festival partners and acknowledge the roles each can play in festival management. They categorise such stakeholder roles as regulator, facilitator, co-producer, supplier, collaborator and audience. Individual partners in fact exhibit a variety of roles for the effective delivery of the festival. As the social, economic and political contexts in which festivals are hosted are modified, the longevity of the relationships accounted for and the changes in internal and external organisational contexts examined, the practical implications of the partnerships become clearer.

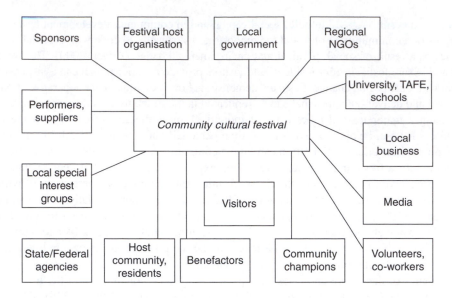

Figure 7.1: Key stakeholders in community festivals. *Source*: adapted from
Allen et al. (2002).

Each festival's programme represents the sum of the interactions between the partners. These partners can sustain local networks after the festival experience. The networks activated breakdown other community infrastructure, bureaucracy or negotiation for the common good. They can promote local solutions to local problems by supporting the establishment of local self-help mechanisms and local community leadership. It also has implications for inter-community or regional collaboration. Healy et al. (2003) suggest the role of social networks between local communities and other communities and key institutions is largely unrecognised in contemporary policy approaches to promoting community resilience and serves as an area of potential further research.

Partnerships that support the host community's sense of itself and its place through festival investment whether in kind, by sponsorship deals, by sharing resources or offering media promotion help build confidence in the life of the festival and ultimately the community. Diverse inputs by partners demonstrate the influence of the relationships and how they enrich the efforts of organisers and encourage local support for each festival. The formal and informal links become known to the potential audience for each event and help consolidate the impression of widespread awareness, satisfaction and value derived for each contributing partner from the relationship.

In this context, social capacity is recognised for the practical opportunities festivals provide for enhanced community communication – meeting neighbours face-to-face in a celebratory atmosphere, developing resident's skills levels through participation in organisation, bringing various parties together for collective decision making, improving infrastructure and liveability and confidence in the amenity of the region for residents and visitors. This discussion is also informed by a philosophical resistance to some aspects of globalisation and the pervasiveness of popular consumer culture that actively works against the distinctive features of regional life that appeals to long-term and recent residents.

Partners demonstrate the principle of active participation, belief in quality of all cultures and the notion of diversity as a social asset (Adams and Goldbard, 2001). The density of civic participation suggests that social capital is not only a product of the region's economy through the exchange of goods and services, but connected vitally to bureaucracies, special interest networks and on a communal level through strong, shared identity (cited in Rolfe, 2006, p. 8).

Methodology

The study exploring community and festival resilience drew on diverse perspectives to create new knowledge about the conduct and impact of festivals. An interdisciplinary approach was required for this research. To better *understand* what occurs when a planned community event materialises, the exploratory or descriptive research builds its findings to predict implications. The focus is on participant observations, interviews, focus groups and model building. The direct experience of key stakeholders in four case study festivals is interpreted. A systematic phenomenology is employed to gain insights. The largely qualitative methods used in the research deliver an understanding of how festivals as cultural products emerge from a community's culture and the contribution they can make to social resilience within the festival organisation and the broader region.

The following brief case studies observe four regional community cultural festivals based in the Northern Rivers region of New South Wales, Australia, and reveal some common characteristics of such events.

Jacaranda Festival, Grafton The Jacaranda Festival was the first floral festival organised in Australia and was based upon spontaneous revelry, music, dance and a celebration for the beauty with which the City of Grafton and district is endowed. The first festival was held on 29 October 1935. Since that time the Jacaranda trees planted throughout the city and their lilac blossoms have become the symbol underpinning the festivities.

The community and the business sectors contribute to the festival. Shop staff dress up in themed costumes, shops are decorated and attract the general public to the shopping precinct. A Queen Crowning Ceremony opens the weeklong festival and a procession along the main street comprising 130 floats ends the festival at the final celebration in the city's Market Square. The site annually hosts thousands of people.

There have been few changes over the years in terms of the content of the festival programme. The lilac blossoms' appearance signals the special time in Grafton. There are day visitors on bus tours to special events like a market, floral displays at the Cathedral, champion gardens, concerts, a car speedway, an aircraft muster, dog agility trials, the fireworks display, greyhound races, the Jacaranda Baby Competition and a vintage car meet.

The volunteer organising committee is reliant on support from individuals, businesses and local government. The non-profit, community-based organisation has sustained this event in Grafton simply by soliciting active individuals who have a vested interest in specific events under the Jacaranda Festival banner. It encourages personal links within the community and succession management has been undertaken on a 'turnabout' model. Numerous office holders have held other community and local government leadership positions. There has been considerable kudos invested in positions of management of the event. The committee is representative of values specifically held by long-term residents – further exemplifying who is local and what locals regard as important.

For more information: www.graftoncity.nsw.gov.au/festjack.htm

Mardi Grass, Nimbin   The Nimbin Mardi Grass promotes itself as the biggest hemp harvest festival in the Western world. It regularly attracts over 10,000 people to the village of Nimbin (normal population 600) in the first weekend in May to celebrate all things hemp, like medicine, fibre, fuel and food. The colourful, loud street parade in the main street of the village is a key attraction with associated activities staged in adjacent parkland. The central icon, the Big Joint, is danced through Nimbin to the sound of jungle drums.

The event was originally conceived as a drug law reform protest. Powerful emotional views are held within the host community about the festival. Volunteers are the backbone of the event and there is a determination to keep the organisation locally based. The Police, local government, the Chamber of Commerce, tourism agencies and regional media are all significant players in how the image of the village is projected beyond the three-day festival.

The programme includes seminars, markets, a hemp trade fair, hemp fashion shows, a pot art exhibition, street theatre and street music. There are seed swaps, a semi-covert judging of the Cannabis Growers Cup (the best heads of the season) and debates about the virtues of bush buds versus the hazards of hydro and health advice for cannabis users. Mardi Grass is a major cultural and tourism asset to the region. Back packer tourism to Nimbin is growing mostly due to media the festival generates and the culture it promotes.

The volunteer management of the event annually undertaken by the *Help End Marijuana Prohibition* (HEMP) Embassy deals with the communal tensions generated. The HEMP Embassy has a major shop front business and tourist attraction in Nimbin. It is part museum (it houses the Big Joint and posters, banners and other art of the Mardi Grass), part drug education centre, part hemp merchandising outlet and part meeting place with Internet cafe and organising office for hemp activists.

For more information: www.nimbinmardigrass.com, www.nrg.com.au/~hemp/

New Year's Eve, Byron Bay   New Year's Eve community celebrations held in seaside Byron Bay are a result of the establishment of a community safety committee. This Council committee sought to redress the image generated by 'chaos' and 'mayhem' resulting during the New Year's Eve street activity in 1993/1994 in the popular coastal town.

The negative national media coverage spurred volunteers to seek solutions of a local nature through strategic partnerships, rebranding the town and the revitalising the annual street celebrations. Extensive work has been undertaken to reorientate the target market, encourage families to return, provide participation opportunities for locals and holidaymakers through workshops to prepare floats for a parade and harmonisation strategies in relation to consumption of alcohol and drugs and innovative waste management to deal with up to 30,000 people.

Extensive community consultation sought to develop an event that reflected the lifestyle of residents, but capitalised on the iconic status of Byron Bay as a tourism destination. The business sector was vital to ongoing negotiations for effective management and monitoring of subsequent events. The volume of summer holiday visitors and day trippers from South East Queensland influenced the strategies employed to diminish pressure on infrastructure in the town's CBD. A programme of entertainment from 6 p.m. to 6 a.m. on New Year's Day is now on the streets and at the beachfront and includes music stages, markets, children's activities, a dance party and fireworks.

Two residents were instrumental in getting Council to convene the Safety Committee, to investigate ways in which a greater community voice could inform the future planning, management and promotion of New Year's Eve celebrations. This couple energetically led interested parties locally and at a state government level in solving the challenges to conduct a safe event for locals and visitors. Their determined advocacy was based on personal experience and attributes in the area of organising, negotiating, networking and documenting local input. Different leaders have followed but the focus remains the same – to reclaim the streets for locals by active de-marketing of the town.

For more information: www.walkabout.com.au/locations/NSWByronBay.html, www.byron-bay.com/, www.byron.nsw.gov.au/policy_public_spaces.shtml

Beef Week festival, Casino   Casino Beef Week commenced in 1981 as an event linked to a specific local economic driver, the beef industry. It satisfied the need to accommodate locals at leisure and ultimately attract visitors. For many years it was actually a 12-day week of activity geared to its established market of beef producers across the eastern states of Australia. Since 2004 the festival has been conducted over five days. The crowning of the Beef Week Queen with up to 10 candidates annually representing a specific cattle breed is a cornerstone to festivities. Each day there is broadly based community entertainment with a cattle theme. The highlight is a parade of cattle, horse drawn vehicles and commercial floats. The main street is converted into a judging ring for hundreds of live steers to compete. The programme has embraced aspects of the timber industry, local arts and crafts, and shop displays. Breakfast with the Butchers is popular to hundreds of locals who come into the main street.

In 2007 the management committee chose not to stage Beef Week. 'Burn out' of a diminishing number of volunteer organisers and a lack of sponsorship were cited as reasons. The festival had enjoyed strong support from the local Council, business and the media since its inception. Its demise and resurrection in an altered guise after 26 years helps us understand the importance of sound governance, leadership of volunteer community-based organisations and their capacity for resilience.

For more information: www.casinobeefweek.com.au

Findings

In the community festivals examined in the Northern Rivers region of New South Wales, Australia (Derrett, 2007), it was found that stakeholder relationships need to work when partners are challenged or during times of positive interaction. In Table.7.2 community resiliency processes are represented in the column headed 'role' and suggest that a collective response for a festival is not only sought, but that parties understand the importance of their shared ability to negotiate and navigate the trials that may emerge as a solution is sought to a problem. This experience can then be translated into other formal and informal ways to assist community development in the future.

Each festival initially had strong links with their respective communities, but the growing number of visitors brought stress on infrastructure, pressure on internal relationships and sometimes resentment about the influx of outsiders. Issues of community carrying capacity become a concern to organisers, Council planners and businesses (Beeton, 2006; Dredge, 2003). Again, the spectrum across the case study festivals reveals differing levels of response to these issues. Organisers commented on the way the festivals contributed to a social multiplier through increased understanding of organisational activity and skills development in project management, leadership, public and private collaboration (Derrett, 2007).

Organising a major festival takes a lot of individual and collective effort. To get the job done the organisers have to be able to give a lot of time personally and be able to call in a lot of favours

Table 7.2: Stakeholder roles in fostering festival and community resilience.

Stakeholder	Role in partnership
Host community – the impacted audience, paying customers and sometimes special guests	• Produce and consume festival • Act as host for visitors • Free access to most of festival as audience • Contribute and celebrate cultural diversity • Traditional and new settler exchange of rituals, volunteer support and >75% of participants • Interest in creating a legacy • Target market supporting image of festival and identity for its promotion
Community champions – facilitators	• Individuals providing vision and leadership, generating enthusiasm, delivering advocacy and attracting respect and loyalty from organisation members and wider community • Bringing goodwill and external recognition to festival
Volunteer co-workers – internal stakeholders	• Demonstrate active participation in community life • Establish and consolidate networks • Local problem solving • Personal skills development and empowerment • Greater understanding of local beliefs, attitudes and values
Festival organisation – internal stakeholder, producers, volunteer and paid staff	• Formal structure emphasises identity and connection to host community • Offers safety and security for participants • Membership comprised of local community • Succession strategies • Community profile
Local government – regulators, sometime co-producers, facilitators	• Policy and planning frameworks • Events officers and project management personnel and infrastructure support • 'In kind' and financial investment • Improve amenities for residents and visitors • Facilitate regional and government alliances and investment • Support tourism marketing initiatives • Reflect community traditions and interests
State and Federal government – often regulators, sometimes facilitators as grant givers	• Provide funding to support elements of festival programmes and value add to economic initiatives and harmonisation challenges
Regional alliances (agencies and organisations representing sectoral interests), collaborators, facilitators	• Desire to respond to locally agreed agendas • Offer financial support and advice • Encourage initiatives with regional outcomes, for example collaborative tourism promotion, arts development, regional cuisine, entrepreneurial initiatives • Some e-technology support
Business community (local and regional), suppliers, vendors	• Be open during festival! • Provide feedback to organisers on economic impacts • Provide sponsorship – 'in kind' or financial • Collaborate in packages and promotion • Active involvement during event highlighting local products and services • Social responsibility

(Continued)

Table 7.2: Continued

Stakeholder	Role in partnership
Sponsors, co-producers	• Demonstrate local corporate goodwill • Share target markets • Establish links to host destination • Share brand • Naming rights
Supplier, performers, merchandisers	• Provide entertainment reflecting local cultural objectives • Offer educational workshops, knowledge sharing and demonstrations • Repeat contributions build loyalty
Special interest groups (local, regional, (inter)national), audience, collaborators, facilitators	• Festival acts as umbrella for diverse but themed pursuits • Consistent involvement brings repeat visitation and builds momentum • Encourages engagement in social action • Provide connection to community issues, concerns and interests • Attracts visitors from further afield • Offers broad network distribution of promotional material
Media (local, regional (inter)national – print, audio-visual, web-based)	• Significant coverage by regional print and audio-visual media, before, during and after festivals • Document and editorialise image and identity, generate archive • Promotion of regional lifestyle • International market reached through web casting, Internet, documentaries • Stimulate debate and controversy • Encourage community responses • Sponsorship
University – audience, participants, researchers	• Provide research and evaluation services to assist with planning and management • Provide an audience for festivals • Provide entertainment for festivals • Provide industry training in event management
Visitors – audience, participants	• Interest in doing what the locals do • Curiosity to learn, discover and interpret local traditions • Repeat visitation substantial because of connection with host community (VFR or reunion) or event • Substantial visitation from South East Queensland • Word-of-mouth value
Benefactors, funders, co-producers	• Nurture formal and informal relationships • Tax deductibility • Anonymity • Celebration • Promotion • Look at structures like foundations

Source: Original Derrett (2005) and Getz et al. (2007).

and/or inspire volunteerism. Celebration can bind a community and it can also be the instrument that keeps community a fresh and constantly renewing experience, an elixir that keeps community relevant and responsive to the needs of the times. Annual festivals create a community of witness that marks the passage of time, notes the changing of the guard as new power relations arise and old ones change.

Discussion

What can be noticed from Table 7.2 is that the stakeholders regularly assume multiple roles in the design, management and delivery of festivals with which they are associated over time. So, for example, local government can be a regulator, a facilitator and a collaborator or partner (according to Getz et al. typology, 2007) simultaneously. Community festivals demonstrate the importance of formal and informal networks amongst stakeholders for the strategic planning necessary for effective festival management and for tactical, operational activities.

Festivals provide service clubs, community special interest groups, local government and businesses with opportunities to raise funds. Some fundraising involves new money as visitors contribute to the common good that encourages investment in infrastructure for residents. Some investment in the promotion of the destination using the festival themes adds to the image and identity developed in each community. The destination-marketing dollar is increased at times connected to the festivals. These in turn influence greater visitation and increased expenditure by visitors, visiting friends and relatives (VFRs) hosts and local business anticipating the influx.

The current level of resilience in each of the host destinations can be established by assessing the experience, resources and time invested in each festival. Each year festival organisers can revisit the baseline assessment to ensure errors are avoided and successes replicated. Intellectually each organisation needs to recognise that the collaboration that takes place in festival making assists community communication and provides a framework for structured and focused approaches to planning. However, being able to translate this into practice effectively is not always easy. This mismatch can place stress on management. Some festival organisations generate a community portrait and document steps in a process to benefit all stakeholders, others get by through ad hoc activity and seemingly come together spontaneously each year, just to enjoy a good time together.

Resilience

Community resilience emerges through the solidarity and co-operation; creativity and adaptability; proactivity; prudence, preparation and planning; responsibility; awareness of environment and where a holistic methodology is present (www.bettertimesinfo.org/7habits.htm, 2006). Festivals can strengthen communities through their own level of resilience.

The resilience sought by festival organisations in regional communities comes from the interaction between three key aspirations – social/cultural well-being, environmental sustainability and economic prosperity. These outcomes result from a greater understanding of the mechanisms that need to be engaged with to ensure a profound sense of place and community is addressed, a realistic image and identity of residents in their place is promoted and that cultural tourism responds to the authentic representation of the hosts.

This can be seen in Figure 7.2 where the interface between the core elements of residents, place and visitors deliver the sense of place and community, the image and identity and cultural tourism that provide a fundamental framework for an investigation into community cultural festivals.

What is exposed is the catalytic nature of community cultural festivals. The interactive 'pace-maker' role of festivals for community resilience is recognised. This is indicated (in Figure 7.2) through the multiple, often overlapping and fluid networks that exist in communities as they face engagement challenges to resilience. Stakeholder groups in communities demonstrate the best and worst of the interaction that occurs when a festival is made. Some demonstrate levels of exclusivity and hierarchical management limiting capacity to generate social capital and well-being. Festivals can also provide evidence of significant benefits accrued from co-operation and collaboration, leadership and advocacy, research, encouragement of participation and partnerships, innovative approaches to funding, technology and increasing infrastructure and capacity building. It is suggested that communities and festivals are more vulnerable to the risk of unsustainability if these positive elements are not in place.

Figure 7.3 is grounded in the model expressed in Figure 7.2. It shows the relationship between festivals and their host community. It indicates the multidimensional interaction and the substantive aspects of festival operation that influence levels of resilience within the festival organisation and the community as a whole when celebrations are held.

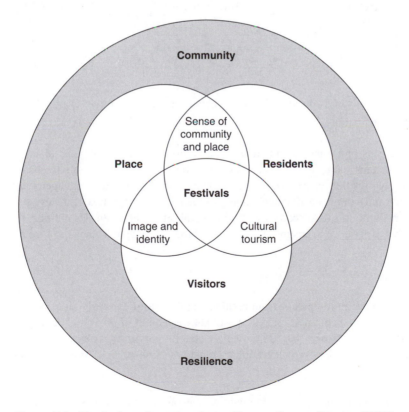

Figure 7.2: Festivals and community resilience. *Source*: Derrett (2007).

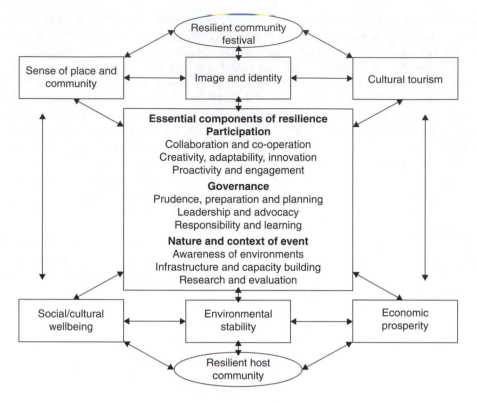

Figure 7.3: Festivals and communities demonstrate resilience. *Source*: Original Derrett (2007).

The arrows in this figure indicate the interconnectedness of all the elements to achieve appropriate celebrations to sustain resilient festivals and communities. The critical factors to ensure festivals contribute to their own resilience and that of their broader community are an engagement with participation, governance and a heightened understanding of the nature and context of the event. The robustness of these elements will inform the capacity of the festival organisation and its partners to use both positive and negative experience to ensure resilience in a broader context. This is the core of the model.

Well-being Component

Through high levels of participation from residents and visitors, festivals give a voice to locals who are brought together by a common interest. Festivals are seen to improve the quality of life and well-being of residents through their shared interactions and by providing a place for people to participate and take some responsibility for celebrations. Dunstan (1994, p. 1) claims that celebration creates community,

> as celebration is the way we humans affirm our connected-ness to each other in meaning, time and place. It is the ritual by which we make and renew our sense of

community whatever and wherever that might be. The converse is also true. A community without a signifying celebration is no "community" at all. The more profound the sharing of meaning in the celebration and the more beautiful the art, the more intimately bonded is that community.

He suggests that celebrations are a measure of the spiritual health of a community and the more a celebration can join people in sharing the core concerns and mysteries of the human condition such as birth, death and connectedness, the more intimately they will realise their shared humanity as a universal brother and sisterhood of all people, a fundamental unity of love, justice and peaceful co-existence.

Such communities, it seems, forge strong and distinct identities, and establish clear rules of inclusion and share information across boundaries. Communities that create social reciprocity using symbols, myths and stories represented in festivals sustain values sufficiently that the community feels familiar. These then become clear building blocks for what is termed 'community well-being' (Wills, 2001). Community well-being can be described as having such outcomes for residents as conviviality, livability, sustainability, viability and vitality (Wills, 2001).

Community well-being incorporates qualities for developing healthy and sustainable communities. The important activity, participation and interaction between people at festival time are seen as 'vitality'. Such elements provide an opportunity to sensitively assess how communities see themselves and measure themselves against a set of criteria that can meaningfully underpin how a sense of community and place contribute to community cultural festivals.

The concept of resilience is a quality aspired to and amply demonstrated by the participants in festival organisations. A sense of place and community help construct resilient communities and networks of people to design each festival. When the Broader community is faced with challenges requiring effective governance, practical leadership and efficient management of logistics, those involved with delivering festivals can come forward and deliver for the greater community good. Despite evidence of stresses within communities represented by specific interests, power struggles, differences in aspirations and levels of participation, economic pressures, festivals provided a level of confidence to function within the internal and external environments. Festivals demonstrate a degree of harmonious partnership and cohesiveness, offering residents' life meaning. They provide interaction or reciprocal relationships between all the determining factors. Festivals show how some things can be worked out through openness and collaboration.

Place-based governance of community cultural festivals may sometimes not succeed in all its objectives, but it is close enough to its constituency to get immediate feedback and can remediate in full public gaze. Such festivals also demonstrate that they fulfil a strategic planning function for regional communities by protecting and enhancing community values, encouraging social cohesion, equity and diversity and care for sacred places. Community resilience becomes viable when a robust festival is shared amongst residents.

Resilience Component

Resilience is essential for community well-being for its capacity to deliver an appropriate quality of life for residents and a level of sustainability for community development. Figure 7.3 shows how resilience is formative and summative, dynamic and responsive to the contexts that arise when communities come together in a shared experience. The strength of the ties between festival stakeholders affects the durability of the networks beyond the festival making. A number of internal variables from these relationships, like trust and reciprocity, influence not only the durability, but also the meaningfulness stimulated by the festival making. This can extend the trust and the loyalty being sustained within the festival organisation and between festival partnerships beyond the delivery of the festival.

Festivals as collaborative entities protect against risk inherent in day-to-day interactions between people. They provide participants with an opportunity to show what they can do rather than feeling restricted as to their options as active residents. This resilience feeds into the well-being framework explored within each case study festival. These frameworks promote the building and nurturing required by communities to address sustainability and productivity challenges from a position of strength and innovation. Festivals offer participants at all levels, opportunities to know what resilience feels like and encourage others in the community to build on it (Benard, 2004). The festival structure and content used in the case study festivals, in turn, influence the capacity residents have to deal with structures around their daily lives.

Festival Tourism Component

Community well-being is important when addressing how residents share their destination with visitors. While in community development terms festival participants have a subjective interpretation of the festivals, it is evident that well-being is a tourism asset (Beeton, 2006, p. 80) when hosts are hospitable. This well-being results from the networks that operate in communities in diverse forms. It is evident that networks can have boundaries that are, in a temporal and spatial sense, open and closed, vertical or horizontal within the community or across the region. These dimensions represent a substantial aspect of the complexity of such festivals.

Characteristic regional hospitality delivers cultural tourism. No two festivals are identical, however some consistent patterns emerge to allow comparisons to be developed and typologies like Getz (2007) to be developed. These diverse and fragmented patterns have their own advantages and disadvantages and it is evident that success or failure is not linked to a particular model for such festivals.

All four festivals mentioned above demonstrate such characteristics as ritual, the showcasing of culture by affirming heritage, active participation by attendees, revelry through excess and exchange of information. A heightened sense of 'festivity' emerges from the communities they serve and is captured for the duration of the event and leaves a positive residual. Each picks up on festive characteristics that best fit their audience including harvest, feasting, holidays, carnival atmosphere, gala functions, diverse entertainments, competitions, games, exhibitions, ritual and spirituality. While there are common elements shared by festivals, the study reveals that each festival is unique because of the nature of the host community, the historical, geographic and cultural context.

How Do Festivals Foster Community Resilience?

Regardless of the transient nature of such experiences, their value is that they induce and sustain a shared sense of occasion and excitement. This connectivity helps build resilience. This glue is demonstrated in three major ways.

These celebrations demonstrate belonging and community resilience through:

1. Participation
2. Governance
3. Nature and context of event.

It suggested that by ensuring each domain is attended to effectively and inclusively, the resulting social/cultural well-being, environmental sustainability and economic prosperity the host community aspires to will contribute to resilient festivals and communities. The integrated nature of festival making needed to be felt by all stakeholders. Indicators for the connection are examined in Table 7.3.

Table 7.3: Indicators of nourishing resilience through community cultural festivals.

Domain	Implications
1. Participation	
Collaboration and co-operation	Partnerships provide intrinsic and extrinsic synergies for positive social action to increase individual and collective capacity to develop and share practical, respectful and spiritual goals
Creativity, adaptability, innovation	Growth of personal and community capacity to accommodate change generates festivities with unique creative characteristics that satisfy participants
Proactivity and engagement	Offering opportunity for volunteerism, social entrepreneurship, storytelling and trusting networks for open dialogue
2. Governance	
Prudence, preparation and planning	Grow the understanding of ethical design and delivery of festivals for the 'common good' reflecting the 'way things are done around here' to the best extent
Leadership and advocacy	Encourage community champions with strong commitment to participative decision making and thinking
Responsibility and learning	Stimulate ownership of festivities through provision of lifelong learning options for joining in and interacting
3. Nature and context of event	
Awareness of environments	Develop alertness to the dynamic social, political, technological, economic, environmental and global influences on local activity
Infrastructure and capacity building	Ensure timely investment from broad stakeholders into hard and soft infrastructure to enhance capacity of residents to reflect and determine their values, interests and aspirations through effective, well-resourced management systems
Research and evaluation	Monitor ongoing activity within community and festivals to ensure responsiveness, durability and best practice to revive and refresh and to replicate success

Source: Derrett (2007) after www.bettertimesinfo.org/7habits.htm and Community Manifesto (2003).

This framework builds on the notion that resilient people with healthy coping skills through clear self-knowledge, optimism and comfort with strong community relationships are best equipped to lead organisations through the challenges that are thrown up when festivals are developed. This model suggests that by keeping the objectives of the festival organisational team in perspective and through practice in problem solving, a robust organisation will emerge. Prior – members of the festival making network will be better placed to deal with complex transitions that deal with multiple partners. Their experience can be applied to not only delivering events, but to social, political, environmental activism that can occur in communities from time to time.

Participation

Partnerships are seen to be a valuable aspect of festival making. The active collaboration and co-operation that can be brought to bear enhances the creative and innovative options available to the festival. They are seen as positive aspects of community development. By taking initiatives in the public domain for a common good, individuals and groups can demonstrate personal and professional skills that can be translated into other aspects of community life. The communication that takes place and the mutual support offered through teamwork are valuable characteristics of resilience.

Governance

Leadership can provide guidance and management to individuals and groups set on a negotiated course. By engaging with people committed to planning worthwhile celebrations with care and attention to detail, organisations are able to handle the responsibility of developing festivals that encourage relationships that are able to deal with challenges both internal and external to the task at hand. These are further characteristics of resilience.

Nature and Context of Event

An appreciation and an understanding of the circumstances in which festivals are developed provide valuable knowledge for organisers. This knowledge interprets and explains the need for sensitivity to partners' needs and aspirations. It has implications for the resources required to ensure the festival can be delivered systematically, in a timely fashion with characteristics that can be replicated.

Conclusion

The social meaning of community festivals needs to be built up through highly contextualised histories. What are observed are independent and interdependent behaviours of individuals and agencies that interact and overlap. Festivals are seen to allow people to reflect and determine a sense of community and place. This becomes the engine that represents their image and identity and contributes to cultural tourism. The importance of festivals in nourishing their own and their community's resilience is revealed through such analysis. Festivals add value to communities. They creatively embed culture. They offer a subtle balance of local community content through authenticity, interest, quality and entertainment to provide the content of the tourism experience. Simultaneously these festivals can be celebrations of community resilience.

The following quote by Taylor (2007) encapsulates the significance of the festival experience that is demonstrated in the four case studies. It recognises many of the forces operating at festival making time and the residual impact festivals have on individuals and communities. This study identified the concept that resilience that emerges from the cultural collaboration transforms the lives of participants.

A creative life. An expressive life. A connected life. A remembered life (Taylor, 2007).

It seems to me that a diverse, rich, and vital cultural ecology in any city, state, or country fosters opportunity for every citizen to inform these elements of their existence. a creative life – The opportunity to make something from nothing, or transform fragments of objects or thoughts into a cohesive whole, is an ennobling and empowering thing. Everyone should have the option to do so, no matter what their stage of life, circumstance, technical ability, or training. an expressive life – Finding your voice and having an opportunity to be heard is an essential quality of being alive and aware in the world. a connected life – The interpersonal and social sharing of meaning is the connective tissue between loved ones, community members, and civilizations. While the arts are not the only means to this sharing, they are among the most powerful and enduring. a remembered life – The accumulated actions and artifacts of our expressive lives are our most vital threads to who we were, who we are, and who we might become. Beyond our children, they are the most compelling evidence that we ever existed at all (Andrew Taylor, 2007).

Through participant observation, interviews, media and document analysis, surveys and photographic images, the research suggests that simple social, economic and environmental festival management issues currently presented in the literature required greater deconstruction. The scholarly investigation enhances understanding of a significant social agenda in regional communities. Festivals add value to communities. They creatively embed culture. They offer a subtle balance of local community content through authenticity, interest, quality and entertainment to provide the content of the tourism experience. Simultaneously, these festivals can be celebrations of community resilience.

References

Adams, D. and Goldbard, A. (2001) *Community Culture and Globalisation*. New York: Rockefeller Foundation, www.communityarts.net/readingroom/archive/25creativecommunity.html.

Adger, W. N. (2000) Social and ecological resilience: Are they related? *Progress in Human Geography*, 24(3), 347–364.

Beeton, S. (2006) *Community Development through Tourism*. Collingwood, VIC: Landlinks Press.

Benard, B. (2004) *Resiliency: What We Have Learned*. Oakland, CA: WestEd Publishing.

Community Manifesto – Valuing Australia's Community Groups (2003) Communities in Control Conference, http://www.ourcommunity.com.au

Derrett, R. (2007) *Regional festivals – Nourishing community resilience: The nature and role of cultural festivals in Northern Rivers NSW communities*, Doctoral thesis, Southern Cross University, Lismore.

Dredge, D. (2003) *Tourism Community Well-being and Local Government*, paper, Australian Regional Tourism Convention, 3–6 September.

Dunstan, G. (1994) *Becoming Coastwise, the Path of Festivals and Cultural Tourism*, Landscape and Lifestyle Choices for the Northern Rivers of NSW, Southern Cross University, Lismore.

Getz, D. (1991) *Festivals, Special Events and Tourism*. NY, Van Nostrand Reinhold.

Getz, D. (2007) *Events Studies, Theory, Research and Policy for Planned Events*. Amsterdam: Elsevier.

Getz, D., Andersson, T. and Larson, M. (2007) Festival stakeholder roles: Concepts and case studies. *Event Management*, 10, 103–122.

Healy, K., Hampshire, A. and Ayres, L. (2003) Engaging Communities for Sustainable Change: Promoting Resilience, published/presented, August, Integrated Learning Network Consultative Policy Development Conference, Canberra.

Kanter, R. M. (1995) *World Class: Thriving Locally in the Global Economy*. New York: Simon & Schuster.

Rolfe, R. E. (2006) *Social Cohesion and Community Resilience: A Multi-disciplinary Review of Literature for Rural Health Research* paper submitted to Social Cohesion and Community Resiliency Working Group of the Atlantic Canada based Rural Centre.

Taylor, A. in Arts Journal (2007), www.artsjournal.com/artfulmanager/main/065478.php

The seven habits of personal, family and community resilience, http://www.bettertimesinfo.org/7habits.htm

Williams, R. (1965) *Culture and Society*, Penguin, London.

Wills, J. (2001) *Just, Vibrant and Sustainable Communities – A Framework for Progressing and Measuring Community Wellbeing*. Townsville: Local Government Community Services of Australia.

Chapter 8

The Buon Ma Thuot Coffee Festival, Vietnam: Opportunity for Tourism?

Lee Jolliffe, Huong Thanh Bui and Hang Thy Nguyen

Introduction

Festivals are known to contribute to the branding of destinations, creating an awareness of the key attributes that can make one destination different from another. Festivals may reflect traditional social celebrations of a community or they may be constructed by the community around a theme connected to the place. Festivals are described as an important expression of human activity that contributes to social and cultural life (Allen et al., 2005). Tourists are drawn to local festivals that celebrate place and identity (MacLeod, 2006). There is some evidence that these festivals contribute to community development and to have some positive local economic impact (O'Sullivan and Jackson, 2002). Event tourism can play a role in the overall tourism strategy of a destination (Allen et al., 2005).

In the case of the capital city of Daklak Province in the Central Highlands of Vietnam, the first Buon Ma Thuot Coffee Festival has engaged community participants, involved a broad range of stakeholders and influenced local thinking about branding the region as a coffee destination. The festival is notable for being the first-ever coffee festival in Vietnam, a country which is the second leading world producer and exporter of the Robusta variety of coffee. The festival has contributed to the potential development of coffee tourism as a niche form of tourism in Vietnam.

Coffee was introduced to Vietnam by the French in the 19th century. Today, the country is known for coffee production and for a thriving café culture. Coffee, a commonly consumed beverage with its own culture, has the potential to be an attraction for potential domestic and international visitors in Vietnam (Jolliffe, 2007a; Jolliffe and Bui, 2006; Nguyen, 2006). Since the Vietnamese love coffee as reflected by their distinct coffee preparation and café culture (Berger, 2005; Sterling, 2000), this coffee theme may appeal to the domestic visitors to the coffee producing province of Daklak. While international tourism arrivals to the area are quite low (less than 5% of the total) at the present these arrivals are predicted to increase and given the global popularity of coffee and its associated culture it is likely that these tourists could be attracted by the coffee theme (Daklak Trade and Tourism

Department, 2007). The media coverage of the first coffee festival reinforced the coffee brand and introduced the concept of visiting the area to experience its coffee.

The region also has the goal of employing tourism for its socio-economic impact by involving local populations in tourism, thus improving livelihoods and contributing to reducing poverty. In an area with tourism resources that compliment the coffee focus (natural resources, ethnic minority life-styles and intangible heritage), it will be necessary to involve the local communities and people. The first coffee festival in 2005 made a start in this direction by including cultural festivities and perform-ances in their four-day programme. For the capital city of Daklak Province and its surrounding coffee producing region both local and international consultants have identified the possibility of positioning the destination as Vietnam's 'Coffee Capital' (Daklak Trade and Tourism Department, 2006).

The coffee festival has a key role to play in developing products for this potential coffee focused tourism. The development of more products to appeal to the potential coffee tourists will be essen-tial and will address a goal of tourism development in the region to diversify the local tourism prod-uct, thus increasing the length of stay and the amount spent by visitors (Daklak Trade and Tourism Department, 2006). During the 2005 festival a coffee tour (visiting coffee farms and production facilities) was piloted by several local travel companies. The overall festival event was voted by the Vietnamese press as one of the most 10 most remarkable festival events of 2005.

This chapter presents a case study of the Buon Ma Thuot Coffee Festival. As this festival is just one of the growing number of festivals linking food and drink to tourism around the world the case study is preceded by a discussion of the context of the festival, both in terms of the relevance of these product themed festivals to tourism and of the relationship of coffee to festivals.

Festival Context

Food and beverage themed festivals have become universally popular (Allen et al., 2005) and are acknowledged as contributing to regional development (Hall et al., 2003). These festivals range from large urban centred festivals incorporating various food traditions to local festivals showcasing local food traditions. Such festivals represent a growing interest in food and drink tourism and are a means of connecting people with local food production (Boniface, 2003). Attending these festivals tourists can directly experience local food and drink traditions. At these festivals it is often also pos-sible to visit farms and to view the processing of local agricultural products. The festivals cater to tourists who are interested in experiencing foods characteristic of the place they are visiting (Goss and Brown, 2006).

Long (2004) notes festivals play a role in framing particular foods as representing culinary herit-age available for tourism. The author recognises realms of such tourism experience ranging from the exotic to the familiar, with tourists associating these attributes with foods and beverages that are edible to inedible and palatable to unpalatable. As experienced with tea and tea tourism (Jolliffe, 2007b) in the case of coffee consumption and experience as tourism many tourists are dealing with a familiar beverage in terms of consumption, but visiting the location of production may be seen as exotic. At these locations tourists may be able to experience different approaches to the preparation, serving and consumption of a beverage that is familiar to them.

Coffee is a beverage with an important social and culinary history that is worthy of celebration. Coffee comes from the fruit of the coffee tree – the coffee bean is inside of the fruit. Now coffee is grown in about 80 tropical countries (Wallengren, 2002). Coffee is a product with established geographical connections to its area of production and the notion of labeling coffee with its country of origin is well accepted, creating a brand equity that may be transferable to tourism.

Coffee is consumed daily by approximately one-third of the world's population (Brenes et al., 1997) both at home and also while away as reflected by the growth of café cultures around the world. Mirroring interest in food and beverage tourism (Boniface, 2003) some tourists may be interested in coffee experiences. Due to the globalisation of food traditions (Pitte, 2002) this experience may be the same or similar to that the tourist would have at home. In other cases tourists may be able to experience local coffee traditions (Berger, 2005) and at coffee producing locations tourists will be able to view coffee landscapes as well as visit coffee farms and production facilities.

Products for tourists in this situation may include visits to coffee interpretation centres on farms as highlighted by the case of Café Brit (Brenes et al., 1997) in Costa Rica or participation in coffee-related festivities. Some countries, such as Columbia and Nicaragua have coffee touring routes. Most coffee is shipped from its countries of origin as green coffee beans with importing countries benefiting from the value added services of roasting, distributing and marketing. In some coffee producing situations in developing countries there is opportunity to diversify through the production of organic and fair trade coffees, for example in Central America (Kilian et al., 2006). These producing countries may appreciate the chance to add value to their coffee resource through tourism, in particular with reference to fair trade and pro-poor tourism. A case of the latter type of tourism that generates net benefits for the poor from Tanzania (Goodwin, 2006) has demonstrated that a small investment in developing a coffee tour and campsite has provided significant new local incomes. A coffee producing cooperative and a local tour operator partnered in this project benefiting the local coffee farmers, tour guides and the local community who receive a percentage of revenues for their community development fund. This case demonstrates best practices in linking coffee with tourism in one country that can be applied in others.

Coffee as a commonly drunk beverage lends itself to the creation of local festivals that celebrate the related history, traditions, cultivation and production. Coffee festivals are reportedly held at a number of coffee producing locations. For example, in Hawaii the Kona Coffee Cultural Festival held annually is the oldest and most successful product festival in Hawaii. The 37th Annual Kona Coffee Festival is scheduled for November of 2007 (Kona Coffee Cultural Festival, 2007). These festivals, also serve the important function of promoting the coffee to the public and introducing potential trade buyers to the product, reinforcing the branding of local coffee. Other coffee festivals are held in coffee consuming countries, such as Ireland, Australia, New Zealand and the United Kingdom. The International Coffee Organization recommends using coffee festivals to encourage consumption. These festivals therefore have various purposes that range from the branding of the coffee to the celebration of coffee culture to encouraging coffee consumption. In some cases the festivals have a dual purpose of contributing to branding, increasing consumption and awareness of coffee and tourism.

Vietnam has a favourable geographic and climatic situation for the growth of coffee, yet it is only in recent years that coffee has become an important export commodity that has been increasingly integrated into the world market (Nguyen, 2006). Using statistics from the International Coffee Organization for 2005–2006 Thorn (2006) reported Vietnam as the world's third largest coffee producer. Vietnam's Ministry of Agriculture and Rural Development subsequently reported that in the first quarter of 2007, Daklak Province, a leader in coffee production, exported more than 115,000 tones of coffee earning a revenue of US$ 168 million almost double that of the same period in 2006 (Daklak Trade and Promotion Centre, 2007a). It is thus evident that coffee production in the province is flourishing.

Coffee consumed in Vietnam and available for tourists to experience is found at either small traditional cafés or in contemporary café settings. The traditional method of brewing coffee in Vietnam involves the use of a small silver filter set on top of the cup into which the coffee slowly drips onto condensed milk. There is anecdotal evidence that tourists value this coffee experience, sometimes purchasing both the equipment and the roasted coffee beans to prepare their own Vietnamese style coffee once they are at home (Berger, 2005; Murray, 2002; Sterling, 2000).

Drinking coffee in Vietnam is also an entertainment. Local people gather at cafés for discussion, for business and for relaxation. The cafés vary in decoration, style of coffee blending as well as different type of music played. Buon Ma Thuot is famous for its coffee production, thus tourists coming to the city may like to experience the local coffee culture. There is a need to survey tourists coming to the city to substantiate this observation. There had been an increase in the number of café establishments in the town in recent years, after the festival in 2005. Since most of the visitors are domestic tourists it is possible that the coffee culture of the town has become an iconic attraction for them. This is related to it being known throughout the country as the homeland of coffee as well as the origin of the most famous café brand in Vietnam – Trung Nguyen. Even though only 10% of the coffee produced is consumed domestically (Nguyen, 2006), the added value for coffee thus comes from the cafés which are successfully blending local coffee into their café culture. In addition branding the locality as a coffee destination might increase the value added for international tourists, a move which could be welcomed by coffee farmers, producers and of course the tour companies.

Methodology

Investigating the first Buon Ma Thuot Coffee Festival the authors traveled to the location to conduct field research. A narrative case study methodology was adopted as such studies are known to be useful for obtaining background information. This is because they are flexible with respect to data-collection methods, may be conducted in practically any kind of social setting and are inexpensive to conduct (Black and Champion, 1976). Interviews were conducted on site during September of 2007 in Buon Ma Thuot using open-ended questions. Yin (1989) advises that case study researchers should seek multiple sources of data, so in addition to interviews, secondary information in the form of media reports, tourism guide books, coffee industry reports, regional tourism plans and related documents were used.

Stakeholders in the Buon Ma Thuot Coffee Festival interviewed included a total of 17 representatives of the local tourism administration, local coffee businesses (cafés and shops), tour operators, complimentary tourism attraction operators and coffee farmers. Using a qualitative research approach suggested by Newman (2006) those to be interviewed were chosen for their relevance to the research topic. Interview questions were designed to elicit stakeholder perspectives and discussion on the first Buon Ma Thuot Coffee Festival which had been held in 2005 as well as on subsequent developments in relation to tourism and coffee in the region. A snowball technique was used to identify stakeholders with those initially interviewed suggesting others who should be part of the process. Respondents were interviewed in Vietnamese and the interview notes were transcribed into English. One limitation of the research is that some information collected is anecdotal, for example, since festival attendance had not been systematically measured as recommended by Getz (1984), attendance levels are only a rough estimate of visitation. Another limitation is that the researchers were investigating the festival 20 months after it was held. This meant that it was only possible to collect anecdotal and impressionistic information from the stakeholders interviewed. This research limitation was addressed in part by the use of documents and media reports relating to the festival.

In terms of the focus of the research it is of note that initially the researcher's primary interest was in the coffee festival as an event connecting coffee and tourism. In a previous paper (Jolliffe and Bui, 2006) the authors had examined the connection between coffee and tourism in Vietnam, identifying the potential of the Buon Ma Thuot Coffee Festival for tourism. However, early in the interview process for the field research the open questions on how the festival should be developed in the future indicated that respondents linked the festival to objectives for developing the destination. This led the researchers to broaden the focus of their investigation and to also examine the important role of the festival in developing and branding the local destination, for coffee and tourism.

After providing essential background on the situation of tourism in Vietnam, in the region and in the city, the detailed case study focuses on the Buon Ma Thuot Coffee Festival. The chapter concludes with an analysis of the festival and suggestions for further research.

Tourism in Daklak Province

Vietnam tourism has taken off since 1995 with an annual growth rate of more than 10% each year. In 2006, the country received 3.6 million international tourists, an increase of 3% over 2005. It is projected that in 2007, there will be 4.2 million international arrivals (VNTA, 2006a, 2007). The country is rich in both cultural and natural resources with four World Heritage sites and two Masterpieces of Oral and Intangible Heritage having been declared by UNESCO.

Daklak is the largest of the five provinces of the Central Highlands of Vietnam. It covers 13,123.5 square kilometers and consists of 12 districts and Buon Ma Thuot, the capital city. The province has a population of 1.7 million and the capital city has a population of over 300,000. The province is home to 44 ethnic minorities out of the 54 ethnic groups of the whole country, who in Daklak make up 30% of the population. The province experiences a temperate climate with an average temperature of 24°C and two seasons, the rainy season from May to October and the dry season from November to April (Daklak Trade and Tourism Department, 2006). The tourist season roughly parallels the dry season.

The province has rich natural and cultural tourism resources. The province is famous for water-based resources reflected by well-known waterfalls such as Dray Sap, Gia Long, Trinh Nu, and lakes such as Lak, Ea Kao, Dak Min, suitable for activities such as sailing, surfing and fishing. The largest national park in Vietnam, Yok Don is around 40 kilometers from the city centre of Buon Ma Thuot. Daklak is known for its rich and original ethnic minority culture, which is less influenced by either Chinese culture (as in Northern Vietnam) or Indian culture (as in Southern Vietnam). The area is famous for its intangible Gong culture, an oral intangible cultural heritage recognised in 2005 (UNESCO, 2005), but also for various types of music instruments made from stones, bamboo and wood, traditional architecture and sculpture, dance and song as well as remarkable epics (stories told in poetry). With this rich culture and a large and varied ethnic minority population in the area festivities and festivals form part of everyday life throughout the year, varying according to the season, the religion and the ethnic minority beliefs. These rich cultural resources provide many attributes to attract tourists.

The region is agricultural with a cash crop focus on coffee (also rubber, pepper, cashews) and 98% of the provincial exports are agricultural. The researchers identified a recent trend of the cash crop companies diversifying into tourism and investing in infrastructure (hotels, resorts, etc.) that will create capacity for tourism. For example, in 2006 it was announced that the Trung Nguyen Coffee Company would invest 30 billion VDN in an agricultural farm ecotourism development in Krong A commune, M'Drak District (VNTA, 2006b). The company also reportedly has ideas for other coffee-related tourism development including a coffee themed resort.

Daklak is still an undiscovered destination in Vietnam, receiving just under 20,000 international tourists in 2006 (Table 8.1). Tourism is just developing in the region (over the last five years), especially after UNESCO declared the Gong Cultural Space as Oral and Intangible Heritage in 2005. Some of the increased visitation also can be attributed in part to the success of Coffee Festival in December of 2005. A provincial proposal for developing tourism in Daklak Province has a focus on developing tourism to the capital city of Buon Ma Thuot and the surrounding area. By 2010 the region is expected to receive 500,000 visitors annually of which 50,000 would be international tourists (Daklak Trade and Tourism Department, 2006).

The tourism objectives of the region (Table 8.2) reinforce a potential move into combining the agricultural sector of coffee production with tourism to brand Buon Ma Thuot as a coffee destination. This is a move that is facilitated and supported by the Buon Ma Thuot Coffee Festival. One of the vehicles for implementing these objectives is the support the local trade and tourism administration provides for local festivals. This includes providing leadership in festival planning and facilitating as well as linking festival activities to other stakeholders, sectors and government departments.

Buon Ma Thuot city has been developing its infrastructure for tourism over the last five years. The city now has 1200 hotel rooms of international standard. In 2006 Daklak's Steering Board for Tourism announced a further 135 million VDN to build hotels, restaurants, entertainment and sports facilities at tourism sites in the province (VNTA, 2006b). In addition, reflecting the local coffee

Table 8.1: International tourist arrivals to Daklak (2000–2006).

2000	2001	2002	2003	2004	2005	2006
7.780	5.759	9.028	9.124	9.632	14.540	19.521

Source: Daklak Trade and Tourism Department (2007).

Table 8.2: Main objectives for tourism development in Daklak Province.

1. Increasing investment in tourism and providing opportunities for all economic sectors to participate in tourism by making the best use of the tourism resources and by diversifying the tourism product.

2. Developing tourism sustainability in relation to the natural environment and the preservation of traditional cultures.

3. Making tourism an important economic sector with socio-economic impacts to include poverty alleviation.

4. Developing tourism products to increase the length of stay and the amount spent.

Source: Daklak Trade and Tourism Department (2006).

culture the city has a wide variety of cafés ranging from small local roadside coffee stands to more sophisticated city centre cafés. Some cafés are recently established since the 2005 festival while others are long established.

In the main coffee producing province in Vietnam it is clear that the provincial government, through Daklak Trade and Tourism Department is committed to developing tourism, linking it with other economic sectors and to ensuring that local communities are involved in this tourism and benefit from it. This commitment is reflected in the following case study.

Buon Ma Thuot Coffee Festival

Vietnamese coffee originated in the area around Buon Ma Thuot where coffee is the main cash crop contributing significantly to the regional economy and accounts for 60% of Vietnam's coffee exports. As noted earlier tourism activities in this area mainly focus on the culture of the ethnic minorities and the rich and native flora and fauna. In a direct effort to promote the local coffee brand and coincidently to diversify the tourism product in this area, the Buon Ma Thuot Coffee Festival was first held here from 2nd to 5th December 2005. At that time this was the only coffee festival that had been held in the context of Vietnam's rapidly growing coffee industry.

The idea for implementing a coffee festival to celebrate coffee in the region originated with the Daklak People's Committee. Having just organised a successful Central Highlands Festival in March the idea for the coffee festival was developed and delivered within seven months by the committee that had implemented the other festival. The stakeholders for this first coffee festival in Buon Ma Thuot included the Department of Culture and Information, the Department of Agriculture and Rural Development, the provincial Daklak People's Committee, the Daklak Trade and Tourism Department, local coffee enterprises, local tourism companies, local cafés, local coffee farmers and traders, and the local population. There were 300 exhibits of which more than 20 were international with famous brand names coffee companies exhibiting.

The Daklak Trade and Tourism Department was the official organiser of the festival. As the department is in charge of both trade and tourism issues, there is support within this department for linking trading activities to tourism. The fact that festival promotes the tourism of the region is also confirmed by an interview with the largest coffee enterprise – Trung Nguyen Coffee Company with its head office based in Buon Ma Thuot.

The main festival purpose was to promote coffee trading, to encourage local coffee culture and to brand the Buon Ma Thuot Coffee. The festival reported approximately 300,000 visitors, averaging 73,000 tourists per day, of which roughly 1200 were international visitors (Jolliffe and Bui, 2006). These figures are based on estimates by the festival organisers. The Buon Ma Thuot Coffee Festival was the first event of its kind in Vietnam that created an opportunity for coffee businesses and visitors to meet discuss coffee.

Observers interviewed noted that the festival proved to be a good coffee-related economic and cultural activity while at the same time advertising the trademark of Buon Ma Thuot Coffee. The local trade and tourism administration and local tourism companies realised, through the festival, the potential for promoting tourism through coffee. Subsequent to the festival the Department of Trade and Tourism began to think more about using coffee to develop a destination focus.

Components of the coffee festival included coffee pavilions, coffee-related seminars, a coffee trading floor, a coffee gastronomy night and cultural activities. According to the organisers a large percentage of visitors were from the coffee trade, with interests in purchasing and ordering coffee, collecting the latest market information, seeking cooperative partners, seeking products agencies and surveying the exhibition to participate next year. Industry specific tours included tours of wet coffee processing facilities and a tour of the powdered coffee processing workshop of the Trung Nguyen Coffee Company Limited in Buon Ma Thuot. A one-day conference was also held on Buon Ma Thuot Coffee. These characteristics make the coffee festival a trade event, although with the addition of events open to the public and the involvement of the local community the festival had added appeal as a tourism event.

The main festival sponsor was the Daklak People's Committee, represented by the Daklak Trade and Tourism Department. In addition the Vietnam National Administration of Tourism and the Vietnam National Coffee and Cocoa Association were acknowledged by the sponsors of the festival. The involvement of the national coordinating body for tourism could be seen as an initial recognition of the potential of the festival for tourism. Nestle Vietnam, a major client for the areas of Robusta coffee was also reported to have been a major sponsor. This reflects the trade interest in and character of the festival.

The festival included some province wide events, including a Central Highlands gastronomy night where 30,000 vouchers were issued for a free coffee drink at 26 coffee shops across the city of Buon Ma Thuot. This free coffee event was coordinated by the Daklak Trade and Tourism Department. Vouchers for a free coffee were distributed by tourism companies, hotels, to festival participants. Participating cafés were able to redeem the vouchers with the administration for 60% of the normal cost of a coffee thus indirectly sponsoring the event. Some cafés appreciated the opportunity to promote their establishments and to have a festival like atmosphere in their cafés with patrons drinking coffee all day. One café owner whose coffee shop had only been open a few months feels that this event contributed to promoting her shop. Other café owners felt the event allowed them to attract new clients who were able to experience the ambience and products of their café through the free coffee promotion. However, of the coffee shop owners interviewed on a random basis during our field work only 50% had participated in the free coffee promotion, and those who did not participate did not see the potential benefits. One of those who participated noted that the coffee suppliers should have borne some of the cost of the cafés providing the free coffee promotion by reducing the cost of the coffee supplied to cafés for the days of the promotion. Because the coffee is offered at a local price the café owners have a low markup on the coffee served.

Complimentary cultural events that included ethnic celebrations and performances at different locations as well as at Don Village with its UNESCO recognised Gong culture music. Attendance at these events was coordinated by a local tourism company (Ban Don Ecotourism Company Limited) who estimates that 2000 visitors participated. Tourism operators interviewed noted that these cultural festivities during the festival contributed to an increased interest in the destination.

During the 2005 festival a coffee farm tour was piloted by both Damsan Travel and Daklak Tourist Company (Nguyen, 2006) during the first coffee festival. The tours included visits to a coffee plantation, viewing the harvesting process and visiting a coffee processing company. Both companies had arrangements to visit the Victoria Coffee Company processing facility. Most of the participants in the tour were also visitors to the festival. This tour marked a cooperative venture between the coffee and tourism enterprises. The coffee producers, although reluctant at first to contemplate continuing the tour admitted recognition of the long-term benefits of exposing tourists to the Vietnamese coffee (Nguyen, 2006). After the festival both travel companies continued to offer these coffee tours. One operator interviewed reported that the interest in these half day tours is from international tourists from Europe and that there has been a continued demand for this product. Local guides lead the tours and the coffee farmers and the coffee company, both of whom are paid a small fee for their participation, often explain the processes to the visitors. However, during the visit to the coffee factory the visitors are not able to see all of the process, as the coffee companies have trade secrets they do not wish to share with visitors. For this reason as well other coffee companies are not willing to receive visitors and this factor could be an impediment to the expansion of coffee-related tours and tourism in the region. The potential for further development of the coffee tour product is reflected by the fact that of the coffee consumers surveyed in Hanoi 90% expressed interest in going on coffee tours to Daklak Province (Nguyen, 2006).

A number of respondents noted that community involvement in the cultural activities and exhibits was a key factor in implementing the coffee festival. Since the community provided a number of the cultural events everything was locally organised. However, in a community that is rich with festival activities and celebrations the coffee festival was also able to piggyback on existing cultural attractions, such as the Gong music performances in Don Village and Lak Lake.

The interviews with those who organised and participated in first festival provided insights into the evolving nature of the festival. The success elements identified by the respondents are summed up in Table 8.3. A conference on coffee and tourism was also held in 2007 and here the idea of developing Buon Ma Thuot as a coffee paradise that would include a coffee museum, a coffee research institute, every kind of coffee and coffee shop and a coffee themed resort was discussed by the entrepreneur behind the Trung Nguyen coffee empire (Daklak Trade and Promotion Centre, 2007b). The proposed coffee resort could act as a promotion for the Trung Nguyen coffee brand and at the same time could enhance the image of Daklak as a coffee destination.

Lessons learned by the festival organisers and the local tourism administration through the 2005 festival and subsequent to it led to plans for coffee weeks promoting Buon Ma Thuot Coffee in both Hanoi and Ho Chi Minh City in November of 2007. The two coffee weeks had six themes, one of which was a participatory coffee processing tours. The festival in Buon Ma Thuot will be held again in December of 2008 and biannually after that. These events reflect the destinations growing commitment to and recognition of coffee as a key driver of not only the local agricultural economy but also of a destination identity for the city and its region.

Table 8.3: Success elements of the Buon Ma Thuot Coffee Festival.

Community involvement	New partnerships and alliances in trade and tourism
Branding of Buon Ma Thuot coffee	Creation of a new product, the coffee tour
Branding of Buon Ma Thuot destination	Input into destination development thinking
Transfer of brand equity from coffee product to destination	Building business of local tourism enterprises
Media coverage of the coffee product, the destination and new 'coffee tourism' focus	Building business and awareness of local cafés

Source: Author interviews in Buon Ma Thuot, September 2007.

Analysis

A situation analysis can be used to gain a detailed understanding of an event's internal and external environment (Allen et al., 2005) and a strengths, weaknesses, opportunities and threats analysis (SWOT) is thus used here (Table 8.4). The points in the analysis reflect stakeholder perspectives and observations the researchers made in the process of field work.

The festival has a number of strengths that can be used by the organisers to diversify the festival product. In particular utilising the rich coffee landscape to develop additional tourism product could address the weakness in product diversification. New products, using existing resources could include coffee bike tours, a coffee trail or route, a coffee school, a coffee interpretation centre or museum, coffee wood carving items and souvenirs, and a coffee guide book. Coffee could also be packaged as a souvenir for tourists to purchase. The Trung Nguyen Coffee Company is one entity that has already recognised the potential for product diversification with their proposal for a coffee themed resort.

Table 8.4: SWOT analysis – Buon Ma Thuot Coffee Festival.

Strengths	Opportunities
• Location in a coffee producing area. • Rich landscape of coffee gardens and farms. • Festive culture of community. • Complimentary cultural tourism activities. • Broad cross section of stakeholder participation. • Community participation in the cultural components of the festival. • Lack of competition from other festivals due to the unique image of the coffee destination.	• Support branding Buon Ma Thuot coffee. • Transfer of the Buon Ma Thuot coffee brand to tourism. • Diversify activities available for tourists by concentrating on those relevant to the local coffee culture. • Create new tourism products, that is festival packages and tours. • Expand the coffee tourism season by extending programming to the coffee blossom time (March and April).
Weaknesses	**Threats**
• Location of destination away from the main tourist sites in Vietnam. • Low profile among domestic and international tourists. • Limited festival awareness beyond Vietnam. • Limited tourism-related activities within the festival. • Low level of understanding of event management. • Government restrictions and low private sector interest. • Lack of community involvement in the planning of the event.	• Competing purposes of trade and tourism. • Maintaining enthusiasm of festival organisers and community participants. • Several sites are not yet opened for tourism.

There are some critical weaknesses in tourism development in the province that will impede the development of the coffee festival and coffee-related tourism. This includes the isolated geographical location from the mainstream tourism flows and restrictions to visiting to places with distinctive natural and cultural tourism resources. As identified through the stakeholder interviews and the authors own coffee tour there is some local resistance towards tourist activities in coffee farms and at local processing facilities. While key stakeholders acknowledged community participation as a strength of the festival there is a lack of local communities' direct participation in the tourism development process. Another weakness may be the lack of festival management knowledge and skills on the part of the organisers, who are an organisation of local government and are not event specialists.

Addressing opportunities for the festival new products noted above could be used to extend the impact of the festival in the local area by encouraging visitors to take pre-festival and post-festival tours. Another opportunity identified by this research is the extension of the coffee event season to include the coffee blossom time in March. This was acknowledged by key stakeholders as the most beautiful season in the Central Highlands. It is significant that the tourist season parallels the cycle of coffee harvesting, production and the blossoming of new flowers for the next coffee crop. This should be seen as an opportunity to expand and extend the focus of coffee tourism visitation to the area beyond the period of the harvest, when most tourists are now encouraged to visit.

The competing purposes of trade and tourism within the Daklak Trade and Tourism Department could be viewed as a strength, as reported by those who were interviewed. However in some cases these dual purposes could work against each other and a few respondents mentioned that the Department sometimes places more focus on trading than on tourism. Another threat is that tourism infrastructure in the region is still being developed so not all areas could serve international tourists with a complete suite of services. Some tourism resources in the area are also not currently accessible to tourists.

Conclusion

The Buon Ma Thuot Coffee Festival is a recently constructed festival. Although initially intended to promote and market the coffee brand of the region, it has definitely had a secondary purpose and an impact as a tourism festival. The festival has numerous stakeholders that include coffee farmers and workers, the coffee trade, local officials and distributors, coffee companies, café owners, tourism companies and tourists, both domestic and international. For each of the stakeholders the festival has a different purpose. The location of the festival is a definite strength. Located in a coffee growing region the area is endowed with a coffee landscape of coffee fields, farms and processing facilities and Buon Ma Thuot also has a thriving café sector.

A review of the 2005 festival highlights the relationship of the festival to the community. The growing relationship between tourism and coffee has been nurtured by the festival. It provides a unique example of the use of a festival as a means to connect different business areas in forming a tourism and leisure product. The case illustrates the use of a festival to enhance both destination and product branding. It also identifies the need for product diversification in the area of coffee and tourism. A significant finding is the fact that the primary coffee tourism season (beginning with the coffee harvest at the end of November and ending with the coffee blossom time at the beginning of March) coincides with the primary tourism season at the location. This opens up opportunities for developing new tours not yet contemplated by the existing tour operators, for example at the coffee blossom time.

The connection between coffee and tourism has been established and is witnessed by the forma-tion of the Buon Ma Thuot Coffee Festival and by its evolution into associated events, contributing to both the branding of the coffee and tourism in the Daklak Province and the Buon Ma Thuot city. Continued study will contribute to understanding the festival as a part of the development of a cof-fee-related tourism destination. This could provide lessons for other agricultural destinations that wish to use the attributes of their major cash crops to brand their destinations as well as for the study of coffee tourism as a niche form of tourism, akin to tea tourism (Jolliffe, 2007b).

Future research could include surveying the visitors to the next festival. Research is needed on the motivations of visitors to the festival as well as of the economic impact of their visit. For exam-ple as Getz (1984) notes, to accurately measure the attribution of spending to the festival it is nec-essary to ask a specific question, such as was the festival the main reason for your visit and what proportion of your trip to this area is attributable to the event? Other aspects of the festival that could be researched include coffee tourism product development in Daklak Province; interests and contri-butions of the private sector to the coffee festival; impacts of this festival on the local community; and promotion of fair trade and pro-poor tourism approaches in this festival. Finally, further research could be undertaken on the feasibility of positioning and branding Buon Ma Thuot as a coffee desti-nation, a strategy that is supported by the case study findings.

Acknowledgements

The field research for this chapter was funded by the University of New Brunswick. The authors would like to thank those interviewed in Buon Ma Thuot and Mr. Nguyen Duc Hoa Cuong, Advisor to Daklak Trade and Tourism Department for commenting on a draft of this chapter.

References

Allen, J., O'Toole, W., McDonnell, L. and Harris, R. (2005) *Festival and Event Management*. Milton, QLD: John Wiley and Sons Australia Ltd.

Berger, A. (2005) *Vietnam Tourism*. New York: The Haworth Press.

Black, J. A. and Champion, D. J. (1976) *Methods and Issues in Social Research*. New York: John Wiley and Sons Ltd.

Boniface, P. (2003) *Tasting Tourism: Traveling for Food and Drink*. Aldershot, Hampshire: Ashgate.

Brenes, E. R., Bolanos, I., Burciaga, R., Jimeno, M. and Salas, F. (1997) Café Britt, S.A. *Journal of Business Research*, 38(1), 23–33.

Daklak Trade and Promotion Centre (2007a) Coffee exports reach 1.3 billion USD in seven months, www.daktra.com.vn, posted 7 August 2007 and accessed 15 September 2007.

Daklak Trade and Promotion Centre (2007b) Coffee paradise a dream come true for Vietnam, www.daktra.com.vn, posted 17 April 2007 and accessed 27 September 2007.

Daklak Trade and Tourism Department (2006) *Daklak Tourism Plan*. Daklak, Vietnam: Daklak Trade and Tourism Department, (in Vietnamese).

Daklak Trade and Tourism Department (2007) *Tourism Statistics*. Daklak, Vietnam: Daklak Trade and Tourism Department, (in Vietnamese).

Getz, D. (1984) Event tourism: Evaluating the impacts. In Ritchie, J. R. B. and Goeldner, C. R. (eds.), *Travel, Tourism and Hospitality Research: A Handbook for Managers*. New York: John Wiley and Sons, Inc., pp. 437–452.

Goodwin, H. (2006) Measuring and reporting the impact of tourism on poverty. Presented at the *Cutting Edge Research in Tourism: New Directions, Challenges and Applications Conference*, University of Surrey, 6–9 June.

Goss, M. J. and Brown, C. (2006) Tourist experiences in a lifestyle destination setting: The roles of involvement and place attachment. *Journal of Business Research*, 59, 696–700.

Hall, C. M., Mitchell, R. and Sharples, L. (2003) Consuming places: The role of food, wine and tourism in regional development. In Hall, C. M., Sharples, L., Mitchell, R., Macionis, N. and Cambourne, B. (eds.), *Food Tourism Around The World: Development, Management and Markets*. Oxford: Butterworth Heinemann, pp. 25–59.

Jolliffe, L. (2007a) Coffee and tourism: A research framework. Presented at *the 2nd International Conference on Tourism and Hospitality*, Universiti Utara Malaysia and the Department of National Heritage, Ministry of Culture, Arts and Heritage Malaysia, Putrajaya, Malaysia.

Jolliffe, L. (2007b) *Tea Tourism: Tourists, Traditions and Transformations*. Clevedon: Channel View Publications.

Jolliffe, L., and Bui, T. H. (2006) Coffee and tourism in Vietnam: A niche tourism product? Presented at the *Travel and Tourism Research Association – Canada Chapter Conference* at Montebello, Quebec.

Kilian, B., Jones, C., Pratt, L. and Villalobos, A. (2006) Is sustainable agriculture a viable strategy to improve farm income in Central America? A case study on coffee. *Journal of Business Research*, 59, 322–330.

Kona Coffee Cultural Festival (2007), http://www.konacoffeefest.com/, accessed 14 September 2007.

Long, L. (2004) *Culinary Tourism*. Lexington, KY: The University Press of Kentucky.

MacLeod, N. (2006) The placeless festival: Identity and place in the post-modern festival. In Picard, D. and Robinson, M. (eds.), *Festival Tourism and Social Change*. Clevedon: Channel View Publications, pp. 222–237.

Murray, S. (2002) Hanoi's café culture. *The Montreal Gazette*, 10 December.

Newman, W. L. (2006) *Social Research Methods*. New York: Pearson.

Nguyen, T. H. (2006). *Coffee and Tourism*, Graduation Thesis, Hanoi University, Vietnam, November.

O'Sullivan, D. and Jackson, M. J. (2002) Festival tourism: A contributor to sustainable local economic development. *Journal of Sustainable Tourism*, 10(4), 325–342.

Pitte, J. P. (2002) Geography of taste: Between globalization and local roots. In Montanari, A. (ed.), *Food and Environment, Geographies of Taste*. Rome: Societa Geografica Italiana.

Sterling, R. (2000) *World Food Vietnam*. Australia: Lonely Planet.

Thorn, J. (2006) *The Coffee Companion*. Philadelphia, PA: Running Press Book Publishers.

UNESCO (2005) The space of the gong culture in the Central Highlands of Vietnam proclaimed as masterpiece of the oral and intangible heritage of humanity. Media Release, Hanoi: UNESCO Vietnam, 25 November.

Vietnam National Tourism Administration (VNTA) (2006a) Tourism statistics in year 2006, at http://www.vietnamtourism.gov.vn, accessed 21 September 2007.

Vietnam National Tourism Administration (VNTA) (2006b) Daklak to invest in 20 tourism development projects, at http://www.vietnamtourism.gov.vn, accessed 27 September 2007.

Vietnam National Tourism Administration (VNTA) (2007) Tourism statistics in year 2007, at http://www.vietnamtourism.gov.vn, accessed 21 September 2007.

Wallengren, M. (2002) Asia's Small Coffee Origins. *Coffee International*, 179(9), Tea and Coffee Trade On-line at http://www.teaandcoffee.net, accessed 15 May 2007.

Yin, R. K. (1989) *Case Study Research: Design and Methods*. Newbury Park, CA: Sage.

Chapter 9

Tasting Australia: A Celebration of Cultural Identity or an International Event?

Graham Brown and Shirley Chappel

Introduction

Since 1997 the city of Adelaide in South Australia has hosted Tasting Australia, a biennial festival that attracts Australian and international celebrities who share an interest in food and drink. It can be regarded as an invented tradition, constructed to showcase Australian produce and promote Adelaide as a tourism destination. The emergence of tourism as a potentially important component of the South Australian economy necessitated the search for attractions that would serve to differentiate the state. Taking account of the South Australia's natural and cultural resources, the tourism authorities decided that the state should be positioned as a lifestyle destination, based on food, wine and festivals.

The addition of Tasting Australia to South Australia's ritual calendar is a component of the identity the state has invented for itself since the 1960s when, through the establishment of the international Festival of Arts, South Australia branded itself as the Festival State. Programmes presented at the festival indicate that its organisers have shown a preference for high culture and performances that challenge audiences to consider new ideas, non-European cultures and innovative approaches to artistic performance. Such programmes do not have universal appeal but do provide a pathway for those who see advantage in engaging in such cultural experiences to build up their cultural capital at a time when people's consumption practices are an indication of their preferred identity. An examination of the programmes for Tasting Australia suggests that it is like a gastronomic Festival of Arts and a survey of the history of the food and drink culture in South Australia, particularly in Adelaide, indicates the emergence of an elitist approach to food and wine from the 1980s onwards. However, the tastes of the mainstream population have not been neglected and South Australians have enthusiastically supported many of the events that have captured and focused international attention. They include the Grand Prix, the Tour Down Under and WOMAdelaide. The Fringe Festival that runs concurrently with the Festival of Arts has proven to be so successful that it is now held annually rather than only biennially.

International Perspectives of Festivals and Events
Copyright © 2009 by Elsevier Ltd.
All rights of reproduction in any form reserved.
ISBN: 978-0-08-045100-8

The chapter aims to show how Tasting Australia is a manifestation of recent developments in South Australia's socio-cultural and economic life. An analysis of the development of a food and drink culture in Australia provides the context for the discussion that will conclude by examining the extent to which Tasting Australia has emerged from a base, rooted in the local culture, to become an event of international significance.

Festivals and Place Identity

In his contribution to *Hosts and Guests Revisited: Tourism Issues of the 21st Century*, MacCannell (2001, p. 389) poses the question: 'As every destination comes increasingly to resemble every other destination, why leave home?' MacLeod (2006, p. 227) also notes the homogenisation of tourist destinations in her discussion of the 'place-less' post-modern festival. Festivals, she argues, take place in 'cities across the world that increasingly have more in common with each other than with the towns and villages of their own countries'. Furthermore, she asserts, festival organisers 'increasingly use common (and often interchangeable) themes and elements of spectacle to appeal to an increasingly international audience' (MacLeod, 2006, p. 228). Formerly, food was a marker of place and season at destinations but this need no longer be the case. Camporesi (1998, p. 202) asserts that refrigeration has compressed time and space so that, in relation to food provision, it can be any season of the year at any time and anywhere; 'the sea lies at the kitchen doorstep, distant lands are just a few metres away'. At the same time, cities compete with one another to stage events to attract festival-goers. George Lewis (1997, p. 77) suggests that 'rationally constructed' festivals have the potential to promote destinations successfully. The creators of such festivals identify the characteristics of a place and then invent a festival that takes account of those characteristics. In time, the 'rationally constructed' festival may become a tradition from which the destination gains an identity.

The identity of a place is 'that which provides its individuality or distinction from other places and serves as the basis for its recognition as a separate entity' (Lynch, 1960, p. 6 in Relph, (1976, p. 45). Relph identifies three components of place identity: the physical setting, the activities of the people, and the meanings people attach to the place (ibid.). Human activity complements the physical setting and is influenced by it (Relph, 1976, pp. 46–47). Relph (1976, p. 58) distinguishes between the public and the mass identity of a place. The public identity comprises the agreement of local people concerning its physical features 'and other verifiable components' (ibid.). The mass identity of a place, however, is 'assigned by "opinion-makers", provided ready-made for the people, disseminated through the mass media and especially by advertising' (ibid.).

Since the advent of tourism as a major economic activity, the 'opinion-makers' have identified South Australia as a festival state. Beginning with the Adelaide Festival of Arts in 1960, high culture was the focus for the Festival State. As time went on, food and wine festivals and multicultural festivals were added to South Australia's public rituals. The creators of these festivals used the natural and cultural characteristics of the state in the construction of the events. Tasting Australia is a 'rationally constructed' festival that reflects South Australia's constructed identity as a festival state in which the emphasis is on food and drink experiences. In the brochure for the first Tasting Australia in 1997, Adelaide was described as being 'renowned for its restaurants and café lifestyle' (Tasting Australia, 1997). Long-term residents of the city would have known that this identity was of recent origin.

South Australia – the Festival State

The development of South Australia's identity as the Festival State in the 1960s owed much to the initiative of music professor, John Bishop. Inspired by the Edinburgh Festival, Bishop played a leading role in the establishment of the biennial Adelaide Festival of Arts in 1960. The event has been held ever since. Like Edinburgh, Adelaide is regarded as the 'the ideal size for a major celebration of all arts' (Campbell, 2001, p. 26). The size of the city also enables festival-goers to move easily between venues. Like many other festivals with which Adelaide has become associated, the Festival of Arts takes advantage of the city's mild Mediterranean climate (although somewhat affected now by climate change), thus enabling many events to be held outdoors. To enhance Adelaide's status as the focal point of the Festival State, the government of South Australia also gave its approval to the building of a Festival Centre. The Centre's location on the lawn-fringed banks of the River Torrens takes advantage of the scenic beauty of the city as a backdrop for festive activities. According to Campbell (2001, p. 27), the Adelaide Festival of Arts 'changed city and state from a cultural whistlestop to one of the world's leading arts destinations'. By the time of the inauguration of Tasting Australia in 1997, Adelaide had come to accept its image as an international destination for the arts, including food and drink, as aesthetic experiences.

In the development of its identity as the Festival State, South Australia has also identified community-based content for its festivities. Its fame as a wine-producing state has enabled it to develop local festivals in the tradition of harvest festivals in other times and in other parts of the world. These festivals combine the wine experience with food, cultural heritage and the scenic beauty of the locations where they are held. In doing so, they have contributed to the state's gastronomic reputation now exemplified in Tasting Australia.

Australia's Food and Drink Culture

Australian interest in food and drink experiences as an aspect of the 'finer things of life' is a relatively recent development. In the early days of European settlement in Australia, except in the homes of the affluent, the life of the pioneers was difficult, leaving little opportunity for the enjoyment of food as an aesthetic experience. Meat played a dominant role in the culinary culture of the time. 'To have the full taste of meat [in the nineteenth century] was to be an Australian' (Blainey, 2003, p. 202). Oysters, now a component of a fine dining experience, 'were not a food for the wealthy or those arranging a celebration' (Blainey, 2003, p. 304). Oysters were a popular working-class dish. The heavy manual labour of the times caused Australians to rejoice 'in meat and potatoes more than lettuces and salads because their hunger was thereby satisfied' (Blainey, 2003, p. 311). Gourmets were not, however, totally absent from colonial Australia. Symons (2007, p. 266) notes their presence in Australia during the gold rush. Nor was the cuisine totally Anglo-Celtic at that time. Even before the gold rush of the 1850s which brought large numbers of Chinese to Australia, Chinese cooks worked on sheep and cattle stations cooking mainly western-style food but, at the same time, introducing some Chinese flavours and dishes (Shun Wah and Aitkin, 1999, p. 11). The arrival of German immigrants in South Australia in the 19th century also added a foreign element to the food culture. The café society, regarded as an important component of Australia's contemporary food and drink culture, flourished in the period 1890–1910 but did not survive the economic hardships of the period of World War I (Blainey, 2003, pp. 405–406).

In colonial Australia, wine and coffee, major components of contemporary food and drink culture, were the drinks of non-Anglo-Celtic Australians while tea was the most popular beverage (Blainey, 2003, pp. 349 and 367). Coffee, in fact, was sometimes used as a disinfectant rather than as a beverage (Blainey, 2003, p. 368). In the late 19th century, most Australians did not drink wine. Beer, instead, was the drink of the working-class and its consumption became a mark of Australian male identity. 'The idea of mateship [allegedly an Australian core value] virtually demands a male-dominated barroom scene for its expression – and a round of beers' (Dunstan, 1988, p. 107). Australians in the 19th and early 20th centuries had a reputation for drunkenness and, consequently, a strong temperance movement developed (Dunstan, 1988, p. 120). Another outcome of the problem of drunkenness was the six o'clock closing of hotels which resulted in the 'frantic, disgusting effort to drink as much as you could before the pub closed' (Dunstan, 1988, p. 120). Downes (2002, p. 11) attributes this so-called 'six o'clock swill' to Methodism and brands it as 'the hallmark of a culture that encouraged the worst kind of drinking in the name of promoting sobriety'.

In the period following World War II, for a number of reasons, this culture underwent significant changes. The travels of Australians in Europe in the post-war period taught the travellers that 'there was more than steak and eggs, and chips and tomato sauce' (Symons, 2007, p. 261). Young Australian travellers in Europe noted 'the civilised use of table wine as an everyday beverage, a practice with which their parents were as a rule totally unfamiliar' (Beeston, 1995, p. 202). Young Australians travelled in Asia and, often because local food was cheap, tried it and liked it. The change in culture is also attributed to Australia's post-war migration policy which brought to the country large numbers of people from continental Europe. This influx resulted, among other things, in the establishment of European-style restaurants in which the serving of table wines was commonplace. With this example and with the discretionary income made available by the prosperity of the 'lucky country', Australians began to experiment with 'lifestyle' (Beeston, 1995, p. 192). For many Australians, of course, adapting to the new ways was challenging. Social researcher, Hugh MacKay (1993, p. 166), notes the experience of one of his interviewees who did not believe that his wife was serious when she presented him with a bowl of spaghetti instead of his meat and vegetables and he admitted that it took him some time to become accustomed to the new diet. Nevertheless, the new food and drink practices eventually became widespread within the Australian community and fused with the food styles of Asia to create a distinct Australian cuisine.

In South Australia, the revolution in the food and drink culture became associated with the idea of 'lifestyle', which became a major selling point for the tourism industry. The Premier of South Australia, Don Dunstan, inspired South Australians to be gastronomically adventurous through his 'frank public admissions of a love of food and wine and fine living' (Downes, 2002, p. 51). He removed the 'six o'clock swill' liquor laws and encouraged South Australians to engage in outdoor eating. He published his own cookbook and established his own restaurant (Downes, 2002, p. 51). Believing that South Australia's economic future would be enhanced by promoting a 'lifestyle economy', he encouraged the establishment of a School of Food and Catering and made Adelaide 'the cradle of Australian cooking' (ibid.). He looked forward to the development of an Australian cuisine that would meld 'the cooking techniques of our Asian neighbours' and 'the European traditions' with which Australians were now more familiar (Downes, 2002, p. 54). The presence in Adelaide at the time of several important chefs assisted in the achievement of this dream.

Food historian, Michael Symons, added an elitist note to the food and drink culture being fostered in South Australia. Believing that people needed to do more talking and philosophising about food and its cultural significance, he joined with people of like mind in organising dinners at which the diners simulated the philosophical discussions of the thinker, Epicurus, in ancient Athens (Downes, 2002, p. 117). The crowning achievement of this development was the convening of the First Symposium of Australian Gastronomy in Adelaide in March, 1984.

Tasting Australia is the inheritor of an invented tradition that began with the inauguration of the Adelaide Festival of Arts which was designed to bring international visitors to Australia to enjoy high culture. Since that time, South Australian communities, wishing to engage in the tourism economy, have examined the state's cultural and natural resources in order to identify potential attractions. From this examination has emerged the idea of the lifestyle destination in which the enjoyment of food and drink plays a key role. At the same time, interest in the study of food and drink has grown steadily as is evident in the availability of university courses, books and television programmes about food and drink as well as wine-tasting courses and cookery schools at international tourist destinations. These factors, combined with the fostering of a gastronomic culture in Adelaide by identities such as Don Dunstan and Michael Symons, made Adelaide an ideal destination for the staging of Tasting Australia.

Tasting Australia as an International Event

The Festival Programme in 2003 claimed that Tasting Australia has 'become a must-do-event on the world's gastronomic calendar' (Tasting Australia, 2003) but can an event which has such a strong national theme and which is supported, unashamedly, by local food and wine products, be considered to be an international event? This question will be discussed in the remainder of the chapter by examining criteria related to participation, the type of events that form part of the festival and the origin of sponsors and people who attend the festival. The information used in the discussion is drawn from a number of sources including a report by consultants that included the findings of interviews conducted with 522 people at the festival and a post-event telephone survey of 1000 local residents. Additional information is drawn from research projects conducted by students studying the Master of Management degree at the University of South Australia, interviews by the authors with festival organisers and sponsors and analysis of festival programmes and event brochures.

The Festival was certainly international in its conception as the idea was formed when the Event Director, Ian Parmenter, was in France in 1996. He was in Dauville to receive an award for his television show, Consuming Passions, at the Festival Internationale de la Tele-Gourmande where he canvassed the level of interest among the international media in attending a food festival in Australia. The establishment of the World Food Media Awards as part of Tasting Australia became the vehicle to entice the media to the event that was held for the first time in 1997. By 2003, it was claimed that 170 food and wine media 'from all over the world converge in Adelaide, and are feted and taken on day trips around the region to taste Australia' (Howells, 2003). In 2005, media coverage was estimated 'to be worth $10 million in key markets such as the United States, Germany and New Zealand' (Love, 2005).

Participation by overseas food and drink professionals has been a prominent theme in event promotion. Although the programme in 2003 revealed that only 19 of the 74 listed participants were from overseas, this does not accurately reflect the scale of international contributions. Many of the 55 participants who now live in Australia were born, trained and gained professional experience in other countries, particularly France, Germany and Italy. The international profile of participants and the blending of Australian and overseas contributions have remained strong features of the festival. The latter is illustrated by a local newspaper report of the event that marked the opening of the 2005 Festival.

He had come from the other side of the globe to cook, chat and flash his familiar generous Italian smile. She had driven from the Barossa valley, full of the joys of spring and seasonal bounty. Together, the pair of world- famous foodies, Antonio Carluccio and Maggie Beer, turned on the burners yesterday in a special demonstration kitchen at David Jones Food Hall to serve the first course of this year's food, wine and beer festival (Love, 2005).

They prepared a 'classic Italian veal cutlet dish using fresh local herbs, Murray River pink salt, and SA verjuice' that was described as a 'collaboration between Australia and Italy' (Love, 2005). The geographical mix of participants in 2007 was similar to that of 2003 but, once again, international visitors were highlighted in promotional activities. The greatest prominence was accorded to the Indian writer Madhur Jaffrey, Antonio Carluccio from Italy, Rick Stein from England and Rachel Allen from Ireland.

It is not surprising that a relationship is evident between participant characteristics and the events that form part of Tasting Australia. However, with over 100 events in the festival a wide variety of topics are included, reflecting issues at different geographical scales. The range of local food and wine products and information about their quality and use are reflected in a large number of events with a local focus, as illustrated in Table 9.1. An opportunity to interact with local producers features prominently and seven Farmers' Markets, held in regions of South Australia, are included in festival.

Regions outside the host state were represented by entrants in the Australian Regional Culinary competition. The teams of chefs, apprentices and trainees had three hours to produce a three-course menu with an emphasis on food and produce grown in the regions they represented. The festival included many cooking demonstrations and while some focused on indigenous produce that is unique to Australia others presented overseas traditions as reflected in sessions titled Tastes of India, Celtic Connection, The Italian Job and C'est Francais. However, the impact of globalisation on food and wine may render irrelevant an attempt to determine the relative importance of geographical regions to Tasting Australia. Presenting food as a journey may be more relevant, as illustrated by an event devoted to the method of yakitori at which 'the 12 courses are served, tracing this cuisine's epic journey from Spain and Portugal, to Japan, and, 250 years later, to Adelaide, Australia' (Tasting Australia, 2007).

Table 9.1: Events with a local focus.

Title of event	Program description
Meet the Producers of McLaren Vale	Meet – local cheese-makers, butchers, sausage makers and grape growers for a hands-on day exploring wine and seasonal organic food
Gourmet Retreat Lunch with Madhur Jaffrey	Using the best of the Fleurieu Peninsula spring produce and matched with wines from the Chapel Hill winery range
Five Tastes from Richard Gunner's Coorong Angus Beef	Featuring various cuts from the famed Coorong Angus Beef to highlight the individual flavour and texture
Taste of Success – a Gala Event	Feast on the finest South Australian food and wine
A Sumptuous Taste of South Australia Dinner	Celebrating South Australia as the Gourmet State. Showcasing award-winning food producers matched with Penfolds Premium Bin wines.

The Australian Regional Culinary competition has been sponsored by the Lifestyle Food Channel since 1991 as it was considered to be an excellent vehicle to enhance the credibility of the channel with the food industry (Hook, 2003). A number of sponsors have agreed to remain as sponsors for 'the next two or three events' (Fleming, 2007) and media organisations such as television channels and magazines that feature food and wine are natural sponsors of Tasting Australia as are local food and wine producers. So, the involvement of Fox Creek Wines, Haigh's Chocolates and the olive oil producer, Cobram Estates, is not surprising. These local companies are joined as sponsors by the South Australia Museum, the Hyatt Regency Adelaide and the training and educational organisation, TAFE SA, which serve as venues for the events. Very few international organisations have sponsored Tasting Australia which is owned and underwritten by the Government of South Australia.

The World Food Media Awards offers an attractive sponsorship platform and Jacobs Creek, Wolf Blass and Le Cordon Bleu have acted as sponsors of the Awards in 2003, 2005 and 2007, respectively. The sponsorship manager of Jacobs Creek has claimed the Awards placed the wine company in front of the world's leading food and wine media and had 'huge reach' with:

- Entry forms sent around the world
- Applications judged by international experts in food, wine and the media
- The Awards ceremony serving as a showcase and networking opportunity
- The sponsor's name appearing on the 'ladles' awarded to winners and on the logo that could be used by winners for two years (Ramke, 2003).

In 2007, Australia provided 41% of nominees for the awards and the remaining 59% came from 10 different countries, dominated by the United Kingdom, with 22%, and the United States, with 19% (Table 9.2). Not only are these the same countries that have dominated the awards in previous years but certain companies and individuals feature prominently on each occasion. This pattern may support the view that the awards have become the exclusive domain of a group of regular participants who encourage applicants from within the group and their network of contacts. However, despite the host country bias and the dominance of applications from English-speaking countries, the title World Awards can be justified as entries are encouraged from around the world and thirteen countries were represented by the 77 people who judged the awards. Members of the jury came from a diverse range of countries including India, Malaysia, France, Italy, the Netherlands, Ireland, the United Kingdom and the United States. The nature of the presenters and recipients at the Awards ceremony help create an international atmosphere and the after-party has been described by the event's director as 'a cross between the Logies and the Oscars' (Fleming, 2007). Inclusion of the World Food Media Awards represents one of the main justifications for Tasting Australia to be accorded the status of an international event.

Another important measure of whether Tasting Australia can be classed as an international event is the extent to which the festival attracts overseas visitors. It has been estimated that approximately 70,000 people attend Tasting Australia events of which approximately 30,000 attend the large public event, Feast for the Senses, on the banks of the Torrens River (Howells, 2003). A survey of people attending the event found that 84% were residents of Adelaide. Respondents recorded high levels of satisfaction with the festival (48% – very satisfied, 38% – satisfied) and there was strong agreement with the statement that 'Tasting Australia is a good way of showing South Australia to the rest of the world' (strongly agree – 54%, agree – 36%) (Howells, 2003). This demonstrates strong local interest in the festival but this is in contrast with the demand expressed by international tourists. Only 3% of people attending Tasting Australia come from overseas (Howells, 2003).

Table 9.2: 2007 World Food Media Awards-Country of Nominees.

Best Food and/or Drink Photography		Best Drink Photography		Best Food Photography	
Website					
USA	2	USA	4	UK	3
Australia	2	Australia	1	Australia	2
UK	1	New Zealand	1	USA	1
New Zealand	1			Belgium	1
Best Children's Cookery		**Best Health and Nutrition**		**Best Professional**	
Cookbook		*Book*		*Book*	
UK	2	Australia	3	Belgium	2
Australia	2	UK	2	Australia	1
		USA	1	New Zealand	1
		Canada	1		
Best Drink Guidebook		**Best Food Guidebook**		**Best Wine Book**	
Australia	4	UK	2	USA	2
		Australia	2	UK	2
		Malaysia	1	Australia	1
				Canada	1
Best Drink Journalist		**Best Food Journalist**		**Best Restaurant Critic**	
UK	2	Australia	3	Australia	3
Australia	2	UK	2	UK	2
USA	1	USA	1	USA	1
Canada	1	Canada	1		
New Zealand	1				
Ireland	1				
Best Food and/or Drink		**Best Food and/or Drink**		**Best Food Magazine**	
Section in a Newspaper		*Section in a Magazine*			
Australia	3	Australia	3	Australia	4
USA	1	New Zealand	2	USA	2
New Zealand	1	USA	1	New Zealand	1
Best Drink Magazine		**Best Food and/or Drink**		**Best Food and/or Drink**	
		Television Show		*Television Segment*	
Australia	2	USA	4	Australia	2
USA	1	Australia	3	Switzerland	1
New Zealand	1	UK	1		

(Continued)

Table 9.2: (Continued)

Best Soft Cover		Best Hard Cover		Best Food Book	
Recipe Book		*Recipe Book*			
Australia	4	Australia	6	UK	5
UK	2	UK	4	Australia	2
New Zealand	2	USA	4	Canada	1
Canada	1	Singapore	2		
South Africa	1				
Belgium	1				

Conclusion

It has been suggested that one of the challenges for events is how to function in an increasingly global environment while expressing the uniqueness of local communities (McDonnell et al., 1999) but food and wine festivals are ideally suited to achieve these mixed objectives. Tasting Australia is, in many ways, a very successful event. It is a product of a local culture that has been shaped by globalisation and, while many of the events that form part of the festival remain inextricably linked to local products, information about South Australia is communicated across the globe. The information that is projected serves to promote the local products and the resources on which they depend.

The participation of overseas food and wine professionals and media representatives helps create a cosmopolitan atmosphere at many of the events but Tasting Australia has failed to capture the attention of international tourists. This is a missed opportunity and the situation is unlikely to change unless a targeted promotional campaign is conducted. The scale and complexity of the festival will require the development of packages that are designed to meet the needs of clearly defined groups, with segmentation based on levels of consumer involvement with food and wine. The packages could be promoted to clubs and societies as well as through more traditional media vehicles such as food and wine magazines.

The World Food Media Awards may be considered to be another missed opportunity. It is very successful in terms of its reach to people in a number of countries who are members of the Tasting Australia food, wine and media network and the Awards ceremony is enjoyed by those who are invited to attend. The opportunity does not concern making the Awards ceremony open to the public; it concerns making the event more visible. By communicating more information about the World Awards and the food and wine celebrities who attend the ceremony, an opportunity is afforded to enhance beliefs about South Australia's international status and its position as Australia's food and wine state, thereby reaffirming this aspect of cultural identity for local residents.

References

Beeston, J. (1995) *A Concise History of Australian Wine* (2nd edn). St. Leonard's, New South Wales: Allen and Unwin.

Blainey, G. (2003) *Black Kettle and Full Moon: Daily Life in a Vanished Australia*. Camberwell: Victoria, Viking.

Campbell, L. (2001) Adelaide festival of arts. In Prest, W., Round, K. and Fort, C. (eds.), *The Wakefield Companion to South Australian History*. Kent Town, South Australia: Wakefield Press, pp. 26–27.

Camporesi, P. (1998) *The Magic Harvest: Food, Folklore and Society*. Cambridge, U.K.: Polity Press, Translated by J.K. Hall.

Downes, S. (2002) *Advanced Australian Fare*. Crow's Nest, New South Wales: Allen and Unwin.

Dunstan, D. (1988) Boozers and Wowsers. In Burgmann, B. and Lee, J. (eds.), *Constructing a Culture: A People's History of Australia since 1788*. Fitzroy, Victoria: McPhee Gribble/Penguin, pp. 96–123.

Fleming, K. (2007) Tasting success. *Adelaide Matters*, October(10), 18.

Hook, S. (2003) Interview with the General Manager of the Lifestyle Channel. *Sydney*, September(17).

Howells, H. (2003) *Evaluation of Outcomes Associated with Tasting Australia*. Harrison Market Research Consultants.

Lewis, G. H. (1997) Celebrating asparagus: Community and the rationally constructed food festival. *Journal of American Culture*, 20(4), 73–78.

Love, T. (2005) Top tastes attract 70,000 for festival. *The Adelaide Advertiser*, October(22), 3.

Lynch, K. (1960) *The image of the city*. Cambridge, Mass: MIT Press.

MacCannell, D. (2001) Remarks on the commodification of cultures. In Smith, V. L. and Brent, M. (eds.), *Hosts and Guests Revisited: Tourism Issues of the 21st Century*. New York: Cognizant Communication Corporation, pp. 380–390.

MacKay, H. (1993) *Reinventing Australia: The Mind and Mood of Australia in the 90s*. Pymble, New South Wales: Angus and Robertson.

MacLeod, N. E. (2006) The placeless festival: Identity and place in the post-modern festival. In Picard, D. and Robinson, M. (eds.), *Festivals, Tourism and Social Change: Remaking Worlds*. Clevedon, U.K.: Channel View Publications.

McDonnell, I., Allen, J. and O'Toole, W. (1999) *Festival and Event Management*. Milton, Qld: John Wiley & Sons.

Ramke, S. (2003) Interview with the Sponsorship Manager, Jacob's Creek, Adelaide, September(23).

Relph, E. (1976) *Place and Placelessness*. London: Pion Limited.

Shun Wah, A. and Aitkin, G. (1999) *Banquet: Ten Courses to Harmony*. Sydney: Doubleday.

Symons, M. (2007) *One Continuous Picnic: A Gastronomic History of Australia*. Carlton, Victoria: Melbourne University Press.

Tasting Australia (1997) *A Feast for the Senses*. Festival Program, Government of South Australia.

Tasting Australia (2003) *Taste the Magic*. Festival Program, Government of South Australia.

Tasting Australia (2007) *Ten years and growing*. Festival Program, Government of South Australia.

Chapter 10

Festivals and Tourism in Rural Economies

Emma H. Wood and Rhodri Thomas

Introduction

Creating a programme of festivals and events is often seen by local policy makers as an imaginative response to creating distinctiveness. This is seen as important in an age where 'place competition', or competition for visitors between destinations, is high on the economic-development agenda. The challenge seems to have become not whether events can produce positive returns to the local economy but how to differentiate one programme, and what it says about a place (in reality what it *can do* for a place), from another. This is not surprising. After all, there is considerable evidence of positive (but also negative) legacies arising from investment in events and they certainly have scope for attracting media attention if the 'right' choices are made.

Much of the research on the impacts of festivals has been undertaken in urban contexts. However, in practice, rural economic policy makers struggling to encourage tourism have also joined the bandwagon; building festivals around local produce, art forms and sport. For many, it seems that festivals have become the elixir of rural economic regeneration.

This chapter examines the impact of small-scale festivals of rural economies by way of an evaluation of three contrasting case studies. What emerges is a clearer understanding of the type of festival which most benefits the local economy in terms of visitor expenditure and a valuable insight into the other, often greater, benefits to local people. The chapter begins by reviewing very briefly some of the conceptual issues that are germane to impact assessments and the existing research on the impacts and importance of rural festivals. This discussion is followed by the case studies, each of which is located in different parts of rural Wales. Data were gathered from interviews with the organiser of the events, those attending the events, local businesses (at the events and within close proximity), and residents who did not attend. The research focuses on issues affecting the community as well as the local economy.[1]

---

[1] The research reported here was part of a wider project undertaken with colleagues at UKCEM (Thomas et al., 2006).

International Perspectives of Festivals and Events
Copyright © 2009 by Elsevier Ltd.
All rights of reproduction in any form reserved.
ISBN: 978-0-08-045100-8

Understanding the Impacts of Events

Official justification for public expenditure on festivals and events is usually couched in economic terms. Benefits are said to arise both directly and indirectly from the increased number of visitors attracted to an area who then spend locally. Figure 10.1 represents a typical summary of how the economic impacts of events are often presented. This kind of income multiplier is useful because it highlights the importance of recognising the role of imports and savings (i.e. they reduce the impact of expenditure) but the diagram is still an incomplete representation of the impacts of event expenditure. It is partial because it fails to draw attention to other potentially important considerations. It ignores the question of whether the event has displaced expenditure elsewhere, for example. Clearly, there are no net economic gains locally if people have simply switched from spending in one part of the locality to another. These and other considerations need to be borne in mind when estimating the impact of events on a local economy. (For a full discussion of economic multipliers, see Crompton, 1995 and Richardson, 1985.)

There have been a number of studies in the last decade that have attempted to quantify the economic benefits to the local area associated with hosting a rural festival or event. These have used a variety of measures building on input–output models and economic multipliers. The results appear to suggest that the economic benefit is often less than is justified by the public expenditure on the event. For example, Jones and Munday (2001) and Yu and Turco (2000) identify, via examination of several case studies, that rural communities will not benefit significantly from the indirect and induced expenditure accrued through events unless they have a developed hospitality and transportation infrastructure. If not, they may well achieve high visitor numbers but the additional expenditure leaks out through outsourced suppliers and out of area accommodation. Moreover, as Yu and Turco (2000, p. 147) put it: 'This leakage problem is particularly obvious in remote and rural communities where the current levels of service-oriented infrastructure and industry are not adequate to

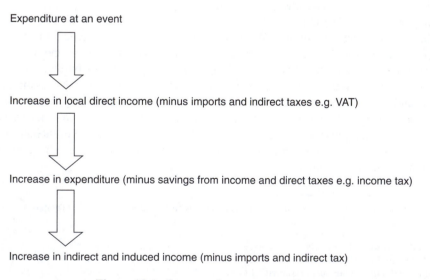

Figure 10.1: Impact of events expenditure.

capture visitor spending.' The policy challenge is how to develop this kind of 'infrastructure' before, or simultaneously with, generating a market demand.

Chhabra et al. (2003) undertook a detailed study on the economic impact of two Highland games held in rural South Carolina. Although there was a positive economic impact, it was found to be relatively small. Income multipliers were low as a result of substantial leakages from the local economies. Although a small number of sectors benefited from the games, there was limited interaction among the sectors, and there was a tendency to purchase inputs from other regions.

Felsenstein and Fleischer (2003, p. 391) used a new framework to evaluate the economic impacts of two local festivals in rural Israel. Rather than a significant economic benefit, they found that local festivals have an 'important "signaling" effect that may in some instances complement or equal the more tangible economic effects with which they are commonly associated'. They suggest that 'the continued high levels of public support for festivals and the relatively modest levels of local economic growth that they yield seem to indicate some form of non-market benefit (such as local image creation) associated with the festival'. However, this continued public investment could just as easily be due to policy makers' lack of understanding of the likely economic benefits due to a lack of strategic planning and investment in post-event evaluation and realistic impact studies (Thomas and Wood, 2003). Felsenstein and Fleischer conclude that economic development practitioners and policy makers need to incorporate non-market measures of value when analysing festivals as instruments of tourism promotion.

One such measure of value is the festival's propensity to change the image of the area both within and outside the local community. Jago et al. (2003) used a number of workshops to investigate current issues and practice around events and destination marketing. One of the findings suggests that a barrier to using events to promote and build destination image successfully is a lack of cooperation between tourism policy makers and event managers but that such organisational cooperation was seen to be higher in small rural towns. It should be noted, however, that even highly successful large-scale festivals may have little impact in changing long-standing perceptions of a region (Prentice and Anderson, 2003).

In New Zealand, a survey of rural event organisers showed that despite a proliferation of events and an apparent willingness to modify traditional events in order to maximise event tourism benefits there is little strategic planning. The authors suggest that with initiative and a close working relationship between local authorities and tourism organisations, 'rural event producers can work cooperatively to create an integrated regional event tourism product to further serve the interests of the region' (Higham and Ritchie, 2001, p. 48).

There are, of course, far greater benefits to these 'home grown' community festivals than mere economic growth (O'Sullivan and Jackson, 2002). They can also provide a showcase for local talents and outlets for local products, 'create a positive image of the host community, instill community pride, promote clean-ups and fix-ups and make business sponsors happy' (Mayerfield and Crompton, 1995, p. 41). Janniskee and Drews (1998) also argue that rural festivals attract tourists who would otherwise go elsewhere and through this influx of newcomers serve to strengthen the communities and enrich the quality of small town life. However, commodification of traditions may also represent a threat and ultimately lead to less tourist interest arising from the dilution of community history and practices (Xie, 2004).

The community themselves must also be willing to embrace tourist interest generated by their traditional and non-traditional events. Wilson et al. (2001) studied six rural communities in Iowa, USA, and found that those who were deemed to have been successful at generating increased tourism

Table 10.1: Summary of potential tangible benefits and costs of hosting events and festivals.

Tangible benefits	Tangible costs
• Increased revenue to local economy, mainly via local businesses • Job creation • Positive media coverage and images • Sponsorship opportunities • Revenue generation from charges	• Cost of essential services such as police, cleaning, etc. • Costs of promotion • Direct costs of staging the event such as entertainers

Sources: Carlsen (2004), Daniels et al. (2004), De Bres and Davis (2001), Dwyer et al. (2001a, b), Fredline et al. (2003), Gursoy et al. (2004), Hall (1992), Jones (2001), Mehmetoglu (2002), Wood (2005), Wood and Thomas (2005).

Table 10.2: Summary of potential intangible benefits and costs of hosting events and festivals.

Intangible benefits	Intangible costs
• Enhanced or maintained community pride • Cultural renewal • Increased interest and investment in the host destination • Enhanced commercial and residential property values in the long term • Development of social capital (networks, interpersonal trust) • Development of human capital (various organisational and other transferable skills) • Inter-cultural contact	• Crowding and inconvenience to residents • Noise and visual pollution • Crime • Poor reputation and image if the event is badly organised • Potential for inter-cultural misunderstanding

Sources: Carlsen (2004), Daniels et al. (2004), De Bres and Davis (2001), Derrett (2003), Dwyer et al. (2001a, b), Fredline et al. (2003), Gursoy et al. (2004), Hall (1992), Lee and Crompton (2003), Ryan and Lockyer (2001), Wood (2005), Wood and Thomas (2005).

had also developed special events associated with local tourist attractions, such as 'fishing tournaments for communities with outdoor tourist recreation attractions and historical festivals for towns with historic sites'. They conclude that these 'special events not only have drawn tourists to the area but have helped promote local tourism as a package'. However, it is not clear whether the events followed or preceded the development of tourism in the region. It appears, in many cases, that festivals are developed to meet the presumed needs of an existing tourist market rather than as a catalyst to develop tourism first.

Tables 10.1 and 10.2 highlight commonly accepted benefits and costs of hosting events and festivals. The precise blend of benefits and costs will vary on a case-by-case basis.

Clearly, tables such as these cannot capture the full extent of potential impacts of events and festivals. Their value is that they demonstrate that the intangible benefits and costs may be significant, and that these often transcend the economic.

From a policy perspective, a number of issues arise from the research insights introduced above. First, an immediate and tangible return on investment is unlikely. The second is that the tourism and hospitality 'infrastructure' in the area needs to be developed to leverage potential economic benefits from rural festivals. Finally, engaging in strategic planning of festival programmes, service sector development and oganisational integration over a wider region will help gain increased benefits from festival hosting.

Case Studies

Very few studies have been undertaken to determine the impact of smaller scale events on rural communities. This section considers the impact of three types of event – a food festival, a music festival and an arts festival held in different areas of rural Wales. The findings of these case studies are summarised below. Each study used survey data collected from festival visitors, stallholders, sponsors, local businesses and local residents to provide an indication of the social and economic benefits and costs associated with each case study event. The net economic benefit quoted for each case is based on average expenditure per person which was in addition to normal expenditure within the area and adjusted for those who spent less because of the festival (i.e. avoided shopping locally).

Case 1: Llangollen Food Festival

The eighth Llangollen Food Festival took place at the Royal International Pavilion, Llangollen on 15 and 16 October 2005, and was sponsored by European Union (EU) LEADER+, Cadwyn Clwyd, Snowdonia Cheese Company, Denbighshire County Council, Flintshire County Council, Food Wales, Regional Development Wales and Village Dairy. The event, advertised as one of the first and most successful food festivals in Wales, exhibited the produce of over 70 local and Welsh speciality food producers, together with producers from as far away as Italy, Portugal, Sweden and Poland. Growth in the event is demonstrated by the move from the hall to the main arena at Royal International Pavilion in order to accommodate increasing exhibitors and visitor numbers. The festival was originally launched to help the developing cluster of food companies in Denbighshire showcase their Welsh produce, but has broadened in recent years to incorporate an increasing range of International produce, some representing towns and regions from European countries where relationships are developing. Llangollen Food Festival is identified in the Denbighshire County Council 'Visitor Economy Strategy for the Dee Valley' (September 2005) as having the potential to expand and develop further, while with additional promotion, it may provide an opportunity to encourage the short-break tourist market.

The results of a number of surveys undertaken in and around the festival indicate that:

- Visitors to the festival were typically part of a couple (58%) aged between 45 and 64 (48%), and lived locally (72% lived in the Llangollen and surrounding postal area).
- The vast majority of visitors (86%) enjoyed the event very much, rising to 99% when those enjoying it to some extent are added.
- Forty-six per cent of the respondents would have been spending money in the area had there not been a festival.
- The Llangollen Food Festival had an estimated positive net impact on expenditure in Llangollen to the value of £58,560.

- Exhibitors were positive about the benefits of the event, noting particularly its impact on the awareness and custom for their organisation and the image of the area.
- Local businesses also endorsed the value of the festival and tended to emphasise indirect benefits such as image enhancement, attracting new visitors as well as increased money to the town.
- The vast majority of residents who had not attended the event considered it to be desirable, with more than 90% considering the festival to be good for the image of the area and a valuable means of attracting new visitors.

The Llangollen Food Festival appears to have had a net positive impact on the local economy. Most of the benefits appear to be derived from direct expenditure at the event with little additional visitor spending taking place outside the festival's boundaries. The evidence is also suggestive of longer term benefits by supporting local producers and providing a showcase for their produce.

The case study also shows a broad consensus – from the exhibitors, local businesses and residents – that Llangollen Food Festival is good for the image of the area and brings new visitors to the area. Those people who attended the festival were very positive about the experience and many were motivated by the desire to support their local festival. Many of those who did not attend were not aware that the festival was taking place, but were considering attending in the future. When combined, these findings indicate the potential value, both economic and social, of supporting local festivals, through bringing new visitors into the area and enhancing the image for both local communities and visitors.

Case 2: North Wales International Music Festival

North Wales International Music Festival organised by North Wales International Music Festival Limited has been held regularly at St. Asaph Cathedral. Now in its thirty third year, the festival took place between 16 and 24 September 2005, and was supported by the Arts Council of Wales, Denbighshire County Council, North Wales Tourism, Cadwyn Clwyd, Theatre Elwy, Welsh Development Agency, View Creative, EU LEADER+, Thomas Hwolle and St. Asaph City of Music project, together with a host of other sponsors and supporters.

According to the organiser, the main aim of the event is to bring classical music to the community, to promote Welsh music and artists and to provide musical education, with the local community and schools benefiting from the event. The event has developed over the years, for example, through increasing the number of events and, in 2005, introducing eight community events. Future plans envisage that it may become more integrated with St. Asaph's Art Centre and Glan Clwid School.

The findings summarised from the surveys undertaken in 2005 show that:

- Visitors to the festival were typically attending with one other person (54%), aged between 45 and 64 (67%), and lived locally (64% lived in the Llangollen postal area).
- The vast majority of visitors (73%) enjoyed the event very much, rising to 96% when those enjoying it to some extent are added.
- Only 24% of the respondents would have been spending money in the area had there not been a festival.
- The North Wales International Music Festival had an estimated positive net impact on expenditure in St. Asaph area to the value of £25,791.
- Local businesses endorsed the value of the festival and tended to emphasise business-related benefits such as bringing in new customers for their business and bringing in non-local customers, though this had not translated directly into the increases in turnover.

- The vast majority of residents who had not attended the event considered it to be desirable, with more than 90% considering the festival to be good for bringing the community together and an opportunity for new experiences, while 88% believed that the festival provided a good image for the area.

The North Wales International Music Festival appears to have had a net positive impact on the local economy. Most of the benefits appear to be derived from direct expenditure at the event, accommodation and transport, with limited additional visitor spending taking place in other business sectors. The evidence is also suggestive of longer term benefits by apparently bringing the community together, and, perhaps, providing a good image for the area, together with bringing new visitors into the area.

The case study also shows that the festival provides the opportunity for new experiences through providing access to classical music for the community and local schools, thus demonstrating the value of supporting events and festivals in rural Wales through the broadening of cultural horizons.

Case 3: Art on the Railings, Chepstow, Monmouth

Art on the Railings, Chepstow, is organised by four active members of the local community. It started more than a decade ago as a means of enabling local artists to display their work in a manner accessible to the local community and visitors. Six Art on the Railings exhibitions were held during the summer of 2005. The event held in September was studied for this project. During that event, 39 artists displayed their work; the majority at Church Walk, with the remainder in the town centre. Eleven of the exhibitors lived and worked in the Chepstow.

The event is self-funding (by charging stallholders rather than visitors) but grant aid is also used for specific purposes such as leaflet production and purchase of a canopy to protect the art from the elements.

Research undertaken in 2005 shows that:

- Visitors to the exhibition typically came alone (42%) or as part of a couple (40%). Most of them were whites and aged between 25 and 64 (68%), though a quarter of those interviewed were older. Fifty-seven per cent lived in the immediate postal area.
- The vast majority of visitors (72%) enjoyed the event very much, rising to 93% when those enjoying it to some extent are added.
- Forty-seven per cent of the respondents would have been at home had they not been attending the event.
- Average expenditure at Art on the Railings was £11.38. When displaced activity was taken into account, the exhibition had a negligible positive net impact on expenditure in Chepstow.
- Exhibitors were extremely positive about the benefits of the event, noting particularly its impact on the image of the area.
- Local businesses were supportive of Art on the Railings but tended to emphasise indirect benefits accruing to the town generally. Few considered there to be serious disadvantages for hosting this event.
- More than 90% of the non-attending residents interviewed identified at least one positive outcome for the town. Reasons for their own non-attendance were divided principally between not knowing the exhibition was being staged (35%), not being interested in the event (35%) and other commitments/too busy (30%).

Art on the Railings has little net positive impact on the local economy. Nevertheless, the majority of stakeholders interviewed – attendees, non-attendees, exhibitors, organisers and local businesses – were positive about the contribution it makes to enhancing visitors' and residents' perception of Chepstow, which may contribute to longer term positive economic and social returns.

Summary

A number of generalisations can be made from the festivals studied. First, it is apparent that local businesses did not feel they benefited financially, unless directly involved as stallholders, but nevertheless remained supportive due to the perceived community benefits. This is a similar picture for local residents who chose not to attend but were still supportive of the event.

The direct economic returns appear to be marginal for the events studied. Any additional spending is usually at the event itself (tickets, merchandise, purchases from stallholders) with very little being spent in the locality. The main beneficiaries, therefore, tend to be the organisers and the participants. The North Wales International Music Festival, in particular, demonstrates that an event can attract tourists successfully yet have little economic impact on the host community. For several of these festivals, a greater benefit will be felt within the local area if effort is put into leveraging and extending the 'event experience' to create a longer term and wider reaching 'tourist experience'.

However, even though the economic tourism benefits are often minimal for this type of smaller scale rural event the longer term image and awareness benefits – or at least local perceptions of these matters – can be greater. The more intangible community benefits may also be substantial but are often overlooked by both funders and organisers.

Economic benefits can be increased by encouraging greater involvement by local businesses as suppliers, participants and through wider initiatives linked to the event. These opportunities are currently being missed by event organisers. Although most residents and businesses surveyed in the case studies were supportive, a number of negative impacts were noted. These ranged from traffic congestion and parking problems to feelings of exclusion and marginalisation. Clearly, if these types of event are to maintain community support, negative perceptions need to be managed via effective communication and involvement.

Although the conclusions above have been drawn from good quality survey data and wider sources, it is important to recognise the limitations of the research. It appears that many of the local businesses tend to play down any financial gain (or attendees exaggerate) as often their account of increased turnover did not match attendees' expenditure figures. The benefits and costs were provided as statements for agreement or disagreement and this may have led to a tendency to 'agree'. The findings also reflect only 'perceptions' of benefits rather than 'real' benefits and further research would be needed to substantiate these. Although the surveys provide a useful snapshot of the impacts of each festival there is a need to build on this type of research through following longer term impacts and by investigating some of the issues through more in-depth qualitative methods.

Conclusions

It is clear from this research and studies undertaken elsewhere that events and festivals now play a central role in many local strategies designed to enhance economic and community development.

As the case studies demonstrate, all key local stakeholders – residents, exhibitors, local businesses – are supportive of community events within their localities. Positive statements were provided consistently, though these tended to emphasise most strongly, indirect and potential future economic benefits and a sense of strengthening community cohesion, rather than direct financial gain.

The economic impacts of rural events vary. For example, in one case, Art on the Railings, the impact was negligible, whereas for most others there was some degree of direct economic impact. Given the relatively small scale of the events, it is not surprising that the returns are modest. The differences of the outcome are accounted for by several factors:

- *Nature of the event being studied*. Exhibitions such as Art on the Railings, where there is no entrance fee and where the art can be appreciated without purchase of a picture (in the same way as a gallery might), are less likely to generate significant expenditure than product-based events such as food festivals.
- *The extent to which the event is established*. Those events that have established reputations locally (and especially regionally or nationally) are more likely to deliver more significant economic benefits. Perceptions of community benefits, on the other hand, do not seem to be related to how long the event has been going on.
- *Marketing and promotion*. This is a key factor in delivering economic benefit if promotion extends beyond local borders because economic benefits are more likely to arise when visitors from outside the locality are attracted to spend at the event as well as at local residents.

The challenge facing policy makers is to establish a blend of events locally that will deliver a boost to the local economy as well as providing for greater community cohesion. In the light of these findings and the wider literature, the former will be more challenging than the latter.

References

Carlsen, J. (2004) The economics and evaluation of festivals and events. In Yeoman, I. et al. (eds.), *Festival and Events Management: An International Arts and Culture Perspective*. Oxford: Elsevier.

Chhabra, D., Sills, E. and Cubbage, F. W. (2003) The significance of festivals to rural economies: Estimating the economic impacts of Scottish highland games in North Carolina. *Journal of Travel Research*, 41, 421.

Crompton, J. L. (1995) Economic impact analysis of sports facilities and events: Eleven sources of misapplication. *Journal of Sports Management*, 9(1), 14–35.

Daniels, M. J., Norman, W. C. and Henry, M. S. (2004) Estimating income effects of a sport tourism event. *Annals of Tourism Research*, 31(1), 180–199.

De Bres, K. and Davis, J. (2001) Celebrating group and place identity: A case study of a new regional festival. *Tourism Geographies*, 3(3), 326–337.

Derrett, R. (2003) Making sense of how festivals demonstrate a community's sense of place. *Event Management*, 8, 49–58.

Dwyer, L., Mellor, R., Mistilis, N. and Mules, T. (2001a) A framework for assessing tangible and intangible impacts of events and conventions. *Event Management*, 6, 175–189.

Dwyer, L., Mellor, R., Mistilis, N. and Mules, T. (2001b) Forecasting the economic impacts of events and conventions. *Event Management*, 6, 191–204.

Felsenstein, D. and Fleischer, A. (2003) Local festivals and tourism promotion: The role of public assistance and visitor expenditure. *Journal of Travel Research*, 41, 385.

Fredline, L., Jago, L. and Deery, M. (2003) The development of a generic scale to measure the social impacts of events. *Event Management*, 8, 23–37.

Gursoy, D. et al. (2004) Perceived impacts of festivals and special events by organisers: An extension and validation. *Tourism Management*, 25, 171–181.

Hall, C. M. (1992) *Hallmark Tourist Events: Impacts, Management, and Planning.* London: Belhaven Press.

Higham, J. E. S. and Ritchie, B. (2001) The evolution of festivals and other events in rural southern New Zealand. *Event Management*, 7, 39–49.

Jago, L., Chalip, L., Brown, G., Mules, T. and Shameem, A. (2003) Building events into destination branding: Insights from experts. *Event Management*, 8, 3–14.

Janniskee, R. and Drews, P. (1998) Rural festivals and community re-imaging. In Butler, R., Hall, C. and Jenkins, J. (eds.), *Tourism and Recreation in Rural Areas.* Chichester: John Wiley.

Jones, C. (2001) Mega-events and host region impacts: Determining the true worth of the 1999 Rugby World Cup. *International Journal of Tourism Research*, 3(3), 241–251.

Jones, C. and Munday, M. (2001) Tourism and Local Economic Development: Three Case Studies *Paper for European Regional Science Association 41st Annual Meeting 'European Regional Development Issues in the New Millennium and their Impact on Economic Policy'*, Zagreb, Chamber of Economy, Croatia, August.

Lee, S. and Crompton, J. L. (2003) The attraction power and spending impact of three festivals in Ocean City, Maryland. *Event Management*, 8, 109–112.

Mayerfield, T. L. and Crompton, J. L. (1995) Development of an instrument for identifying community reasons for staging a festival. *Festival Management and Event Tourism*, 2(3), 37–44.

Mehmetoglu, M. (2002) Economic scale of community-run festivals: A case study. *Event Management*, 7, 93–102.

O'Sullivan, D. and Jackson, M. J. (2002) Festival tourism: A contributor to sustainable local economic development? *Journal of Sustainable Tourism*, 10(4), 325–342.

Prentice, R. and Andersen, V. (2003) Festival as creative destination. *Annals of Tourism Research*, 30(1), 7–30.

Richardson, H. W. (1985) Input–Output and economic base multipliers: Looking backward and forward. *Journal of Regional Science*, 25(4), 607–661.

Ryan, C. and Lockyer, T. (2001) An economic case study: The South Pacific Masters' Games. *Tourism Economics*, 7(3), 267–276.

Thomas, R. and Wood, E. (2003) Events-based tourism: A survey of local authority strategies in the UK. *Local Governance*, 29(2), 127–136.

Thomas, R., Wood, E., Bowdin, G. and Robinson, L. (2006) The contribution of community festivals and events to the local areas and the Welsh economy. LEADER + Programmes: PLANED, Adventa, Northern Marches Cymru and Cadwyn Clwyd, Wales.

Wilson, S., Fesenmaier, D.R., Fesenmaier, J. and van Es J. C. (2001) Factors for success in rural tourism development. *Journal of Travel Research*, 40(2), 132–137.

Wood, E. (2005) Measuring the economic and social impacts of local authority events. *International Journal of Public Sector Management*, 18(1), 37–53.

Wood, E. and Thomas, R. (2006) Measuring cultural values: The case of residents' attitudes to the saltaire festival. *Tourism Economics*, 12(1), 137–146.

Xie, P. F. (2004) Visitors' perceptions of authenticity at a rural heritage festival: A case study. *Event Management*, 8, 151–160.

Yu, Y. and Turco, D. M. (2000) Issues in tourism event economic impact studies: The case of the Albuquerque International Balloon Fiesta. *Current Issues in Tourism*, 3(2), 138–149.

PART 3

AUDIENCE AND PARTICIPANT EXPERIENCE

Adele Ladkin

The third part of the book introduces four chapters that explore the experience of events with reference to both audience and participant experiences.

In Chapter 11, Frost, Wheeler and Harvey explore commemorative events, specifically relating to issues of identity and dissonance. The starting point for this work is to remind us that whilst commonly events are defined as celebration, not all are festive. In commemorative events the focus is on remembering, usually with the intention of reflection on the past as a means to reinforce national or ethnic identity. However, there is often a disagreement in interpretations of history by different groups, which can cause tensions and difficulties in the staging of commemorative events. As a consequence, the nature of commemorative events can present specific challenges and difficulties for event organisers who seek to create a positive event experience for both audiences and participants. The interpretation of history and how this is presented is an area of intense debate involving many different stakeholders, and this chapter examines the complexities through the exploration of three case studies of Australian commemorative events. The first of these is the Eureka Stockade (1854) involving gold miners at Ballarat who rebelled against government maladministration. The second is the capture of the bushranger Ned Kelly (1880) which has been the subject of much destination marketing publicity and festivals. The third is the World War I battles at Gallipoli (1915) and Villers-Bretonneux (1918), commemorated through Anzac day celebrations. The detail of the three events presented in this chapter leads to four issues for discussion. The first is that they are a highly emotive theme of sacrifice. Second, the events are commemorations not celebrations which raises the issue of what types of activity are appropriate. Third, each event involves multiple stakeholder groups with a high degree of dissonance, much of which is associated with claims of ancestry and perceptions of how each group is connected to the event. The fourth is the extent of government involvement in the events, which although well meaning can often increase conflict. The complex issues associated with commemorative events have significant implications for event organisers.

Chapter 12 by Shipway and Jones meanwhile turns the attention to a very different type of event, sporting events. The research focuses on participant experiences at sporting events through a quasi-ethnographic examination of a group of distance runners participating in two distance running events, the Cyprus International four-day Challenge and the 2007 Flora Marathon. The concept of 'serious sport tourism' provides the background to this study. In carrying out this research, the authors have sought to demonstrate a framework by which 'serious' sport tourism activities can be described and explained. Through the adoption of a social identity-based approach the work explores the characteristics of the participants in order to understand their motives for undertaking and what they achieve from such events. A range of qualitative findings are presented including identities and running careers. The research discusses the potential for further qualitative research on active sports participants, and argues this is a potential way forward to better understand the social settings in which this type of participant operates.

Chapter 13 by Morgan and Wright continues the sports theme and examines elite sports tours. Although large sports mega events are familiar in research, interest in a diverse range of other types of sporting events is growing. As a result of this general trend, there has been a growth in the number of elite sporting competitions, many of which involve touring associated with the movement of those participating in, watching or involved with the sporting event. As a consequence of this movement which often crosses regional boundaries and involves many different stakeholders, this type of event has specific challenges. Using a case study of the 2005 British and Irish Lions Rugby Union Tour of New Zealand the chapter explores these challenges, including the experiences of host communities and supporters of the events. The research contains evaluation of both the regional tourism planning surrounding the event and the experience of travelling supporters in attendance. The chapter concludes that elite sports tours provide challenges and opportunities to tourism destination management in terms of both planning for and managing the event.

To end Part 3, Chapter 14 by Stone examines the phenomenon of the British Pop Music Festival. There is increasing demand and support for all kinds of music festivals in the United Kingdom and those involving popular music are no exception, with many becoming significant socio-cultural and historic landmark events. Despite this and in contrast to the amount of research into conventional music events, little research has been undertaken on British pop festivals. Following an examination of the nature and characteristic of pop festivals, this chapter explores the issues relating to markets and demand, motivations for attendance, operational dimensions and trends in provision. The role of pop festivals as tourist destinations is also considered. The understanding of the motivations for attendance at festivals are explored through a discussion of research from a range of different disciplines. The research concludes that the pop festival is now an accepted part of British culture and adds to the diverse range of events available to consumers.

Chapter 11

Commemorative Events: Sacrifice, Identity and Dissonance

Warwick Frost, Fiona Wheeler and Matthew Harvey

Introduction

While events are commonly defined as celebrations, not all are festive. Some are staged to commemorate an historic anniversary. Their emphasis is on remembering rather than mere celebrating. They are usually intended to reinforce a sense of national or ethnic identity through encouraging reflection on the past. However, they may be highly dissonant, with various groups contesting interpretations of history. Accordingly, commemorative events present special difficulties and challenges for event organisers. This chapter examines these complexities through a trio of case studies of Australian commemorative events. These are the anniversaries of the Eureka Stockade (1854), the capture of the bushranger Ned Kelly (1880) and the World War I battles at Gallipoli (1915) and Villers-Bretonneux (1918).

Literature Review

The limited literature on commemorative events has tended to focus on anniversaries of a nation's founding (Bennett et al., 1992; Frost, 2001; McDonald and Methot, 2006). These studies suggest that such events appeal to both domestic and tourist markets, a theme also increasingly pursued in studies of attractions linked to national identity (Light, 2007; Pretes, 2003). However, the range of commemorative events extends well beyond such national anniversaries. Military conflicts are a common subject for commemorations, often used to reinforce national identity but also providing a great scope for contests over their meanings (Buchholtz, 2005; Lloyd, 1998; Ryan and Cave, 2007).

In contrast to official commemorations, some events utilise significant dates to protest against government policies, for example, Hiroshima Day and Australia's Sorry Day. There is also an increasing emphasis on commemorative events inspired by popular culture. Dublin, for example, hosts an event called Bloom's Day on 16 June each year, this being the day on which the story of

James Joyce's Ulysses is set. In 2007 events were staged to mark the 30th anniversary of the death of Elvis Presley, the centenaries of the births of actors John Wayne and Gene Autry and the 40th anniversary of the release of the Beatles' Sergeant Pepper's Lonely Hearts Club Band.

The corporatist model of events focuses on operational planning in order to satisfy the objectives of formal stakeholders such as sponsors. Commemorations illustrate how events may have meanings which are outside this corporatist model, that is their interpretation and staging are of critical importance to groups who are not part of the formal planning. Such events reshape how societies see themselves and their identity (Picard and Robinson, 2006; Street, 2004). Accordingly, it may be that the meanings of an event are distinct from (and far more important than) the objectives of the organisers.

The meanings of an event may be multiple, contested and irreconcilable. Commemorative events often provoke heritage dissonance. Tunbridge and Ashworth (1996, p. 20) coined this term to describe situations where cultural heritage provoked a 'discordance or a lack of agreement and consistency' amongst the community. The term dissonance originally denoted music played in contrasting and jarring styles. Tunbridge and Ashworth argued that this was an apt analogy for the differences we hear from the community in relation to their heritage.

Such disagreements may be seen as unsettling and disruptive, calling for action to resolve or cover them up (Frost, 2005). The temptation with commemorative events is to fashion one single interpretation while ignoring other perspectives. However, such an approach is wrong, for Tunbridge and Ashworth (1996, p. 21) argued that dissonance 'is intrinsic to the nature of heritage ... It is not an unforseen and unfortunate by-product of the heritage assembly process'.

Heritage dissonance is closely linked with ideas of heterogeneous community and identity. Under such circumstances, it means that while, 'heritage benefits someone ... [it also] disadvantages someone else' (Howard, 2003, p. 4). While making, 'some people feel better, more rooted and more secure ... [it] simultaneously makes another group feel less important, less welcome and less secure' (Howard, 2003, p. 147). Accordingly, 'heritage battles are not just against vandals, but also those who would also claim the same heritage' (Lowenthal, 1998, p. 230). This leads to the development of guardians of heritage, committed to presenting their version of history as true and excluding or suppressing the claims of rivals (Fawcett and Cormack, 2001; Frost, 2005).

For organisers of events with historic themes, contested authenticity becomes a dilemma as they grapple with the issues of what to include or leave out (Bennett et al., 1992; Buchholtz, 2005; Frost, 2001; Getz, 1994; Ryan and Cave, 2007). Whatever interpretation is constructed by organisers, the resultant meanings are often a 'co-construction'. A study of tours at the Gettysburg Battlefield in the United States concluded that:

> The resulting narratives are contested by tourists and become subject to negotiation. During the performance of the story, tourists are not passive readers of the text. Rather, they are actively engaged by using their prior background, negotiating, filling gaps, and imagining. Hence, service providers do not simply teach history and tourists do not only learn about the past (Chronis, 2005, p. 400).

Methodology

In this chapter we will focus on three annual commemorative events involving Australia. These are Eureka Day, the anniversary of Ned Kelly's capture and Anzac Day. All are staged annually and commemorate sacrifice in conflict. Most importantly, all three are highly dissonant, with different stakeholders laying competing claims to the meanings and significance of the events commemorated.

A comparative case study approach is utilised. This methodology is being increasingly used to identify differences and similarities (e.g. see Frost, 2005 and Pretes, 2003). Information was gathered via a combination of published sources (including newspapers and event programmes), stakeholder interviews and participant observation. Newspapers in particular can be a valuable source for tracking public reactions to events. Statements made in newspapers may be especially revealing, both through the opportunities for reply by other parties and the journalistic convention of trying to include at least two perspectives in any article (Frost, 2008).

Findings

Eureka Day

In 1854 disgruntled gold miners at Ballarat rebelled against government maladministration. Refusing to pay the fees for their miner's licences, they raised the Southern Cross Flag, took up arms and constructed a rudimentary stockade in Eureka Gully. In the early morning of 3 December 1854, the stockade was attacked by British troops. In 15 minutes, about 30 miners were killed. However, the miners were ultimately triumphant. A jury acquitted their leaders of treason and a Royal Commission led to the introduction of democracy (Frost, 2007).

Over time Eureka has been commemorated in many ways, including monuments, processions and re-enactments. A 1917 re-enactment was watched by a crowd which may have been as large as 50,000. In some years there were no commemorations at all. Beginning in the 1930s, commemorations became highly politicised as Eureka was appropriated by the Left. Staging the centenary in 1954 at the height of the Cold War provoked strong reactions (Beggs Sunter, 2001).

In 1979 the Eureka Commemorative Organisation was formed. It was intended to be 'a local Ballarat organisation and it deliberately aimed to disassociate Eureka from political and ideological causes' (Beggs Sunter, 2001, p. 55). In 1993 a local historian began a Dawn Lantern Walk following the route taken by the soldiers. In 1998 the organisation of this event passed to the Ballarat Fine Art Gallery, custodians of the original Southern Cross Flag. During the 1988 Bicentenary of European Settlement, a new organisation was founded called Eureka's Children. Its members were the descendants of the miners at Eureka and it aggressively claimed exclusive ownership of the right to commemorate and interpret Eureka (Button, 2004; Frost, 2007).

Eureka's Children were especially indignant that the Art Gallery's Dawn Lantern Walk commemorated the soldier's route to battle. They labelled it 'offensive in the extreme because it commemorates the march and attack by soldiers on innocent men, women and children' (quoted in Beggs Sunter, 2001, p. 56). In opposition to the Dawn Lantern Walk, Eureka's Children created their own dawn procession, following the route taken by the miners between the hill where the flag had first been raised and the stockade site (Button, 2004).

These tensions came to a head in the organisation of the 150th anniversary in 2004. For the first time, the State Government sponsored the commemorations, but in turn, it required unity. A single Dawn Commemoration Service was held on the anniversary date and this was at the site of the Eureka Stockade. The Dawn Lantern Walk was 'bumped' to two days after.

Further controversy arose when the 'leading light' was announced for the Dawn Lantern Walk. Each year, its organisers invite someone to lead the walk and address the walkers 'about what it means to defend rights and liberties today' (Anon, 2004). For 2004 the choice was Terry Hicks, the father of David Hicks, an Australian at that time imprisoned by the United States in Guantanamo Bay. Accordingly the Dawn Lantern Walk gained more media and political attention than any other part of the commemoration. Those vocally critical of linking a current issue to a historical commemoration included the Federal and State Governments, the City of Ballarat (all funding bodies of the anniversary) and the great-great grandson of the miner's leader (Anon., 2004; Flanagan, 2004).

The other major issue ignited by the commemoration was the location of the miner's flag – the Eureka or Southern Cross Flag. Since the 1970s this had been on display at the Ballarat Fine Art Gallery, which is located on the site of the soldiers' camp. The flag had been donated to it by the descendants of a soldier who had souvenired it after the battle (Beggs Sunter, 2007). The occasion of the 150th anniversary ignited a campaign to move the flag. Many stakeholders deemed the site of the soldiers' camp as completely inappropriate. As Professor John Molony, the leading historian of Eureka, forcefully put it, the current location 'stands where the soldiers and police danced, spat and urinated on it when they returned from their work at Eureka' (Molony, 2004, p. 2). Eureka's Children, in particular, used the anniversary to gain publicity for their campaign for it being moved (Brown, 2004; Button, 2004).

Ned Kelly

The notorious bushranger Ned Kelly is Australia's greatest cultural icon and 'the closest thing Australia has to a national hero' (Seal, 1996, p. 145). Outlawed on trumped up charges in 1878, he and his gang engaged in daring robberies and eluded the police for two years. In 1880 he was captured while trying to derail a police train at Glenrowan and subsequently executed. Kelly had escaped, but returned to try to rescue his comrades besieged by police in the Glenrowan Hotel. This was the occasion he wore his famous armour, making him impervious to bullets, but weighing him down so badly he was unable to aim his gun.

The story of Ned Kelly has been celebrated through folklore, song, art and cinema (Betrand and Routt, 2007; Holland and Williamson, 2003; Seal, 1996). *The Story of the Kelly Gang* (1906) was the world's first full length feature film. It has been followed by a further nine films. The Ned Kelly Prize is awarded for Australia's best crime fiction. Ned Kelly was the only identifiable person featured in the Opening Ceremony of the 2000 Sydney Olympics. Through the paintings of Sidney Nolan, the stylised image of a helmeted Kelly is widely known and is increasingly being used in destination marketing (see Figure 11.1).

Nonetheless, there has been ongoing official disapproval of such interest. In the 1920s films about him were banned and the play *Ned Kelly* was rejected for inclusion in the 1956 Olympics cultural programme. In 1980, the Victorian State Government complained when Australia Post released a Ned Kelly commemorative stamp. In 2003, the Victoria Police were mortified when a Kelly family member called on them to finally acknowledge that Kelly had been unjustly treated (Holland and Williamson, 2003; Seal, 1996).

Interest in Ned Kelly has stimulated tourism, particularly to the small country towns associated with him (Beeton, 2004; Frost, 2006; Pearce et al., 2003). His tourism manifestations include trails (the Ned Kelly Touring Route and the Ned Kelly Wine Trail), attractions (an animatronic theatre, a giant statue) and destination branding (Benalla is the 'Hometown of Ned Kelly'; Beechworth is

Figure 11.1: Welcome Sign for Glenrowan utilising reproduction of Sydney Nolan's
iconic painting of Ned Kelly.

'Australia's best-preserved Ned Kelly town'; Glenrowan is 'Keeping Place of the Kelly Legend'). Increasingly, Ned Kelly has also been the subject of commemorative events.

1980 was the centenary of Ned Kelly's capture at Glenrowan. Despite intense resistance (allegedly including threatened sabotage) from some members of the local community, a number of Glenrowan residents and business-owners took it upon themselves to organise a re-enactment. Members of the Melbourne Historic Re-enactment Society were recruited to play the police in period uniform. An old house stood in for the Glenrowan Hotel in which the Kelly gang were cornered and as a culmination of the re-enactment this was set on fire (as had been done 100 years before). A vintage steam train was used to transport people from Melbourne. The event was a great success receiving extensive media coverage and reportedly attracting around 5000–6000 people (Griffiths, 1987). However, despite this success, efforts to repeat it have failed.

Commencing in 2001, local enthusiasts began an annual commemoration. The centrepiece was the Annual Commemorative Kelly Siege Dinner. For the first couple of years the dinner was held in a marquee in the town. However, in 2004 it was transferred to the Bailey's Winery, located a couple of kilometres outside the town. Each year saw a different theme for the dinner, such as that of early settlement (2004) with dishes typical of the period (e.g. Irish stew) and a Chinese theme (2005) to commemorate the connections between Kelly and the Chinese mining community.

Attendees tended to be a mix of local residents and business operators (who received half price tickets), historians and journalists, as well as visitors to the area. Many of those who attended had a keen interest in the Kelly story and used the opportunity to share their own researches. This extended to displays of privately owned relics, in particular there were several showings of the armour worn by Ned's lieutenant, Joe Byrne.

In 2005, the 125th anniversary of the Siege, a number of additional events were organised, including a debate and discussion about the Kelly story, a play depicting the story through the eyes of the Kelly women, screenings of old Ned Kelly movies, an art exhibition on a Ned Kelly theme and tours of the local area. These events attracted a diverse range of attendees from far and wide, including many Kelly enthusiasts, historians, the media as well as local community members, indicating the extent of the resonance of the Kelly story.

However, in 2006, the commemorative events fell flat – the 6th Annual Commemorative Dinner was cancelled by the local council just before the event. Interviews with the local Glenrowan community suggest that there were insufficient resources devoted by the local council to organising and promoting the event. For the 2007 anniversary, the council declined to organise anything, and instead members of the local Glenrowan community have taken it upon themselves to organise a BBQ on site at Glenrowan. While visitors are welcome, interviews suggest that the objective of this year's commemoration is to make it much more of an event for 'locals'.

It appears that Glenrowan is at a stage of transition with regard to its commemorative events. A core group of local 'champions' face a number of challenges such as intense resistance from some community members for whom the events of 1880 continue to hold significant, deeply felt meaning, as well as a lack of support and tangible resources from the local municipality which is based in the city of Wangaratta, 15 kilometres away. It also seems that plans for a A$15 million Ned Kelly Interpretive Centre at Glenrowan are unlikely to proceed due to a 'reprioritisation' of funds towards a new performing arts centre in Wangaratta.

The larger town of Beechworth was the centre of the police hunt for Ned Kelly. Upon capture he was brought there for a preliminary trial, before being transferred to Melbourne. It still retains its civic precinct of impressive stone 19th century buildings, including courthouse (recently restored) and gaol. In 2005 it held a festival to commemorate the 125th anniversary of Kelly's capture. Strongly supported by the local council and business community, this has become an annual event.

In 2006, the festival included The Great Debate, promoted as 'Australia's most significant Ned Kelly event'. The debate topic was "Ned Kelly – An inappropriate hero for Australia". The debaters included Kelly historians, members of the Melbourne legal profession, the Victorian Police Commissioner and media identities. It was claimed by the organisers to be an unprecedented success with over 400 attendees at the debate itself, while the weekend festival attracted an unexpected 5,000 visitors to the town. The 2007 festival attracted 2,500 visitors, with much media publicity focusing on the recreation of Ned Kelly's trial (Kissane, 2007; see Figure 11.2). With the collapse of Glenrowan event, Beechworth has taken over as focal point for commemorations.

Anzac Day

On 25 April 1915 troops of the Australia and New Zealand Army Corps (Anzac) landed at Gallipoli in Turkey. This was part of an ill-fated attempt to break the deadlock of the Western Front through an invasion of Germany's ally Turkey. Though unsuccessful, the campaign became symbolic of the identity of Australian soldiers and nationhood. Commemorations of Anzac Day began in 1916, in 1919 it had become a public holiday in Western Australia and by 1923 it was a public holiday

Figure 11.2: Ned Kelly Festival Beechworth, re-enactment of police taking Kelly
through town to court.

throughout Australia. Such was its status between the wars that were even attempts to adopt it as
Australia Day or Nation Day (Seal, 2004, pp. 106–108).

Anzac Day was highly popular up to the 1950s. However in the 1960s and 1970s it was increasingly seen as reactionary and irrelevant. Such views were widely reflected in popular culture, such as in the play *One Day of the Year* (1958) by Alan Seymour. Focusing on the confused ideology and drunkenness of returned soldiers on Anzac Day, it was banned by the Adelaide Festival in 1960, but eventually would be widely featured on schools syllabi. Just when it seemed that Anzac Day would wither away, its popularity rose again in the 1990s and 2000s. A significant feature of this revival was the crowds of up to 20,000 tourists (mainly young backpackers) attending Dawn Services on Anzac Day at the Gallipoli battlefield in Turkey (Hall, 2002; Scates, 2006; Slade, 2003).

The revival of interest in Anzac Day has been credited to a number of sources. These include a craving for rituals in a secular society, the passing of the last veterans, changing reflections on the Vietnam War and Australia's current military involvement in Iraq and Afghanistan (Hall, 2002; Scates, 2006). One major change is that while visitors to Gallipoli in the 1920s and 1930s tended to express pro-imperial sentiments, the new generation are more likely to be anti-British (Scates, 2006, pp. 115–116).

Recent Anzac Day commemorations have stimulated a great deal of debate over the motivations and behaviour of participants. While many visitors see themselves as solemn pilgrims, there is a tendency to criticise others as being too celebratory and accordingly loutish and disrespectful. Gallipoli is now part of a well-worn backpacker circuit. Established tour companies including

Contiki, Compass and Allsun operate tour taking in the Dawn Service. There is excessive consumption of alcohol and the crowd has been likened to like one for a rock-concert (Scates, 2006). Such an analogy seemed particularly apt when official organisers screened music videos on a big screen to entertain the crowd waiting for the Dawn Service.

The growing doubts about the contemporary meanings of Anzac Day were well illustrated through recent comments by the actor Mark Lee. He and Mel Gibson were the leads in Peter Weir's popular film *Gallipoli* (1981). He was concerned that for backpackers in Turkey for Anzac Day:

> The film gets shown before they go and get pissed and sit on Anzac Cove, turning it into a party. They'd watch in on buses going there, getting primed, and you think: What are you watching? What are you actually absorbing? (quoted in Dow, 2007, p. 40).

Villers-Bretonneux is a small town of about 1500 residents, 15 kilometres from Amiens and 80 kilometres from Paris. In 1918 a massive German offensive threatened Amiens, the last bastion before Paris. On 25 April Australian troops launched a successful counter-attack against the Germans at Villers-Bretonneux.

In 1938 Australia constructed a National War Memorial at the site of the battle to commemorate its 20th anniversary. The Australian connection is a major part of the town's identity. The town's symbol is a kangaroo and its website contains an English language section especially targeted at Australian visitors (Villers-Bretonneux, 2007). Each year an Anzac Day commemoration is held on the Saturday closest to 25 April. The local primary school, destroyed during the war, was rebuilt with donations by Australian schoolchildren. It features a large sign stating 'N'oublions jamais les Australiens' (Let us never forget the Australians). A number of streets are named after Australia (Rue de Victoria, Rue de Melbourne).

On the eve of Anzac Day 2007 the Australian Government announced an initial funding allocation of A$2.8 million for an interpretive centre at Villers-Bretonneux. The funding is for consultation with French authorities and the development of preliminary designs. Further funding allocations will be made as the project progresses.

In announcing the centre, the Australian Minister for Veterans' Affairs stated that:

> Australia has a proud history of involvement in the battles of the Western Front during World War I and the centre will be a fitting tribute to more than a quarter of a million Australians who served on the Western Front … A centre providing international standard interpretive facilities will strengthen Australia's presence in the area, foster European relations and provide a focal point for visitors from Australia and other nations (Billson, 2007a).

While styled an interpretive rather than a visitor's centre, the funding announcement made connections to tourism and events. It noted that the Western Front battlefields attracted 350,000 visitors annually and that 'we are in the process of commemorating the 90th anniversary of the many extraordinary battles of the Western Front and not too far away from the 100th anniversary' (Billson, 2007a, emphasis added).

Later in 2007, it was announced that Australia would stage a Dawn Service at Villers-Bretonneux to mark the 90th anniversary in 2008. This would be Australia's first Dawn Service in France and would parallel the ceremonies held at Gallipoli. In announcing this event, Paul Stevens, Director of the Australian Office of War Graves noted that it 'marks a huge shift for Australia's commemorative tradition … but the 90th anniversary is the year to make the break with tradition' (quoted in King, 2007). The traditional Anzac Day commemorations at Villers-Bretonneux, now termed 'the annual community ceremony', will continue on the closest Saturday each year (Department of Veterans' Affairs, 2007).

The new commemoration may be viewed in two ways. First, the anniversary is being used to improve the recognition of the Western Front battlefields. While, many more Australians fought and died in France than in Turkey, this has tended to be overlooked. The developments at Villers-Bretonneux are an attempt to rectify that inbalance. As the Minister for Veterans' Affairs emphasised, 450,000 Australians visit France each year, but only 5,000–7,000 visit the area containing the World War I battlefields (Billson, 2007b). Second, concerned about capacity, behaviour and security at Gallipoli, the Australian Government may be seeking to channel the commemorative events and visitors towards Western Europe.

Conclusion

In examining these specific case studies and other commemorations in general, four main trends and patterns are apparent. The first is that they are connected by a highly emotive theme of sacrifice. Each of the three events commemorate young people who laid down their lives. Event attendees may also reflect on complementary concepts of tragedy, injustice, freedom and comradeship. It is then not surprising that some visitors see their participation in terms of a pilgrimage. Of course not all commemorative events have such emotional links, though they are strongly linked to anniversaries of conflicts.

Second, these are commemorations not celebrations. Certainly, there is scope for commemorations to have festive components. Ryan and Cave (2007) examined how Armistice Day at Cambridge (New Zealand) contained elements of fun and parody. Seal (2004) invoked Faludi's concept of festivals inverting the normal social order, to explain the drinking and gambling associated with traditional Anzac Days in Australia. The recent growth of backpacker trips to the Dawn Service at Gallipoli has given that event a festive, almost rock-concert, ambience (Hall, 2002; Scates, 2006). However, such behaviours draw strong criticism as not being appropriate to the nature of the occasion.

Third, these events involve multiple stakeholder groups who often have conflicting ideas of the meaning of what is being commemorated, how it should be organised and even where it should be staged. In some cases, this proprietorial attitude may extend to notions of exclusion of other groups. Such gatekeeping is based on perceptions of participants' connection to the heritage commemorated. As Poria et al. (2003) argued, interest in heritage derives from one's personal connections, for example, religion or ethnicity. These cases extend that concept by highlighting that gatekeepers will make value judgements on personal connections and their appropriateness for being involved.

Accordingly, dissonance at Eureka is magnified by the claims of those who can trace ancestry to the miners. Through that connection, they seek to be custodians of all associated events and interpretations. There is much irony in the paradox between their claims of national significance and exclusive control. For Ned Kelly, there is a struggle between the competing claims of two towns. Recent Anzac Days are characterised by much public commentary on the behaviour of attendees.

Such comments reveal judgmental attitudes about degrees of solemnity and moral worthiness. Parallels may be drawn with research by Cohen (2007) on Beatles themed festivals in Liverpool. She found sharp divisions and tensions between attendees who saw themselves as serious fans as opposed to those they characterised as shallow and there just for a good time.

Fourth, this dissonance creates potential pitfalls for government agencies used to corporate approaches to events. At Eureka, government chose one stakeholder group's dawn procession over another's. When one of the events featured a speaker on current political matters, government officials quickly distanced themselves from it. The Ned Kelly commemorations involved two local councils. At Glenrowan the local council from nearby Wangaratta took little interest, resulting in the decline of the event. In contrast, at Beechworth, the local council has enthusiastically embraced the event as a tourist attraction. At Anzac Day at Gallipoli, organisers have been criticised for providing entertainment and for the behaviour of the crowd. Indeed, government action in trying to smoothly manage these events by discouraging conflict, may even have contributed to increased dissonance.

References

Anon. (2004) As Eureka flag flies, Hicks' role sparks a flutter. *The Age*, News section, 3 December, pp. 1–2.

Beeton, S. (2004) Rural tourism in Australia – has the gaze altered? Tracking rural images through film and tourism promotion. *International Journal of Tourism Research*, 6, 125–135.

Beggs Sunter, A. (2001) Remembering Eureka. *Journal of Australian Studies*, December, 49–59.

Beggs Sunter, A. (2007a) Contesting the flag: The mixed messages of the Eureka Flag. In Mayne, A. (ed.), *Eureka: Reappraising an Australian Legend*. Perth: Network, pp. 45–60.

Bennett, T., Buckridge, P., Carter, D. and Mercer, C. (1992) *Celebrating the Nation: A Critical Study of Australia's Bicentenary*. Sydney: Allen and Unwin.

Betrand, I. and Routt, W. D. (2007) *The Story of the Kelly Gang*. Melbourne: The Moving Image.

Billson, B. (2007a) *$2.8 Million to Progress an Australian Interpretive Centre on the Western Front*. New York: Media Release from Australian Minister for Veterans' Affairs.

Billson, B. (2007b) Transcript of radio interview on ABC radio, 24 April 2007, www.minister.dva.gov.au/speeches/2007/apr/Interpretive_Centre_Villers-Bretonneux, accessed 11 September 2007.

Brown, J. (2004) The flag was stolen … it must return. *Royal Auto*, 72(10), 22–23.

Buchholtz, D. (2005) Cultural politics or critical public history? Battling on the Little Bighorn. *Journal of Tourism and Cultural Change*, 3, 18–35.

Button, J. (2004) Eureka, the 150 Year war: How children of the rebellion maintain the rage. *The Age*, News section, 27 November, pp. 1 and 10.

Chronis, A. (2005) Coconstructing heritage at the Gettysburg storyscape. *Annals of Tourism Research*, 32(2), 386–406.

Cohen, S. (2007) *Decline, Renewal and the City in Popular Music Culture: Beyond the Beatles*. Aldershot: Ashgate.

Department of Veterans' Affairs (2007) 2008 Dawn Service at Australian National Memorial Park, Villers-Bretonneux, France, www.dva.gov.au/commem/events/villersbret08/index, accessed 10 September 2007.

Dow, S. (2007) Mark of Cain. *Sunday Age*, M Section, 26 August, p. 40.

Fawcett, C. and Cormack, P. (2001) Guarding authenticity at literary tourism sites. *Annals of Tourism Research*, 28(3), 686–704.

Flanagan, M. (2004) By the fires of dawn, the first diggers are honoured. *The Age*, News section, 4 December, p. 7.

Frost, W. (2001) Golden anniversaries: Festival tourism and the 150th anniversary of the Gold Rushes in California and Victoria. *Pacific Tourism Review*, 5(¾), 149–158.

Frost, W. (2005) Making an edgier interpretation of the Gold Rushes: Contrasting perspectives from Australia and New Zealand. *International Journal of Heritage Studies*, 11(3), 235–250.

Frost, W. (2006) *Braveheart*-ed *Ned Kelly*: Historic films, heritage tourism and destination image. *Tourism Management*, 27(2), 247–254.

Frost, W. (2007) Refighting the Eureka Stockade: Managing a dissonant battlefield. In Ryan, C. (ed.), *Battlefield Tourism: History, Place and Interpretation*. Oxford: Elsevier, pp. 187–194.

Frost, W. (2008) Popular culture as a different type of heritage: The making of AC/DC Lane. *Journal of Heritage Tourism*, 3(3), 25.

Getz, D. (1994) Event tourism and the authenticity dilemma. In Theobald, W. F. (ed.), *Global Tourism: The Next Decade*. Oxford: Butterworth-Heinemann, pp. 313–329.

Griffiths, T. (1987) *Beechworth: An Australian Country Town and its Past*. Melbourne: Greenhouse.

Hall, C. M. (2002) ANZAC Day and secular pilgrimage. *Tourism Recreation Research*, 27(2), 83–87.

Holland, A. and Williamson, C. (2003) *Kelly Culture: Reconstructing Ned Kelly*. Melbourne: State Library of Victoria.

Howard, P. (2003) *Heritage: Management, Interpretation, Identity*. London: Continuum.

King, J. (2007) Anzac Day dawn service to be held on French soil. *The Age*, News section, 8 September, p. 3.

Kissane, K. (2007) Victim or villain? Ned Kelly comes to life in Beechworth'. *The Age*, News section, 6 August, p. 6.

Light, D. (2007) Dracula tourism in Romania: Cultural identity and the state. *Annals of Tourism Research*, 34(3), 746–765.

Lloyd, D. (1998) *Battlefield Tourism: Pilgrimage and the Commemoration of the Great War in Britain, Australia, and Canada, 1919–1939*. Oxford: Berg.

Lowenthal, D. (1998) *The Heritage Crusade and the Spoils of History*. Cambridge: Cambridge University Press.

McDonald, T. and Methot, M. (2006) That impulse that bids a people to honour its past: The nature and purpose of centennial celebrations. *International Journal of Heritage Studies*, 12(4), 307–320.

Molony, J. (2004) Dawn of a democracy. *The Age*, Review section, 27 November, pp. 1–2.

Pearce, P. L., Morrison, A. M. and Moscardo, G. M. (2003) Individuals as tourist icons: A developmental and marketing analysis. *Journal of Hospitality and Leisure Marketing*, 10(½), 63–85.

Picard, D. and Robinson, M. (2006) *Festivals, Tourism and Social Change: Remaking Worlds*. Clevedon: Channel View.

Poria, Y., Butler, R. and Airey, D. (2003) The core of heritage tourism. *Annals of Tourism Research*, 30(2), 238–254.

Pretes, M. (2003) Tourism and nationalism. *Annals of Tourism Research*, 30(1), 125–142.

Ryan, C. and Cave, J. (2007) Cambridge Armistice Day celebrations: Making a carnival of war and the reality of play. In Ryan, C. (ed.), *Battlefield Tourism, History, Place and Identity*. Oxford: Elsevier, pp. 177–186.

Scates, B. (2006) *Return to Gallipoli: Walking the Battlefields of the Great War*. Cambridge: Cambridge University Press.

Slade, P. (2003) Gallipoli Thanatourism: The meaning of ANZAC. *Annals of Tourism Research*, 30(4), 779–794.

Seal, G. (1996) *The Outlaw Legend: A Cultural Tradition in Britain, America and Australia*. Melbourne: Cambridge University Press.

Seal, G. (2004) *Inventing Anzac: The Digger and National Mythology*. Brisbane: University of Queensland Press.

Street, J. (2004) This is your Woodstock: Popular memories and political myths. In Bennett, A. (ed.), *Remembering Woodstock*. Aldershot: Ashgate, pp. 29–42.

Tunbridge, J. E. and Ashworth, G. J. (1996) *Dissonant Heritage: The Management of the Past as a Resource in Conflict*. Chichester: Wiley.

Villers-Bretonneux (2007) Villers-Bretonneux specially for Australians, www.Villers-Bretonneux.com/Australian, accessed 9 September 2007.

Chapter 12

Running Commentary: Participant Experiences at International Distance Running Events

Richard Shipway and Ian Jones

Introduction

Existing sport tourism and sporting events research has been subject to claims of lacking coherence, theoretical underpinning, and lacking empirical support. This chapter addresses these issues and advances event sport tourism research through a quasi-ethnographic examination of a group of distance runners participating in two distance running events – the *Cyprus International 4-day Challenge*, and the *2007 Flora London Marathon (FLM)*.

Although the volume of scholarly work on event sport tourism has increased over recent years, this subject area is, arguably, still in its infancy in terms of development, with a coherent and usable body of knowledge slow to emerge (Weed, 2006). A number of limitations can be identified in much existing work. Firstly, most studies are essentially descriptive in nature, providing information on what is taking place but generating little in the way of understanding or explanation (Gibson, 2005; Weed, 2005), and with an overemphasis upon developing typologies of participants (Green and Jones, 2005), leaving the important questions, those of understanding and explanation largely unanswered (Gibson, 2005). This argument is echoed by Weed (2005), who suggests that existing work on sport tourism experiences specifically is generally descriptive, and fails to address issues such as why the event sport tourist experience is enjoyable, or why participants would like to repeat the experience. This appears to be an outcome of the predominance of positivist, quantitative research designs that are often devoid of any theoretical discussion. This lack of theoretical underpinning is the second limitation to be identified. Weed (2005) argues that sport tourism is an area of study that, in many cases, does not employ clear theoretical perspectives to underpin what is largely descriptive research. He highlights the concern that the development of social science knowledge has been random, and has produced many studies that are simply added to existing research without any consideration into how such studies further the construction of a coherent body of theoretically grounded knowledge. Finally, almost a third of the literature lacks any form of primary data collection (Weed, 2006), and is, arguably, more speculative in drawing conclusions, than empirically supported.

International Perspectives of Festivals and Events
Copyright © 2009 by Elsevier Ltd.
All rights of reproduction in any form reserved.
ISBN: 978-0-08-045100-8

This chapter aims to address some of these issues through an examination of one particular group of event sport tourists – distance runners – and their experiences 'within the field', relating these experiences to the concept of 'serious sport tourism' (Green and Jones, 2005), focusing specifically upon one particular aspect of serious sport tourism, that of the social identities related to that particular activity. This will facilitate deeper insight into the culture of one significant event tourism social world, so that a more informed discussion of the sociology of sporting events, sport tourism, and sport-related subcultures can be developed. The findings both describe and, more importantly, explain participants' behaviours within the context of two distance running events, firstly, the *Cyprus International 4-day Challenge* and secondly, the *2007 FLM*, described by Bryant (2005, p. 11) as the 'Great Suburban Everest'. It explores whether the actors involved within these particular events have different social constructions of their activity than many of the existing descriptive event sport tourism studies might predict.

Literature Review – 'Serious Event Sport Tourism'

The term 'Serious Leisure' was introduced by Stebbins to describe leisure activities that are 'sufficiently substantial and interesting in nature for the participant to find a career there acquiring and expressing a combination of its special skills, knowledge, and experience' (Stebbins, 1992, p. 3), thus providing a framework by which leisure could be acknowledged to be more substantial than as simply 'free time' or 'free choice', both of which conceptualisations have extremely limited value (Stebbins, 2007). Serious Leisure is defined by six distinctive qualities, these being:

1. A need to persevere, and negotiate constraints to participation.
2. The development of a long-term 'career' within the activity, involving progression through stages of achievement.
3. The use of significant effort, based upon skills, knowledge, or ability, to undertake the activity.
4. The durable benefits that accrue as a result of participation. These include benefits such as those relating to self-esteem, self-actualisation, self-expression, and social interaction.
5. The unique ethos, related to the 'social world' (Unruh, 1980) of the activity, demonstrated, for example, through the dress, language, and behaviour distinctive to that activity.
6. The strong sense of identification that participants' have with the activity. Thus, individuals' will describe themselves in terms of that activity, and view the activity as providing a valued social identity.

Whilst the concept of Serious Leisure has been applied to a variety of contexts, it has yet to be extensively applied to tourism (Frew, 2006), and even less so to event tourism or sport tourism, with perhaps Kane and Zink (2004) providing the only detailed exploration to date. They examined the experiences of kayaking tourists, demonstrating how such tourists became embedded within their own 'social world' during the trip, which, in itself, was a significant marker in terms of the 'career progression' of participants. Using the Serious Leisure framework, they were able to describe the 'social world' of adventure kayakers, although with limited explanation of the reasons why participants behaved in the ways that they did. This limitation is arguably a consequence of the concept of Serious Leisure, in that it is largely a descriptive tool, representing a Weberian 'ideal type', rather than providing an explanatory framework. It therefore fails to tackle the issues of why Serious Leisure participants behave as they do. This was a point addressed by Jones (2006), who suggested that by conceptualising Serious Leisure as leisure that provides the participant with a valued social identity, and focusing upon this single defining characteristic, rather than the six outlined by Stebbins, a more effective framework with which to explain both the attraction of certain activities, as well as the subsequent behaviour of individuals taking part in such activities is provided.

Social identity theory has gained increasing prominence in terms of its ability to explain behaviour in a variety of contexts, ranging from terrorism to sports fandom (Jones, 2006). Essentially, a social identity is formed when the individual becomes aware of their membership of a social group, where such membership involves some emotional or value significance (Tajfel, 1972). Social identities are important for a number of reasons. They provide the individual with a sense of belonging, a valued place within their social environment, a means to connect to others, and the opportunity to use valued identities to enhance self-worth and self-esteem. 'Casual' leisure (such as passive event sport tourism) is unlikely to provide a significant social identity (Stebbins, 2001), however Serious Leisure activities, such as 'active' sport tourism (running the London Marathon or the Cyprus International Running Challenge) have the potential to do so (Green and Jones, 2005). Once the individual has a social identity, then there may be a reciprocal relationship between this identity and Stebbins' other five defining characteristics of Serious Leisure, in that these five defining characteristics are, to some extent, an outcome of the valued social identity. In return, the social identity itself is reinforced by each of the characteristics. This framework allows the behaviours of participants to be both described and, more importantly, explained. This chapter develops this idea, probing the concepts of identity and 'serious event sport tourism', to two particular sporting event contexts.

Methodology

A quasi-ethnographic design was adopted to explore the experiences of the runners participating in both the events. This empirical research was part of a larger ethnographic project involving full immersion in the culture of the distance runner. To access social meanings, observe behaviour, and work closely with informants, several methods of data collection were used as advocated by Brewer (2000), including participant observation, in-depth interviewing, the use of personal documents, and discourse analyses of natural language. This particular approach enabled the researchers to explore the structures and interactions within a cultural context, and to explore the meanings that participants' gave to their cultural environment through first hand experience (Holloway and Todres, 2003). The main aims of the data collection were to access and understand the social meanings of distance runners, observe their behaviour, work closely with key informants, and to actively participate in the sporting 'field' with them at the two events. Within this design, a qualitative approach was used in this chapter given its association with an interpretative viewpoint, exploring the way people make sense of their social worlds, and trying to understand social reality from the point of view of participants engaging in the sporting activity. It was important for this fieldwork to study active participants in their natural settings, attempting to make sense of, or interpret, this phenomenon in terms of the meanings people bring to the activity (Denzin and Lincoln, 1998, p. 3).

Data Collection and Research Settings

The past decade has seen a steady expansion of marathons and similar endurance running events providing for the needs of distance runners, as a substantial subgroup of the sporting events market.

There are clearly extensive event sport tourism opportunities for destinations that choose to target a wide range of running-related activities by offering a diverse range of events from smaller scale 10-kilometre runs, up to the big city marathons such as Berlin, Chicago, London, New York, or Boston, to name but a few.

Gratton et al. (2005) argue that the *FLM* is not only a prestigious and high profile event in the United Kingdom sporting calendar, but it also leaves a hidden but significant economic legacy. Their study demonstrated that the Marathon is a successful business venture that generates in excess of £58 million in associated expenditure. In contrast to that quantitative study, this chapter takes an alternative, qualitative analysis, and interpretation of the Marathon, by looking at the 'experiences' of participants in the event. Engaging in a sport-related event, such as the *2007 FLM*, as an active participant, allows the runner to be at the centre of what Morgan and Watson (2007) describe as an 'extraordinary experience'. These are experiences that simply cannot be replicated by passively observing the event, and therefore make them uniquely distinctive and incredibly intense.

Data collection in London started on the Friday morning, 48 hours before the start, at the London Marathon Expo held in London's Docklands, where the researchers engaged in both semi-structured interviews and observational studies. On the Saturday, the day prior to the event, the authors spent the day with approximately 30 Marathon participants from a variety of UK-based running clubs, who formed an integral part of the data collection. The researchers also contacted several people who had previously been interviewed for the Cyprus element of this study, which was an additional opportunity to follow up and develop some of the emerging themes connected to the experiences of distance runners. On the Sunday, the race day, one researcher completed the Marathon and adopted the role of immersing themselves in the event as a competitor, while the second researcher observed the Marathon at different locations along the route. The post-race evening provided an opportunity to talk and observe runners who had completed the race, and follow up emails and phone conversations were held with Marathon participants in the two weeks following the event.

The second event studied was the *Cyprus 4-day International Running Challenge*. The central locations for the Running Challenge were the Akamas Peninsula and the town of Paphos. The Cyprus event consisted of a mix of different types of running from traditional road running to spectacular trail running, including a 6-kilometre time trial, a hill race involving a 500-metre climb over 11 kilometres of trails, a trail half marathon running across the Akamas National Park, and finishing with a standard, flat road 10 kilometre through the tourist resort of Paphos. The Headquarters for the race series and the main location for data collection was the Coral Beach Hotel. The hotel is located near to Paphos, and was the base for the British Olympic Association (BOA) prior to the Athens 2004 Olympic and Paralympic Games. The race hotel provided an ideal site for both participant observation and interviews with participants in the *Cyprus Challenge*.

The two researchers adopted differing roles, following the idea that adopting differing methods (in this case observation and participant observation) may be useful in developing a more holistic and contextually grounded assessment of the phenomenon (Jick, 1979). One of the authors, whose own experiences within this specific world as an 'experienced insider', became an integral part of the data collection, whereby their own experiences could be used to illuminate and explain key issues (e.g. see McCarville, 2007) that may not be apparent to a more 'scientific' approach (Bale, 2004). The non-participant observer, however, adopted the role of 'outsider', critically questioning the meanings and interpretations of the participant, as well as collecting data from the etic perspective. This approach was preferred to one confined to the use of the self as the only data source, with the possibility that a predominantly auto-ethnographic approach would be too self-indulgent, introspective, and narcissistic (Sparkes, 2000). The methodology used in this fieldwork allowed the researchers to enter inside the experience and systematically document the moment-to-moment details of sport tourism activity. Participants in the study were all entered for either the *Cyprus Challenge* or the *FLM*, and classified as 'serious' sport tourists based upon the level of ability required to complete the two events. Sampling of specific participants was opportunistic, based upon access at appropriate times. Extensive field notes were taken, and subsequent data were coded, both in terms of open and axial coding (Miles and Huberman, 1994), seeking data that were related to the Serious Leisure framework, both confirmatory and disconfirmatory. This data was then channelled into general dimensions based upon the defining qualities of Serious Leisure. Data were not quantified at any stage, as the intention was to explore the issues of 'why', and 'how'. As Krane et al. (1997, p. 214) suggest:

> *placing a frequency count after a category of experiences is tantamount to saying how important it is; thus value is derived by number. In many cases, rare experiences are no less meaningful, useful, or important than common ones. In some cases, the rare experience may be the most enlightening one.*

For the purposes of this chapter, the researchers were aware that it is the voices of the participants that are discussed, and such a realistic approach may be considered as 'author-evacuated' (Sparkes, 2002, p. 51), however it is useful that the credentials of the researchers are given, so that 'credibility' may be ascertained.

Findings and Discussions – Running as Serious Event Sport Tourism

The following findings and discussions suggest a diverse range of motivations for actively participating in the two events. The key finding, which is explained in this section was the strength of identification that participants had with the activity of running. This sense of identification is used to explain the unique ethos of runners, the need for personal effort to complete the events, the perseverance of participants, the durable benefits obtained by the runners, and the career structure associated with the social world of the distance runner.

An underlying theme which was constantly emerging during this fieldwork was the serious, almost professional approach towards the activity adopted by all participants towards their racing, preparation, training, and overall attitude towards distance running in general. A key aspect of the experience was that both running events provided access to a social environment of like-minded people – whilst Serious Leisure is generally perceived in terms of being a group activity (Stebbins, 1992), much of the day-to-day training of the competitors away from the *Cyprus Challenge* or the *London Marathon* was undertaken in isolation. Thus the distance running events allowed participants a period of interaction with other participants. Participants, although event tourists, were certainly not 'on holiday', and their activities could not be viewed in terms such as casual, escape, or relaxation but rather as serious, committed, and activity driven, thus fulfilling the criteria by which Stebbins (1992) distinguishes serious from casual leisure.

Identification as a Distance Runner

Perhaps the clearest finding from the fieldwork was the extent to which participants identified with the activity of distance running, thus confirming the idea that both active and event-related sport tourism could provide a valued social identity. Self-presentation of this identity was a clear feature of the data. The vast majority of participants at both events wore clothing identifying them as runners, most notably in terms of T-shirts containing logos or insignia demonstrating participation in past running events. Much of this clothing holds special nostalgic or sentimental values to distance runners, while also acting as a 'badge of honour', representing the possession of 'subcultural capital' (see below) to demonstrate either their identity as a club athlete or as having completed another marathon, multi-event race, or endurance competition. These T-shirts were often used as conversation ice breakers and as a way of engaging in conversation with other participants, with the club vest or race T-shirt breaking down barriers which may have otherwise existed outside the running 'event' environment. For example, two competitors from relatively close clubs in Wales identified each other immediately after arriving at the 'Blue Start' area of the Marathon in Blackheath, due to the clothing they both wore, a T-shirt from the 2006 Swansea 10-kilometre event.

Running apparel as a statement of people's identity as a runner, was reinforced by the special meaning and association attached to the vest, T-shirt, rain jacket, or sweatshirt that many of the participants wore throughout the duration of the London Marathon weekend, as evidenced through the stories associated with each garment told by some of the runners. Running clothing was clearly apparent at the London Marathon Expo, held on the four days prior to the event, where participants collected their race number and had the opportunity to purchase merchandise associated with the event. There were also opportunities to obtain information on other international running events, and purchase a diverse range of running-related clothing, electronic equipment such as heart rate monitors or GPS technology equipment, and footwear from major sponsors and sportswear manufacturers. One participant commented '*The Expo was great. I felt like a kid in a candy shop!*' The 'finishers' T-shirt from the Marathon was positively received by most participants, and several wore them on the Sunday evening in central London for the post-race meal, as a sign of their achievement in completing the Marathon. One female runner commented '*I was really pleased with the finishers T-shirt. Instead of the usual XXL white cotton joke, we all got a proper, "technical" shirt – it's great!*' However, another competitor moaned:

> *Why was the T-shirt in the goody bag sized to fit an elephant? Runners are supposed to be lean and fit right? I'm a bit annoyed that I won't be able to run in it, to show it off, because it comes down to my knees.*

Runners also talked continually about past performances and past events that they had taken part in, and discussion of previous experiences was by far the most dominant topic of discussion in the days leading up to, during and after the *Cyprus International 4-day Challenge*. This storytelling was a key aspect of establishing the credentials of individuals within the group, and may also have served the function of reinforcing the individual's own sense of identity (Clark and Salaman, 1998). Interestingly, however at a post–London Marathon social event on the Sunday evening, participants while still talking about their Marathon experience, demonstrated less commitment to their running identity after the event finished, focusing partly upon other identities, such as work or family, although still predominantly focusing upon the running identity. This not only supported Foster's (1986) findings that social interaction was focused by a lack of time and the structured daily routines during an event, but also Green and Jones' (2005) suggestion that participants were able to escape their enduring identities associated with their home lives (which was not the case when simply training, or competing close to home).

Both distance running events provided a setting whereby participants were able to undergo an 'identity transformation' (in reality, a shift in identity salience) and become 'serious', almost professional runners. As one participant in London observed *'Where else can you finish 27,532th, and still feel as if you were in an Olympic final?'*, while another competitor explained *'I was stood on the start line at Blackheath, only five metres from both Stefano Baldini, the 2004 Olympic champion from Athens, and the current Marathon world record holder Paul Tergat from Kenya'*. Thus, the very act of travelling to the two events allowed the running identity to become more salient, and more enduring (at least for the four-day duration of the Marathon weekend or the seven-day Cyprus trip) than other identities, that became less salient as participants were distanced from them. This in itself seems to provide an attraction for such events, in that most of the other events for these runners, even for those at a relatively skilled level, were often short-lived, whilst a prolonged visit to Cyprus or London provided a unique opportunity for a period of extended enactment of a particular identity. The consequences of possessing such a valued social identity have been explored within a variety of contexts. These consequences can now be related to the five remaining characteristics of the Serious Leisure framework to demonstrate that they are outcomes of a valued social identity (Jones, 2006).

The Unique Ethos of the Running World

Once a valued social identity exists, then there is generally a strong desire to present it to others (Leary, 1995), especially 'frontstage' where a receptive audience (of both runners and non-runners) exists (Jenkins, 1996). As well as the individual social identities of the runners, a group identity was evident in the homogeneity of behaviour, appearance, and language amongst participants from varied social backgrounds that separated them from non-runners (the runners and non-runners were clearly distinguishable to the researchers in the field, even demonstrating clear differences to other athletes staying at either the hotel in central London or the Coral Bay Hotel in Cyprus). The unique ethos was strongly related to the 'social world' (Unruh, 1980) of the runners. The findings supported the suggestion by Green and Jones (2005) that group members would accentuate their membership through both dress and language, especially where the social identity is not readily apparent. The running identity, unlike identities such as race, or gender, is not necessarily immediately identifiable as such, and hence the use of signifiers such as clothing and language can be seen as a consequence of the desire both to portray a certain social identity, but also to conform to the role identity associated with that group. Some of the language used was specific to the running world, for example competitors spoke of *'blowing up'* or *'hitting the wall'* after some of the Cyprus Challenge events, or needing to get more *'miles in your legs'* in preparation for the Marathon. A spouse of one competitor interviewed in Cyprus noted *'I'm actually fed up with his incessant running speak about mileage, races and diet'*. One participant recalled that:

> *I turned into the type of person to avoid in the months leading up to the event. I had only one topic of conversation and would waffle on about carb-loading, tapering and race days plans to anyone who had the misfortune to listen.*

The need to separate the socially identified 'in-group' from non-runners can be seen as not only descriptive, in that the competing runners invariably wore the same 'uniform' whilst not competing (a T-shirt or cap signifying participation in a past race and either shorts or tracksuit bottoms), and discussed the same issues in the evenings after the Cyprus challenge events (overall time, perception of their personal performance, breaking down the race into constituent parts, comparisons with past races), but also *prescriptive*, in that the social identity prescribed a way to behave, to demonstrate unity with the group. For example, in the days after the Marathon, the majority of club members from one running club all met at a pre-arranged pub on the Thursday evening following the Marathon to embark on a short training run, to help aid recovery. Those who failed to conform, for example one runner who failed to adhere to these group 'standards' was noticeably ostracised as a consequence, confirming the need for group conformity.

The Requirement for Significant Personal Effort

The requirement for significant effort was evident amongst all runners, not only in terms of the physical effort required to undertake both endurance events, but also the evident underlying knowledge demonstrated through the discussion between participants of training routines, nutrition, equipment, and strategy. This was supported by many of the competitors stating that they had undergone an active process of education, for example, in undertaking *UK Athletics* coaching awards, as well as more informal processes of learning, for example one competitor suggested that '*Naivety played a big part. If I had known how bad I was going to feel during the last few miles, I'm not sure I would have gone into the Marathon with the same amount of enthusiasm*'. Another participant indicated:

> I spent hours researching nutrition and strategy. I decided to start slowly and finish strongly when everyone else was tiring. Marathon pace judgment is a skill you develop and learn. I found that it's all about mental toughness. The biggest learning experience from it all was how mental a marathon is.

This characteristic is, arguably, implicit within all Serious Leisure, as more casual activities requiring little in the way of skill are unlikely to provide a valued social identity (Stebbins, 2001). There seems to be a reciprocal relationship here, in that the activity needs to involve significant effort to provide a valued identity, and when that identity is obtained, then individuals will undertake efforts to maintain that identity.

A Need to Persevere

Perseverance generally involves the negotiation of constraints, such as risk, danger, and so on. In this instance the *London Marathon*, the *Cyprus Challenge*, and other longer distance events by their very nature, all require perseverance simply to complete. The main sources identified were not, however, solely related to the personal effort in completing the two running events, but also in various other ways. These included the training schedules that all participants had undertaken, involving high mileages for many months beforehand, the need to save money throughout the year to participate in other running events, including overseas training trips such as Cyprus, and the requirement to balance the time and financial commitments with the need to maintain a balanced family and work life.

Linked to the positive attributes of Serious Leisure, the fieldwork also identified negative aspects of serious sport tourism amongst the distance running community. Discussions with several participants in the *Cyprus Challenge* displayed an interesting balance of priorities in life, often with family and work being ranked behind, or on an even par with their commitment to running as a Serious Leisure activity. As one runner in Cyprus commented

> *My husband can't understand why I have to run on a Tuesday night, club night, when we might have an invite to go out for a drink with friends after work. He often gets annoyed with me and my obsessive need to train. He's not a runner, so he doesn't really understand why I have to run 10 miles tonight.*

This demonstrates the separateness of the runners' social world to even close family. One runner, for example, had forgone the opportunity to go on a family holiday, instead preferring to undertake the Cyprus Challenge event and then prepare and to train for a spring Marathon in Paris, France.

During both running events, extreme cases of perseverance were evident, for example numerous runners suffering from extreme heat exhaustion and dehydration during the events. Normally, such weather conditions would prevent many runners from participating; however many runners persevered, explaining that the nature of the events actually meant that such an act was not even considered. In London, many runners were actually forced to withdraw, not through choice, but through medical conditions which prevented them continuing. One runner reflected:

> *The mask of pain etched on faces was the common denominator. My legs were in spasms of agony and my left thigh had given up and gone numb. My head was screaming 'stop you stupid man, this isn't healthy, enough is enough, but then another little voice kept nagging me saying it hurts more walking than running – nearly there – just keep those legs moving.*

This again can be explained with the need to maintain the social identity, to be seen as someone who completed the Marathon, providing that runner with sub cultural capital that would extend far beyond the duration of that given Sunday in April. One runner in the Cyprus event commented that '*Pain is temporary, failure lasts forever*', or similarly '*Pain is temporary, while glory lasts forever*'. On the theme of suffering, another runner observed '*Pain is simply weakness leaving the body*'. For these runners, the importance was not how they completed the two events in either London or Cyprus, but that they did so. In this way, pain, physical exhaustion, or injury also provided physical evidence of commitment to the group, and become 'badges of honour' among runners (cf. Thornton, 2004). Bale (2004) notes how pain can actually be a source of emotional satisfaction and enjoyment, reaffirming commitment to the social world of the runner. Thus, pain was not actually something necessarily to overcome, but something to value for members of the group.

The unusually warm weather conditions for both events resulted in many participants having to run in conditions they were unfamiliar with, over the various distances. One participant, disappointed with their performance in the heat in London commented:

> *The heat played mind games – it was too hot, there was no breeze, and people were dropping like flies. I just went into preservation mode. The reflected temperature on the tarmac tipped 28 degrees, somewhat higher than the sub zero temperatures I had been used to back home. Docklands was an oven. My mind was on all the effort and pain, and for what? All I achieved was sunburn and a very slow time. It was hot enough to put off cutting the grass, let alone running 26.2 miles.*

The perseverance can be explained from a social identity perspective. Firstly, once a valued social identity exists, then there are a number of mechanisms that 'protect' this identity, for example the development of in-group favouritism, whereby participants view fellow in-group members (in this case, runners) favourably, whereas non-runners (the out-group) were generally perceived in negative terms, often in terms of lack of fitness, being 'couch potatoes', or lacking the motivation to undertake an activity that required no particular skills. Such perceptions make it difficult for in-group members to cease participation and become part of the derogated out-group. Secondly, the self-presentation of such identities to others makes it difficult to cease such activities, due to the expectations of others, and how runners may feel they will be perceived if they stopped the activity (Shamir, 1992). One runner highlighted before the Cyprus events that '*I got flu, and basically lost four weeks of training, which is why I'm probably going to struggle. I just don't want to fail after training so hard, I just don't want to let my family and friends down*'. Thus runners are, to some extent, socially committed to the activity once others are aware of their social identity.

The Development of Running Careers

The concept of serious event sport tourism suggests a career path whereby particular stages of the activity are achieved. For many runners participating in both Cyprus and London, the events were often seen as a career progression, representing an advance from smaller scale, or shorter events, to a more 'professional' event. Several of the group commented before the events that they were a '*major step up*', thus for some this was a significant 'career marker', representing a confirmation of their progression to confirmed 'serious' runner. For others, however, it was actually a 'step back' from, or training session for more advanced events such as the *Marathon des Sables* (an ultra marathon across Moroccan desert). For these runners, a clear 'career' development had occurred over time, and was perhaps less important if they had extensive experience.

The challenge of the two events studied was especially important as a career marker for less experienced participants, providing them with sub cultural capital (Green and Jones, 2005), in that participation in the events actually raised their level of identification and credibility with other runners, through having taken part in such an event, especially for those who had competed at a more local level, or who had yet to complete longer races, such as a Marathon. For many, these events were the pinnacle of their running career, as one participant in London commented:

> I have done several half marathons, but this was my first full Marathon. The 'London' was one of the best and worst things I have done in my life. I now have the bug. I told myself during the race to just get back in one piece and don't worry about the time, however upon reflection I'm disappointed. I am even more determined now to get the time I wanted. I'm determined to get round in less than five hours.

This collection of sub cultural capital, related to the valued social identity was an important motivator for many runners however. As part of this, a strong motivation for participation was the desire to travel and 'collect places', as advocated by Urry (2002) with the 'Big Five' of London, New York, Berlin, Boston, and Chicago mentioned by several competitors. An important element of this aspect was the subsequent tradition of storytelling, as highlighted by McCarville (2007), whereby the rigours and exertions undertaken were discussed, and debated.

Durable Benefits

The durable benefits of participation within both events were evident through both observation and interviews with participants. Some of these were generic, such as developing and overcoming personal challenges, experiencing a heightened sense of achievement and self-esteem, fun and happiness, healthy living, weight loss and physical well-being, injury rehabilitation, addiction and obsession, induced euphoria, excitement and adrenalin, pride, overcoming pain and exhaustion, spirituality and testing the mind, body and spirit, freedom, space, place-specific attractions, enhancing personal performance, and non-aggressive competition. Generally, however, feelings of accomplishment were mentioned as being of a greater magnitude than home-based events, such as 10-kilometre road races or half marathons, for two main reasons. Firstly, the nature of the Marathon event (over 42 kilometres of continuous running) or the Cyprus Challenge (four hard races over four consecutive days) was, for many competitors, more than they had experienced during their running careers. Secondly, the actual nature and route of the *London Marathon* and the *Cyprus Challenge* as events, in terms of unfamiliar routes, the unseasonably warm climate, and difficulty provided challenges beyond that faced by the runners at home. This was identified by one London Marathon runner who said that:

> *The worst part was finding the horrible mess that was lying in wait beneath my socks on Sunday evening, and having to scramble around on my backside all day on Monday. I had niggles in places that I have never had niggles before – my whole body just felt so jarred and achy. Three days later and I was still walking like a penguin. Despite this, blisters last a week, but the memories will last a lifetime.*

The second key benefit identified through the fieldwork was that of the self-esteem benefits accrued as a consequence of participation in both running events. Clear evidence of 'basking in reflected glory' (Cialdini et al., 1976) was observed though participants wearing artefacts that positively associated them with previous events (notably the Paris Marathon and the New York Marathon). One runner commented upon completing the Cyprus Challenge – '*I made it, and I got the medal – now I'm wallowing in self pride*'. One London Marathon finisher noted:

> *I ran down the Mall with the announcer telling us that we were achieving something only 1% of people in Britain will achieve. It was chaos afterwards. Finding my family and friends was very difficult, but when I did I had hero status. This carried on the next day when I arrived at the office, as all my colleagues came to have a look at the medal that I proudly wore at work all day. I felt like a real champion, and was still buzzing from it all five days later, and I'm happily telling my story to anyone and everyone who will listen. However, I'm now suffering from PMD –Post Marathon Depression!*

Another rather weary Marathon finisher, sat outside a pub in central London, less than an hour after completing the event observed:

> *When the medal was put around my neck I forgot all those hard miles; they melted into the background as I looked dazed and confused at the medal. I had done everything I had ever dreamed of. I have never felt more pride and happiness and I knew that moment would stay with me forever.*

Discussion of past successes was an evident focus of social interaction, especially during the months of preparation for the two events. A key finding was that some individuals were able to protect their self-esteem as runners through emphasising injury, lack of preparation, or simply suggesting minimal effort was to be undertaken during the events. This was generally done in either the few days prior to the Marathon or in the days surrounding the Cyprus Challenge, and could be viewed as 'cutting off future failure' (Wann et al., 1995), a strategy utilised to anticipate and account for potential dangers to the running identity of the participant. For example, on the day before the Marathon, one male competitor observed '*I think I might have a nightmare day tomorrow though. If that happens, I'll just put it down to lack of preparation, lack of fitness, injury and the curry and beers we had last night*'.

Given the focus upon the running identity during the days before the events, this strategy appeared to be a key element of 'protecting' that identity, so that performances not congruent with the identity portrayed (e.g. failing to complete the Cyprus Challenge, or finishing the Marathon in an unsatisfactory time) did not impact upon the salient identity. One female runner, interviewed at the finish of the London event observed:

> *I had an excruciating hamstring pain at 20 miles, which slowed me down. Also at 18 miles, I heard that Haile Gebreselassie (the famous Ethiopian athlete) had pulled out, and my instant thought was that if he can't make it, then I'm stopping too.*

The durable benefits again relate to the social identities held by the runners. Benefits such as those which accrued through basking in reflected glory are only available when there is a strong connection between the self and the activity. Thus, casual runners are unlikely to gain benefits from occasional participation if the activity holds no value for them. Serious runners are, however, more likely to benefit from successes related to their sense of membership.

Conclusions

The main aim of this chapter was to demonstrate a framework by which 'serious' sport tourism activities could be described and explained. Stebbins' (1992) Serious Leisure framework provides a useful tool with which to describe the characteristics of such behaviour. As noted, however, the key limitation is that it fails to explain these behaviours. By adopting a social identity based approach, however, this chapter has provided a preliminary explanation of the characteristics of 'serious event sport tourism' based upon a quasi-ethnographic study of distance runners. By confirming the valued social identities held by participants, the subsequent unique ethos of the group, the perseverance of its members, the requirement for personal effort, the careers of the runners, and the subsequent durable benefits can be explained to some extent.

A key emphasis of this chapter was to speak with event participants rather than speaking for or about them. Outcomes from the fieldwork suggest that the dominant positivist, scientific model of research in sport tourism (and also in much event tourism in general) fails to understand or capture the real nature of social settings (Atkinson and Hammersley, 1994). While the existing typologies of sport tourism are extremely useful, limitations lie in their inability to account for event sport tourists who cut across typology classifications, based on the unique aspects of their chosen activity, be it rugby, football, tennis, swimming, golf, skiing, distance running, or any other form of event sport tourism activity. In order to understand the social world of event sport tourism, future research needs to be qualitative in its nature rather than conceptualising sport tourism in terms of variables and the relationship between them.

There is extensive scope to explore some of the key themes that emerged from this observational research in order to develop a deeper understanding of the social world of distance running. Future research opportunities are most notable in the link between Serious Leisure, identity, and distance running. In the wider context, this chapter attempts to illustrate the extensive potential for qualitative research on 'active' sport tourism participants at both major and smaller scale sporting events. This chapter in itself does not address all of the issues related to current event sport tourism research, but is one of a series of forthcoming open ended field studies that are linked, leading to cumulative advances in knowledge and understanding of distance runners as active sport tourists.

References

Atkinson, P. and Hammersley, M. (1994) Ethnography and participant observation. In Denzin, N. and Lincoln, Y. (eds.), *Handbook of Qualitative Research*. London: Sage, pp. 248–261.

Bale, J. (2004) *Running Cultures: Racing in Time and Space*. London: Routledge.

Brewer, J. (2000) *Ethnography: Understanding Social Research*. Buckingham: Open University Press.

Bryant, J. (2005) *The London Marathon: The History of the Greatest Race on Earth*. London: Arrow Books.

Cialdini, R., Borden, R., Thorne, A., Walker, M., Freeman, S. and Sloan, L. (1976) Basking in reflected glory; Three (football) field studies. *Journal of Personality and Social Psychology*, 34(3), 366–375.

Clark, T. and Salaman, G. (1998) Telling tales: Management gurus' narratives and the construction of managerial identity. *Journal of Management Studies*, 35(2), 137–161.

Denzin, N. and Lincoln, Y. (1998) *Handbook of Qualitative Research*. London: Sage.

Foster, G. (1986) South Seas cruise: A case study of a short lived society. *Annals of Tourism Research*, 13(20), 215–238.

Frew, E. (2006) Comedy festival attendance: Serious, project based or casual leisure? In Elkington, S., Jones, I. and Lawrence, L. (eds.), *Serious Leisure: Extensions and Applications*. Eastbourne: LSA, pp. 105–122.

Gibson, H. (2005) Towards an understanding of 'why sport tourists do what they do'. *Sport in Society*, 8(2), 198–217.

Gratton, C., Shibli, S. and Coleman, R. (2005) The economics of sport tourism at major sports events. In Higham, J. (ed.), *Sport Tourism Destinations: Issues, Opportunities and Analysis*. Oxford: Elsevier Butterworth-Heinemann, pp. 233–247.

Green, C. and Jones, I. (2005) Serious leisure, social identity and sport tourism. *Sport in Society*, 8(2), 198–217.

Holloway, I. and Todres, L. (2003) The status of method: Flexibility, consistency and coherence. *Qualitative Research*, 3(3), 345–357.

Jenkins, R. (1996) *Social Identity*. London: Routledge.

Jick, T. (1979) Mixing qualitative and quantitative methods: Triangulation in action. *Administrative Science Quarterly*, 24(4), 602–611.

Jones, I. (2006) Examining the characterisitcs of serious leisure from a social identity perspective. In Elkington, S., Jones, I. and Lawrence, L. (eds.), *Serious Leisure: Extensions and Applications*. Eastbourne: LSA, pp. 47–60.

Kane, M. and Zink, R. (2004) Package adventure tours: Markers in serious leisure careers. *Leisure Studies*, 23(4), 329–345.

Krane, V., Anderson, M. and Stean, W. (1997) Issues of qualitative research methods and presentation. *Journal of Sport and Exercise Psychology*, 19, 213–218.

Leary, M. (1995) *Self Presentation: Impression Management and Interpersonal Behavior*. Boulder: Westview.

McCarville, R. (2007) From a fall in the mall to a run in the sun: One journey to Ironman Triathlon. *Leisure Sciences*, 29, 159–173.

Miles, M. and Huberman, A. (1994) *Qualitative Data Analysis*. Thousand Oaks: Sage.

Morgan, M., Watson, P. (2007) *Resource Guide in Extraordinary Experiences: Understanding and Managing the Consumer Experience in Hospitality, Leisure, Events, Sport and Tourism*, Higher Education Academy [On-line]. Available at: http://www.hlst.heacademy.ac.uk/resources/guides/extraexperiences.html, accessed on 16/06/2007.

Shamir, B. (1992) Some correlates of leisure identity salience: Three exploratory studies. *Leisure Studies*, 24(4), 301–323.

Sparkes, A. (2000) Auto ethnography and narratives of self: Reflections on criteria in action. *Sociology of Sport*, 17, 21–43.

Sparkes, A. (2002) *Telling Tales in Sport and Physical Activity: A Qualitative Journey*. Champaign: Human Kinetics.

Stebbins, R. (1992) *Amateurs, Professionals and Serious Leisure*. Montreal: McGill-Queen's University Press.

Stebbins, R. (2001) *New Directions in the Theory and Research of Serious Leisure*. Lewiston: Edwin Melllen.

Stebbins, R. (2007) *Serious Leisure: A Perspective For Our Time*. New Brunswick: Transaction.

Tajfel, H. (1972) Experiments in a vacuum. In Israel, J. and Tajfel, H. (eds.), *The Context of Social Psychology: A Critical Assessment*. London: Academic Press, pp. 69–119.

Thornton, A. (2004) Anyone can play this game: Ultimate frisbee, identity and difference. In Wheaton, B. (ed.), *Understanding Lifestyle Sports: Consumption, Identity and Difference*. London: Routledge, pp. 175–196.

Unruh, D. (1980) The nature of social worlds. *Pacific Sociological Review*, 23, 271–296.

Urry, J. (2002) *The Tourist Gaze*. London: Sage.

Wann, D., Hamlet, M., Wilson, T. and Hodges, J. (1995) Basking in reflected glory, cutting off reflected failure, and cutting off future failure: The importance of group identification. *Social Behaviour and Personality*, 23(4), 377–388.

Weed, M. (2005) Sports tourism theory and method – Concepts, issues and epistemologies. *European Sport Management Quarterly*, 5(3), 229–242.

Weed, M. (2006) Sports tourism research 2000–2004: A systematic review of knowledge and a meta-interpretation of methods. *Journal of Sport and Tourism*, 11(1), 5–30.

Chapter 13

Elite Sports Tours: Special Events with Special Challenges

Michael Morgan and Richard Wright

Introduction

The past two decades has seen a considerable amount of research into the implications for tourism of large-scale, urban-based, sporting competitions, with numerous case study-based explorations of the Olympic Games in particular. However, while the periodically held 'mega' event remains the world's most recognisable type of sports competition, it is important to recognise the diverse, and transient, nature of the rapidly expanding global sports event market. For example, at any one moment in time, somewhere in the world, a professional sports event will be either starting or coming to a conclusion. Regardless of its size, status or general appeal, this event will not only be attended by those participating, but also those watching from the stands.

   With the emergence of a truly global sports event industry, there has also been a noticeable growth in the number of elite sporting competitions that involve some kind of touring itinerary necessitating the movement of those in attendance (i.e. teams, entourage, supporters) from one locality to the next. In doing so, they often cross regional boundaries and so require the involvement and collaboration of several political, administrative and sporting authorities. In general, the majority of these travel movements tend to be from one venue to another in the same host nation, but the soaring financial costs involved in securing and staging high profile sporting tournaments has resulted in an increase in the number of major events being co-hosted by neighbouring countries. Examples of the latter include football championships co-hosted by Belgium and Holland (2000), South Korea and Japan (2004); Rugby World Cups by France and Britain (1999 and 2007) and the Cricket World Cup spread across the Caribbean nations in 2007.

   This chapter will examine the special challenges that these touring events, crossing regional or national boundaries, present to key stakeholders involved in both the supply-side and the demand-side of sports event tourism. In addition to discussing the actions of public and private sector operators, it also highlights the experiences of the host communities and the supporters that travel to attend such events. The challenges will be illustrated by the case of the 2005 British and Irish Lions Rugby Union Tour of New Zealand. In doing so, it draws on the authors' individual research into the regional tourism planning that surrounded the six-week tour (Wright, 2007) and the experience of the travelling supporters in attendance (Morgan, 2007). Wright interviewed representatives of 11 Regional Tourism Organisations (RTOs) responsible for maximising the benefits to the local visitor economy from the tour, while Morgan reflected on the insights into the nature of the sports tourism experience provided by participant observation of the Lions' fans. In comparing the findings, the authors considered that some of the issues raised by this kind of elite touring sports event were not covered in any depth by the existing literature. This chapter is intended to identify and explore these issues.

Background

Staging special events is widely regarded as a unique, and infrequent, opportunity for host destinations to generate substantial global media attention, while at the same time attracting a significant amount of short-term, but high-yielding, visitors (Hall, 2001; Getz, 2003). Within the realms of sport tourism, 'elite' events are defined by Hinch and Higham (2004) as competitive fixtures in which the number of passive participants (spectators) significantly outnumbers the number of active participants (competitors, officials and coaching staff). The diversity of products and experiences offered by sports event tourism has been a key ingredient in its rapid emergence as an important segment of the world's tourism market (Bjelac and Radovanovic, 2003; Pigeassou, 2004). At the start of the 21st century, the net worth of all sports events was estimated to be almost 30% of all international tourism-generated revenue (Kurtzman, 2001).

Examples of urban-based sports event research can be found across a variety of academic disciplines (Getz, 2003). In general, the majority adopt a case study approach, targeting quantifiable/statistical data in order to calculate the socio-economic value of sports event tourism to the host destination (Bramwell, 1997). As the world's largest periodically held sporting competition, the Olympic Games are without doubt the most cited, and well-documented example of tourism-generating 'mega' or 'hallmark' events, and have been the subject of research conducted across a wide range of academic disciplines including economics, geography and the social sciences (Madden, 2002; Waitt, 2001).

While it is necessary to stage certain Olympic sports (e.g. Equestrian, Sailing, etc.) in peripheral or coastal locations away from the host city, the majority of participants and supporters still tend to locate themselves in, or at least around, a single base for the duration of the event. As a result, much of the existing research into the implications of hosting the Olympic Games has tended to be heavily focused on the impacts generated within the single 'host' destination. As a result, the potential ramifications on the wider/surrounding region or nation as a whole is often overlooked or ignored.

Existing sports event tourism studies appear to overlook the growing prevalence of other types of sporting competitions which not only last longer but also take place over a greater geographical area. For well over a century, regular international cricket and rugby 'Test' series have been contested by touring teams that stay in the host country for a number of weeks and play in several different cities or regions. The Football (Soccer), Rugby and Cricket World Cups, have since the 1930s chosen to schedule their fixtures across a number of destinations within the host country, in contrast to the single city formula utilised by the Olympics. Finally, examples of national and international sporting circuits and individual touring events can be found among a range of professional sports, most notably cycling and rally driving. The domestic and international travel movements generated immediately before, during and after these events present a wide range of research issues worthy of further study.

The sheer size and scale of the global sports event market makes any attempt to categorise such competitions an arduous challenge in itself. For the sake of this chapter, we have identified three major types within the elite sports tours sector; the Test Series, the Cup Finals and the Road Tour. The evolution of each group is described in the following section.

The History of Elite Sports Tours

The Test Series

The earliest examples of what we term the 'elite sports tour' date back over a 100 years to the lengthy excursions first undertaken by cricketers in the late 19th century. These first tours included several months at sea, and typically involved teams travelling between the Mother Country and the colonial settlements of the British Empire. India and Australia were the traditional opponents for England's cricketers, whilst New Zealand and South Africa were the major origins and destinations of Rugby tours. As a result of the long transit times, and the high costs involved, each touring party would remain in the host country for several months at a time. Whilst there, they would play a series of provincial matches (against regional sides) and 'Test' matches (against the national side). A 'Test' series, in both cricket and rugby, would typically involve either three or five games at various different venues located around the host country. The number of provincial fixtures played varied depending on the size of the host country and the length of the tour.

While the development of air-travel has increased the accessibility of these and many other destinations, the basic formula adopted by the touring sides has altered very little over the course of the past century. What has changed as a result of the improved transport links between the traditional touring nations has been the increased frequency on which the tours take place and the decreased duration of time spent in each location. While cricket Test series continue to be over two or three months in duration, international rugby teams have, since the game went professional in 1995, tended to make shorter tours with few or no provincial warm-up games. The British and Irish Lions, used as the main case study in this chapter, are the exception, a specialised touring team that maintains, in a truncated form, the traditional pattern of the provincial tour.

The British and Irish Lions.   In almost all international sporting codes (including Rugby Union) the constituent countries of the British Isles compete as separate national teams. However, over the past 119 years, the leading rugby players from England, Wales, Scotland and Ireland have regularly come together, putting national allegiance to one side in order to travel and compete as a team representing the British Isles or latterly Britain and Ireland. The first official tour was the visit to New Zealand in 1888 and lasted 9 months, including the 14-week return journey by sailing ship (Lions Rugby, 2005). Due to the large costs involved, many of the earliest trips incorporated matches in both Australia and New Zealand. Knight (2005) notes that, while the 'Lions' nickname first emerged during the 1930s, it was not until the 1950 and 1955 tours – of New Zealand and South Africa respectively – that it began to be widely used in the media.

With the introduction of the Rugby World Cup (in 1987) and the subsequent professionalisation of Rugby Union (in 1995), the number of traditional-style tours have noticeably declined (Maguire and Tuck, 1998). While it is still common for travelling cricket and rugby teams to have a couple of warm-up matches against local sides, the British Lions is now the only international sporting side that continues to combine a full series of provincial matches within their travels. However, as a result of the World Cup, and a general increase in international Test matches, these tours are now obliged to operate on a much more disciplined schedule, alternating every four years between Australia, New Zealand and South Africa at the half way point between each World Cup year. The most recent tour of New Zealand, in 2005, lasted 36 days with 11 matches in 9 regional locations and included 3 Tests in Christchurch, Wellington and Auckland.

While the duration, and frequency, of such tours have been heavily reduced, the number of people travelling to follow these fixtures has increased significantly as long-haul tourism has become affordable to a larger proportion of the population. The 2001 Lions tour of Australia, for example, brought an estimated 10,000 fans to the country (Mintel, 2004). Similarly, in 2005, an estimated 20,400 travelling supporters followed the largest ever Lions squad to New Zealand (Vuletich, 2005).

Arguably, it is the dramatic increase in travelling support that has not only helped to ensure the sustainability of the Lions tour concept, but also made them one of the most recognisable brands in sport. Though these types of sports tours have always attracted large crowds from within the host destinations, their newly found 'unique' status, along with the increase in accessibility, has firmly secured their place as a major tourism-generating sports event.

The Cup Finals

The second type of multi-centred events is the final stages of a World Cup or European Cup competition. Typically this involves a series of pool matches played in locations around the host nation, followed by quarter-finals, semi-finals and a final. Thus, as in the sports tour, competing teams have to move from location to location during the tournament. Football's (Soccer) World Cup undoubtedly provides us with the best, and most cited, example of these events. First held in 1930, it takes place once every four years and is the most widely viewed sporting event in the world. FIFA, the sport's governing body, recently estimated a global television audience of approximately 715.1 million watched Italy defeat France in the 2006 tournament final (FIFA, 2006). The right to host the finals is awarded in a similar manner to the Olympics, with several nations bidding for the honour years in advance. FIFA policy also prevents two countries from the same continent hosting the event on back to back occasions, giving the event even greater scarcity value.

The matches are traditionally held in a number of locations around the host country. However, in 2002, the tournament was co-hosted for the first time by neighbouring Japan and South Korea. Though the number of nations and amount of global exposure involved varies significantly, the basic principles of a knockout tournament formula – which incorporates a round-robin group stage followed by several elimination rounds – has been copied on numerous occasions within football and a number of other team sports. The UEFA European Championships, for example, operates similar formats, as do tournaments periodically held in Africa, Asia and the Americas.

Following the example of soccer, other sports have established similar World Cup formats including Rugby League (in 1954), Rugby Union (in 1987) and Cricket (with the inaugural One Day International in 1974 and, more recently, the first Twenty/Twenty World Cup in 2007).

The Road Tour

A third category of elite sports tour is what we have termed the road tour. These tend to occur on an annual schedule but share the key characteristic of the movement of teams, entourage and spectators from place to place across regional or national boundaries. The Tour de France is, by far, the most commonly cited example of this type of event. First developed in 1903, the 22-day, 20-stage cycle road race is usually run over more than 3,000 kilometre around France and its neighbouring countries. De Knop (2006) claims the Tour is unmatched by any other elite sports event in generating tourism revenue, attracting several million spectators along the route. This audience in turn results in a long procession of sponsors' vehicles preceding the cyclists through each town. Towns and cities bid for the honour and unprecedented publicity that comes with the passage of the 'peleton', so the route varies from year to year. As a result, for an individual locality the arrival of the tour may have the rare and infrequent value noted in the other two types of elite tour. For example, the BBC (2007a) reported that at least 500,000 people 'flocked' to see more than 189 riders start the 2007 tour from central London for the first time in the event's history. In addition, it was also estimated that around two million people lined the streets along the following day's London to Canterbury stage (BBC, 2007b). For the dedicated fans, the Tour is a participative as well as spectator event, with many taking several days holiday to camp in the mountains alongside the route of the key stages, or to ride the same routes as their professional heroes (Berridge, 2006). A similar pattern to the Tour is found in other cycle races, along with the various national and international rallying events that annually make up the World Rally Championship.

Distinguishing Characteristics of Elite Sports Tours

From an analysis of these three main categories within the elite sport tours sector, the features which distinguish them from other types of elite sports events are shown in Table 13.1. For destination management, the key implications are:

- Matches or stages take place at a succession of different venues within numerous host locations over a short period of weeks.
- These locations tend to be spread across the host country, often for economic and political reasons as well as purely sporting ones.
- The teams and their entourage (management and support staff) are often required and expected to move around the country.
- To follow their team, supporters also have to travel from one centre to another, as opposed to remaining in one destination and/or staying at the same accommodation throughout the event's duration.
- The planning, management and exploitation of such events therefore involve key local authority representatives and industry stakeholders from more than one region.

In addition to the distinguishing features listed above, the elite tour also can be seen to share the following characteristics in common with other major sports events:

- From the viewpoint of the host country, or at least the host region, the tour is a one-off event and/ or one that occurs very infrequently with a gap of many years between.

Table 13.1:   Distinguishing features of elite sports tours

	Elite sports tours	Mega sports events	Professional sports circuits
Occurrence	Infrequent	Infrequent	Annual
Location	Series of venues across regional or national boundaries	A single city, plus satellite locations	International: One event in each country
Competitors	Move from venue to venue	Based in a single place	Permanently 'on the road'
Typical duration	Three to six weeks tour	Programme of events over two to four weeks	Discrete events over six to twelve months
Examples	Rugby, cricket tours; Soccer, Rugby, Cricket World Cups; cycle tours and car rallies	Olympic and Commonwealth Games, Americas Cup, Ryder Cup	Golf, tennis, motor racing

- The event is of major significance to followers of the sport, thus attracting large numbers of international and often trans-continental tourists.
- The event will also attract a significant amount of domestic and international media attention/ exposure, providing unique opportunities for host destinations to (re)brand and (re)position their region on an increased, potentially, global scale.

These features together distinguish these infrequent inter-regional tours from sports events which occur on annual international circuits. Examples of these would be the various Grand Prix (in Athletics and Motorsport), in addition to golf and tennis tournaments, which continually move from country to country over the course of a year or season. Unlike the tour events we have covered above, those incorporated into an established circuit not only involve different national sporting and governmental authorities, but also are unlikely to attract spectators able to follow the whole series. Each individual tournament, or round, is therefore regarded as being a separate national event in its own right. For example, although they are a coordinated part of a series of competitions on the ATP and WTA pro-tennis circuits which form the basis for a world ranking, the annual tennis tournaments at Melbourne Park, Roland Garros, Wimbledon and Flushing Meadows are all equally discrete and distinguishable elite events in their own right.

We also distinguish between the World Cup format spread over a number of different venues and other sports' World Championships, for example Athletics, which are still held within a single host city or host region in a similar style to the Olympics or Commonwealth Games format.

The Challenges of Elite Sports Tours

The transient and infrequent nature of these elite tour events presents a number of challenges to the many different stakeholders involved in the initial planning and subsequent management of each fixture. In this chapter, we have separated some of the key issues identified in our research into four individual, but inter-related, areas worthy of further discussion. These are:

1. Choice and scheduling of host locations.
2. The need for inter-regional tourism planning.
3. Unpredictable patterns of demand.
4. The changing nature of the sports tourism experience.

Choice of Locations

The logistical elements of an elite sports tour are typically arranged by the sport's national governing body (e.g. New Zealand Rugby Football Union NZRFU), the governing bodies of the visiting team (in the 2005 Lions' case a management team appointed by the English, Welsh, Scottish and Irish Rugby Unions) and the sport's independent world governing body (e.g. the International Rugby Board). Together, these top-level organisations not only determine the specific timing and duration of the event, but also the unique schedule and structure of the competition. The individual sporting criteria to be used in determining the allocation of various host locations is also discussed and decided by these key players. A major issue under negotiation, for example, is the need for all regional 'warm-up' games to be against suitable teams of the right level of competitiveness. In addition, the specific requirements of the touring party, in terms of accommodation, travelling times and training facilities must be considered. Finally, the seating capacity and overall standard of the grounds to be used has also become a major issue over the past decade, especially with the growth in demand shown by travelling supporters and the increased concern for safety and security.

From a purely economical perspective, those responsible for funding the events are increasingly under pressure to maximise the economic revenue gained through ticket sales/gate receipts. In the case of the 2005 Lions tour, the various Regional Rugby Unions (Rufus) were invited by the NZRFU to bid for a provincial fixture, with the support of their regional or municipal governments. The choice of location for the three Test matches was a much less complex process, with the games being awarded only to the New Zealand sporting venues – and to a certain extent destinations – deemed large enough to cope with the perceived demand (i.e. influx of visitors).

The potential economic benefits and impacts of hosting a match mean that the decisions are also a matter of major political concern for various government authorities. City, regional or national governments are often heavily involved with bids, particularly if there is a need for investment in venues and infrastructure (Jones, 2001). This can give them leverage in influencing the choice. As Higham (2005, p. 97) says; 'one recurring challenge relating to sport tourism planning is [determining] where government responsibility and institutional arrangements for sport and tourism lie'. Furthermore, the choice is often influenced by a combination of existing sporting and regional politics. For example, in their bid to host the 2007 Rugby World Cup in France, the Fédération Française de Rugby were supported by their counterparts in Wales and Scotland against a rival bid from England, as a reward for which, some matches were also awarded to both Cardiff and Edinburgh. Within France, the choices of Lens and Marseille were made partly to introduce the sport to cities without a rugby tradition.

The Need for Inter-regional Tourism Planning

Once the final decision on the various host locations has been made, the management and exploitation of the tourism flows generated is likely to involve significant input from a range of potentially competing local and national authorities. As Hinch and Higham (2004) point out, planning for sports event tourism, at any level, can often take place at various spatial levels and within various organisations from both the public and private sectors. Successful planning for sport event tourism at an inter-regional level requires a high degree of supportive cooperation received from key stakeholders (Dobson and Sinnamon, 2001; Getz, 2003; Hall, 2000; Higham, 2005; Hinch and Higham, 2004; Webb, 2005; Weed and Bull, 2004; Whitson and Macintosh, 1996).

While an integrated management approach can assist event tourism planners, to achieve it requires a significant amount of coordination, cross-sector communication and cooperation from a range of local industry stakeholders, many of whom are also actively fighting against each other within the highly competitive regional tourism market (Getz, 1997, 2003; Higham, 2005). Getz (1997) identified the destination, the consumer, the event organiser and the event sponsor as four of the most active stakeholders found within regional event planning. Unsurprisingly, each were found to have their own perspectives, agendas and personal priorities, making the challenge of planning tourism generated through sports events even more daunting for destination managers. More recently, Getz (2003, p. 50) suggests; 'many stakeholder groups can be involved with sport events, therefore tourism goals must be complimentary to those relating to sport and community development, corporate marketing, and the physical environment'.

The lack of coordination between independent sport agencies and regional tourism authorities has been the focus of many studies within the realms of sport, tourism and sport tourism literature. Weed and Bull's (1997) in-depth study into regional sport and tourism policies in England, for example, remains a prominent warning of the lack of integration that exists between sport agencies and tourism organisations at a regional government level. In a similar study, focusing on public and private sector organisations, Gibson (2002, p. 114) also found 'a lack of coordinated policy and practice', including a series of conflicting goals among individually motivated operators and agencies.

At present, the responsibility for planning mega sports events has largely fallen on the shoulders of national government-backed agencies within sport and economic development (Hall, 2005). Existing event planning procedures have therefore tended to utilise a distinctly 'top-down' approach of governance and promotion, with little consideration for the long-term consequences, particularly with regards to the negative impact and implications that staging such events can have on the host communities (Dobson and Sinnamon, 2001; Hiller, 1998; Hodges and Hall, 1996; Olds, 1998; Shapcott, 1998). While events can be controlled, organised and driven from outside the region, this has been shown to amplify negative effects in a manner that local authorities are unwilling or unable to mitigate (Hall, 1997; Hiller, 1998; Jones, 2001).

In the case of the 2005 Lions tour, RTOs only became involved after the itinerary of matches had been agreed. With support and guidance from Tourism New Zealand, the majority of RTOs began planning between 18 and 12 months in advance. The underlying motive was generally the desire to 'cash in on the good will for New Zealand' through the maximisation of visitor spend and global media exposure gained. The generation of future business opportunities was also high on the agenda. The event was regarded as a 'golden' or 'once-in-a-lifetime' opportunity to 'showcase' New Zealand's regional diversity to one of their biggest overseas markets. With regards to repeat visitation, many of the RTOs aimed to ensure that every visitor not only wanted to return, but also returned to the United Kingdom as 'walking brochures' for their region. As a result, broad or generic objectives were created at an early stage and subsequently followed up by a series of more flexible/reactive plans implemented on a more ad-hoc basis.

While the social and environmental implications were briefly discussed, the principal, short-term targets all tended to be financially motivated. The main long-term objectives were generally based around the maximisation of the future benefits, especially those attached to the extensive global media coverage/attention expected to follow the Tour. Many regions argued that this is much more important than the pre-event promotion itself. However, due to the lack of experience or reliable data, the first course of action taken by the RTOs generally involved the development of regional working groups or steering panels. The groups all included representatives from both the public sector (e.g. economic development agencies and local authority departments) and the private sector (e.g. local business operators from within the transport, accommodation and hospitality sectors). The extent to which the different RTO were involved tended to vary, depending on the size of the organisation. However, in general, these stakeholders were considered to be active and accurate representatives for the local community as well as their industry.

Unpredictability of Demand

With regards to planning for the 2005 Lions tour, the biggest challenge faced by the 11 New Zealand RTOs was forecasting how many supporters were actually going to need accommodating and entertaining within their region.

Overall, the problems experienced across New Zealand's hosting and non-hosting regions are seen as being typical of such elite sports tours. The unique transient features of these special occasions, along with the long periods of time that lapse between such events makes it almost impossible to predict patterns of demand with any accuracy. Forecasting sports tourism is always difficult. In football (soccer), after the success of the 1998 World Cup, which was reported to have attracted 900,000 fans to France, both the 2000 European Championships in Belgium and Holland and the 2002 World Cup in Japan and South Korea failed to meet their forecast numbers. According to Mintel (2004) this was due to a mixture of macro-economic factors, the perceived threats of terrorism, over-pricing of accommodation and purely sporting reasons such as which teams qualified for the competitions.

With the Lions only touring once every 4 years, to New Zealand, South Africa and Australia in turn, this results in a gap of 12 years between their return visits to each particular destination. Clearly, the lack of recent data on which to base forecasts plays a major role in the problems facing event planner both at a national and a regional level. The 2005 series was the Lions first tour of New Zealand since 1993. All the RTOs agreed that the previous Lions tours to New Zealand, and the last South African (Springboks) tour to New Zealand in 1994, were too long ago to have any relevance to how they approached the 2005 series. Likewise, the inaugural Rugby World Cup, co-hosted (and won) by New Zealand back in 1987 was also discounted due to the significant growth in long-haul sports tourism and the professionalisation of rugby over the past two decades. Looking to the future, the respondents were equally insistent that the impact of the 2005 event would also have little bearing on the way the next New Zealand-hosted Lions Series would be prepared for when (or if) it takes place in 2017.

The nearest precedent was the last Lions tour, to Australia in 2001, which had brought an estimated 10,000 fans to that country, exceeding the number of British and Irish sports tourists for the Sydney

Olympics the previous year. The growth in sports tourists continued with the 2003 Rugby World Cup, also in Australia, attracting 32,000 followers from the United Kingdom alone (Mintel, 2004).

Interest in the Lions New Zealand tour was expected to be higher than ever following the appointment of Sir Clive Woodward, manager of the winning England 2003 World Cup team, as the Lions manager. The victory of Wales in the 2005 Six Nations Championship, earlier that spring, was also reported to have led to a rush of Welsh supporters to book to follow their star players in the Lions team. As well as these sport-specific factors, awareness and interest in New Zealand as a tourism destination had been growing significantly because of the film trilogy *Lord of the Rings* (2001–2003).

As the media-fuelled anticipation began to take hold of the small rugby-obsessed nation of New Zealand, predictions of international visitor numbers for this 'once-in-a-lifetime experience' increased dramatically, reaching as high as 40,000 at one stage (Wright, 2007).

Having said that, at the other end of the scale, several less-optimistic sources within the local media and tourism industries publicly argued that the tour was being drastically over-hyped and would actually struggle to attract anymore than 15,000 overseas guests. These figures were largely based on the high financial cost associated with travelling across the world for a six-week sport series (official UK-based package prices, for example, started at around £4000 for the three weeks). Despite having little information to work with, the majority of RTOs expected the final inbound visitor numbers to be around 20,000 and, in the end, they were largely proven correct with the actual overseas visitor numbers reported as being around 20,400 (Vuletich, 2005).

If predicting the overall numbers was difficult, predicting how long the visitors were going to stay in each host destination was described by the RTOs interviewed as 'a logistical nightmare'. In Australia the Lions had played all their games in 5 cities, in New Zealand they were to play in 12 towns and cities. Some tourists came for the full 5 weeks and attended all the provincial games. Others arrived only for the Test matches in the last 15 days. In addition, many of the RTOs were unsure of what local recreational amenities and tourist activities/attractions would prove to be popular with those following the tour. As a result of this uncertainty, regions were forced to base entire action plans on unsubstantiated information passed on from various industry sources based outside their area.

The Changing Nature of the Sports Tourism Experience

The challenges facing the local planners and tourism businesses were also complicated by the changing expectations and behaviour of the sports tourists. Rather than being package tourists only interested in the sport, many were independent travellers seeking to experience as much as possible of the country during their stay.

The growth in Rugby Union-related sports tourism has been matched by rising prices for the matches themselves. For example, while tickets for the 1999 Rugby World Cup Final cost £75, in 2007 prices for the same event started at £200 (and became considerably higher on the black market). These figures would appear to illustrate what Pine and Gilmore (1999) call the growth of the experience economy. They use figures from the United States which show that admissions to recreational events have out-performed other services and goods (in terms of price inflation, employment and GDP) as evidence that people will willingly pay premium prices for experiences they perceive to be unique. To compete in this experience economy, these authors say, organisations should therefore exploit the unique drama of their business to attract and involve the consumer (Grove et al., 1992; Pine and Gilmore, 1999). Similarly Jensen (1999) predicts that the company's most valuable assets will not be products or services but stories that engage the customer's emotions and touch their aspirations, hopes and dreams. In the field of tourism, this has been taken up by King (2002) who criticises destination marketing organisations for being too focused on promoting the physical attributes of the destination, despite travel being 'increasingly more about experiences, fulfilment and rejuvenation than about places and things'. Williams (2006) also calls for the emphasis to be less on destinations than on the contemporary consumers themselves.

The growth of sports tourism can be seen as evidence of the appeal of sporting stories such as that of the British Lions. Their long history, unique traditions and the rarity of their encounters with the Southern Hemisphere's best three teams – including most notably New Zealand's All Blacks – along with the drama inherent in any sporting encounter, give these tours a significance and value that most other brands would envy. Such experiential products appeal to what Poon (1993) called the new tourists, better educated, confident about travelling, money-rich but time-poor (Schor, 1992) wanting high value experiences during their limited leisure time, turning away from conventional beach holidays to more active special interest forms of tourism (Cooper and Lewis, 2001).

In general, the Lions supporters that travelled in 2005 can be seen to match this profile. Many were on their second or third long-haul rugby tour having been to Australia with the 2001 Lions or for the 2003 World Cup (Morgan, 2007). The official Economic Impact Assessment commissioned by New Zealand's Ministry of Tourism reported that, demographically, 84% were male, spread evenly over working-age groups from 20 to 60 years (Vuletich, 2005). In addition, due to the substantial costs involved and the upscale profile of rugby generally (Mintel, 2004), they also tended to be in well-paid jobs with generous holiday allowances.

One of the characteristics of the new tourists, as Cooper and Lewis (2001) noted, is that they are turning away from the conventional distribution channels of package holidays to interact directly with suppliers to create their own itineraries. This was certainly true of the 2005 Lions fans, of whom less than 40% arrived on any form of package tour and an estimated 12,400 (61%) travelled independently, often without tickets for the three Test matches (Vuletich, 2005). What is more, many of the 8000 visitors on package deals still remained largely semi-independent, with accommodation only pre-booked for the Test weekends. For many of these people, the aim was to find a way of following the Lions and experiencing the country as cheaply, but as completely, as possible (Morgan, 2007). They took a pride in having found the cheapest air-route and the most affordable accommodation. Press estimates ranged between 500 and 2000 campervans hired by Lions fans. Others hired cars and stayed in backpacker hostels. From the way people talked about it, this was not just a solution to the accommodation problem; it was part of the fun and a way of optimising the experience. On a trip of a lifetime they wanted to do everything that was on offer – bungee-jumping, white-water rafting and skiing for the young, walking, birding and photography for older travellers.

The growth in the number of sports tourists travelling independently by hire car, campervan or public transport also means that the tourism flows generated will not necessarily follow the itinerary of the team they are supporting. Major tours of this kind are, for many of the tourists, perceived to be once-in-a-lifetime opportunities to see the host country. As a result, having spent considerable amounts of money to get there, they are likely to want to see and experience as much of it as possible. Significant numbers of 2005 Lions visitors were often observed in regions, and at fashionable visitor attractions, located considerable distances away from the nine official host destinations. For example, remote tourist areas such as the West Coast glaciers and Fiordland National Park proved extremely popular with both groups and independent travellers. Out of all the RTOs contacted, the one claiming to have gained the biggest net profit from the 2005 tour – in terms of revenue gained, after expenditure – was actually one of the non-hosting South Island regions, located adjacent, and within easy reach, to three hosting destinations. This kind of tourist behaviour distinguishes the supporters of these major long-haul sports events from those who travel shorter distances (domestically and internationally) for single sporting fixtures and are unlikely to visit other tourist attractions during their trip.

Implications for tourism planning.   From a logistical planning perspective, tourism is always much easier to manage when the tourists arrive in pre-organised and pre-paid package groups. As with most other major spectator-driven sporting events, large proportions of the ticket and bed allocations for the 2005 Lions tour of New Zealand were given to a handful of inbound tour operators, including Gulliver's, Mike Burton Travel and Titan Tours. However, as we have already established in this chapter, the number of pre-booked all-inclusive package tourists was greatly overshadowed by the number of independent travellers. As a result, when it came to trying to gauge the demand in which the local accommodation, bars and restaurants needed to provide for, the RTOs were unable to rely too heavily on the estimates made by the package tour operators. Instead, many had to use other major sports events of a similar status as benchmarks.

In general, the two Auckland-based Americas Cup regattas of 1999/2000 and 2003 proved the most relevant sports event in New Zealand's recent hosting history. The only other precedents were past and/or current national or trans-Tasman sporting events annually held in New Zealand, many of which were also rugby-based.

Lack of Resources to Cope with the Surge in Demand

The sudden and largely unpredictable surge in short-term visitor numbers created by elite sports tours can severely stretch the often limited resources of the regional tourism industry. Fundamental to this are the logistical and capacity problems preparing for an unknown influx of people all wanting to stay in the same cities at the same times. The capacity of hotel accommodation in many of the New Zealand host destinations was widely criticised for being inadequate for the numbers of fans expected. As a result of this shortage, a P&O cruise liner was leased and drafted in as an additional package option and chance for several destinations to provide extra beds. Likewise, the majority of inbound tour companies made use of out-of-town hotels to accommodate some of their groups.

For existing major sporting events, such as the Olympic Games or various World Cups, considerable regional investment in transport infrastructure, sports facilities as well as accommodation is often essential. Such building projects and capital expenditure inevitably attract local and national opposition, which in the case of multi-centred events can also be compounded and complicated further by strong inter-regional rivalries. For example, the last minute decision to award Auckland's Eden Park stadium with a provincial tour game as well as the final 2005 Lions Test match, proved somewhat unpopular in both Christchurch (whose region were only awarded a Test match) and Wellington (the only destination originally due to host two games).

The sudden influx also strains the resources of the tourism organisations to coordinate planning to cope with it. While the NZRFU had a team of over 30 working on Lions tour-related projects, at the other end of the spectrum, one of the smaller RTOs could only justify allocating one employee working on a part-time/ad-hoc basis. Overall, by the start of 2005, all of the host regions had at least one full-time employee specifically focusing on the tour. Early planning was justified in 'non-mainstream' destinations with the recognition that they would have to 'fight a bit harder' to attract their share of overseas visitors. Unlike some of the larger commercial operators, the RTOs were forced to develop campaigns that fitted within their limited annual budgets. Major promotions were kept to a minimum, with the primary focus of attention falling largely on entertaining the local community as much as the travelling supporters.

Whilst Tourism New Zealand expected the various RTOs to focus on promoting local interest within their areas, many wanted to avoid over-selling or raising expectations too high within their community. Most of the independently orchestrated promotions were not brought into operation until the eve of the event itself. With regards to the information made public, many reactive decisions were made, amended and/or subsequently dropped completely during the build-up stages. Local media sources were by far the preferred method of targeting the local community and tackling any of the misleading publicity coming from the commercial sector (Wright, 2007). The drawn out nature of the 2005 Lions Series, allowed for information to progressively flow from pre-tour into tour time planning. Regions were able to pass on guidance, based on their own experience, allowing those areas yet to come into direct contact with the visitors the opportunity to change and adapt their plans accordingly. For many, this was the first and only time they had received any accurate information, especially regarding the size and behavioural characteristics of the travelling fans.

Impact on Local Businesses

While elite sports tours can present an opportunity for local businesses and entrepreneurs, the reasons given above effectively highlight that any attempts to exploit the event can be perilous. Local traders, for example, particularly in the hospitality sector, had to make many of their Lions tour-related business plans without any reliable forecasts on which to base it. In general, small businesses need to avoid being swept along in the mood of excitement generated by often grossly exaggerated stories in the local media. The New Zealand media in 2005, for example, proclaimed the advent of a Barmy Army of hard-drinking fans intent on a good time:

> If New Zealand suspected it wasn't quite sure just what hosting a Lions tour these days actually means, then I have news for you. When the Barmy Army hit your beaches, life will never seem the same again. Of course, they will target your wives, daughters, pubs and cheap hotels and guest houses! Some will be there already, picking fruit in some quiet location in an attempt to build up their funds for what is certain to be the best supported Lions tour in history (Bills, 2005).

The Barmy Army was the name given by Australian journalists to the large number of England cricket supporters in 1994/1995, because of their inexplicable loyalty to a losing Ashes team. The fans retaliated by adopting the nickname as a chant and, by the end of the tour, 8000 items of merchandise had been sold and the name was registered as a trademark not long after (Morgan, 2007). The Barmy Army, according to Parry and Malcolm (2004) represent 'Laddist male culture', a vocal and colourful reaction to the conservatism and restrained manners of the cricket establishment. Their activities are designed to have fun, influence the play on the pitch and express a strong partisan English nationalism. More controversially, it has subsequently evolved over the past decade from a spontaneous and anarchic ethos to become an organised commercial undertaking. (Parry and Malcolm, 2004). Today the Barmy Army has a database of 25,000 names as well as running a community website for cricket fans and selling T-shirts and song sheets, it is also an Official Travel Agency for international cricket tours. Another activity is arranging deals with bars or other venues where the Army can meet and drink before and after matches. As these places have big television screens, they also offer the opportunity for fans without tickets to watch the sport and experience the atmosphere (Barmy Army, 2007).

In 2005, the New Zealand media were quick to adopt the term 'Barmy Army' to describe the impending 'invasion' of the Lions rugby supporters (Bills, 2005). One Barmy Army representative, Freddie Parker, arrived in the country amid great publicity to set up base camps in all the host destinations included on the tour. By far the largest was a 6000 capacity tented village in Auckland's fashionable Viaduct Harbour, sponsored by Lion Breweries and managed by a local event company (Dearnaly, 2005). Adopted as the Barmy Army's HQ, it offered an opportunity for RTOs to promote their regions and provided visitors with themed bars, shops, Internet cafes and a host of free activities, such as horizontal bungee-jumping and rock-climbing. In addition to the various bases, 30,000 booklets were printed to hand out at major airports, containing details of these base camps including songs, jokes and other 'advice' (Morgan, 2007).

The strategic operation conducted by the Barmy Army in New Zealand contains all the ingredients of the Pine and Gilmore (1999) recipe for experience management. Special sets decorated with flags and banners were provided, in which the fans were expected to perform to scripts (the songbooks) issued by the experienced directors. To add to the spectacle, fans wore costumes that were not only a replica of the Lions rugby shirts but also waterproof cagoules and other red clothing issued by the major tour operators. Ultimately, however, many of these attempts to 'experientialize' sports tourism, as Pine and Gilmore would put it, were not received with unanimous approval by the tourists themselves. As Berridge (2006) says, while event managers can plan for certain experiences, the way individuals respond to them is unpredictable.

Many of the 2005 Lions supporters objected to, and subsequently rejected, the attempt to draft them into Freddie Parker's Army. They did not want to be associated with an image which had nothing to do with their own culture and traditions:

> "Sadly the image that this self-styled 'supporters group' has cultivated for itself is more suited to an 18–30 holiday in Ibiza than a genuine rugby supporters tour to the world's greatest rugby nation."
>
> Richard Lewis quoted Morgan (2005)

> The leaders of the Barmy Army seemed to have tried to hijack the tour here in NZ. They are primarily an England cricket supporters group and I find it a little disconcerting how the whole of the NZ media now refer to every potential Lions fan as a member of Freddie Parker's 'Barmy Army'. Lions' fans have never needed any help singing before. I doubt they need it now.
>
> Nick Hall on BBC website (2005)

A basic objection was that the English-based Barmy Army had the wrong target market. The age range of the 2005 Lions supporters was evenly spread between 15 and 60 years and, more importantly, 45% were not from England (Vuletich, 2005). For these and other reasons, Parker's New Zealand base camps were widely reported to be underused. A bar-owner in Dunedin who was persuaded, against the advice of the local RTO, to organise around the clock live music and entertainment ended up sending 77 kegs of beer back and lost several thousand New Zealand dollars. In Palmerston North, another local organiser complained that most people who were part of the Lions support group went

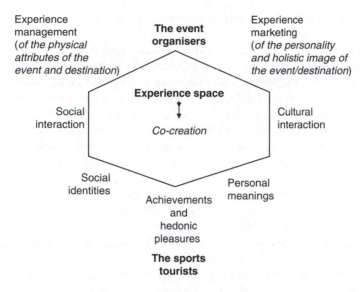

Figure 13.1: The experience space: Interactions between organisers and sports tourists (Morgan, 2007). *Source*: Based on Kapferer (1998).

to different sorts of bars (Morgan, 2005). In general, many of the Lions fans rejected the stage-managed experiences provided for them and went in search of different spaces, perhaps looking for those which were perceived as more authentically local (such as Galbraith's Real Ale Brewery in Auckland) or in which they could create their own social interactions and experiences (Morgan, 2007).

This would seem to support critics of the experiential marketing concept such as Prahalad and Ramaswamy (2004) who say companies need to go beyond 'experiential marketing 'a la Disney ... which is still production centric' and which sees the customers as ' human props in a carefully staged performance'. They suggest that company strategies should be grounded in the interaction between the firm's supply network and communities of consumers to 'co-create' value through personalised experiences. Arguably, true co-creation only occurs when firms create 'experience spaces' where dialogue, transparency and access to information allow customers to develop experiences that suit their own needs and level of involvement. Figure 13.1 (from Morgan, 2007) shows how destination and event management provides the space for social and cultural interaction, from which the sports tourist can derive their personal benefits and meanings. An example of the creation of such a space would be the way in which the Tourism New Zealand website catered for the independent Lions supporters, suggesting itineraries to explore New Zealand between the matches. Visitors to their site could click through to more detailed descriptions of individual towns and attractions, and then select accommodation through direct links to hotel, motel and hostel websites, all of which allowed them to book on-line or by email.

Conclusions

The Lions tour is an example of what we have labelled an elite sports tour. These can be defined as major spectator-generating sports events which require the temporary movement of players, entourage and spectators between a number of geographically separate locations, often spread across regional or national boundaries.

Like other major sporting events, they not only attract a temporary surge of international visitors and international media attention, but also present destination managers with a host of logistical, capacity and marketing challenges. However, what distinguishes elite sports tours from other events is that the potential benefits (and impacts) are spread over a number of regional centres, as opposed to one single host location. Before the itinerary is decided, there may be vigorous competition between cities and regions to secure the fixtures and their expected benefits. However, once the decision is made, a considerable amount of cross-sector and cross-border collaboration/cooperation is required in order to fully exploit the unique opportunities available. Ultimately, the international sport tourist, incoming travel trade and global media will not recognise or acknowledge local boundaries of demarcation when it comes to evaluating their experience of the country as a whole.

The 2005 Lions supporters exemplify the trend towards independent travel even in special interest segments such as sports tourism. While the move away from package tours undoubtedly makes visitor flows and demand for specific amenities harder to predict, it does creates opportunities for a wider range of businesses to benefit from the event. For example, many non-sports-based attractions and tourist locations away from the Lions tour fixtures were visited by supporters on numerous occasions before, during and immediately after the six-week sports series.

An elite sports tour typically represents an infrequent event of great significance, especially to those willing to pay significant amounts of money and travel substantial distances just to be part of it. They are therefore likely to be looking for other 'once-in-a-lifetime experiences' outside the stadium(s), sampling whatever memorable sights and activities the host destination(s) has to offer. To pay for these peak experiences, however, they may seek to economise by shopping around (on-line) for cheaper travel and accommodation options. Thus, there will be potential demand for a wide range of tourism products in all price segments. With this in mind, competing destinations and industry sectors will therefore need to work together to enable the sports tourists to co-create their itineraries and experiences to suit their own interests and budgets. Websites such as Tourism New Zealand's, which link together the tourism supply network and the community of travelling supporters, can be regarded as a model of good practice for managing the tourism potential of other elite sports tours.

In summary, elite sports tours represent both an opportunity and a challenge to tourism destination management. Planning for such events would be aided by further research into the motivations, expectations and impacts of this specialised sports tourism market.

References

Barmy Army (2007) England's Barmy Army/History. http://www.barmyarmy.com/history.cfm, accessed 31 March 2007.

BBC (2007a) *Fans flock to Tour de France race.* http://news.bbc.co.uk/2/hi/uk_news/england/london/6280274.stm, accessed 26 July 2007.

BBC (2007b) *Carnival across Kent for Le Tour.* http://news.bbc.co.uk/2/hi/uk_news/england/kent/6281688.stm, accessed 26 July 2007.

Berridge, G. (2006) *Event Design and Experience.* Oxford: Butterworth Heinemann, p. 279.

Bills, P. (2005) Barmy Army ready to storm NZ. *New Zealand Herald*, Tuesday, 24 May 2005.

Bjelac, Z. and Radovanovic, M. (2003) Sports events as a form of tourist product, relating volume and character of demand. *Journal of Sport Tourism*, 8(4), 260–269.

Bramwell, B. (1997) Strategic planning before and after a mega-event. *Tourism Management*, 18(3), 167–176.

Cooper, C. and Lewis, J. (2001) Transformation and trends in the tourism industry: Implications for distribution channels. In Buhalis, D. and Laws, E. (eds.), *Tourism Distribution Channels*. London: Continuum.

De Knop, P. (2006) Sport and events tourism. In Buhalis, D. and Costa, C. (eds.), *Tourism business frontiers: Consumers, products and industry*. Oxford: Elsevier.

Dearnaly, M. (2005) Barmy Army secures its base camps. *New Zealand Herald*, Wednesday, 01 June 2005.

Dobson, N. and Sinnamon, R. (2001) A critical analysis of the organisation of major sports events. In Gratton, C. and Henry, I. P. (eds.), *Sport in the City; the Role of Sport in Economic and Social Regeneration*. London: Routledge.

FIFA (2006) Info Plus: Number One Sports Event (2006 FIFA World Cup TV Coverage) Federation International de Football Association, Zurich http://www.fifa.com/mm/document/fifafacts/ffprojects/ip-401_06e_tv_2658.pdf, accessed September 2007.

Getz, D. (1997) *Event Management and Event Tourism*. New York: Cognizant Communication Corporation.

Getz, D. (2003) Sport event tourism: Planning, development and marketing. In Hudson, S. (ed.), *Sport and Adventure Tourism*. New York: Haworth Hospitality Press.

Gibson, H. J. (2002) Sport tourism at a crossroad? Considerations for the future. In Gammon, S. and Kurtzman, J. (eds.), *Sport Tourism: Principles and Practice*. Eastbourne: Leisure Studies Association, pp. 111–128.

Grove, S. J., Fisk, R. P., Bitner, M. J. (1992) Dramatising the service experience: A managerial approach. In Swartz, T. A. Brown, S. and Bowen, D. (eds.), *Advances in Services Marketing and Management*. Greenwich, CT: JAI Press Inc.

Hall, C. M. (1997) *Hallmark Tourist Events: Impact, Management and Planning*. Chicester: Wiley.

Hall, C. M. (2000) *Tourism Planning: Policies, Processes and Relationships*. Harlow: Prentice-Hall.

Hall, C. M. (2001) Imaging, tourism and sports event fever: The Sydney Olympics and the need for a social charter for mega-events. In Gratton, C. and Henry, I. P. (eds.), *Sport in the City; the Role of Sport in Economic and Social Regeneration*. London: Routledge.

Hall, C. M. (2005) Sport tourism planning. In Higham, J. E. S. (ed.), *Sport Tourism Destinations: Issues, Opportunities and Analysis*. Oxford: Elsevier Butterworth-Heinemann.

Higham, J. E. S. (2005) Introduction to sport tourism destination policy and planning. In Higham, J. E. S. (ed.), *Sport Tourism Destinations: Issues, Opportunities and Analysis*. Oxford: Elsevier Butterworth-Heinemann.

Hiller, H. H. (1998) Assessing the impact of mega events: A linkage model. *Current Issues in Tourism*, 1(1), 47–57.

Hinch, T. D. and Higham, J. E. S. (2004) *Sport Tourism Development*. Clevedon: Channel View.

Hodges, J. and Hall, C. M. (1996) The housing and social impacts of mega-events: Lessons for the Sydney 2000 Olympics. In Kearsley, G. (ed.), *Tourism Down Under II: Towards a More Sustainable Tourism*. University of Otago: Dunedin Centre for Tourism.

Jensen, R. (1999) *The Dream Society*. New York: McGraw Hill.

Jones, C. (2001) Mega-events and host-region impacts: Determining the true worth of the 1999 Rugby World Cup. *International Journal of Tourism Research*, 3, 241–251.

Kapferer, J-N. (1998) *Strategic Brand Management*. London: Kogan Page.

King, J. (2002) Destination marketing organizations – Connecting the experience rather than promoting the place. *Journal of Vacation Marketing*, 2(8), 105–108.

Knight, L. (2005) Heart of the lions. In Alexander, M. (ed.), *Mighty Pride: The Tests*. Auckland: Customs Publishing.

Kurtzman, J. (2001) Economic impact: Sport tourism and the city. *Journal of Sport Tourism*, 6(3), 45–65.

Lions Rugby (2005) History of the Lions. http://www.lionsrugby.com/, accessed 16 May 2005.

Madden, J. R. (2002) The economic consequences of the Sydney Olympics: The CREA/Arthur Anderson Study. *Current Issues in Tourism*, 5(1), 7–21.

Maguire, J. and Tuck, J. (1998) Global sports and patriot games: Rugby Union and National Identity in a United Sporting Kingdom since 1945. In Cronin, M. and Mayall, D. (eds.), *Sporting Nationalisms: Identity, Ethnicity, Immigration, and Assimilation*. London: Frank Cass Publishers.

Mintel (2004) Sports tourism – International. *Travel and Tourism Analyst*, October 2004. Mintel Group.

Morgan, G. (2005) Where's your army, ask NZ barmen. *Western Mail*, 6 July 2005, accessed at http://icwales.icnetwork.co.uk/0500rugbyunion/0900lions/tm_method=full%26objectid=15703961%26siteid=50082-name_page.html, March 2007.

Morgan (2007) We're not the Barmy Army: Reflections on the sports tourism experience. *International Journal of Tourism Research*, 9(5), 361–372.

Nick Hall: BBC website (2005) Messages on BBC Sport-Rugby Union website posted 31/5/05 1255 BST http://news.bbc.co.uk/sport1/hi/rugby_union/default.stm

Olds, K. (1998) Urban mega events: Evictions and housing rights, the Canadian case. *Current Issues in Tourism*, 1(1), 2–46.

Parry, M. and Malcolm, D. (2004) England's Barmy Army: Commercialization, masculinity and nationalism. *International Review for the Sociology of Sport*, 39(1), 75–94.

Pigeassou, C. (2004) Contribution to the definition of sport tourism. *Journal of Sport Tourism*, 9(3), 287–289.

Pine, B. J. and Gilmore, J. H. (1999) *The Experience Economy: Work is Theatre and Every Business is a Stage*. Boston, MA: HBS Press.

Poon, A. (1993) *Tourism, Technology and Competitive Strategies*. Wallingford: CAB.

Prahalad, C. K. and Ramaswamy, V. (2004) *The Future of Competition: Co-creating Unique Value with Customers*. Boston: Harvard Business School Press.

Schor, J. (1992) *The Overworked American: The Unexpected Decline of Leisure*. New York: Basic Books.

Shapcott, M. (1998) Commentary on 'urban mega events: Evictions and housing rights, the Canadian case by K. Olds. *Current Issues in Tourism*, 1(2), 195–196.

Vuletich, S. (2005). *The Economic Impact of the 2005 DHL Lions Series on New Zealand*. Report prepared by Covec Limited. Auckland, October 2005.

Waitt, G. (2001) The Olympic spirit and civic boosterism: The Sydney 2000 Olympics. *Tourism Geographies*, 3(3), 249–278.

Webb, S. (2005) Strategic partnerships for sport tourism destinations. In Higham, J. E. S. (ed.), *Sport Tourism Destinations: Issues, Opportunities and Analysis*. Oxford: Elsevier Butterworth-Heinemann.

Weed, M. and Bull, C. (1997) Integrating sport and tourism; A review of regional policies in England. *Progress in Tourism and Hospitality Research*, 3, 129–148.

Weed, M. and Bull, C. (2004) *Sports Tourism Participants, Policy and Providers*. Oxford: Butterworth-Heinemann.

Whitson, D. and Macintosh, D. (1996) The global circus: International sport, tourism and the marketing of cities. *Journal of Sport and Social Issues*, 23, 278–295.

Williams, A. (2006) Tourism and hospitality marketing: Fantasy, feeling and fun. *International Journal of Contemporary Hospitality Management*, 18(6), 482–495.

Wright, R. (November 2007) Planning for the Great Unknown exploring the challenge of promoting regional sports event tourism. *International Journal of Tourism Research*, 45–65.

Chapter 14

The British Pop Music Festival Phenomenon

Chris Stone

Introduction

The first modern popular music festivals were staged in the later 1960s, the best-known early examples being outdoor events in the USA including the Monterey Pop Festival of 1967 and Woodstock and Altamont in 1969. These and British events, such as the 1968–1970 Isle of Wight festivals and the internationally famous Glastonbury festival (first staged in 1970), have risen in prominence to become important socio-cultural and historic landmarks of the 21st century. The number staged in Britain grows each year indicating that, as a species of event, pop festivals are increasingly popular, and the country is developing an international reputation for them. Despite this, however, and in marked contrast to the number of studies of more conventional musical events, little research investigating the British pop festival phenomenon has been published. This chapter sets out to investigate the music festival, defining such events and providing a brief review of relevant academic research before locating the phenomenon in an historical context and outlining the nature and characteristics of these events. It then considers markets and demand, trends in provision, success factors, motivations for attendance, and operational considerations. Finally, mention is made of the environmental impacts of such events, and festivals' roles as tourist destinations assessed.

The Pop Music Festival – A Definition

While it is easy enough to identify the British pop music festival at first hand, a robust working definition of what is a relatively variable type of event is required. However, those few in the extant literature are inadequate for the present purposes, and it has therefore been necessary to devise a definition suited to the present purposes.

A pop festival is defined as 'a performance event comprising two or more live performances of pop music over one or more days and at recurring periods, which is packaged as a coherent whole' (After Mintel International Group Limited, 2006a; Paleo and Wijnberg, 2006).

Here, the term 'pop' is used in an inclusive manner to cover the full range of popular music presented at festivals and elsewhere. Not all music at all such events is 'live' in the commonly accepted sense; the term 'live' extends the nature of performance to include the work of DJs, for instance, the use of pre-recorded backing music by artists playing musical instruments, and also the use of computer-based sequencers often used in live performance of house and techno music. The definition includes paid-admission and free events, and also music festivals held both indoors and outdoors. This chapter will, however, confine its focus to festivals held outdoors because they are more interesting as events, more intuitively associated with the term 'pop festival' than indoor ones, and being qualitatively different to indoor ones deserve distinct treatment.

Festivals act as intermediaries between producers of live performances and consumers, distributing aural goods ('musical texts') by arranging for artists to deliver their performances, and simultaneously act as retailers, selling these goods to consumers (Paleo and Wijnberg, 2006). Festivals may also be considered as intermediaries between producers of live performances and consumers, acting as distributors and retailers (Paleo and Wijnberg, 2006).

Types and Typologies of Music Festivals

The wide variety of types of music festivals makes them difficult to categorise, but a taxonomy of popular music festivals has been proposed by Paleo and Wijnberg (2006) (Table 14.1).

To explain the elements of the taxonomy:

1. Character distinguishes between competitive and non-competitive festivals. The former include public 'Battle of the Bands' events in which performers compete in order to be chosen as winners by a jury; at non-competitive festivals, the performers don't compete, at least not in such an explicit manner.
2. Purpose relates to whether the festival was conceived as a for-profit or a not-for-profit event. Not-for-profit festivals include events like the Truck Festival and also those staged by public bodies such as local authorities.

Table 14.1: Taxonomy of popular music festivals

Character	Competitive	Non-competitive
Purpose	For-profit	Not-for-profit
Range	Wide	Focused
Format	One-track Non-ranking Aural goods only	Multivenue Ranking Multidisciplinary
Degree of institutionalisation	High	Low
Degree of innovativeness	High	Not innovative: Mainstream
Scope	Local – Regional – National	International

Paleo and Wijnberg (2006).

3. Range refers to the composition of the audience. There is a self-evident relationship between particular types of consumers and particular genres, and a festival with a broad range would feature relatively mainstream acts that are popular across a variety of subcultural communities, while one with very narrow range would focus on one particular niche market/genre.

4. Format covers the types of festival goods which are presented and the ways in which they are presented. Some display artists and aural goods sequentially – a 'one-track' festival – while at a 'multivenue' festival different aural goods are displayed simultaneously, perhaps presenting different genres at different venues. 'Ranking' refers to whether an explicit ranking of acts is reflected in the format, the stars on the main stage while lesser acts perform at smaller venues. A further dimension of format is the extent to which the festival presents aural goods only or is 'multidisciplinary', encompassing other types of cultural goods. Glastonbury festival is best known for music, but the full title of the event is 'The Glastonbury Festival of Contemporary Performing Arts' and it features dance, comedy, theatre, circus, cabaret, and street performance amongst other arts. The 2005 Big Chill festival featured a library from which festivalgoers could borrow books.

5. Degree of institutionalisation – relates to connections between the festival and other suppliers of aural goods (music labels, record companies, agents, and artists), sponsors, audiences, and others including TV and radio stations, magazines, and websites.

6. Degree of innovativeness – some festivals are dedicated to new artistic forms but a majority schedule relatively well-known aural goods, providing an experiential product consumed by audiences seeking familiarity (Prentice and Andersen, 2003). The late BBC Radio One DJ John Peel complained that the Glastonbury festival no longer presented much 'cutting edge' music.

7. Associated with but distinct from range, scope refers to the spatial area from which performers are drawn, whether local, regional, national, or international. Some festivals present only local talent, while the WOMAD festival, for example, sets out to present music, art, and dance artists from countries and cultures all over the world.

A more market-oriented classification has been employed by the UK Festival Awards. 'Curated' by virtualfestivals.com since 2004, festival awards are made based on the outcome of a public vote held in September. Categories for the 2006 awards, with some of the events nominated for each, were:

- major festival – the Carling Weekends, the V Festivals;
- medium-to-large festival – Bestival, WOMAD;
- small festival – Beautiful Days, Cambridge Folk Festival;
- one-day festival – Creamfields, Monsters Of Rock;
- grass-roots festival – Green Man Festival, Solfest;
- new festival – Bloom, End Of The Road Festival;
- dance music festival – Global Gathering, The Big Chill;
- fan-friendly festival – Cambridge Folk Festival, Isle of Skye Festival;
- family festival – Beautiful Days, Wychwood Festival.

Adapted from Virtualfestivals (2006).

Festivals and the Event Life Cycle

An event life-cycle model has been proposed by Beverland et al. (2001), in research focused upon events staged to attract tourists to wine-producing regions. The model draws upon the concept of life-cycle stages in organisations, describing and explaining their development over time, and also the 'tourist area cycle of evolution' model of Butler (1980) comprising five stages, itself inspired by the marketing notion of the product life cycle. The model postulates an event life cycle of six stages:

1. Conception – organisers develop the concept and objectives of the event and gain support from stakeholders.
2. Launch – the 'birth' stage, involving building awareness of the event and gaining a critical mass of consumers and thereby media attention.
3. Growth – when the event has gained a critical mass, the key task for organisers changes to a growth-stage one, brand building and retaining loyal customers while attracting new ones.
4. Consolidation – at this stage the task is to focus on the original spirit and key objectives of the event, retaining a 'point of difference' without instituting radical change.
5. Decline – failure to consolidate can lead to decline. Customers' perceptions of the quality of the event deteriorate, and a decision needs to be made whether to revive the event or cancel it.
6. Revival – a new image and focus must be developed for the event that attracts customers and stakeholders.

Beverland et al. (2001)

While the biggest and best-known events maintain a position at the consolidation stage of the event life cycle, most are not successful and proceed to decline.

Festivals-History and Research

The term 'festival' is a synonym of 'carnival', traditions of which date from pre-Christian times, and which in more recent times has referred to the season immediately preceding Lent in Roman Catholic countries. 'Carnival' denotes a time or event characterised by revelry, riotous excess, and indulgence overstepping the bounds of decorum, and while this may be a more fitting description of at least some music events than 'festival', the latter term is more widely used for the events under study. The meaning of the term 'festival' spans both the appointed day(s), and the nature of the event-public entertainment, and often on a large scale. The great folk culture carnivals of medieval Europe were regarded by Bahktin as anarchic and liberating periods when the authority of Church and state was reduced, but carnival traditions declined in Europe from the Renaissance, and in Britain the Victorians abolished many of the festivals which had until then been highlights of popular British cultural life in the name of economic efficiency (Harrowven, 1980). The modern British pop music festival dates from the late 1960s (McKay, 2000), and Table 14.2 provides a list of major British pop music festivals since that time.

Despite the scale of the phenomenon in Britain, only a limited volume of research into the pop music festival has been published. Part of the explanation may be that, of all the arts, music has attracted the least interest from the major social and political theorists (Smith, 1997). The relative neglect of popular music by researchers reflects a focus on elite culture derived from a view that popular culture is trivial, ephemeral, and not worthy of serious consideration (Kong, 1995). Also, despite the successful political mobilization in support of music festivals achieved by their supporters since the 1970s (Clarke, 1982), the image of these events remains a negative one in certain sections

Table 14.2: Landmark British pop music festivals

1968–1970	Isle of Wight Festival
1970	Bath Festival of Blues and Progressive Music
1970	Present – the Glastonbury Festival
1971	Weeley Festival
1977–1980	Reading Rock Festival
1972–1975	Windsor Free Festival
1974–1979	Knebworth Festival
1979–1980	Loch Lomond Rock Festival
1970s	Cambridge free festivals
1980–1996	Monsters of Rock at Castle Donington
1981–1986	The Elephant Fayre
1982 – Present	WOMAD festivals ('World of Music, Arts and Dance')
1980–84	Stonehenge Free festivals
1980–87	The Reading festival

of society, with lingering perceptions of associations with licentiousness and general abandon, however inappropriate.

Methodology

This chapter integrates a review of academic research with the results of an original empirical investigation which obtained data from a variety of sources. The relatively few relevant academic papers that exist are scattered across a range of academic journals including *Event Management*, *Journal of Travel Research*, *Annals of Tourism Research*, and *European Journal of Clinical Microbiology & Infectious Diseases*. The majority of the data upon which the study is based was gained from semi-structured interviews with festivalgoers and current and former pop festival organisers. Inevitably, given its longevity and popularity, Glastonbury festival featured prominently in respondents' accounts. In addition, secondary material was sourced from commercially published market research reports, the popular press, and the Festivals Unit at the Department for Culture, Media & Sport (DCMS).

Pop Festivals in Britain

There exist little definitive data on the British pop festival market, neither on the number of events staged each year nor on the total national audience for such events. The number of music festivals has been increasing each year for the last decade or so, and it is estimated that about 300 were held in Britain in 2007. However, many events – probably a majority – fail to attract a capacity crowd, indicating that the British market may be becoming saturated as competition intensifies, a trend similar to that identified in the Netherlands (Leenders et al., 2005).

The largest pop festivals are very large indeed, constituting some of the biggest single events of any type in the United Kingdom. In 2007, the Glastonbury festival attracted 137,000 paying entrants and a further 40,000 staff, volunteers, and traders, making it by far the largest, and the Carling Weekend between 70,000 and 80,000 to each of the two centres at which it was held (Reading and Leeds). The medium-sized Big Green Gathering in Wiltshire attracted about 20,000 in 2006, while around 4000 people enjoyed the two-field Ragged Hedge fair in the Cotswolds. By comparison, the biggest festival in western Europe is said to be the Sziget festival, which is staged on an island in the Danube in the centre of Budapest and attracted 317,000 in 2007, and the biggest in the world is said to be the Milwaukee Summerfest in Wisconsin, an urban-based music festival which lasts for 11 days and attracts almost one million people each year. Popular festivals usually grow in size over time: Glastonbury started with an audience of 1,500 in 1970 (at an admission price of one pound) and has exhibited a sustained growth in audience numbers of a factor of over 100 since then (see Figure 14.1). Successful music festivals are usually staged annually, but less successful events which fail to consolidate (in terms of the event life cycle – Beverland et al., 2001) may continue for a few years after launch before static or dwindling ticket sales force organisers to seek to merge with one or more other similar events in an effort to continue in operation, or lead to its cancellation. Reasons advanced to explain why festivals fail include poor marketing and planning, the weather, competition, and a lack of sponsorship (Getz, 2002).

The duration of individual music festivals varies considerably. Some run for only a few hours over the course of a single day or perhaps overnight, while many such events continue for two, three, four or even more days, usually over weekends. Organisers of successful festivals often seek to extend their duration: until 2006, 'T In The Park', the biggest Scottish pop festival, was a highly successful two-day event, and in 2007 it was extended to three days, and sold out rapidly – again. In the United Kingdom, the festival licence specifies the hours between which music (live or recorded) may be played, typically 11 in the morning to 12 midnight or 2 a.m. Recently, however, some festivals

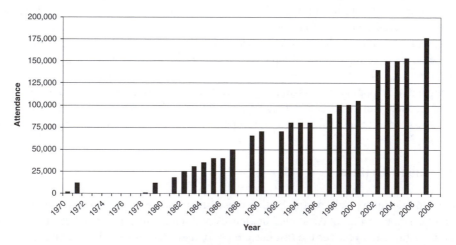

Figure 14.1: Licensed attendance figures for Glastonbury 1970–2007. Figures include tickets on sale to the public, and those for traders, staff, and local people. No festivals were held in the years 1972–1977, 1980, 1991, 1996, 2001, and 2006. The large numbers of ticketless entrants in the 1980s and 1990s mean that the figures for those years probably under-represent the actual number of people at the event. *Source*: Glastonbury Festival of Contemporary Performing Arts (2001).

have acquired 24-hour licences, under which smaller music stages may operate throughout the night, along with some food and beverage outlets.

The success of outdoor music festivals is closely associated with the prevailing weather. Summer is the festival season in the United Kingdom for outdoor events, when the weather is normally warm enough between late May to early September for camping, and the day length conducive to outdoor activities which often stretch into the evening and night. Indoor events may of course be held at any time of the year, though tend to be scheduled outside the summer months. The weather of the British Isles is unpredictable, however, and the extended period of unusually poor weather during the summer of 2007 led to a washout at Glastonbury and was the reason adduced to the cancellation of several other festivals. The final day of the Ashton Court event in Bristol was cancelled because the site was deemed unsafe for the public due to poor ground conditions after heavy rain during the previous night. Organisers stated that they were unable to guarantee access to the site for emergency services. Refunds in the event of bad weather are usually specifically ruled out in the terms of sale of festival tickets. Several festivals are scheduled to take place annually on or around the date of the summer solstice (21 June in 2007) which marks the first day of the season of summer, when the sun is at its maximum elevation. The solstice is a time of spiritual significance for some groups and is celebrated annually by thousands of people at Stonehenge, a gathering which developed into a sizeable – and, to some, notorious – free countercultural festival from the 1970s to the mid-1980s, when a court ruling led to its demise.

A majority of British pop music festivals are staged in the southern half of the country, and particularly south of the River Thames. This can largely be explained by reason of markets and the prevailing weather: the south of the country is more heavily populated and wealthier, and the weather tends to be significantly warmer and less prone to rain. Northern regions have markedly fewer festivals, and few large ones. Once an event has been successfully held on a site, the organisers will usually aim to stay there for several years because of the cost and effort involved in identifying an alternative site and gaining the necessary agreements (and acceptance by local residents), and the cost of any investments necessary for infrastructure or other site modification. As a result, festivals tend to become identified with their geographic locations, which in turn become venerated because of the event. However, holding any mass outdoor event regularly on the same site inevitably entails environmental degradation, and to address the problem, environmental management measures may be necessary, and events may be cancelled on occasion to 'rest' the site for a year.

'The line-up is everything', says pop promoter Vince Power, playing as it does a critical role in determining prospective festivalgoers' perceptions of each event, its reputation, and the markets to which it will appeal. The British music scene is presently enjoying a vibrant and diverse period, and as the popularity of dance music fades the revival of epic melodic rock music produced by bands like Coldplay, Oasis, and Keane may be better suited to big-stage shows in fields. At a big festival people can 'see' much of their entire record collection in one weekend. The identity of a music festival is closely dependent upon the line-ups of successive editions of the event, and organisers signal, certify and classify competing aural goods for their chosen market(s) (Paleo and Wijnberg, 2006). Music festivals act as selectors in a way comparable to that of radio DJs. The place of the artist in the line-up, as an opening or a closing act, for instance, serves as a signal of their status, as well as their physical location at a multivenue festival, whether on the main stage or at a less auspicious venue. By bringing an act to the attention of the public, and especially by signalling the quality of the artist, the festival may have a significant effect upon their economic performance and/or career, in terms of music product sales as well as a live performer. Additionally, by programming in a particular way the festival implicitly categorises artists as belonging together, producing in aggregate the kind of aural goods the festival organisers expect will appeal to their audience, typically the music genres the festival implicitly or explicitly specialises in. Offering a set of aural goods as a meaningful whole can contribute to the construction of music genres: founded in 1995, the Big Chill festival has undoubtedly contributed to the success of the 'ambient' niche music genre, and to the partial restoration of folk music to fashionability.

Pop festivals operate in an increasingly competitive market, and recent market entrants seek to differentiate their offer from others enabling audiences to regard each festival as unique and with the potential to offer a distinctive experience (Paleo and Wijnberg, 2006). Major festivals frequently aim to appeal to a mass market, and often seek to put on the biggest current bands, which can be very expensive. However, some festivals like Glastonbury are able to attract major international artists like David Bowie and Shirley Bassey despite paying relatively low fees by capitalising on the status and reputation of the event. Some big-name acts even waive their fees for the prestige of playing the event. There is evidence, however, that newer, niche festivals have the potential to attract large audiences. The music festival industry is one with low barriers to entry, and success may be achieved through devising new formulas which deliver unique experiences addressing developing tastes in the marketplace (Leenders et al., 2005). Such focused, niche events may not need to book a line-up of big names because staging very popular artists may not be in the best interests of their brand. Instead, they often concentrate upon less well-known performers in their chosen genre, partly for reasons of cost and also in an effort to attract an enthusiastic audience and making the *event* the focus rather than any single act.

Festivalgoers

The market for pop festivals has grown and changed dramatically since the late 1960s, during which time their image has changed and their appeal broadened. Until the later 1980s these events were generally regarded as the preserve of ageing hippies and hardcore music fans, a market prepared to endure significant privations on often badly designed and badly-managed sites in order to enjoy their kind of music. Mass-media coverage of the relatively few events that then existed was limited and mostly centred upon Glastonbury, which was consistently portrayed negatively and in disapproving tones by TV and other news sources. Since then, the image of British pop festivals has been transformed from their being disreputable events attended by quasi-criminal low-life (see for instance Clarke, 1982) to major cultural events with an increasingly mainstream appeal, both in terms of the sheer size of their appeal in terms of audience numbers and the range of social groups motivated to attend.

Little firm information about the profile of the typical individual drawn to pop festivals is available, and as this type of event grows in number and becomes more diverse in character it is increasingly difficult to generalise. Live music of all kinds increasingly attracts a broad range of the population, including families and people in their 50s and 60s. However, in general the market for these events is comprised of individuals:

- aged 25–44;
- in employment;
- drawn from ABC1 social groups.

Tomljenovic et al. (2001)

By 2007 the mass-market British conservative tabloid newspaper the *Daily Mail* was able to describe pop festivals as 'an unmissable social fixture of British summer time'. In late spring of that year, the paper listed six such events which its readers might enjoy, ordered by the paper's perception of the characteristics of the fractions of their readership which might be interested in each:

- dancing queens;
- rock chicks;
- posh stock (upmarket readers);
- yummy mummies ('…chilled rose wine for adults. Ginger beer for the kids…');
- new rave fashionistas;
- hippy chic readers.

Anon (2007)

The upmarket nature of pop festival audiences may occasion some surprise, but at £145 for a weekend ticket the 2007 Glastonbury festival was expensive by any measure. The cost of admission needs to be considered in context, however: some tickets for single gigs by international stars like the Rolling Stones and U2 are comparably priced, and when former festival favourites Led Zeppelin reformed for a single London show in 2007 more than one million fans attempted to buy tickets at £125 each. Further spending upon essential items including alcoholic drinks and food – both more costly at festivals than elsewhere – is usually inevitable, the likely total expenditure being proportionate to the duration of the event and the willingness of individual festivalgoers to go to the trouble of purchasing such items more cheaply beforehand and carrying them into the event. One survey reported that more than one-quarter of festivalgoers spend in excess of £500 enjoying outdoor pop festivals, including expenditure on new clothes, camping equipment, and food and drink (Freeview Playback, 2007).

The rise in the popularity of pop festivals and a gradual growth in governmental regulation have been paralleled by a professionalisation of the conception, organisation, and management of pop festivals. The process has disenchanted a section of the audience they are designed to attract (Ritzer, 1999), notably those who identify music festivals with the 'counterculture' movement since the 1960s, and brought accusations of a loss of authenticity, aestheticisation, and creeping commercialisation. The new social movements (the 'New Left') of the later 1960s sometimes sought to 'prefigure' and embody the egalitarian and fraternal values and ways of a 'better society' (Breines, 1982), and staging music festivals may have been viewed as one means of prefiguring, however small scale or temporary in nature. But values and tastes have changed, and as the profile of the counterculture of the latter half of the 20th century sinks to almost imperceptible levels the growth in the popularity of pop festivals has necessitated better organisation and management of such events, particularly the largest and most popular. The culture of the last 25 years may be characterised by a growth in consumerism in the context of neoliberal capitalism, and the changing market for music festivals reflects this broader societal change, as well as the vicissitudes of fashion. Pop festivals are market-driven events, and need to respond to market change in order to continue to exist. Festivalgoers are now drawn from a broader range of society than in the past, and many would refuse to tolerate the amateurish event management and poor living conditions that prevailed at some of the pioneer pop festivals of the late 1960s and 1970s. The meaning of authenticity with reference to music festivals has changed since the late 1960s, and processes of aestheticisation have made these events safer, more pleasant, and more interesting places to be than before.

Commercialisation was perhaps inevitable, impacting as it has upon most types of event and parallelling the growth of disposable incomes and consumerism in more general terms. Commercialisation is increasingly evident at many music festivals but certainly not all, and most festival organisers are keenly aware of the phenomenon and its associated issues.

Demand

A key characteristic of the biggest and best-known pop festival events is the extraordinarily high levels of demand for tickets. The biggest and best-known events sell out very rapidly. The popularity of live music in general terms barely needs substantiation: live music is the fastest-growing part of the music industry, and an estimated 37% of the national population attend at least one 'gig' each month (Live Music Forum, 2007), and nearly half (44%) of UK students go to live pop music events (Mintel International Group Limited, 2006b). All 137,000 tickets for the 2007 Glastonbury festival, said to be the largest 'greenfield' music and performing arts festival in the world, sold within two hours on 1 April of that year – at £145 each – over two months in advance of the event and before any acts had been announced. About one-quarter of a million people failed to obtain tickets. In 2004, Glastonbury tickets were being offered by agencies for as much as £477, over four times their face value of £112, and such is the demand for this mega-event that the festival has subsequently instigated measures to stop tickets being sold at inflated prices. For 2007, prospective festivalgoers were required to go though a pre-purchase registration system, and a photograph of the rightful bearer was reproduced on each ticket. Some very popular events are able to make ticket sales one year in advance: Bestival commenced selling 'Early Bird' tickets for the 2008 edition five days after the end of the 2007 event, which itself had sold out in advance.

The World Wide Web has played a significant role in expanding the demand for music festivals, and has also made finding out about them much easier. While improvements in recording and reproduction technology have meant that any objective need to attend performances has declined (Earl, 2001), demand for live music has grown in recent years and former city centre 'superclubs' are being refurbished and used again as concert halls. The web has made it easier to find out about new music, encouraging the desire to see the groups that produce it and in turn promoting the thrill of congregating with like-minded humans at non-virtual cultural experiences such as music festivals. The rapid success of the Arctic Monkeys, an indie-rock band from Sheffield, benefited from the availability of their music on websites likes MySpace (a site originally created by their fans) and the iTunes Music Store. The band subsequently played at the Reading and Leeds festivals in 2005, on a relatively small stage devoted to lesser-known bands, where they were met with an unusually large crowd singing along songs which at that point were only available as web-sourced 'demos'. The web has made information about music festivals much more available, too: in the past, the average potential festivalgoer might be aware only of a few of the larger festivals, and perhaps those in their immediate region. Now, even small scale, specialist events may be publicised to a wide audience, particularly with the advent of national listings sites like Efestivals (www.efestivals.co.uk) and Virtual Festivals (www.virtualfestivals.com). One slightly perverse result of this is that a few music festivals go to considerable lengths *not* to be publicised in this manner, to maintain secrecy or a sense of exclusivity. Glastonbury is regularly broadcast on British media including radio, television (since 1994), and webcasts, providing glimpses of the event which may heighten demand and help to quell misgivings about attendance.

The British Pop Music Festival – Motivations and Satisfactions

The best outdoor music festival events provide a 'leisure, social or cultural experience outside the normal range of choices or beyond everyday experience (Getz, 1991). As places for celebration and consumption they have a place alongside other 'cathedrals of consumption', and are 'enchanted settings' (Ritzer, 1999) even though as events theirs is a temporary existence. Certainly many festivals can be characterised as playgrounds for adults, and in their provision of spaces devoted to hedonism and largely uninhibited play and fun over relatively extended periods they are a unique type of event.

For some, pop festivals represent marginal, liminal zones, places outside the normal constraints of daily life, representing 'a liberation from the regimes of normative practices and performance codes of mundane life' (Shields, 1991). One characteristic of people experiencing liminality together at such events can be the fostering of 'communitas', a term employed in cultural anthropology and the social sciences to describe an intense community spirit resulting from shared experience, associated with an atmosphere of social equality, sharing, intimacy, and togetherness (Turner, 1982). Barbara Ehrenreich considers that humans are born to indulge in 'the incommunicable thrill of the group deliberately united in joy and exultation' (Ehrenreich, 2007). A festival trip may be interpreted as an act of pilgrimage (Turner, 1982), involving preparation, the journey and arrival, the beginning, culmination and ending of the long-anticipated event, and finally departure and reflection. Festivalgoing may also be associated with ritual: to cite an extreme example, the act of constructing and finally ceremonially burning a large wooden sculpture of a man at the end of the annual Burning Man festival in the Black Rock desert of Nevada has clear ritualistic connotations.

For some people, identity-affirmation is a major motivation for festivalgoing. Many are drawn to festivals in order to collectively celebrate a group identity. Members of the subcultures to be observed at festivals are by definition in a/the minority in their day-to-day lives across Britain and may identify as outsider groups, marginalised to a degree by a dominant ideology. The social function and symbolic meaning of the event are closely related to the community's values, historical continuity, and physical survival (Falassi, 1987 cited in Getz, 2007). In congregating for the duration of a music festival they gain a voice, and validation of their identities that may be withheld by mainstream society. An instructive example of a community with a shared worldview uniting at a music festival is provided by the Bulldog Bash, 'Europe's No. 1 Biker Party', held at a drag strip raceway in Warwickshire. Attracting about 30,000 people each year, Bulldog features heavy rock bands alongside custom bike and car shows, wrestling, a 'beer gut' competition, and 'Run What You Brung', a rare chance for the everyday biker to flog their own machine down a quarter-mile dragstrip at full throttle.

Music is only part of the attraction of music festivals. While the dominant reasons for attending events relate directly to the theme of each and the specific attractions on offer, event socialisation is also important. Research has suggested that festival organisers should not rely on music alone, or specific artists, to draw large crowds (Bowen and Daniels, 2005) and, for many people, wandering around the site, meeting like-minded enthusiasts and soaking up a festive and celebratory ambience are also important motivations (Nicholson and Pearce, 2001). Indeed, one piece of research concluded that budgets and star line-up are largely insignificant predictors of success (Leenders et al., 2005), seemingly contradicting promoter Vince Power's assertion that 'The line-up is everything'. Organisers need to focus on creating a fun and festive atmosphere offering social opportunities (Tomljenovic et al., 2001) and new, non-musical experiences. The simple enjoyment of spending extended periods outdoors is another part of the attraction of pop music events, providing a welcome break from the urban-based lives led by many and, for some, an introduction to the joys of camping. Overnight camping, with the attendant risks of cold and inclement weather, can be interpreted in terms of individual festivalgoers making an investment in and commitment to the success of an event. A taste of camaraderie and egalitarian and fraternal values may be had at many music festivals, and Michael Eavis, the organiser of Glastonbury, has referred to a 'Dunkirk spirit' evident in the presence of adversity at the festival.

Linked to the themes of group identity-affirmation is the concept of cultural capital, part of the function, and symbolic meaning of festival. Championed by Bourdieu (1986), the concept distinguishes the assets of particular social groups between conventional material wealth and *cultural* assets in an effort to explain the ways in which children of elite groups seem more likely than others to succeed in contemporary society, with clear implications for attitudes towards leisure pursuits. Individuals frequenting festivals are undertaking a 'performance activity', making status-positioning statements to others (Rojek, 1999) and accumulating popular cultural capital (or 'subcultural capital'). The social functions of such capital, validated within informal or subcultural networks, parallel those functions associated with dominant, conventional cultural captial (Fiske, 1992).

Festival Sponsorship

Sponsorship is of global importance in the events sector (Getz, 2007), and its increased availability is making staging music festivals easier and more lucrative. Sponsors who formerly targeted major sporting events now seek to associate their products with the cool cultural capital associated with pop music festivals, as well as aiming to directly increase product awareness and sales. However, the majority of sponsorship revenue accrues to the largest and most mainstream festivals. The brewer Carling is a major sponsor, spending £6 million on live music events in 2005 alone (Balakrishnan 2006). Tennents, another brewer, sponsors the Scottish T In The Park event, and the mobile phone operator O2 the Wireless festival in Hyde Park. Sponsorship effectively functions as co-branding, with positive impacts for both sponsor and event: the sponsor requires big-name headliners to make their effort worthwhile, which in turn gives the festival a higher profile in the market. Opportunities for live performance are usually seized by bands, and notably by many of the biggest: only 4 of the top 35 earners in pop music make more money from recordings than live appearances (Connolly and Krueger, 2005). In addition, lucrative sponsorship deals enable bands to demand more money than usual to play events. Record companies' top artists can be seen by up to one million people over a single summer, and artists like Bjork schedule CD releases for the start of the festival season, a period now more important in sales terms than Christmas in some countries.

Corporate sponsorship of pop music festivals has been identified as an issue of concern, however, because of the risks of 'goal displacement' (Getz, 2007) when in the admixture of business and culture the interests of commercial sponsors come to dominate an event. The issue is more prominent at some of the major, more 'institutionalised' events. At the Carling Weekends for instance, sponsors' logos are omnipresent, inducing an uncomfortable perception of over-commercialisation in some fractions of their audience. Some festivals reject any form of corporate sponsorship, notably smaller events with independent ethea including, for instance, the Beautiful Days event and the Green Man festival. Other events are highly selective, including Glastonbury, the policy of which is to welcome sponsorship from organisations 'which do not compromise festival values' (Glastonbury Festival of Contemporary Performing Arts, 2002). In September 2006, the Advisory Council on the Misuse of Drugs proposed that alcohol companies be prohibited from sponsoring music events attended or watched by under-18s in an effort to tackle the perceived 'binge drinking' culture in young people (ACMD, 2006), and while Glastonbury will 'work with alcohol sponsors, [it] will not accept a high-profile on-site presence from any alcohol manufacturer'. Neither does the event accept sponsorship from tobacco companies, nor those with a poor environmental record or who have traded unfairly in less developed countries.

Festival Licensing and Management

Pop music festivals are required to gain a licence from their respective local authorities, with the aim of ensuring that such events are carefully planned and managed, before they are able to operate. A tragic accident that occurred at the Roskilde festival in Denmark emphasises the importance of safety measures at music festivals. This large-scale festival had been operating for 20 years and was considered well-organised, but at the 2000 edition the site was wet, muddy, and slippery, and 9 people died in front of the stage and a further 26 required medical treatment in a crowd-trampling incident. Local authorities are responsible for festival licensing under the provisions of the Licensing Act 2003, and require a detailed event management plan as part of each licence application. Each festival is licensed for a specified maximum audience number, and all applications must address:

- The prevention of crime and disorder.
- Public safety.
- The prevention of public nuisance.
- The protection of children from harm.

Securing suitable sites for outdoor music festivals is often difficult, frequently because of opposition expressed by local residents. During the period from the mid-1980s and well into the 1990s, media reports about the Stonehenge Free Festival, troubles at Glastonbury, and the advent of the oft-unlicenced 'rave' party-festival made it particularly difficult for organisers to obtain sites. Many festival licences are valid for a single year only, but in 2007 the Glastonbury Festival was granted a four-year licence which secured the event's future until 2010. It permitted an expansion in numbers of 27,500–177,500 on a larger site with a new campsite and entertainment area. Part of the licence conditions included a requirement that the festival organisers hold public consultation meetings with local residents both before and after the event.

When seeking sites, festival organisers favour relatively remote locations with few residents living nearby and access roads with the capacity to handle large volumes of vehicles without causing excessive disruption to local traffic. Onsite, the layout of stages, roads, walkways, and retail areas is carefully planned with the aim of preventing overcrowding or congestion at any specific point or time. Noise is usually a major concern for local residents, and if managed incorrectly the issue may cause difficulties for future licence applications. Careful site selection and exploitation of the topography can minimise off-site complaints arising from noise, and stages are carefully oriented to ensure that the sound is not intrusive for local residents. Rogue sound systems playing out in campsites at night may be noisy enough to be audible off-site, and are dealt with by festival security teams. Some events offer to pay for the temporary relocation of local residents for the duration of the event.

At bigger events, popular acts are often cross-scheduled across different stages and start and finish times staggered in order to prevent excessive numbers of people gathering for any one performance and sudden mass crowd movements which might jeopardise safety. Provisions are made for stopping performances mid-way, and for emergency evacuation of the site, if necessary. At Glastonbury, the topsoil in front of the main 'Pyramid' stage was removed and thousands of tonnes of hardcore laid before the soil was replaced in order to avoid the dangers associated with deep mud there.

Volunteers occupy a special place in event management (Getz, 1997) and are widely used to 'steward' pop festivals, even at the biggest and most commercial events. They are engaged to supervise traffic and people at the various gates, check tickets and passes, monitor campsites and safety in arenas, and generally ensure the welfare of festivalgoers. The international aid charity Oxfam recruited, trained, and managed 1400 stewards for the 2007 edition of Glastonbury, each of whom worked for three eight-hour periods over the course of the festival weekend in exchange for a festival ticket. In 2005, the festival donated £200,000 to Oxfam for their work. Higher risk activities, including perimeter security, crowd control at the front of stages, dealing with any violent incidents and ejections from the site are undertaken by professional security staff.

Security is a concern at all music festivals but particularly at the most popular events, many of which exercise an almost magnetic draw for some people. For several years, Glastonbury suffered mass invasion by the ticketless: in 2000, for instance, between 30,000 and 100,000 gained free entry through various means including fence-climbing, the use of ladders, and tunnelling. The additional numbers at the event overloaded the facilities, made crowd control difficult, and contributed to an occasionally sour atmosphere. Licence conditions relating to maximum attendance numbers were regularly broken, and the authorities insisted that the event responded with appropriate measures, so in 2001, a 'fallow' year during which the festival was not staged, a 3.5-metre-high fence was erected around the site at the cost of one million pounds. The 'superfence' dealt very effectively with the long-running perimeter security problems, and was probably essential to enable the event to continue to gain an operating licence. Elaborate arrangements have been developed over the years to monitor the number of people in the main arena.

Far less crime occurs at festivals than is popularly imagined. The House of Lords heard that the number of crimes committed at Glastonbury in 2004 was about 20% less than that occurring in a comparable area of the sedate City of Bath over the same period – 478, compared to 566 in Bath (Hansard [House of Lords], 16 June 2005, column 1334). About half of the criminal incidents recorded at the festival comprised thefts from tents. As part of general security measures at the festival, certain individuals are barred from entering the event (Hughes, 2000). High-tech crowd surveillance methods are increasingly being employed, raising issues about the balance between public security and personal privacy at licensed events. In 2007, police used a remote-controlled miniature helicopter to survey the crowds at the V Festival for the first time at a major public event. The battery-operated flying surveillance device carried high-resolution still and colour video cameras, and had night vision capability. It is less than 1 metre in length, inaudible once above 50 metre in height, and invisible to the naked eye above 100 metre. The declared purposes for the use of the device were to monitor people thought to be acting suspiciously in car parks – perhaps attempting to break into vehicles – and to gather intelligence on individuals in the crowd. It was not flown over the main arena because of fears that a crash might cause injuries. Closed-circuit television (CCTV) was also employed to monitor the festival site throughout its duration.

Public health is a further dimension of the public safety issue. Several articles in medical journals examining disease outbreaks at festivals serve perhaps to reinforce the perception of some sectors of the public towards the conditions at these events. Conditions conducive to outbreaks of disease may develop wherever large gatherings of people are living in close proximity outdoors and with relatively basic services, circumstances which may also render the control of any outbreaks difficult. Glastonbury suffered an outbreak of *E. coli* in 1997, a species of bacteria living in the lower intestines of mammals which can cause diarrhoea and urinary tract infections if ingested (Crampin et al., 1999), and shigellosis, a form of dysentery, was reported at an outdoor festival in Michigan, USA in 1988 (Lee et al., 1991), for instance. Such disease problems may be exacerbated by mud contamination in fields often more normally used for grazing cows, inattention to personal hygiene, and the limited availability of handwashing facilities.

Trends in Provision

The growth in the number of British pop music festivals has been paralleled by a blossoming of diversity in the event genre in response to the changing market environment (see Table 14.3). The structure of the industry is straightforward: there are relatively few major events, including well-known mass-market ones like Glastonbury and the Carling Weekends, and a larger number of medium-sized festivals, but the majority of all such events are small scale, perhaps of the order of 1000–3000 attendees. While the biggest and best-known events continue to dominate public perceptions of the pop festival, arguably the most creative developments are at the small-scale end of the event genre. A phenomenon of 'festival evolution' is discernible, whereby over the course of time some former festivalgoers themselves become festival organisers, staging the type of events that they themselves would wish to patronise. When the Stonehenge Free Festival was banned in 1985, former festivalgoers helped conceive the Green Fields section of Glastonbury, and subsequent discussions between like-minded individuals there identified a common desire for a similar but smaller festival with an explicit focus on green issues. This in turn led to the establishment of the Big Green Gathering festival, the first edition of which was held in 1994, attracting 1600 people. In 2006, 20,000 people attended the event, now described as 'Europe's Biggest Green Gathering'.

Small events can recapture the sense of fun and freedom often missing at big festivals, and the philosophies behind the selection of their line-ups frequently prioritise artistic innovation and risk-taking. Many small events are staged simply to satisfy the passion of the organisers and their social circle, without expectations of making a profit, and bands may not be paid for playing. Technological developments have made staging music at small-scale alfresco events quicker, easier, cheaper, and with much greater quality than in the past. As a result, small music festivals can often seem more like large parties than the often seemingly over-organised large-scale ones. At Farmageddon, alcoholic drinks from the bar are free – until all have been drunk, after which the audience is expected to turn to its own supplies. Small festivals are frequently able to operate with only minimal security, and may even dispense with perimeter fences.

Environmental Impacts of Festivals

Music festivals inevitably entail environmental impacts, and the general atmosphere of partying and gaiety is not particularly conducive to environmentally responsible behaviour. Festivalgoers' travel to and from music events produces environmental impacts, and in an attempt to address the issue, Glastonbury recommends the Liftshare.com website, through which people make contact and agree to share transport. The festival estimates that the service reduces the number of car journeys made by up to 15,000. An alternative approach is taken by the Big Chill, which providing dedicated coach services from several British cities and subsidises fares by 50%. Further impacts include traffic congestion, noise pollution, and the carbon footprint and emissions associated with the process of setting up, running, and taking down any major event.

The environmental impacts produced by large numbers of people cohabiting in a restricted space become very obvious very quickly. On-site environmental impacts derive from the generation of refuse and sewage, and impacts upon the appearance and ecology of the festival site. The 'A Greener Festival' organisation (www.agreenerfestival.com) researches and audits many of the major music events and while many have instituted environmental policies or 'environmentally friendly practices'

Table 14.3: Recent trends in pop festival provision

Type	Description
The regional festival	Exploiting market opportunities for new events held in the regions of the United Kingdom.
The religious music festival	Promoting and celebrating religions through the medium of contemporary pop music.
The urban festival	Music festivals held both indoors and outdoors (in parks and open spaces) in towns and cities.
The holiday destination festival	Staged at locations outside the United Kingdom and promoted to the British (and other nationalities) for inclusion in peoples' annual holiday plans Examples include the Festival Internacional de Benicassim on the Spanish Mediterranean coast between Barcelona and Valencia, and the Festival Au Desert held at the oasis of Essakane in Mali each January.
The premium festival product	Upmarket events aimed at more mature festivalgoers prepared to pay premium prices for some of the creature comforts lacking at many pop festivals.
The secret festival	Events which are deliberately not publicized widely in an effort to promote an intimate and friendly atmosphere by attracting only 'the right sort of people'.
The teenagers' festival	The conditions of most festival licences prohibit entry by unaccompanied children aged under 16, and the teenagers' pop festival has emerged in response to demand from a market segment that is often unable to access live music at all.
The deliberately constrained festival	With only limited numbers of tickets available in response to perceptions that major events such as Glastonbury have become commercial, predictable, and simply too big.
The boutique festival	Small scale, intimate, elegant, and stylish, these niche-type events prioritize quality over quantity. Even the music often tends to take a back seat.
The womens' festival	Typically espousing feminist philosophy and featuring female bands. Some are aimed particularly at lesbian feminists, promoting a positive collective identity for that social group (Eder et al., 1995).
The green festival	Perhaps the closest to the 'hippy festival' of popular imagination, green festivals often emphasize the provision of opportunities for debate by audiences interested in environmental issues, and may be powered by renewable energy sources.
The family festival	Aimed at attracting family markets, the music at such events generally comes second to trampolining, circus skills workshops and communal bedtime stories for festivalgoers' children.
The dual-location festival	Demand for the Carling Weekend rock festival at Reading proved so great that in 1999 a twin festival was established 200 miles further north near Leeds, capitalizing on the popularity of event amongst audiences there. The line-up of Reading plays Leeds the following day and vice versa.
The economy festival	Events for price-conscious markets staging line-ups of 'cover' bands alongside some new acts.
The political festival	Popular music festivals staged to promulgate political messages.
The no-camping festival	To overcome the problem of outdoor festivals being at the mercy of the British weather, and to provide for those who dislike camping.
The virtual festival	A recent development exemplified by the Secondfest music festival. This is staged in the web-based virtual world Second Life, and provides opportunities to 'dance' virtually with others to the music of professional entertainers in a festival-shaped virtual space.

(EPFs) the organisation has challenged all to do so in future. Such initiatives could be viewed as assisting with the positioning of some festivals as much as their value in ethical terms, in the same way as sponsorship and branding. Waste separation bins similar to those used for domestic purposes have become a familiar sight at many pop festivals, and the T In The Park festival claimed to have recycled 75% of cardboard cups and 40% of the total waste generated at the 2007 edition of the event.

After some pop festivals, organisers have to cope with large numbers of tents abandoned in the camping fields. The price of camping equipment has fallen dramatically in recent years, and five-berth tents can be now bought for as little as 20 or 20 pounds; indeed, in 2007 the British budget retail chain Argos advertised a 'disposable' two-person tent for £7.94! The low price of equipment, coupled with the often considerable effort required to strike camp and carry everything from camping fields to car parks or pedestrian exits, encourage some festivalgoers to leave their tents in situ upon departure, especially after wet and muddy festivals. Over 3000 tents were abandoned after the Reading and Leeds festivals in 2006. At the 2007 edition of Glastonbury festivalgoers were asked to donate unwanted tents and other camping equipment rather than abandoning them. The equipment was collected and re-used for children camps and humanitarian work in less developed countries (the 'Give Me Shelter' project).

The British Pop Festival and Tourism

Music festivals act as cultural tourist destinations, and many or most festivalgoers are effectively tourists. Music festivals, 'where people travel, at least in some part, because of music', have been described as the oldest and the most common form of music tourism (Gibson and Connell, 2005). At most pop festivals, audiences stay only for the duration of the scheduled entertainment, making their trip behaviour comparable to that of short-break tourists. However, for some people these events are so enjoyable that a weekend is insufficient, and in recognition of this a few festivals permit festivalgoers to stay much longer. Large numbers of people arrive at the Big Chill in Herefordshire on Thursday, fully 24 hours before the weekend programme commences, for instance. Glastonbury is now 'open' for a full week from Wednesday before the scheduled Friday midday start, meaning that festivalgoers may remain on the camping grounds until the following Tuesday. In 2007, about 80,000 people had arrived by the day before the event commenced, nearly half the total capacity. Some make visits to one or more music festivals a feature of their summer holidays.

A successful music festival can have a substantial impact upon the economy of the area in which it is located. The expenditure necessary to stage an event constitutes an injection of additional demand into the local economy; audiences often go shopping locally before the event; and a music festival can extend the tourist season in its locality (Gibson and Connell, 2005). Estimates suggest that the gross expenditure at the 2007 edition of Glastonbury totaled more than £73m (including two other linked events, the much smaller Glastonbury Abbey Extravaganza, and the Equinox Party) (Baker Associates, 2007). Staging the events cost £21.2m, of which around £18m was spent with local suppliers and service providers in accordance with festival policy to retain festival-related expenditure within the locality as far as possible. £25.6m was spent on-site by festivalgoers and traders, and a further £26.5m was spent off-site (hundreds of festivalgoers stay in hotel and bed and breakfast accommodation in the local area during the festival period, for instance). The net impact on the local economy of Mendip Direct was about £35.8m, rising to about £45m over the wider south-west of England, and 929 FTE jobs were generated in Mendip alone. It is estimated that Glastonbury accounts for over one-seventh of the total annual visitor spend for tourism in Mendip District.

As a result, local authorities and other public sector agencies with responsibilities for economic development and place promotion take an interest in some music festivals. Public assistance may be offered to organisers, and festivals may be organised partly or wholly by local authorities (Felsenstein and Fleischer, 2003). The direct economic effects may be augmented by the image-production role of festivals, whereby such events can contribute to place marketing, raising the profile of areas as destinations and distinguishing them from others.

Some major British music festivals including Glastonbury and the Carling Weekends have an international reputation, but British tourism authorities have been slow to capitalise on their popularity. The Slovakian-based SkyEurope low-cost airline advertised flights from Poland to Glastonbury festival in 2007 priced from 19 Euro per trip, although closer inspection seemed to indicate that Eastern European festivalgoers would actually be flying into Stansted, London's third airport, a distance of 270 kilometre from the festival site. The DCMS, responsible for government policy on tourism, evinces a generally positive attitude towards live music events in general and recognises festivals as part of the creative industries sector, which it defines as those based upon individual creativity, skill and talent, and with the potential to create wealth and jobs (DCMS, 2007). Visit Britain, the national agency that promotes Britain internationally, now lists festivals on its www site, including Glastonbury as well as several smaller events. Similarly, Enjoy England, the domestic marketing division of the agency, launched a marketing campaign in 2007 entitled 'England Rocks' aimed at persuading more Britons to holiday at home by promoting music festivals amongst other music-related destinations and events.

Conclusion

This chapter has investigated the phenomenon of the British pop music festival, a hugely popular and diverse type of event with a reputation extending internationally but which nonetheless has largely been neglected by researchers. Contemporary events bear little resemblance to their often poorly organised antecedents, and the largest constitute some of the biggest events of any type held in the United Kingdom. A revised definition of the pop music festival has been advanced, types and typologies enumerated, and the concept of the event life cycle introduced to a new context. Pop festivals exhibit many parallels with the carnivals of pre-Christian and medieval Europe, events characterised by revelry, excess, and indulgence. The pop festival has made a remarkable transition from being considered disreputable to become a major cultural event type with mainstream appeal, though it has attracted criticism for perceived loss of authenticity and creeping commercialisation along the way.

Markets and provision are expanding, and the best-known events experience high levels of demand for tickets. Key trends in provision are the growth in the number of festivals and a blossoming of diversity, with small events setting out to recapture an atmosphere of fun and freedom, making them seem more like large parties than the major festivals. Some events rely upon their line-up to achieve success, but some researchers contend that it is not necessarily a predictor of success; many niche events concentrate on devising new formulas in an effort to attract an enthusiastic audience by making the event the focus rather than individual acts. The festival phenomenon has been boosted by a growing interest in live music, improved information availability through the web, and the broadcasting of music festivals on TV and radio. Uniquely, many festivals serve as adult playgrounds, representing marginal, liminal zones devoted to hedonism and largely uninhibited play and fun. Identity-affirmation is also a major motivation for attendance, linked to the accumulation of 'popular cultural capital'. Environmental impacts are inevitable at events involving large numbers of people cohabiting in a restricted space, and many events are attempting to address these, both on- and off-site. As most pop festivals function as tourist destinations, and many festivalgoers are effectively tourists, government tourism agencies are starting to promote them to national and international markets.

It seems likely that the growth in the number of pop music festivals observed over recent years may decline in the foreseeable future, but this exciting, fun, sociable, and essentially unique type of event has become an established addition to the range of popular cultural diversions available to thrill-seekers in 21st century in Britain and elsewhere.

References

ACMD (2006) *Pathways to Problems*. London: Home Office.

Anon (20 May 2007) Your guide to getting the most out of summer festivals. *Daily Mail*, 37.

Balakrishnan, A. (28 August 2006) How the summer rock festivals became one big branded beer tent. *The Guardian*, 7.

Baker Associates (2007) *Glastonbury Festivals 2007 – Economic Impact Assessment*. Bristol: Baker Associates.

Beverland, M., Hoffman, D. and Rasmussen, M. (2001) The evolution of events in the Australasian wine sector. *Tourism Recreation Research*, 26(2), 35–44.

Bourdieu, P. (1986) *Distinction: A Social Critique of the Judgement of Taste*. London: Routledge.

Bowen, H. E. and Daniels, M. J. (2005) Does the music matter? Motivations for attending a music festival. *Event Management*, 9(3), 155–164.

Breines, W. (1982) *Community and Organisation in the New Left, 1962–1968: The Great Refusal*. New Brunswick, New Jersey: Rutgers University Press.

Butler, R. W. (1980) The concept of a tourist area cycle of evolution: Implications for management of resources. *The Canadian Geographer*, 24(1), 5–12.

Clarke, M. (1982) *The Politics of Pop Festivals*. London: Junction Books.

Connolly, M. and Krueger, A. B. (2005) *Rockonomics: The Economics of Popular Music, NBER Working Papers 11282*. Cambridge, MA: National Bureau of Economic Research, Inc.

Crampin, M., Willshaw, G., Hancock, R., Djuretic, T., Elstob, C., Rouse, A., Cheasty, T. and Stuart, J. (May 1999) Outbreak of *Escherichia coli* O157 infection associated with a music festival. *European Journal of Clinical Microbiology & Infectious Diseases*, 18(4), 286–288.

DCMS (2007) *Definitions*, at www.culture.gov.uk/Reference_library/Research/det/glossary_abbreviations.htm, accessed 10 September 2007.

Earl, P. E. (2001) Simon's travel theorem and the demand for live music. *Journal of Economic Psychology*, 22(3), 335–358.

Eder, D., Staggenborg, S. and Sudderth, L. (1995) The national women's music festival: Collective identity and diversity in a lesbian-feminist Community. *Journal of Contemporary Ethnography*, 23(4), 485–515.

Ehrenreich, B. (2007) *Dancing in the Streets: A History of Collective Joy*. London: Granta Books.

Falassi, A. (1987) *Time Out of Time: Essays on the Festival*. Albuquerque: University of New Mexico Press.

Felsenstein, D. and Fleischer, A. (2003) Local festivals and tourism promotion: The role of public assistance and visitor expenditure. *Journal of Travel Research*, 41(4), 385–392.

Fiske, J. (1992) The cultural economy of fandom. In Lewis, L. A. (ed.), *The Adoring Audience: Fan Culture and Popular Media*, London: Routledge, pp. 30–49.

Freeview Playback (2007) Pack your wellies and your wallet: "Kate Moss effect" sends festival costs soaring, press release, 20 June 2007, at http://www.freeview.co.uk/press/pr200607, accessed 26 September 2007.

Getz, D. (1991) *Festivals, Special Events and Tourism*. New York: Van Nostrand Reinhold.

Getz, D. (1997) *Event Management and Event Tourism*. New York: Cognizant Communication Corporation.

Getz, D. (2002) Why festivals fail. *Event Management*, 7(4), 209–219.

Getz, D. (2007) *Event Studies: Theory, Research and Policy for Planned Events*. Oxford: Butterworth: Heinemann.

Gibson, C. and Connell, J. (2005) *Music and Tourism*. Clevedon: Channel View Press.

Glastonbury Festival of Contemporary Performing Arts (2001) *Student information pack: Attendance numbers*, at www.glastonburyfestivals.co.uk/uploadedFiles/Information/Student_Information_Pack, accessed 23 November 2007.

Glastonbury Festival of Contemporary Performing Arts (2002) *Sponsorship*, in supporting documentation to licence application for Glastonbury Festival 2002, at www.glastonburyfestivals.co.uk/uploadedFiles/Information/Student_Information_Pack/25%20Sponsorship.pdf, accessed 23 November 2007.

Harrowven, J. (1980) *Origins of Festivals and Feasts*. London: Kaye and Ward.

Hughes, H. (2000) *Arts, Entertainment and Tourism*. London: Butterworth-Heinemann, 223.

Kong, L. (1995) Popular music in geographical analyses. *Progress in Human Geography*, 19(2), 183–198.

Lee, L. A., Ostroff, S., McGee, H., Johnson, D., Downes, F., Cameron, D., Bean, N. and Griffin, P. (1991) An outbreak of shigellosis at an outdoor music festival. *American Journal of Epidemiology*, 133(6), 608–615.

Leenders, M. A. M., van Telgen, J., Gemser, G. and Van der Wurff, R. (2005) Success in the Dutch music festival market: The role of format and content. *The International Journal on Media Management*, 7(3&4), 148–157.

Live Music Forum (2007) *Findings & Recommendations*. London: DCMS.

McKay, G. (2000) *Glastonbury: A Very English Fair*. London: Gollancz.

Mintel International Group Limited (2006a) *Music Concerts and Festivals: UK*. London: Mintel.

Mintel International Group Limited (2006b) *Student Lifestyles: UK*. London: Mintel.

Nicholson, R. E. and Pearce, D. G. (2001) Why do people attend events: A comparative analysis of visitor motivations at four south island events. *Journal of Travel Research*, 39(4), 449–460.

Paleo, I. O. and Wijnberg, N. M. (2006) Classification of popular music festivals: A typology of festivals and an inquiry into their role in the construction of music genres. *International Journal of Arts Management*, 8(2), 50–61.

Prentice, R. C. and Andersen, V. A. (2003) Festival as creative destination. *Annals of Tourism Research*, 30(1), 7–30.

Ritzer, G. (1999) *Enchanting a Disenchanted World: Revolutionizing the Means of Consumption*. London: Pine Forge Press.

Rojek, C. (1999) *Leisure and Culture*. Basingstoke: Palgrave Macmillan.

Shields, R. (1991) *Places on the Margin: Alternative Geographies of Modernity*. London: Routledge.

Smith, S. J. (1997) Beyond geography's visible worlds: A cultural politics of music. *Progress in Human Geography*, 21(4), 502–529.

Tomljenovic, R., Larsson, M. and Faulkner, B. (2001) Predictors of satisfaction with festival attendance: A case of Storsjoyran rock music festival. *Tourism*, 49(2), 123–132.

Turner, V. T. (ed.) (1982) *Celebration: Studies in Festivity and Ritual*. Washington: Smithsonian Institute.

Virtualfestivals (2006) UK Festival Awards 2006 – The Winners!, at www.virtualfestivals.com/latest/news/3044, accessed 23 November 2007.

PART 4

MANAGING THE EVENT

Jane Ali-Knight

This final section of the book offers five chapters each addressing various critical aspects of the management of festivals and events. The role of planning; effective human resource management; event analysis and implementation are examined. One theme common to all these chapters is the need for effective planning and design to ensure successful events for the destinations and host communities.

In Chapter 15 Elbe presents a model for analysing the development of public events. The model deals with three central aspects of the development process: how the different activities of the event are coordinated, how the resources needed are mobilised and finally, what motivates the different stakeholders, to contribute to the realisation of the event. The chapter reveals how the tool aids understanding and knowledge of how events develop and is useful to anyone working in the public and private events sphere.

Chapter 16 addresses the essential human resources issues of events. Human resources are seen as a critical success factor in the events industry and to date little attention has been paid to the human resources element. Davidson outlines the importance of effective human resource planning to remaining competitive in a crowded events market. He also focuses on the importance of attracting and retaining professional staff and how this contributes to the securing of events for their city or country. The ability to recruit and retain professionals of the right calibre into key destination marketing positions is also explored. Business events such as conventions and incentive trips are also examined in this context. Finally the chapter explores the issue of education and career development of professional staff in destination marketing organisations, with particular emphasis on those who are responsible for attracting business events to their destinations.

Chapter 17 changes focus to consider the role of 'micro-events' and their contribution to local communities. Dickson and Milne examine the planning and development of such events and the economic and social benefits that are presented to the communities that host the events. The chapter outlines the development of a web-based system to permit event managers, local communities, businesses and planners to better understand and estimate event-related economic impacts. In this chapter, issues affecting the leveraging of micro-events for economic impact, as well as its measurement, are discussed. The Tourism Research and Community Empowerment (TRACE) Events project is then presented as a solution to some of the issues identified. TRACE is shown to facilitate improved understanding of economic impacts as well as the promotion of networks and knowledge sharing between event stakeholders and presents data from four New Zealand sporting events used as part of the calibration process. This chapter finally highlights the important role that ICT, and particularly the Internet, can play in helping to build closer relationships and linkages between New Zealand communities, businesses and sports tourism.

In Chapter 18 we move from micro to mega-events as Lovell and Stuart-Hoyle again address the important role of planning and implementation in the event cycle. A case study of the hosting of the first stage of the 2007 Tour De France is examined. The chapter aims to analyse the relationship between the heritage city and mega-event, assessing the processes involved in planning and implementing the event, using the staging of the Tour de France in Canterbury as a case study. The chapter explores the planning and management issues of staging the Tour De France in a historic environment highlighting the contribution of meticulous preparation in the design and establishment of the event to the level of success by the event organisers. Canterbury's cultural policy initiatives and heritage city constraints are identified and the chapter finally establishes how the event reinforced a 'sense of place' for the destination.

In the final chapter of the book Paraskevas introduces a topical and timely aspect of event management that has been little researched to date – the safety and security aspects of events in the face of increased global terrorist activities. This chapter explores, through the use of extensive case study examples, the nature of the events industry and the reasons why it attracts terrorist groups and then proposes a structured approach to counter-terrorism planning to be used as a guide by event planners and other event professionals. A framework for special event counter-terrorism planning, calling for a joint intelligence process from all event stakeholders, offers event planners a structured approach to undertaking this task. Paraskevas finally concludes offering a word of caution highlighting the subjectivity of all threat assessments and event criticality/vulnerability evaluations. The assumption of intimate knowledge and understanding of terrorist groups and accurate information about the event, the venues and the potential perpetrators is key.

Chapter 15

A Model for Analysing the Development of Public Events

Jörgen Elbe

Introduction

In this chapter, a model for analysing the development of public events is presented. The model deals with three central aspects of the development process: how the different activities of the event are coordinated, how the resources needed are mobilised and finally, what motivates the actors, that is the different stakeholders, to contribute to the realisation of the event. The theoretical foundations of the model can mainly be found in the network approach to business activities developed by the so-called Industrial Marketing and Purchasing group (Axelsson and Easton, 1992; Håkansson and Snehota, 1995; Ford, 1997), but also in economic sociology (Granovetter, 1973, 1985; Suchman, 1995; Weber, 1914/1983).

The model was developed in a previous research project, the aim of which was to create a better understanding of the role events play in tourist destination development and how these events are developed and organised (Elbe, 2002; Elbe et al., 2007). By using the model in research, new insights into the processes involved in organising events can be revealed. It can produce results answering questions such as: Why do different types of actors participate with resources or in activities in events? In what ways can resources be mobilised? How are activities controlled and linked to each other?

The model may also be used for comparative studies, researching issues such as what differences exist between one-off and recurrent events or between different types of events. It can also be used in longitudinal studies, when researching how the aspects the model focuses on develop and change over time. The results may be systematised and structured to produce new knowledge. Such knowledge can increase our theoretical understanding, but also help organisers and other stakeholders involved to be better prepared for the challenging task of organising and staging public events.

In the next section, the rationale behind developing a model in this field is discussed, that is the model is positioned in relation to existing models. Then, in the following section, the theoretical frame of reference on which the model is based is introduced. Thereafter, the model is presented in detail. Following that section, examples of some of the findings produced when the model has been

International Perspectives of Festivals and Events
Copyright © 2009 by Elsevier Ltd.
All rights of reproduction in any form reserved.
ISBN: 978-0-08-045100-8

used in research are described. Finally, in the last section, the chapter is summed up and possible use of the model in future research is discussed.

Literature Review

Organising and mobilising resources for public events is often a complex task. This is particularly true of major events, since major events usually involve a magnitude of activities, resources and actors. Many of these events, such as different sports and cultural events, are often organised by local, non-profit organisations that lack the expertise, routines and resources needed. However, there are a number of books offering advice on how to organise events (see e.g., Bowdin et al., 2006; Getz, 2005; Watt, 1998). Although the books differ somewhat in structure and content, the approach they offer is based more or less on the same rationale, namely the rational planning process. In general, models on the rational planning process can be divided into four steps. The first step is to decide on goals; in the next step, an analysis of the organiser's and the stakeholder's strengths and weaknesses as well as the opportunities and threats to the environment is carried out; in the third step, a strategy based on the analysis is developed and, in the last step finally, the plan is implemented and later evaluated.

Using models on rational planning is of course helpful for any organiser of major events, but these models also have their limitations. As stated by Simon as far back as 1957, all planning is associated with uncertainty since planning requires the collection and interpretation of often ambiguous information, and in addition to that, it often involves several stakeholders with varying and sometimes even conflicting interests (Simon, 1957). Another criticism involves a basic assumption in the rational planning models. When using planning models, it is assumed that there is a dividing line between the planning unit, that is the organiser and his/her partners, and the environment, and that the planning unit is able to control what is happening inside the unit while it has to adapt to the environment outside its limits. But according to Håkansson and Snehota (1989), it is irrelevant to talk about a dividing line between actors, in this case the organiser and the environment. They mean instead that every actor is part of a wider network: they are interconnected with other actors, directly and indirectly, through different types of relations. To define where a network starts or ends is then irrelevant since there is no given outer limit for the network. This means that an actor does not adapt to the environment, instead the actor has to act and react to the actions of interconnected actors in a network. The relations may, in other words, create opportunities as well as constraints.

This certainly holds true for events. As pointed out by Bowdin et al. (2006) among others, major events involve a number of stakeholders from different sectors, such as the government and community sectors as well as the corporate and non-profit sectors. The participating actors from these sectors are all interconnected with yet other actors, which directly or indirectly can influence the processes involved in carrying out the event. There are also studies indicating the role relationships play when carrying out events (Larson and Wikström 2001; Mount and Niro, 1995; Wicks, 1995), as well as the role events have in developing relationships between actors (Long, 2000).

In other words, the model presented does not focus on the planning process as such but, rather, on how an event is actually carried out. While rational planning models can be said to be normative in character, that is, they are developed in order to find a solution to a practical problem by suggesting solutions based on a theoretical idea (March, 1978), the aim of the model suggested here is to be exploratory and to use the actions occurring in reality as a basis for explanation and increased understanding.

The Theoretical Frame of Reference

As already mentioned, the model is based on a relationship and network perspective. The network perspective highlights the interdependencies and the role of the relationships between business actors (Håkansson and Johanson, 1992; Håkansson and Snehota, 1995). An actor is here defined as anyone who is perceived to take action; it may be an organisation, a department or an individual. It is not assumed that the actors act individually and independently of each other, which is the normal assumption in economic theory. Rather they are seen to be part of a context, a network of interdependent and related actors. This means that they are dependent on other actors' actions while the other actors are dependent on theirs. In a network perspective, the actors are not just dependent on those with whom they have a direct relationship. They may also be affected by processes in relations with which they are indirectly connected.

The relationships between the actors are developed over time and they may consist of gradually developed links between their different activities, ties between their resources and of social bonds between individuals. The character of the activity links and resource ties influences the degree of connectedness and the relationships create opportunities to develop activities and to mobilise resources. However, relationships between business actors may be symmetric or asymmetric (Elbe, 2002). A symmetric relationship is characterised by interdependence and by the development of trust between the actors. In a symmetric relationship, both parties have an interest in developing the relationship, and hence, more or less the same opportunities to influence development. In an asymmetric relationship, one party is dependent on the other. This means that the dependent party lacks the possibility to influence the relationship and it must accept the changes that the other party makes. The stronger party can exercise power over the weaker party.

Thus, a network consists of different types of connected relationships between different types of actors. A network may have different kinds of structures as a consequence of the character of the types of relationships that are included in the network (Axelsson, 1996). The number of actors included may differ; the structure may be tight or loose (it may be easier or more difficult to be connected or disconnected); and the power may be concentrated in one or more actors or it may be spread to several. The cooperative climate may differ. It may be characterised by openness or by closeness between actors or between groups of actors. The structure of the network and the functions of the relationships will affect the efficiency of the network when it comes to developing new activities and to mobilising resources for these new activities.

There are certain advantages to be derived from analysing events from a relationship and network perspective. An event consists of a number of related activities that have to be carried out during a limited time. The activities require different types of resources, which have to be mobilised. In other words, different actors are needed in order to perform and coordinate the activities as well as to contribute resources. The purpose of using the model introduced below is to provide answers to the question of how this is done.

Introducing the Model

The model consists of two dimensions and the analysis is made in two steps in accordance with these two dimensions. The first dimension, and subsequently the first step in the analysis, is aimed at mapping out the structure of the event. This description of the event is needed in order to be able to analyse the development processes in the next step. The three concepts: activities, resources and actors are used for this purpose. These concepts are, as already discussed, central in models developed to analyse business relationships and networks within the network approach (Håkansson and Johanson, 1992; Håkansson and Snehota, 1995).

To begin with, the central activities in the event are mapped out. Then, the resources needed in order to carry out the activities are identified. Next, the actors participating in the activities and/or with resources are identified. By systematically revealing the structure of the event according to the three concepts, a basis for analysing the development processes is created.

The second dimension concerns the actual analytical part, which is carried out in order to understand the development processes behind the realisation of an event. The focus here is on analysing how the structure of the event has developed. The concepts: coordination, mobilisation and interests are developed for this purpose. These concepts correspond to the structural concepts in the first dimension, in the following way: activities – coordination, resources – mobilisation and actors – interests. In this step, coordination captures how the activities are carried out; mobilisation, how the resources have been made accessible and the interests concept, finally, captures the motives of the actors in connection with their participation.

For logical as well as practical reasons, we suggest the analysis be carried out in the following sequence. In the first step, the three concepts are used in the order presented above: activities, resources, actors. A logical starting point is to map out the activities first, in order to understand what the event consists of. When the activities are known, the resources needed in order to carry out the activities may be identified. Then the actors participating in the activities and contributing resources can be mapped out. But in the second step, it makes more sense to start with how the resources have been mobilised in order to perform the activities. The analysis continues by finding out what interests the different actors have in contributing resources, and finally, finding out how the whole event, with all its different activities, is coordinated. Before the concepts are presented in detail, the model with its two dimensions and two analytical steps is described graphically in Figure 15.1.

The Structural Dimension

Activities   An activity is considered as a sequence of acts aimed towards a goal (Håkansson and Snehota, 1995). How we choose to consider an activity depends on what we want to achieve with the analysis. Activities can be analysed on different levels. An event consists of a number of activities. They may be stage or sport performances, security measures, traffic and first aid arrangements, catering, rubbish disposal, ticket sales and so on. Depending on the purpose of the analysis, the appropriate

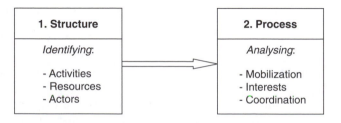

Figure 15.1: The two steps.

level of analysis must consequently be decided. In some cases whole events are analysed, while in others, perhaps in larger hallmark events (Hall, 1992), attention is focused on a specific part of the event and what seems to be one activity might be subdivided into several, limited activities.

The whole event (or a specific part of it) can be seen as an activity pattern, where the activities are connected in different ways. They may for instance be vertically and sequentially connected, like in a chain. Where one activity ends, the next will follow. Or they can be performed in parallel or partly overlap each other. Some can go on for a long time, before, under and after the event or even become permanent between events, as in some recurring events. In complex, major events, one can expect to find a number of different activities, vertically connected as well as parallel.

Resources   Every activity requires resources. In the network approach, resources are defined as all elements that can be put into productive use in an activity (Håkansson and Snehota, 1995). In order for an element to be a productive resource, it must be combined with one or several other elements. Resources are, in other words, considered to be heterogeneous and variable. For instance, let us assume that in a sports event the results of thousands of athletes have to be reported as quickly as possible after the competition. In this example, equipment for timing and computers are needed, as well as electricity and channels to communicate the results also being necessary. But without combining these elements with each other and without the human skills required to build systems and operate those systems, the resources would not be of much help.

Although resources are variable and heterogonous, it may be useful, for analytical reasons, to categorise these into a generic classification. Grant (1995) as well as Axelsson (1998), suggests three categories: tangible, intangible and human resources. Both authors have categorised financial resources as a tangible resource, but Axelsson suggest that financial resources may be a category on their own, since financial resources are considered to be a more flexible resource than other tangible resources. This makes sense since financial resources can easily be transformed into other kinds of resources through market transactions. It also makes sense to separate financial resources from other tangible resources for another reason. Tangible resources can often be put to productive use more than once in a while, once money is spent, it cannot be used again unless resources are sold. In addition, the value of tangible resources (except financial resources) may also be calculated in more or less arbitrary ways. This means that we end up with four categories. The four categories, with examples of resources within each category, are presented in Table 15.1.

Most of the resources exemplified in the table are probably obvious, but a few comments may be appropriate. Relationships and contacts are considered to be an important human resource, since such connections are often used in order to mobilise resources. Legitimacy (image and reputation) is seen as a valuable intangible resource. A positive perceived legitimacy may often be a prerequisite

Table 15.1: Examples of resources within four resource categories.

Categories	Examples of resources
Tangible	Land, facilities, equipment
Intangible	Systems, routines, legitimacy
Human	Labour, competence, relationships
Financial	Financial means

when it comes to attracting actors to an event. This will be discussed in more detail when the concept of mobilisation is presented below.

Actors   Actors are people who take action; they contribute resources and perform activities. Theoretically it is only individuals who can act. But in reality we have different roles and usually we act according to these roles. We often act on behalf of some perceived entity, for example an organisation, or perceive that organisations can take actions (Weber, 1914/1983). This means that we ascribe an identity to those organisations, based on the experiences and perceptions we have of them (Håkansson and Snehota, 1995). Different organisations will then be perceived differently; we ascribe different characteristics and identities to them and they will consequently have a different meaning and importance for us. The importance is related to how dependent we, as individuals or as representing organisations, are on these organisations. If they are dominant within the field they operate in, they will be perceived as central actors and important to relate to (Pfeffer and Salancik, 1978).

To summarise, organisations are mental constructions to which we ascribe identities based on how we perceive them. According to this view, nations, companies, authorities, departments as well as individuals can be considered as actors as long as they have an identity. But the meaning behind the actions must always be searched for in the individuals who perform them, and interpreted with their perceptions in mind.

The Process Dimension

Mobilisation   Resources are needed in order to carry out the activities. Access to resources can be established in different ways. An organiser may have control over some of the resources by reason of ownership or employment. If not, the resources have to be mobilised. One way of getting access to resources is to acquire or lease them through market transactions. That is possible if the organiser has the necessary financial means but, for many organisers, this is not the case. This is often the situation for non-profit organisations such as many sport clubs and cultural associations. As pointed out by Getz (2005), many organisers are dependent on contributions from donors or on exchanges with sponsors. In other words, they have to mobilise resources through other actors.

This can be done by networking, that is by developing and using social relationships and contacts to get access to others resources (Jarillo, 1988). One prerequisite for networking is to be perceived as a legitimate organiser organising a legitimate event, that is to have a positive reputation (cf. Pfeffer and Salancik, 1978; Thompson, 1967). Legitimacy can be defined as follows (Suchman, 1995):

> Legitimacy is a generalized perception or assumption that the actions of an entity are desirable, proper, or appropriate within some socially constructed system of norms, values, beliefs, and definitions.

Legitimacy is something that can be achieved within a certain field, where the actor or the event operates, and it is something that can increase but also decrease over time, depending on whether the organiser or the event is deemed to be 'desirable, proper, or appropriate' within the field (cf. Powell and DiMaggio, 1991). If not perceived as legitimate within the field, it is important to be able to refer to persons and organisations that are identified by the counterpart as legitimate (Håkansson and Snehota, 1995).

Sometimes it is not possible to mobilise crucial resources from actors that are within or are familiar with the field of the event and the organiser. Instead, resources have to be sought elsewhere. It is then useful to distinguish between strong and weak ties (Granovetter, 1973). Strong ties are the ones we have with our regular social contacts (i.e. within the field in this context), while weak ties are contacts that function as connections to other groupings (in other fields) where necessary resources can be accessed. Thus, the resources required for an event can be mobilised through relationships, through a network of actors, using either strong or weak ties. These actors may be mobilised by the organiser, but also by other actors connected to the event (Hellgren and Stjernberg, 1995). This means that the outer limit of the network may be beyond the control of the organiser.

When resources are mobilised through social contacts, both parties generally have an interest in the relationship. Relationships based on some form of interdependency can be denoted as symmetrical. Yet another way to mobilise resources is by exercising power, by using a stronger position in an asymmetrical relationship. Power can be used if an actor has a specific power base, which another party is dependent on (Axelsson, 1998). One example of using a power base is when a major sponsor of an event makes its sub-suppliers sponsor the event by threatening, explicitly or implicitly, to stop buying from them. In other words, power can be used to make actors contribute to the event, which they would not have done otherwise. To sum up, apart from the possibility to use his/her own resources for the event, the organiser can acquire them through market transactions, use legitimacy-building and networking or use the exercise of power.

Interests   One way to better understand the mobilisation process is by viewing it from the perspective of the participating actors, that is trying to understand the various motives for their participation. The motives can be categorised in accordance with Weber's (1914/1983) classification of interests underlying purposeful action. Weber suggests four categories: material, idealistic, traditional and affective interests. A material interest is the driving force behind instrumental actions with the purpose of achieving something beneficial or to gain advantages. Commercial activities are based on a material interest. Sponsors have this interest when they participate in order to promote their brands and products. Actors whose participation is based on ideological, patriotic or religious beliefs are guided by an idealistic interest. Participation because of strong beliefs in the purpose of the event or in order to support the local community reveals examples of idealistic interests (examples of the latter two can be found in Mount and Niro, 1995; Wicks, 1995).

A traditional interest reflects a commitment to the continuation of institutionalised activities. An event may be an important symbol and constitute a part of a local identity, which actors may be interested in supporting. The affective interest, the fourth and final one, is based on emotional motives, which might be the case if actors find it exciting or amusing to participate. Different types of interests can of course operate in combination. An individual can act both on behalf of some kind of organisational interest, let's say a material interest, and be motivated by personal interests, for instance idealistic reasons. Apart from the four interests discussed here, actors may, as mentioned above, feel obliged to act in a certain way if they perceive they are under the influence of another actor's power. A similar situation occurs if actors participate because they are ordered to do so, for instance by their employer. In such cases also the motives are linked to the implicit or explicit exercise of power.

Coordination   Activities aimed towards a goal to be achieved by several actors need to be coordinated. According to Alter and Hage (1993) coordination refers to the method used in order to regulate the actions in a social system. Thompson (1967), in his classical text, argues that we can distinguish between three general principles of coordination. These three are: standardisation, coordination by plan and coordination by mutual adjustment. Standardisation is suitable if the activities are sequential and vertically linked; that is one activity must be performed before the next one. Such an activity structure is rather predictable, and hence, easy to standardise. When the activities are parallel and interdependent, instead, coordination is more complex. Such situations require planning of the activity structure in order to make the activities function in relation to each other. This is something that can be applied over time in recurrent events, but it is obviously much harder to achieve in a one-off event. For many events, the number of activities and their relation may be even more complex. There may be vertical and sequential as well as parallel and interdependent activities, which have to be performed under uncertain conditions and adapted to new circumstances. In such situations, the most successful coordination principle is probably mutual adjustments between the actors. In other words, complex activity patterns cannot be standardised and it is difficult to plan their implementation.

There are some differences between when coordination occurs within a hierarchy (an organisation) and when it occurs in a network of several actors (as it does in most events). A hierarchy can use command and reward systems, which is not possible in a network. The network consists of more or less autonomous, although often interdependent, actors. A large number of them also participate on a voluntary basis. This means that the prerequisites for coordinating the activities are not the same as in a classical hierarchy. Generally speaking, coordination is influenced by several factors: the number and types of actors, the interests of the actors and the number, complexity and interdependency between activities, and whether the event is recurrent or a one-off affair.

The Model

We have now come to the point when it is time to sum up the discussion on the model. The analysis is made in two steps. In the first step, the structure of the event is revealed (1) by mapping out the

Table 15.2: A summary of the model.

1. Structure		
Activities	*Resources*	*Actors*
• One or several, parallel and/or sequential with different purposes	• Tangible • Intangible • Human • Financial	• Individuals, businesses, public and voluntary organisations
2. Process		
Coordination	*Mobilisation*	*Interests*
• Standardisation • Planning • Mutual adaptations	• Legitimacy • Relationships and social contacts • Power	• Material • Idealistic • Traditional • Emotional

activities that are carried out, (2) by identifying the resources needed for the activities and finally (3) by identifying the actors that contribute and participate with the resources.

In the second step, the process behind the development of the event is analysed. This step starts with an analysis of (1) how the resources are mobilised for the activities, and then with an analysis of (2) the interests underlying the actors' decision to participate and finally (3) the coordination of the activities is analysed.

In Table 15.2, the two dimensions of the model are summarised, this time, not in the practical, analytical order but in the order the concepts are related to each other, that is activities – coordination, resources – mobilisation and finally, actors – interests.

Findings

Two Cases

The model has been tested on two major public events that took place in two small communities in Sweden (Elbe, 2002; Elbe et al., 2007) and is currently also being used for a study of a third event, the world's largest cross-country ski race, Vasaloppet – an annual Swedish hallmark event. Some of the results derived from the two previously investigated cases are reported here in order to illustrate some of the results that may be achieved by using the model. Both events concern sports but, nevertheless, differ in character.

The first study deals with the international competition in orienteering, O-Ringen in Gästrikland in central Sweden, an event that was arranged on just one occasion within this region. This competition is held every year but is organised by a new committee at a new location on each occasion. Gästrikland, where the event took place, is a province with approximately 200,000 inhabitants and with one major town, Gävle. The event may be considered as a one-off event. The second event is an international football tournament for young players, the Dalecarlia Cup. This event is repeated every year within the same area, Borlänge, and is consequently considered to be a recurrent event. Borlänge is a town with some 45,000 inhabitants in central Sweden. The O-Ringen competition attracted some 20,000 people, while the football cup attracts some 4500 participants every year. The purpose of the studies was to research the development processes, but also to see how the one-off event developed the first time and to see what patterns and routines are created over time in the recurrent event.

Methodology

The organising committees in the two events were regarded as focal actors. A focal actor is an actor with a central role and position in the case studied. Within every focal actor, one or more persons in central positions functioned as key informants, with whom several interviews were carried out. These persons also contributed with their viewpoints on the interpretations and analyses made.

New actors and informants to interview were chosen by the so-called snowball sampling or chain sampling (Patton, 1990). In the beginning, the key informants connected with the focal actors, recommended new actors and informants. In turn, these new actors recommended other actors, and so on. The process went on until a saturation level was reached, that is, when no additional actors were mentioned who had not been mentioned previously by other informants, and when no new central information was obtained through the interviews (Taylor and Bogdan, 1984).

An interview guide, covering the issues in the model, was used during the interviews. The interviews often turned into long conversations and discussions around these issues. This means that the interviews can be considered as semi-structured. In order to check factual statements, counterchecks were made and the sources were evaluated. All information was documented in a case-study database, which was used continuously during the analysis.

Activity Coordination

Both of the events investigated involved a number of activities, parallel as well as sequential. There were organising committees involved in both O-Ringen and Dalecarlia Cup, each responsible for coordination. However, their influence over the coordination of the activities was rather limited. Much of the coordination of activities in O-Ringen, the isolated event, was planned by the organising committee, but in reality, much of the coordination was achieved through mutual adjustments made by the actors. In reality, the organising committee had no chance to foresee what kind of coordination was needed. Instead, this was solved by initiatives taken by the actors involved.

To a large extent, coordination in Dalecarlia Cup, the recurrent event, was accomplished through standardised systems and routines that have been gradually developed over the years. In most of the cases, these systems were not implemented by the organising committee. Instead, they were developed as a consequence of the learning and the mutual adaptations that occurred among the actors. The existing actors also took care of new contributing actors, by introducing them to the existing routines.

Resource Mobilisation

A huge amount of resources was needed in order to carry out all the activities. In both events, most of the resources were mobilised through social relationships. In the isolated event, where social relationships were not so well developed as in the recurrent event, other forms of mobilisation could also be found, such as through application for different grants and through regular purchasing procedures. But also, in a few cases, the exercise of power was used.

From the point of view of those who provide the resources, a great deal of the resources mobilised through the network of social relationships may be considered marginal. These are resources that various actors can spare during periods when the resources do not have a productive function in the actors' normal operations (Elbe et al., 2007). This means that the value of these resources may be high for the organiser, that is they would not be able to afford them by means of regular market transactions, while the value for the producer is limited. The resource providers often considered a connection with the public event to be valuable.

For instance, land was made available for the O-Ringen competition by Stora, a major forestry company. They liked being connected with sports which can be associated with forests and also with their concern for the environment. The value of lending out this resource was probably marginal to the company, while it was a crucial resource for the organiser. In Dalecarlia Cup, a company selling cars lent vehicles to the organiser, vehicles that were used in order to provide transportation during the event. The cost of doing this during one summer week was limited for the company, but it was very valuable for the organiser. The company participated due to their interest in showing goodwill in the local community.

Actors' Interests

The resources used in the two events were obtained from many different kinds of actors, such as clubs, companies, authorities and private individuals. The interests underlying the actors' participation were less materialistic and more idealistic, such as the interest in sport or commitment to the local community. This was also the case for many of the companies who were participating as sponsors. Among these actors, a combination of commercial (materialistic) interest together with some kind of idealistic interest was often found. This combination of interests was particularly strong among local firms (cf. Mount and Niro, 1995; Wicks, 1995). But emotional and traditional interests were also found, such as the joy of seeing old friends again or preserving valued traditions (Dalecarlia Cup).

Some actors were recruited because they were perceived to strengthen the legitimacy of the events, that is it was important to be connected to actors that others wanted to be related to. But mobilisation requires legitimacy. It was important that the organisers of the events were well connected and that people were recruited who could act as bridges to different clusters of actors controlling important resources. The Dalecarlia Cup had been able to establish such a network over the years, while O-Ringen had to find legitimate actors from the start. This was done by recruiting individuals with a reputation and position that were considered to be a valuable asset for the organiser.

Discussion

The two cases presented show a similar pattern in that resources are mainly mobilised through social relationships and contacts. Many of the actors in both events were attracted to participate due to a combination of interests: idealistic and emotional interests seemed to play a specifically important role. But there were also differences. More time and effort were needed to build legitimacy and create contacts in the one-off event than in the recurrent event. The network around the recurrent event was already well established. In the recurrent event, the different actors knew each other and they took responsibility for the event by solving problems, by recruiting new actors, by mobilising their resources and by coordinating the activities. Thus, the recurrent event could benefit from its history and use previous experience and learnt behaviour among the actors involved. This simplified the mobilisation and coordination processes.

The studies also indicate that it is possible for an organiser in a small community to organise rather large events, even if they lack the financial means needed. But mobilising resources for such events requires a network of contacts. This is obviously important for finding actors with suitable skills and resources and who have some kind of interest in the event, but also for finding actors who match each other. In other words, the most crucial asset for an organiser is being well connected and acquiring legitimacy.

Conclusion

Understanding and possessing knowledge of how events develop is important to everyone in the field: to organisers and their stakeholders, and to students and researchers of event management. The aim of this chapter is consequently to present and offer a model which can be used as an analytical tool in systematic research on the process of the developments of events.

In the chapter, some results generated by the model are presented, that is examples of how resources are mobilised, how activities are coordinated and what interests the different actors have in participating and contributing to the events. These results are interesting but require, of course, validation through more research. The results also indicate that more focused research into the different areas of the model may be fruitful. More qualitative in-depth studies are required in order to better understand the role of social connections in mobilising resources for events, but also in order to increase our understanding of how events may foster social connectedness by bringing actors together. Another area is to get a better understanding of the interplay between interests, and also the exercise of power, underlying the different actors' decision to participate.

References

Alter, C. and Hage, J. (1993) *Organizations Working Together*. London: Sage.

Axelsson, B. (1996) *Professionell marknadsföring*. Lund: Studentlitteratur.

Axelsson, B. (1998) *Företag köper tjänster*. Stockholm: SNS Förlag.

Axelsson, B. and Easton, G. (eds.) (1992) *Industrial Networks: A New View of Reality*. London: Routledge.

Bowdin, G., Allen, J., O'Toole, W., Harris, R. and McDonnell, I. (2006) *Events Management* (2nd edn), Oxford: Elsevier, Butterworth-Heinemann.

Elbe, J. (2002), Utveckling av turistdestinationer genom samarbete (Developing tourist destinations through cooperation). Doctoral Thesis no. 96, Department of Business Studies, Uppsala University, Uppsala.

Elbe, J., Axelsson, B. and Hallén, L. (2007) Mobilising marginal resources for public events. *Event Management*, 10(2–3), 175–183.

Ford, D. (ed.) (1997) *Understanding Business Markets*. London: The Dryden Press.

Getz, D. (2005) *Event Management and Event Tourism* (2nd edn), New York: Cognizant Communication Corporation.

Granovetter, M. (1973) The strength of weak ties. *American Journal of Sociology*, 78, 1360–1380.

Granovetter, M. (1985) Economic action and social structure. The problem of embeddedness. *American Journal of Sociology*, 91(3), 481–510.

Grant, R. M. (1995) *Contemporary Strategy Analysis*. Oxford: Blackwell.

Håkansson, H. and Johanson, J. (1992) A model of industrial networks. In Axelsson, B. and Easton, G. (eds.), *Industrial Networks: A New View of Reality*. London: Routledge.

Håkansson, H. and Snehota, I. (1989) No business is an island. The network concept of business strategy. *Scandinavian Journal of Management*, 5(3), 187–200.

Håkansson, H. and Snehota, I. (1995) *Developing Relationships in Business Networks*. London: Routledge.

Hall, C. M. (1992) *Hallmark Tourist Events. Impacts, Management and Planning*. London: Belhaven Press.

Hellgren, B. and Stjernberg, T. (1995) Design and implementation in major investments – A project network approach. *Scandinavian Journal of Management*, 11(4), 377–394.

Jarillo, C. J. (1988) On strategic networks. *Strategic Management Journal*, 9, 31–41.

Larson, M. and Wikström, E. (2001) Organizing events: Managing conflict and consensus in a political market square. *Event Management*, 7, 51–65.

Long, P. (2000) After the event: Perspectives on organizational partnerships in the management of a themed festival year. *Event Management*, 6, 45–59.

March, J. G. (1978) Bounded rationality, ambiguity, and the engineering of choice. *Bell Journal of Economics*, 9(2), 587–608.

Mount, J. and Niro, B. (1995) Sponsorship: An empirical study of its application to local business in a small town setting. *Festival Management & Event Tourism*, 2, 167–175.

Patton, M. Q. (1990) *Qualitative Evaluation and Research Methods*. Newbury Park: Sage.

Pfeffer, J. and Salancik, G. R. (1978) *The External Control of Organizations: A Resource Dependence Perspective*. New York: Harper & Row.

Powell, W. W. and DiMaggio, P. J. (1991) The iron cage revisited: Institutional isomorphism and collective rationality in organizational fields. In Powell, W. W. and DiMaggio, P. J. (eds.), *The New Institutionalism in Organizational Analysis*. Chicago: The University of Chicago Press.

Simon, H. A. (1957) *Models of Man*. New York: Wiley.

Suchman, M. C. (1995) Managing legitimacy: Strategic and institutional approaches. *Academy of Management Review*, 20, 571–610.

Taylor, S. J. and Bogdan, R. (1984) *Introduction of Qualitative Research Methods. The Search for Meanings*. New York: Wiley.

Thompson, J. D. (1967) *Organizations in Action. Social Science Bases of Administrative Theory*. New York: McGraw-Hill.

Watt, D. C. (1998) *Event Management in Leisure and Tourism*. Dorchester: Addison Wesley Longman.

Weber, M. (1914/1983), Ekonomi och samhälle. Förståendesociologins grunder. Translated by Lundqvist A. Argos: Lund. (Original work published 1914.)

Wicks, B. E. (1995) The business sector's reaction to a community special event in a small town: A case study of the 'autumn on parade' festival. *Festival Management & Event Tourism*, 2, 177–182.

Chapter 16

Human Resources in the Business Events Industry

Krzysztof Celuch and Rob Davidson

Introduction

The extent to which any city or country may be successfully branded, positioned and promoted as an events destination depends largely on the availability of a wide range of resources within the destination itself. These may include infrastructural, natural and cultural resources. However, increasingly, attention is focusing on *human* resources as a critical success factor in the events industry in general and the business events sector in particular. The dedication, expertise and creativity of all events professionals operating in any destination are clearly of great importance in determining that destination's level of success in this industry. But while this has been widely acknowledged in the case of the men and women who conceive, plan and deliver the actual events (with job titles such as events managers, events planners and events coordinators), far less attention has been paid to the human resources element represented by those professionals who are responsible for marketing their destinations as attractive places in which to hold events. As competition to 'win' events of all types intensifies worldwide, it is becoming clear that the degree of success of any city or country in attracting such events depends partly on recruiting and retaining professionals of the right calibre into these key destination marketing positions. Destinations that are eager to succeed as places that host highly lucrative business events such as conventions and incentive trips need to attract and retain professional staff capable of using their initiative and innovative skills to secure these types of events for their particular city or country.

Nevertheless, despite the widely acknowledged importance of the role played by marketing professionals in attracting events to their destinations, very little is known about how these vital stakeholders are educated and trained for, as well as recruited into, such positions. This chapter therefore explores the issue of the education and career backgrounds of professional staff in destination marketing organisations, with particular emphasis on those who are responsible for attracting business events to their destinations. It examines the extent to which the educational community is contributing to preparing young people for employment in these organizations, and investigates the career paths that currently lead to this particular occupation.

Literature Review

Business Events

Also commonly known as the MICE (Meetings, Incentives, Conferences and Exhibitions – or Events) sector, *business* events represent a major element of the events portfolio of many destinations. Some of these may be qualified as business-to-business events, when they involve company employees meeting with employees of other companies in order to conduct business of some kind, as in the case of, for example, trade shows and exhibitions; others may be designated as corporate events, when all of the participants are employed by a single company, for instance incentive trips, management conferences or off-site staff training sessions; and other types of business events – often the largest events and therefore those of most interest to destinations – comprise the meetings of professional or trade associations, local, regional, national or international, for their annual conferences.

When considered as a form of tourism activity, business events such as these have been called the 'blue chip' (McCabe et al., 2000) segment of the tourist market, due to the economic benefits they bring to the destinations in which they are held. Many authors (Davidson and Cope, 2003; Davidson and Rogers, 2006; Dwyer and Forsyth, 1997; Dwyer et al., 2000) have highlighted the tangible and intangible benefits that business events bring to the destinations in which they are held, emphasising in particular the valuable economic contributions that corporate and association conventions bring to the destinations in which they are held.

Destination Marketing Organisations

These economic benefits explain, in part, why growing numbers of destinations worldwide are investing in promoting themselves to win those business events that may be described as 'discretionary', in other words, those that are mobile and therefore capable of being held in a different destination each time they take place. Crouch and Weber, in Weber and Chon (2002, p. 57), state that: 'The attractiveness of convention tourism has spurred destinations to proactively pursue the meetings and conventions market. Modern, sophisticated marketing techniques are now being used by destinations to serve this segment'.

Destination marketing organisations (DMOs) play a key role in securing large conferences and exhibitions for the countries and cities they represent. Destination marketing for the purpose of attracting business events occurs at various geographic levels, from the local to the national (Rogers, 1998); and the structures created for this purpose may be operated under the title of Convention and Visitor Bureau (CVB) or of other organisations, such as National Tourism Offices or city Tourist Boards. They may be funded publicly or privately, or using a combination of both types of funding.

Authors have emphasised the essential role of DMOs in attracting business events (Davidson and Cope, 2003; Davidson and Rogers, 2006; McCabe et al., 2000) and the wide range of tasks they undertake in this respect. Gartrell (1994, p. 16) identified the CVB as 'the single most important marketing organisation for a community, projecting an image for that destination into the various target markets', and describes their primary purpose as 'to solicit and service conventions and other related group business and to engage in visitor promotions which generate overnight stays for a destination, thereby enhancing and developing the economic fabric of the community' (Gartrell, 1994, p. 21).

From creating an attractive brand for the destination, to lobbying and leading the bidding process, DMOs play a crucial part in the decision-making process that lies behind the choice of destination for business events. Yet very few academic studies have focused on these structures (Weber, 2001), and even less is known about the human resources element of DMOs.

In particular, there has been very little systematic and comprehensive research into the education and training backgrounds of the professional-level staff of DMOs or the career paths that they have taken, leading them to such employment. This is a significant gap in our knowledge of this element of destination marketing, since it may convincingly be argued that the skills, knowledge and creativity of those charged with the promotion of their destinations for business events are a critical success factor for countries and cities that are competing in this market.

Education and Career Paths in the Business Events Industry

While research into the specific area of the career paths and education and training backgrounds of DMO professionals is practically non-existent, some light may be shed upon this topic from the studies of human resources issues in the business events industry in general. Yet even these are extremely rare. Yoo and Weber (2005), in their analysis of the content of 115 articles with a convention-related theme and published in 14 leading hospitality and tourism journals from 1983 to 2003, found that only 5 out of 115 of those articles had focused on human resources issues in the field of business events. Over half of the articles focused on the area of marketing in this sector.

Nevertheless, authors investigating human resources issues in the business events industry in general (Schreiber and Beckmann, 1999; McCabe, 2006; MacLaurin in Weber and Chon, 2002) have identified a number of common themes. Prominent among these is the fact that management positions in the business events industry are frequently taken up by people from other related industries with individuals moving between industry sectors in order to achieve their overall career objectives. McCabe's (2006) research presents evidence of the strategies used by individuals in their career planning and development in the business events industry as a whole: professional conference organisers, those employed in purpose-built convention and exhibition centres, venues and hotels, and those working for CVBs. CVB staff represented 10% of her sample.

> There was ... evidence of extensive intra-sectorial, inter-sectorial and inter-industry mobility. For example, intra-sectorial mobility where individuals currently employed in professional conference organizations indicated that they had previously worked in the 'venue' sector, 'other' MICE suppliers and 'purpose-built convention and exhibition centres,' whilst those in 'government' and 'convention and visitor bureaus' may have previously been employed in 'venues', 'other MICE organisations' and 'professional conference organisations'... There was also evidence of inter-industry mobility with over one third of all respondents indicating that they had been employed in 'other' areas outside the convention and exhibition industry at some time in their careers. What was apparent was that an individual may have entered the convention and exhibition industry after a number of jobs in an unrelated industry or as a young or new employee' (McCabe, 2006, p. 63).

A further theme of the research into this topic is the absence of specific education and training opportunities to prepare individuals for employment in the business events sector. MacLaurin in

Weber and Chon, 2002, p. 79 argues that although 'the (global business events) industry has grown rapidly in recent decades, supported by tremendous infrastructure and technology advancements, … the improvements in education and professional development programs were, if evident at all, only sporadic and ad hoc'. The same author, as well as Rogers (1998) and McCabe et al. (2000) provide examples of the limited provision of university courses that have business events as their focus of study. In the absence of widespread provision of such courses, entrants to the business events industry are often recruited for their generic skills (Schreiber and Beckmann, 1999) which means that they have to learn about the industry 'on the job'.

Linked to the lack of educational provision for the business events sector is another issue commonly acknowledged to be a characteristic of human resources in this industry, the absence of a recognised career path for professional staff. Rogers (1998) maintains that clear career structures should be introduced, to ensure that experience and expertise are retained within the industry. He thus suggests a direct connection between the absence of a recognised career path and the high level of staff mobility rates and turnover in this industry, an issue also identified by McCabe (2006). This appears to be compounded by a further characteristic of employment in this sector, relatively at low remuneration rates. Martin Kinna, former Dean of Meetings Professionals International's Certificate in Meetings Management programme (CMM), is quoted by MacLaurin in Weber and Chon (2002) as noting that in addition to clear career progression opportunities, an attractive reward system must also be in place to prevent employees from leaving.

A final area of agreement between commentators on this topic is the perceived lack of public awareness of career opportunities in the business events industry (Rogers, 1998, MacLaurin in Weber and Chon, 2002). Unlike that sector of the industry comprising 'public' events such as those in the realm of sports and culture, business events are generally the reserve of those in employment – and mainly employment at the managerial/professional level. Consequently, young people's direct experience of business events as consumers is severely limited. This lack of public awareness may be aggravated by a lack of knowledge of the business events sector as a career option on the part of those who are responsible for guiding young people towards vocational training, a choice of university subject or job opportunities – high school and university careers counsellors. An exploratory research project by Beaulieu and Love (2004), examining the characteristics of the *meetings planning* sector of the business events industry, overwhelmingly concluded that high school careers counsellors in the United States were not making students aware of opportunities in that sector. It is highly likely that the same situation pertains in the case of the business events industry more widely, including the field of destination marketing.

Methodology

The primary objective of the research project was to investigate the education and career backgrounds of professional staff employed by DMOs responsible for attracting business events to their destinations, while a secondary objective was to determine to what extent these people were satisfied by the jobs they currently hold.

In order to identify suitable subjects for this research, data collection was undertaken through a survey of members of ICCA (the International Congress and Convention Association), a global association of business events professionals established in 1963. ICCA operates through a series of eight discrete categories representing different sectors supplying services to the business events industry. The full list of ICCA Membership Categories appears in Table 16.1.

Table 16.1: ICCA Membership Categories.

Congress travel and destination management companies	A
Airlines	B
Professional congress, convention and/or exhibition organisers	C
Tourist and convention bureaux	D
Meeting information and technical specialists	E
Meetings hotels	F
Convention and exhibition centres	G
Honorary members	H

By definition, any member of ICCA, in whichever category, is involved in the business events sector in some capacity. As Category D members are employed in organisations that are active in promoting their destinations as places where conventions, incentive trips and trade exhibitions may be held, they formed a ready-made, self-selected target group for this research project's survey.

Quest, the web-based survey tool regularly used by ICCA to conduct surveys of its membership, was used to host the online questionnaire for this study. One advantage of this method was the fact that ICCA members were already familiar with using Quest, a tool they closely associated with ICCA itself. Along with the message e-mailed to Category D members by the researchers, explaining the aims of the study, ICCA also sent a message endorsing this research project and encouraging members to participate. The survey was posted from 30 August until 15 September 2006.

In terms of data collection, therefore, the survey used non-probability, convenience, heterogeneous sampling. It may be considered a heterogeneous sample due to the fact that the views and attitudes of all of those destination marketing managers who took part in the survey were included.

Regarding the design of the survey, it included 32 questions, with response options ranging from multiple-choice and fill in the blank to a 1–4 Likert scale. The questions were developed using the literature review and were grouped by different areas: the respondent's employing organisation; their education and career background and their attitudes towards their future career progression in the destination marketing profession.

Results and Discussion

In all 113 usable responses were received, a response rate of 18.5%; 21 of the respondents were employed by DMOs representing entire countries – national DMOs, 21 were employed by DMOs representing regions within countries and 71 worked for DMOs representing individual cities. There were 69 female respondents and 44 male respondents, reflecting the balance of the gender bias prevailing in the business events sector overall.

In order to identify the geographical spread of the DMOs employing the respondents, the latter were asked to indicate the country in which they were operating. In all, 30 countries were represented, although in the vast majority of cases, there were only one or two respondents from each of those countries. The United Kingdom, with its abundance of DMOs at the individual city level, was the country which returned the greatest number of questionnaires. The United States, the country with the most comprehensive network of state-level and city-level DMOs may have been expected to have returned more than one questionnaire. However, an explanation for the low rate of return is almost certainly the fact that ICCA membership in the United States is comparatively low, due to the fact that another professional association, Destination Marketing Association International (formerly the International Association of Convention and Visitor Bureaus) is based in the United States and has an extensive North American membership base. Nevertheless, the wide range of countries represented is a strong indication of the extent to which different destinations around the world are now actively engaged in this market and competing to win discretionary business events Table 16.2.

The responses given in answer to the question, 'How long has your DMO existed?', indicated that the sample included representatives from DMOs that were established less than five years preceding the date of the survey as well as representatives from DMOs created more than 15 years before the survey. The figures confirm that new DMOs which focus on the marketing of their destinations for business events are still being established. Whereas in the middle of the last century, the vast majority of international conventions were held in the cities of Europe and North America, the trend since then has been for increasing numbers of countries and cities in other world regions to enter the market as destinations for business events (Davidson and Rogers, 2006; Spiller in Weber and Chon, 2002). The figures shown in Table 16.3 indicate that a high proportion of the respondents were operating in DMOs created within five years preceding the survey date.

In response to the question, 'What is your highest educational qualification?', 45 respondents indicated that they had a university bachelor degree; 38 had gained a university masters degree; for 20 respondents, a school certificate was their highest educational qualification; while only 1 had a

Table 16.2: Location of DMOs.

Australia 5	Finland 5	Malaysia 1	South Africa 2
Austria 7	France 5	Mexico 3	South Korea 2
Bahrain 1	Germany 5	Netherlands 6	Spain 8
Belgium 5	Greece 1	New Zealand 1	Sri Lanka 1
Brazil 2	Hungary 2	Norway 2	Sweden 2
Canada 2	Ireland 1	Poland 5	Switzerland 7
Croatia 1	Israel 1	Portugal 2	Thailand 1
Denmark 1	Italy 4	Singapore 1	Turkey 1
Ethiopia 1	Japan 3	Slovenia 1	United Arab Emirates 1
			United Kingdom 13
			United States 1

Table 16.3: Age of the DMO.

When was the DMO established?	Number of responses
0–5 years ago	35
6–10 years ago	22
11–15 years ago	18
Over 15 years ago	38

doctorate degree. Those without graduate or postgraduate degree tended to be drawn from the older age-groups of the sample. Of the 20 respondents in this category, 15 were aged over 40 at the time of the survey. In addition, respondents with school certificates as their highest educational qualification tended to be those that had the longest periods of service in their DMOs, suggesting that professional employment in DMOs is now overwhelmingly considered to be a graduate-level and postgraduate-level occupation.

For those respondents who went to university, the subjects most commonly studied by them are shown in Table 16.4.

The prominence of economics/business-related subjects is evident, and these reflect to a great extent the generic skills that are useful for effective performance in DMO employment. The same economics/business-related subjects are often included in courses in Tourism and Hotel Management, the two industry sectors most studied by this sample. However, only two respondents had majored in a subject specifically linked to the business events industry (entitled 'Business Tourism' in both cases). This is unsurprising, given the relatively slow pace at which the provision of specific under-graduate and postgraduate courses in business events related subjects has grown, worldwide.

In response to a question about their experience of specific education and training in destination marketing, 50 respondents, just under half of the total, reported that they had received this in some form; 16 had studied this subject as one element in their university courses and 26 had taken an in-service training course in destination marketing after joining their DMO (two had taken both types of course). The most widespread example of such in-service training was the annual ICCA course for DMOs' and venues' sales and marketing staff (13 responses). Training courses offered by other business events industry associations were also mentioned: provision by the European Federation of Conference Towns (7); Meeting Professionals International (3); and the International Association of Professional Conference Organisers (3). MacLaurin in Weber and Chon (2002) confirms the key role played by the business events industry associations in providing education programmes for this sector and outlines the range of in-service provision offered by the largest and most powerful associations. Given the rapid pace of change in this industry and the constant emergence of unforeseen challenges and new opportunities, it is likely that even if university provision of business events related courses increases, the industry associations will continue to play a vital role in offering education programmes to update their members' knowledge and skills, and to make them aware of key trends and issues affecting this sector.

Table 16.4: Subjects studied at university.

Subject	Responses
Economics	18
Tourism	16
Hotel management	13
Business studies	13
Languages	12
Marketing	11
Communication	8
Political sciences	6

Table 16.5: Previous employment (non-DMO).

Sector	Responses
Marketing	49
Hotels (not marketing)	36
Travel trade	26
Teaching	15
National government	13
Local government	10
Conference planning/DMC	07
Venue management	03

Focusing on the respondents' experience of work prior to joining the DMO, 54 out of the 113 (48%) respondents had no previous experience of employment in such an organisation; and the remaining 52% had previously worked for a CVB or a tourist board in some capacity. Of the other types of work previously experienced by the respondents, marketing, with 49 responses, was the most commonly mentioned occupation. When asked the question, 'Marketing *what*?' of the most frequently mentioned categories, hotels came first with 11 responses, followed by conference venues (7);transport (predominantly airlines) (5); food and beverages (5) and other consumer products (4).

Other types of employment that had preceded the respondents' work in destination marketing were: architecture, interior design, banking, librarianship and the mining industry.

It is perhaps unsurprising that marketing emerges as the occupational activity most commonly engaged in by respondents, prior to their DMO employment. But it is worthy of note that the vast majority of respondents with marketing work experience had been marketing services and facilities closely linked to the business events sector. There was very little evidence of individuals moving from the marketing of manufactured goods, for example, into a career in destination marketing.

The close association between employment in DMOs and work experience in the hospitality and travel industry is evident from the figures in Table 16.5, supporting McCabe's (2006) contention that career development in the business events sector is characterised by a high occurrence of inter-industry movement; while the incidence of work experience in conference venues and, to a lesser extent, conference planning and destination management companies illustrates that individuals are also progressing their careers by moving intra-sectorally.

In order to gauge respondents' level of commitment to their continuing employment in DMOs, they were asked: 'How probably is it that you would change career and move to a completely different profession?'

Responses to this question were balanced only slightly in favour of a commitment to continuing in the field of destination marketing, as shown in Table 16.6.

Finally, those choosing to answer the open question, 'What would be the most likely reason for you moving to a completely different profession?' gave two main reasons for their dissatisfaction with their present employment, as shown in Table 16.7.

It should not be surprising that the outstanding reason for dissatisfaction with DMO employment is the lack of opportunity for promotion. The vast majority of DMOs focusing their activities on the business events market are relatively small in size, and characterised by very flat hierarchies,

Table 16.6: Likelihood of changing profession.

Probability of leaving the profession	Responses
Very probable	8
Probable	40
Improbable	56
Never	8
No response	1

Table 16.7: Reasons for discontentment.

Reason	Responses
Lack of opportunity for promotion	24
Salary too low	18
Too much stress	8
Too much time spent away from home	2

typically consisting of two layers of management – on the one hand, a Director who sets strategic goals and oversees the operations of the DMO; and on the other hand, his/her managers who undertake the professional tasks of the organisation, aided by a number of support/administrative staff members. Given the typical structure of a DMO, it is clear that opportunities for promotion within the organisation are generally limited to moving one step higher when, and if, the Director vacates his/her position. The frustration felt by ambitious DMO managers seeking to progress in their careers is undoubtedly a factor contributing to the high degree of intra- and inter-sectoral movement highlighted by McCabe (2006) in the case of the wider business events industry in general.

The relatively low wages and salaries paid in the business events industry have been discussed by authors such as MacLaurin in Weber and Chon (2002), who partly explains this phenomenon through the close association of this industry with the tourism and hospitality sectors, which are often characterised by comparatively modest levels of remuneration. The increasing number of women working in business events related work (McCabe et al., 2000) may also partly explain why average salaries in this industry appear to be a source of dissatisfaction for so many, as even in countries with equal pay legislation, there often exists a sizeable gap between men's average salaries and those of women.

Given the investment in staff training and the valuable work experience that managers accumulate in their time spent in employment in a DMO, the dissatisfaction with salary levels must remain a cause for concern, if it is adding to the rate of staff turnover in DMOs.

Conclusions

The findings of this exploratory research project have several implications for the ways in which people who market destinations for business events are prepared, by the education system, for such employment and for how they progress through their careers in destination marketing. The results of the project indicate that, in common with other types of business events related occupations such as conference planning, there is no such thing as a standard route into employment in destination marketing of this type. Rather, in common with many types of work in the events industry overall, jobs in business events are largely unregulated, with low barriers to entry.

Those professionals who have the responsibility for attracting business events to their destinations appear to take up such employment either directly from higher education or after following a wide variety of educational and occupational routes. Although much of the prior work experience of DMO professionals was found to be in sectors or occupations with some bearing on the role of destination marketing, such as hotels and venue marketing, other types of previous work experience, such as teaching and government work, indicated a more circuitous route into DMO employment.

The results strongly suggest that the vast majority of people who took part in the survey entered the destination marketing profession by chance, whether directly from education or after years in other types of employment.

Further research on these issues should focus on the role of the education system in preparing young people for employment in marketing destinations for business events. In conclusion to their research into the meetings planning profession, Beaulieu and Love (2004, p. 120) stated that 'The industry needs to grow from being an occupation that people just "fell into" or "learned on the job" to one that has formalised training'. Is there also an argument for specific educational provision focusing on the marketing of destinations for the types of business events that a growing number of countries and cities are eager to win? Is the task of marketing those countries and cities as destinations for business events sufficiently distinct to promoting them as destinations for leisure tourism and sports and cultural events to warrant specialised educational provision for this sector? And if so, to what extent should the curriculum combine sector-specific content with generic business and communications skills, in order to effectively prepare students for a career in marketing destinations for business events?

Future research should also investigate the level of general awareness of business events and the occupation of promoting destinations for the hosting of these. The somewhat circuitous routes taken by many professionals into DMO work suggest that awareness of this occupation in the population in general is relatively low, with very few people making a deliberate and informed choice to enter this field of work directly after higher education. Given the economic importance of business events for a growing number of destinations, a convincing argument may be made in favour of conducting a survey among those counsellors who are responsible for guiding students in their career choices in schools and universities, to determine the extent to which they understand this sector and the skills, attitudes and knowledge that people require to function effectively within it. In the event that careers counsellors' awareness of destination marketing is found to be lacking, a strategy for disseminating to them occupational information on this sector could be devised.

A considerable degree of dissatisfaction, among DMO professional staff, with their opportunities for career progression in this sector was also identified as an issue of concern in this research project. The standard DMO structure is that of a very flat pyramid – a small team of professional staff led by one director. As such structures offer little scope for promotion, DMOs must recognise that in order to retain talented and ambitious individuals, they need to provide ample opportunities for the nurturing and development of their staff to prevent them from moving to another organisation in order to continue to widen their experience. This is particularly the case since professional staff employed by DMOs are very often highly mobile in terms of their employment prospects within the wider business events industry exactly because they have experience of DMO work. Rosvi Gaetos, former Secretary General of the Asian Association of CVBs acknowledges this in his statement that 'NTOs and CVBs are the best places to train new entrants into the industry, with both entities providing a broad insight into the industry' (MacLaurin in Weber and Chon, 2002).

The findings of this exploratory project confirm other researchers' conclusions that there is a high degree of intra-sectorial and inter-sectorial mobility within the business events industry. But how many people are simply lost to the business events industry after a few years because they leave to join other industries unrelated to this field? A future study could further explore the question of staff turnover by investigating the career destinations of staff when they leave employment in a DMO to work in another sector or when they leave the business events industry altogether.

Clearly, attracting and retaining people of talent with initiative and creative skills are crucial to the future of the business events industry as a whole and to the effective marketing of destinations in particular. Given the considerable economic benefits of hosting business events and the growing competition for these, a case may convincingly be made for strategic intervention in this issue, along similar lines to that of Australia's national strategy for its business events industry. That strategy highlights several key priorities in human resource development, including: 'Career paths and opportunities designed to develop the expertise of personnel and encourage their retention in the industry', and 'Industry-specific education so that the industry is able to meet the demand for qualified and trained professionals' (Commonwealth Department of Tourism, 1995).

As competition for business events intensifies, and destinations increasingly recognise that having the right human resources is just as important for success in this sector as being equipped with the right infrastructural resources, it may be expected that other countries follow Australia's example in this regard.

References

Beaulieu, A. F. and Love, C. (2004) Characteristics of a meeting planner: Attributes of an emerging profession. *Journal of Convention and Event Tourism*, 6(4), 95–124.

Commonwealth Department of Tourism (1995) *A National Strategy for the Meetings, Incentives, Conventions and Exhibitions Industry*. Canberra: Commonwealth of Australia.

Davidson, R. and Cope, B. (2003) *Business Travel: Conferences, Incentive Travel, Exhibitions, Corporate Hospitality and Corporate Travel*. Harlow: Pearson Education.

Davidson, R. and Rogers, T. (2006) *Marketing Destinations and Venues for Conferences, Conventions and Business Events*. Oxford: Butterworth Heinemann.

Dwyer, L. and Forsyth, P. (1997) Impacts and benefits of MICE tourism: A framework for analysis. *Tourism Economics*, 3(1), 21–38.

Dwyer, L., Mellor, R., Mistilis, N. and Mules, T. (2000) A framework for assessing 'tangible' and 'intangible' impacts of events and conventions. *Event Management*, 6(3), 175–191.

Gartrell, R. B. (1994) *Destination Marketing for Convention and Visitor Bureaus* (2nd edn). Dubuque, IA: Kendall/Hunt Publishing Company.

McCabe, V. S. (2006) Strategies for career planning and development in the convention and exhibition industry: Results from an Australian study. *Proceedings of the International Convention and Expo Summit 2006*, Milton, Queensland.

McCabe, V. S., Poole, B. and Leiper, N. (2000) *The Business and Management of Conventions*. Brisbane: John Wiley & Sons.

Rogers, T. (1998) *Conferences: A 21st century industry*. Harlow: Addison Wesley Longman.

Schreiber, C. and Beckmann, K. (1999) *Kongress und Tagungsmanagement*. Munich: Oldenbourg.

Weber, K. (2001) Meeting planners' use and evaluation of convention and visitor bureaus. *Tourism Management*, 22(6), 599–606.

Weber, K. and Chon, K. (2002) *Convention Tourism: International Research and Industry Perspectives*. Binghampton, New York: Haworth Hospitality Press.

Yoo, J. J. and Weber, K. (2005) Progress in convention tourism research. *Journal of Hospitality & Tourism Research*, 29(2), 194–222.

Chapter 17

Measuring the Impact of Micro-Events on Local Communities: A Role for Web-Based Approaches

Geoff Dickson and Simon Milne

Introduction

At the 2006 conference of New Zealand Association for Event Professionals, the manager of New Zealand Major Events (NZME) and the Senior Advisor for Events for Sport and Recreation New Zealand (SPARC) provided a joint address to the delegates. The NZME representative spoke about international events such as the New Zealand Open Golf, World Mountain Bike Championships and the Rugby World Cup 2011 and their ability to generate economic development, showcase New Zealand industries to the world, and provide a platform for business exchange. The SPARC spokesperson followed and began his address with words to the effect 'NZME puts on sixteen events per year. I am interested in the hundreds of events that take place in New Zealand each weekend'. In this chapter, the term micro-event is used to describe an event that will typically be located in rural or regional communities and will attract a few 100 (or perhaps a few thousand) visitors. Micro-events are smaller than 'small-scale' events, a term which has been used previously in the literature (Gibson et al., 2003) and are at the opposite end of the events spectrum to mega-events (Gursoy and Kendall, 2006). Despite their smaller size, the same economic and social benefits that present themselves to more populated communities are also available to the communities that host these events so long as these events are used strategically and planned effectively (Chhabra et al., 2003; Wilson, 2006).

For a variety of reasons, organisers of micro-events in local communities are likely to lack the capacity to maximise and measure the economic impact of their events. The purpose of this research was to develop a web-based system to permit event managers, local communities, businesses and planners to better understand and estimate event-related economic impacts. In this chapter, issues affecting the leveraging of micro-events for economic impact, as well as its measurement, are discussed. The Tourism Research and Community Empowerment (TRACE) Events project is then presented as a solution to some of the issues identified. The community informatics (CI) literature is then used to argue that web-based tools can provide robust estimates of the local economic impacts associated with micro-events. In addition, the approach can facilitate improved understanding of

International Perspectives of Festivals and Events
ISBN: 978-0-08-045100-8

economic impacts as well as the promotion of networks and knowledge sharing between event stake-holders. Data is then presented from four events used as part of the calibration process. Particular emphasis is placed upon sharing the early successes and failures of the TRACE Events project.

Micro-Events: Data Collection Issues

Micro-events are often developed and managed by small businesses. Small businesses are often managed by owner-operators and their families (Page and Getz, 1997). Anecdotal evidence suggests that such businesses are characterised by an owner integrally involved in both operational and management duties resulting in few companies being able to implement 'best practice' business management principles on a consistent basis (NZMED, 2001). It is estimated that the New Zealand tourism industry comprises between 13,500 and 18,000 small to medium enterprises (SME) with approximately 80% of these employing less than five people (TSG, 2000). The same report also recognised that upskilling and capability building of sector participants, particularly small and medium-sized businesses was critical to the success of New Zealand tourism. The effectiveness of intermediaries in the tourism sector is limited by poor local networks and local knowledge (Forstner, 2004).

Authors have noted that the ability of a sporting event to contribute to the overall development of a host destination is dependant upon its integration with other tourism products and services (Chalip and McGuirty, 2004). However, the organisations behind rural events are likely to lack the networks, structures and skills to work effectively with tourism providers (Weed, 2003). This is important given that the success of rural tourism development and entrepreneurship is considered to be dependent upon both the participation and the collaboration of stakeholders directly and indirectly involved in tourism (Wilson et al., 2001). Taken together, it is likely that event organisers and their key stake-holders will lack the required knowledge and skill base to effectively maximise the economic impact of events. The development of a decision-support system will provide more opportunities to communities to develop and implement an improved events strategy.

The organisers of sport events and the public authorities who participate in their financing often want to quantify the impact of the event on the economy of the host region, and more specifically income and job creation. This information can assist in gaining the community and governmental support necessary to overcome concerns regarding the possible negative impacts (Milne, 1998). The problem, however, lies in the ability to generate this information in a cost-effective manner. This is important given that the financial costs associated with producing a valid and reliable economic impact analysis are likely to be prohibitive for these types of events. The ability to gain more detailed information on the impacts associated with events can enable planners and communities to develop strategies that will provide more yield per person. Conversations with micro-event managers and local government indicate that they both have a desire to understand the impact of their events. However a shortage of time, resources or knowledge to conduct an event-impact research is also evident. The key issue therefore is 'How do these decision-makers get the information that they need?'

The TRACE Events Project

The TRACE Events project utilises Information and Communication Technologies (ICT) in the assessment of micro-event impacts on host communities. The TRACE model and its associated toolkit provide an effective, low-cost mechanism for collecting event-related data. The TRACE program respects the principle of subsidiarity, meaning the responsibility and decision-making for event-specific initiatives should rest with those 'closest to the action' (Mele, 2005).

The TRACE Events project makes available simple approaches for data analysis. This includes the provision of expenditure estimates and economic linkage data that can be combined simply with estimated visitor numbers to provide baseline estimates for impact. The website (www.trace.org.nz) also offers opportunities for stakeholders to share their experiences in conducting micro-event research. In this manner, the project seeks to move beyond the economic impact studies conducted by professional firms on large-scale sporting events in large population centres and to develop the ability for the stakeholders of small, local sporting events to conduct their own economic impact assessments. This will enable them to work cooperatively with local government and Regional Tourism Organisations (RTOs). This is a strategy considered essential to creating an integrated regional event tourism product to further serve the interests of the region (Higham and Ritchie, 2001).

TRACE Events project differs from the economic impact toolbox made available by New Zealand's Ministry of Tourism (NZMT). Although the NZMT toolbox is distributed online, it is little more than a number of surveys that can be downloaded and distributed by the researcher. NZMT estimate the cost at $5 per survey for the visitor survey and between $15,000 and $20,000 for the business survey. The cost of this research is somewhat ironical given that tourism is an information-intensive industry, and control over information shapes the ability of different stakeholders to participate in, and benefit from, the industry (Milne et al., 2004).

The role of CI in the TRACE Events Project

The TRACE Events project builds on key elements of CI – a discipline that emphasises the design and delivery of technological applications to enhance community development, and improve the lives of residents. Commentators (Gurstein, 2000; Shuler, 1999) identify three strategies for using CI as an enabler of community development: as a marketing tool for local business, as a mechanism to bring together a range of 'linked' resources of value to improving quality of life and as a distributed network that can assist the creation of new relationships and economic linkages (Milne et al., 2004). The CI literature focuses on five key areas in which ICT can enhance community quality of life (O'Neil, 2002). These are (1) the promotion of strong democracy and participation in planning processes; (2) the development of social capital; (3) the empowerment of individuals, especially marginalised groups; (4) the strengthening of community and 'sense of place' and (5) the creation of sustainable community economic development opportunities. In summary, a key driver for the adoption of CI is the need for communities to move beyond having things done for them, and become active participants in their own development. Hence, the word *empowerment* was deliberately incorporated into the overall program name.

CI programs have been criticised for their 'top down' approach with programs often started and run by government agencies and typically aimed at providing generalised 'community benefits' (Loader et al., 2000). While governments and agencies have enthusiastically accepted the need to embrace the 'information society' the success of these projects are mixed at best and often curbed by budget cuts and other factors (Gurstein, 2000). In order to create a 'bottom up' approach to applied CI a 'hook' is needed to interest people in using the new technology (Loader et al., 2000). The objective of the TRACE Events program is to develop a tool that is easy not only to use but also to access and be trained on, open-source in concept and with the methods and approaches being readily available on the Internet.

The first criterion, ease of use, is achieved by enabling local stakeholders to access tools for gathering data and providing simple approaches for data analysis using online survey approaches refined by NZTRI in recent years. The second criterion, ease of access, is achieved through innovative use of the Internet. Not only are data collection and analysis tools available on the web, they are also be able to updated and reworked by participants – who are requested, in turn, to feed their input back into the system. It is this open-source approach to sharing and receiving information that has the potential to increase uptake and generate quality data for the calibration of the model (Surman and Wershler-Henry, 2001). The tool kit comprises survey and other tools that can be downloaded and then used for data collection purposes (see Figure 17.1).

The TRACE Events project uses a model based on neo-Keynesian multiplier theory (see Milne, 1987, 1998), that can provide robust local economic estimates while still being user-friendly enough to enable local communities to gather and/or analyse the research. In order to allow for meaningful comparisons between events and to avoid controversies associated with the use of multipliers, the direct impact attributable to additional expenditure remains the focus. As the number and type of communities and events using the system grows it will be possible for communities to have two choices in developing a better understanding of a sporting event. One will be to use the calculator to

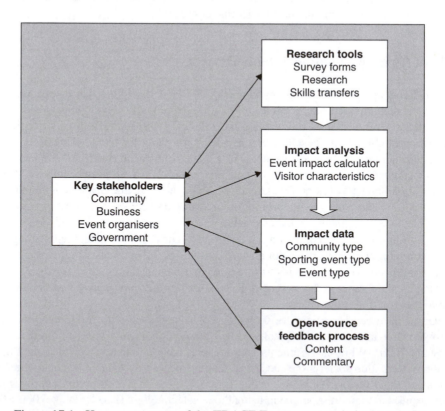

Figure 17.1: Key components of the TRACE Events economic impact model.

search for communities and events that have a similar size, location and characteristics to those of a forthcoming event; in this case a more generic impact figure can be achieved. The second approach will be for the stakeholders group(s) to conduct primary research using the online tool kits and then utilising the economic impact model to derive more accurate findings. As the number and range of studies increases, so will the accuracy and applicability of the more generic approach.

Overview of Calibrating Studies

The research revolves around several key elements: a survey (online) of participants/supporters/spectators with spectator surveys sometimes being conducted by hand; interviews with local businesses and expert interviews with event organisers and local government officials are also used. These are effective and inexpensive methods that enable us to 'triangulate' the data being collected (Oppermann, 2002). All event managers approached to assist in this research agreed without hesitation. All demonstrated an awareness of the role that economic impact studies could play in their negotiations with local councils. This initial enthusiasm for the project augurs well for a successful uptake of the project when it is made available.

The participant/supporter/spectator survey consists of an online questionnaire. Participants were made aware of the questionnaire through: a pre-event email, a short introduction to the study at the race briefing, a written explanation in their race packs and a post-event reminder email. Because of privacy considerations, both emails were written by TRACE Events program members but were sent to participants by the event managers. An example of the surveys used in the research to date can be viewed at the TRACE website (www.tri.org.nz).

Key businesses, from each tourism industry sector in the host community, were interviewed after the event, as were local government event managers and regional tourism organisers. Questionnaires were utilised to encompass the wider business community (Daniels et al., 2004). Pilot trips to each location were undertaken and important local characteristics defined through observation and initial interviews with the event organisers. These trips provide the opportunity to develop contacts and familiarise stakeholders with the research. The surveys and interviews again focused on determining economic impacts. The possibilities of leveraging, leakages, negative event externalities and the importance of tourism to the community (and businesses themselves) were also discussed with business owners/managers.

Applying the Approach: Review of Initial Events

A foundation for the development of the TRACE Events program was provided by studies conducted at four events. The Kururau Krusher is a multisport event (296 participants) located in Taumarunui (population 5136). Adventure Racing Coromandel's 12 and 24 Hour Race (subsequently referred to as the ARC 12/24) was based in Whangamata (population 3858). The ARC 12/24 is considered an adventure race because it involves a navigational element, or in other words, a map and a compass are essential items. The Waiheke Challenge is a multisport event (72 participants) based on Waiheke Island (population 7137). The Special K Triathlon was an entry-level, women's only triathlon based in Taupo (population 20,310). A summary of the initial findings of direct expenditure is presented in Table 17.1.

Table 17.1: Summary of key economic impact and direct spend indicators for five New Zealand events.

	Kururau Krusher	ARC 12/24	Waiheke Challenge	Special K
Average spend ($)	97	62	80	123
Average length of stay	1.6	2	1.6	1.6
Estimated spend ($'000)	135	37	24	586

Table 17.2: Breakdown of participant and spectator spending.

	Kururau Krusher	ARC 12/24	Waiheke Challenge	Special K
Accommodation	43.41	63.77	40.13	48.71
Restaurant/bar	37.29	24.37	49.00	47.77
Supermarket	22.50	17.91	20.87	30.88
Petrol/repairs	34.64	10.73	0	25.15
Recreation	3.39	1.46	8.00	8.73
Shopping	0.09	0.93	0	26.01
Event expenses	11.43	5.25	10.67	8.53

Response rates varied from a low of 15% at the Waiheke Challenge, 19% at the Kururau Krusher, 25% at the ARC 12/24, to a high of 44% at the Special K Triathlon. A key feature underpinning this variation is the quality of the 'web relationship' between the event and the participants. For instance the Special K Triathlon makes extensive use of the internet – race registration is online, the website contains training advice and participants are emailed on a regular basis with words of support and encouragement from the event manager. In comparison, the Kururau Krusher does not utilise the Internet to any significant degree. The race has a static webpage and although the event manager collected email addresses as part of the registration process, it is considered unlikely that these emails would not have been utilised at all, had it not been for the research. Another distinguishing feature of the Special K race was that all participants were females, whereas other events were dominated my male participants. Anecdotally, this suggests that females were more likely to respond to the survey. The greater length of stay evident in the ARC 12/24 is a consequence of the greater amount of time required to complete the race. In order to identify expenditure patterns, the breakdown of expenditure at the different events is summarised in Table 17.2.

Per day spending by participants and spectators ranged from a low of $62 to a high of $123. A number of explanations for this variation can be offered. The relatively high levels of expenditure associated with the Special K race is largely attributable to higher levels of spending in Taupo's bars, restaurants, supermarkets and retail shops. Taupo is an established tourism centre with much to offer in terms of attractions and places to eat. It is also likely that participants in the other events may be more likely to be self-sufficient, in that they bring food with them. The absence of petrol and shopping expenditure is not surprising given that all competitors would have travelled to Waiheke Island by a passenger ferry and the very small retail district on the island.

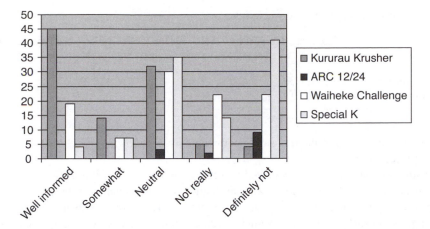

Figure 17.2: Local business awareness of event.

In Figure 17.2 summary statistics describing local business awareness of the event are presented. In the following paragraphs, responses from the surveys administered to local business are reported.

Local businesses were asked the extent to which they felt well informed about the event. The higher than average results for the Kururau Krusher is attributed to the long standing nature of the event and the social networks of the organising committee that permeate through the local community. This event is organised by a non-profit group who are driven by a commitment to make both a social and an economic contribution to their community. The non-profit, community-based approach contrasts markedly with the other events that have a more explicit for-profit orientation. Different explanations for the very low level of event awareness within Whangamata and Taupo can be offered. As noted earlier, Taupo is an established tourism centre with a well-established events calendar. Despite attracting 1600 participants, the event falls well short of some other events in the Taupo events calendar (e.g. Ironman New Zealand, Round the Lake Bike Race) in terms of length of impact and number of visitors to the community. The ARC 12/24 is held in a different township on the Coromandel Peninsula every year. However the 'host community' is only made public two weeks before the starting date. The exact course is made available to competitors at the pre-race briefing the night before the race. For clarification, an integral part of this race is the ability to navigate through the wilderness. If athletes were aware of the trails and terrain to be used in advance, they could familiarise themselves with the aspects of the course. As a consequence this would remove part of the challenge from the event and create an unfair advantage because those athletes who lived in other parts of New Zealand would not be able to familiarise themselves with the course as part of their race preparation. Whilst this is an accepted part of the race it prevents the race from appearing on an annual events calendar and limits the ability for awareness of the race to be diffused in the local community.

As the event is held in a different part of the Coromandel Peninsula every year, there is little in the way of tradition associated with location of the event, which stands in contrast to the Kururau Krusher in Taumarunui. The research indicated that 60% of business respondents agreed that Whangamata could benefit more from hosting such events if the businesses were provided with better information prior to the event. When asked what changes could be introduced to allow their business to benefit

Table 17.3: Turnover change on race weekend.

	Kururau Krusher	**ARC 12/24**	**Waiheke Challenge**	**Special K**
Increased turnover	50	23	4	34
No change in turnover	32	62	96	53
Decreased turnover	14	15	0	12

more from such events, two of the less subtle comments were 'Knowing about such events would be a start' and 'More notification'.

Local business owners/managers reported relatively low levels of awareness event websites. The Kururau Krusher website (Taumarunui) was the highest with an awareness level of 36%. Twenty-one percent of Taupo businesses were aware of the Special K triathlon website, whereas only 14% of the Whangamata (ARC 12/24) and Waiheke business community were aware of their local event websites. These figures, as well as a simple content analysis of the event websites, indicate that there are low levels of collaboration between the race director and local businesses in terms of cross-promotion. When interviewed, event managers consistently commented that their focus was on the race itself rather than promoting the wider destination.

This is not to suggest that event managers were oblivious to their role in promoting local businesses merely that their priority was on the provision of a fair, challenging and safe race. Anecdotal comments by the RDC RTO manager in Taumarunui suggest that information regarding 'things to do' for event spectators in Taumarunui was not sourced from the Internet. She commented that the Taumarunui Visitor Information Centre experienced a significantly greater than normal number of visits on the day of the event and that their volunteer staff struggled to cope with the visitor enquiries.

Event websites can serve as a logical portal to existing community websites and should be redesigned to promote the destination ands its tourist attractions. Possible activities do not need to be restricted to pre- and post-race activities. Multisport events and adventure races do not make for good spectator viewing because of the limited opportunity to actually see participants, let alone their preferred athlete. For these races, there is often a need for activities to be scheduled during the race.

Local business owners/managers were also asked about the extent to which their turnover changed on race weekend relative to other weekends at the same time of the year (refer Table 17.3).

With the exception of the Kururau Krusher, a minority of businesses reported no change or even a decline in turnover. It is not clear as to why businesses in three communities experienced decreased turnover. Road closures were not significant, lasting for only a few minutes at a time and overcrowding was never apparent. It is speculated that local businesses identified that the participants were in the community to race and not to shop (especially in fast food outlets, licensed premises and liquor stores) and associated this with lower levels of expenditure when compared to other types of visitors to the local community. In effect, it is considered that many may have misinterpreted the question as it is not clear how the event served to displace local expenditure or displace a higher yielding visitor group.

As discussed earlier, the largest expenditure categories were in food/beverage and accommodation businesses. A number of business owners/managers were aware of this bias, commenting that the event only brings substantive and direct benefits to restaurants and the accommodation sector. Another issue addressed in the business survey was the perception held by the business owners/managers regarding the extent to which the community (as opposed to their own business) benefited by hosting the event. The results of this question are presented in Table 17.4.

Table 17.4: Local business perception of community benefit from hosting the event.

	Kururau Krusher	ARC 12/24	Waiheke Challenge	Special K
No benefits at all	0	0	8	0
Not much benefit	0	0	8	12
Neutral	5	10	57	22
Some benefit	11	33	8	33
Definite benefits	84	56	19	33

Taumarunui business people were more likely to indicate that their community 'definitely ben-efited' from hosting the Krusher. When prompted to elaborate on the nature of this benefit, 71% of respondents mentioned increased profile for the town. In addition, 29% commented on the possibil-ity of the event changing people's perception of Taumarunui. Fifty percent commented on increased visitor numbers and increased spending in the community by the visitors. Anecdotally, out of all the communities and their respective events, Taumarunui was the community that embraced their event the most. Again, it is thought to be associated with the strong social networks, non-profit orientation of the events organisers. The relatively high level of benefits perceived for Whangamata by local business people (56%) is somewhat surprising given the lower levels of awareness and increased turnover reported by the same respondents. These findings suggest that these events are able to pro-vide some non-monetary benefits to local communities (Misener and Mason, 2006).

In summary, these four events were studied to provide baseline data for the development of an online economic impact calculator as part of the TRACE Events program. These events were found to make varying economic contributions to the local community and were considered by local busi-ness owners/managers as making positive contributions to the local community. While this research is based on small sample sizes and is not statistically reliable, the research provides an insight into the economic and social significance of the event. As more and more events utilise the system, it is anticipated that increased reliability will be achieved.

The high response rates to the survey from local businesses suggest a high level of support for the research. While some business respondents did not perceive much direct benefit to their busi-ness from their community hosting the event, there was widespread appreciation of the event in terms of profiling the community as a desirable destination and a place to live. Businesses consist-ently reported a desire for more information on future events as well as more local involvement, and perhaps encouragement to take advantage of the opportunities the event offers. Clearly, there is unrealised potential for local businesses to leverage off visitors to the events, which will in turn increase the contribution of the event to the local economy (Chalip and Leyns, 2002). This can only be achieved by event managers and local businesses working collaboratively.

Conclusions

The research to date suggests that responses rates upwards of 25% are easily achievable for online survey approaches. The response rates suggest that online surveys will be more successful in those instances where the race director establishes an 'email rapport' with participants. Those events that make their first email contact with the participants to ask them to participate are likely to have lower response rates. An inherent problem is the small sample size, meaning that results can be easily influenced if the respondents are not representative of the entire population.

Sport events are an important component of sporting tourism and it is micro-sporting events that often make their impact felt in more peripheral areas. There is only limited understanding of the true economic impacts of these small events and there is considerable work to be done in creating cost-effective tools for those who want to better understand the economic yield of events and how they can be developed in a sustainable fashion. This chapter has argued that ICT, and particularly the Internet, can play an important role in helping to build closer relationships and linkages between New Zealand communities, businesses and sports tourism. The TRACE Events program has demonstrated an ability to support decision-making processes that involve multiple stakeholders. The TRACE Events model outlined here utilises the basic principles of CI to develop a web resource that is open-source in nature and which facilitates the sharing of knowledge as well as the generation of economic impact figures. Research elsewhere shows that ICT can help in strengthening linkages between visitors and local economies and, in the long term, giving local people and communities more control over the tourism planning process (Hull and Milne, 2001; Mason and Milne, 2002). A key question remains, however, as to how do we not only ensure that local involvement and participation occurs, but that it can be sustained in such a way that it leads to effective development outcomes?

References

Chalip, L. and Leyns, A. (2002) Local business leveraging of a sport event: Managing an event for economic benefit. *Journal of Sport Management*, 16, 132–158.

Chalip, L. and McGuirty, J. (2004) Bundling sport events with the host destination. *Journal of Sport Tourism*, 9, 267–282.

Chhabra, D., Sills, E. and Cubbage, F. W. (2003) The significance of festivals to rural economies. Estimating the economic impacts of Scottish Highland Games in North Carolina. *Journal of Travel Research*, 41, 421–427.

Daniels, M., Backman, K. and Backman, S. (2004) Economic impact results with perspectives from host community business and opinion leaders. *Event Management*, 8(3), 117–125.

Forstner, K. (2004) Community ventures and access to markets. The role of intermediaries in marketing rural tourism products. *Development Policy Review*, 22, 497–514.

Gibson, H. J., Willming, C. and Holdnak, A. (2003) Small-scale event sport tourism – Fans as tourists. *Tourism Management*, 24, 181–190.

Gursoy, D. and Kendall, K. W. (2006) Hosting mega events. Modeling locals' support. *Annals of Tourism Research*, 33(3), 603–623.

Gurstein, M. (2000) Community informatics. Enabling community uses of information and communications technology. In Gurstein, M. (ed.), *Community informatics: Enabling community uses of information and communications technologies*. Hershey, PA: Idea Group, pp. 1–31.

Higham, J. E. S. and Ritchie, B. (2001) The evolution of festivals and other events in rural southern New Zealand. *Event Management*, 7(1), 39–49.

Hull, J. and Milne, S. (2001) From nets to the 'net': Marketing tourism on Quebec's lower North Shore. In Aarsaether, N. and Baerenholdt, J. O. (eds.), *Coping Strategies in the North*. Copenhagen: Nordic Council of Ministers, pp. 159–180.

Loader, B., Hague, B. and Eagle, D. (2000) Embedding the net: Community empowerment in the age of information. In Gurstein, M. (ed.), *Community Informatics: Enabling Community Uses of Information and Communications Technology*. Hershey, PA: Idea Group Publishing, pp. 81–103.

Mason, D. and Milne, S. (2002) E-Commerce and community tourism. In Palvia, P. C., Palvia, S. C. and Roche, E. M. (eds.), *Global Information Technology and Electronic Commerce: Issues for the New Millennium*. Marietta: Ivy League Publishing Limited.

Mele, D. (2005) Exploring the principal of subsidiarity in organisational forms. *Journal of Business Ethics*, 60(3), 293–305.

Milne, S. (1987) Differential multipliers. *Annals of Tourism Research*, 14(4), 499–515.

Milne, S. (1998) Tourism linkages and leakages. *World Tourism Organisation – Tourism Economic Report*. Madrid: World Tourism Organisation, pp. 77–79.

Milne, S., Mason, D. and Hasse, J. (2004) Tourism, information technology and development. Revolution or reinforcement? In Hall, M., Lew, A. and Williams, A. (eds.), *A Companion to Tourism Geography*. London: Routledge, pp. 184–195.

Misener, L. and Mason, D. S. (2006) Creating community networks: Can sporting events offer meaningful sources of social capital? *Managing Leisure*, 11(1), 39–56.

NZMED (2001) *SMEs in New Zealand: Structure and Dynamics*. Wellington: New Zealand Ministry of Economic Development.

O'Neil, D. (2002) Assessing community informatics: A review of methodological approaches for evaluating community networks and community technology centres. *Internet Research: Electronic Networking Applications and Policy*, 12, 76–102.

Oppermann, M. (2002) Triangulation – A methodological discussion. *International Journal of Tourism Research*, 2(2), 141–146.

Page, S. J. and Getz, D. (1997) *The Business of Rural Tourism: International Perspectives*. London: Thomson Learning.

Shuler, D. (1999) *New Community Networks: Wired for Change*. Reading, MA: Addison-Wesley.

Surman, M. and Wershler-Henry, D. (2001) *Commonspace: Beyond Virtual Community*. London: Financial Times/Pearson.

TSG (2000) *New Zealand Tourism Strategy 2010*. Wellington: Office of the Minister of Tourism/Tourism Strategy Group.

Weed, M. (2003) Why the two won't tango? Explaining the lack of integrated policies for sport and tourism in the UK. *Journal of Sport Management*, 17(3), 258–283.

Wilson, R. (2006) The economic impact of local sport events: Significant, limited or otherwise? A case study of four swimming events. *Leisure Management*, 11(1), 57–70.

Wilson, S., Fesenmaier, D. R., Fesenmaier, J. and van Es, J. (2001) Factors for success in rural tourism development. *Journal of Travel Research*, 40(2), 132–139.

Chapter 18

Post-modern Heritage, Chivalry, Park and Ride: *Le Tour* Comes to Canterbury

J. Lovell

Introduction

On 8 July 2007, the 2007 Tour de France (TDF) began with a *Grand Depart* in London and ended the first stage in Canterbury. This opportunity to stage a high-profile mega-event was extremely significant in the context of London's successful Olympic bid, making the Tour de France a pilot for a mega-event, so it was vital that event planning and implementation were effective. This chapter aims to analyse the relationship between the heritage city and mega-event, assessing the processes involved in planning and implementing the event, using the Tour de France Stage One finish in Canterbury as a case study. The first race stage from London to Canterbury was judged by the press as a success, with serendipitous good weather in the midst of a poor summer and a lack of mass major crashes or other negative elements; in contrast to the following day's events at Stage Two in Dunkerque, subsequent doping scandals and rider and team expulsions. The chapter will examine the detail of the planning and management issues of staging the Tour de France in a historic environment and establish the level of design and intention by the event organisers making the 'success' the result of meticulous, labour-intensive preparation. This chapter asks how was the Tour de France managed in the context of Canterbury's cultural policy initiatives, heritage city constraints and the chapter will finally establish how the event and city augmented and reinforced each other's 'glocal distinctiveness' and 'sense of place' (McCabe 2006 in Picard and Robinson, 2006).

Canterbury seems like an obvious race backdrop in terms of the prestige of the Canterbury brand complementing the significance which is the nature of mega-events (Getz, 2005), but tourist-historic cities (Ashworth and Tunbridge, 1990) manifest certain well-documented operational characteristics and specific visitor management requirements (Breakell and Human, 1999; Laws and le Pelley, 2000) which don't make them typical mega-event venues. The limitations of heritage cities, as victims of their own tourism success, are well documented. Their carrying capacity is restricted; the visitor/resident ratio is extremely high; they are tourist traps, susceptible to congestion due to their Medieval

International Perspectives of Festivals and Events
Copyright © 2009 by Elsevier Ltd.
ISBN: 978-0-08-045100-8

layout; they struggle with inadequate, expensive parking, visitor dispersal and cultural diversification; to balance stakeholder relationships they usually have strong city centre partnerships to manage these elements; and the vision can focus on preservation (Ashworth, 1990; Grant et al., 1996; Russo, 2002; Snaith and Haley, 1999; Stuart-Hoyle and Lovell, 2006; Swarbrooke, 2002).

Events can cause a variety of equally well-documented negative and positive social impacts including carrying capacity, congestion, visitor management issues, disruption among the host community, strong partnerships and stakeholder relationships (Bowdin et al., 2006; Shone and Parry, 2004; Yeoman et al., 2004) which mirror the typical management issues of heritage cities. The Tour de France could be classified as a sporting mega-event (Bowdin, et al., 2006) indicating that it is an event of status, national publicity and coverage and requires extensive planning. Despite the constraints of both historic city and mega-event management, the nature of the two combined to provide the unique event experience. Event organisers were highly sensible of the symbolism of the pilgrims' journey from London to Canterbury, fictionalised by Chaucer, and the parallel Tour riders' journey which consolidated the 'sense of place' (McCabe 2006 in Picard and Robinson, 2006) and authenticity (Derrett, 2004 in Yeoman et al., 2004) of both event and city. The Tour de France, itself an emblematic spectacle, heavily layered with traditional and modern meanings and associations, not only underpinned the distinctiveness of Canterbury but also created a new visitor flow within the heritage environment, a new 'time–space compression' (Harvey, 1989), and created a new fusion 'experience', turning the city into a stage for a day (Richards, 2001).

Canterbury Culture

As Ken Livingston (as Mayor of London) pointed out before the race, 'London and Canterbury have been linked for many centuries, first by the Roman built Watling Street and later in Chaucer's Canterbury Tales' (Livingston, 2006). Canterbury Cathedral acts as a globally familiar historical metonym for the city's brand, yet Canterbury's sense of place is rooted both in the historic and inevitable contemporary developments making Canterbury a 'post-modern historic city', rich with contrasts and irony, with the sense of different timescapes encapsulated by the housing of a modern watch shop in one of its most famous medieval pilgrim's inns. Old and new coexist, ambivalently. A bylaw creating the pedestrianisation of the High Street, as opposed to heritage destinations with central traffic flow like Chester, allows the city to create a cosmopolitan atmosphere with restaurant and cafe tables and chairs and temporary market stalls, among the ancient buildings. Canterbury is, however, broadly a typical heritage city, manifesting various social problems such as traffic congestion and crowding detailed above, caused by the number of visitors to the historic core, or tourists clustering at the magnet attraction of the Cathedral (Law and le Pelley, 2000). Of the estimated 6.3 million visitors to Canterbury a year, Canterbury Cathedral draws an estimated 1,100,000 visitors a year in contrast with the Canterbury Tales visitor attraction (approximately 93,000 p.a.) and the Canterbury museums (approximately 20,000 p.a.) (Canterbury City Council, 2004). A variety of tactics are used by the City Council's Tourism Unit to disperse visitors around the city; for example, modern signage fingerposts designed to make the city more 'legible' and pinpoint secondary attractions such as St Augustine's Abbey. Marketing campaigns such as the 'Canterbury Passport' attraction packaging scheme (one entry ticket for four main attractions) are intended to bundle the attractions overshadowed by the Cathedral, and guide books are designed to emphasise the variety of tourist facilities within the city and strive to diversify the product. Despite these efforts, Canterbury

Cathedral remains the 'magnet', and visitor numbers at St Augustine's Abbey have dropped so low that the English Heritage site, part of the World Heritage Site, will only be open one day a week during the 2007/2008 winter, although the Abbey was recently modernised by a Heritage Lottery funded new museum in 2001.

Since Canterbury's 2002 Capital of Culture bid, the city has been politically committed to both improving cultural facilities and hosting events to 'stretch' the historic product and 'liberate' it from the heritage city tag (Lovell and Stuart-Hoyle, 2006) which is reflected in the continual re-examination and evolution of the Council's cultural policy documents. 'Beyond the Vision' was published to establish the Capital of Culture bid event-based legacy and set out how the Council would use the Urban Cultural Fund investment to mount a series of 19 events running until 2006 entitled 'Make It Real'. A new strategy 'Canterbury Culture: In Place, In Motion, Inspired, Involved' created a development framework from 2003 to 2010. In addition, Canterbury had investigated the concept of city quarters for many years and as part of a piece of independent research by a regeneration and economic development consultancy called Yellow Book Ltd., framework document was published in 2005 refocusing the city's cultural perspective, and setting out a cultural State of the Nation. The report recommended that a cultural quarter should not be implemented, but the city as a whole should be treated as a single cultural entity (Yellow Book, 2005). The report went on to say that although the establishment of a Canterbury Cultural Quarter (CCQ) would be 'counter-productive', 'The focus on authenticity means moving beyond the simplistic and superficial conventions of the branded "quarter," an increasingly dated concept, and instead adopting a more sophisticated place marketing strategy, provisionally entitled "Canterbury City of Imagination"' (Yellow Book, 2005, p. 2).

Elements of these strategies have coexisted in some landmark projects. Canterbury was rebranded in 2005 as 'Canterbury, Simply Inspirational' and is upgrading and maintaining some of the main capital facilities of the heritage and cultural product. A £7 million Heritage Lottery Fund application to create a modern art gallery and a £17 million campaign to develop the local theatre were all launched in 2006, possibly causing local fundraising saturation. Canterbury Cathedral has simultaneously launched a campaign to raise £50 million to 'Save our Cathedral' and provide repairs to the roof and reinforce the mission of the cathedral to act as a 'Ministry of Welcome' by providing more comprehensive visitor services. The destination continues, therefore, to develop and enhance its cultural product in capital projects and through the cultivation and implementation of events.

Events in Canterbury

Against this backdrop, Canterbury could be described as running a 'festivalisation' strategy (Van Elderen, 1997 in Stevenson, 2003) with thriving investment in events and a policy of event development, following the 2002 bid to be a European Capital of Culture. This is due in part to the sensitive nature of the historic environment, which requires versatile, temporary visitor attractions that do not impact directly and long term on the fabric of the city, making the transient entertainment and maintenance provided by events an appealing prospect. Events in Canterbury are organised by a variety of public and private sector bodies, which each provide a specialist part of the events calendar. Canterbury first created a multi-partner agency, the Canterbury City Centre Initiative in 1994, established to enable strategic visitor management when Canterbury was receiving a peak, unsustainable number of up to 18,000 coaches per year (Laws and le Pelley, 2000). Canterbury City Centre Management has since evolved from a basic city partnership into a limited company and in 2007 was absorbed back into Canterbury City Council as 'frontline management of council to business relationships in Canterbury City Centre' (Canterbury City Council, 2007). Its central function is to link and balance the interests of partners including the Canterbury Independent Traders Association (CITA), the major department stores and the Whitefriars shopping centre, which has a separate city manager. Events act as a cohesive, uniting force between these partners. The Canterbury City Centre Co-ordinator manages specific retail and food events in the Canterbury calendar such as the Euromarket Food and Drink Festival. The cathedral has a specifically religious-based events roster including the Lambeth Conference and Mystery Plays and is used as a venue for various 'appropriately themed' city centre events including University graduations and classical concerts by local choirs. The cathedral has resisted offers to expand into popular culture and has refused opportunities such as providing the Harry Potter set for Hogwart's, or hosting Canterbury's Christmas Food Festival in its precincts, in an attempt to preserve its integral position as home of the Church of England. Canterbury Festival is managed by a separate organisation and specialises primarily in special interest theatre-based and music events during October.

Whitefriars shopping centre offers a recent base for collaboration; the centre was constructed in 2003, with a layout including squares and piazzas specifically designed for events, for example, street performers and German Christmas stalls and a new events budget intended to improve city cohesiveness and draw people in to the retail product. Canterbury City Council events teams organise events such as the Global Bandstand, Heritage Open Days and art exhibitions at the museums. A new Canterbury Culture organisation was formed in 2006, with the objective of building greater cohesiveness in the creative community including local artists and writers. A 'Cultural Olympiad' Fine Arts Group has linked the arts departments of Canterbury Christ Church University, the University of Kent and the University College of the Creative Arts and aims to bid for a wide portfolio of projects during the build-up to the Olympics. The Museums run events such as exhibitions and road shows, and the Marlowe Theatre also hosts events such as Street Theatre. This approach is fragmented, but effective, filling the calendar with a variety and selection of events, although not presented under a single theme, unlike historic cities like Winchester, which use umbrella themes such as sculpture, or Spain to add cohesiveness to the city event product.

A gap analysis study of events could indicate that Canterbury has no central medieval pageant, procession or historic re-enactment event, such as Il Palio in the historic city of Sienna, or the Mercantia in Certaldo, but attempts a strong sense of traditional detail. Medieval cooking is displayed at the annual food festival, pendants have been manufactured for one of the most significant heritage streets, Palace Street, during events, to reinforce a sense of place. Bringing *Le Tour* to Canterbury meant that the authenticity of the historic environment and ideal of chivalric sportsmanship worked well in combination, creating a romantic imaginary and a sense of modern cosmopolitanism, while invoking old rivalries and battles, or a touch of the Field of the Cloth of Gold, where Henry VIII met Francis I of France. '...a Tour de France fought out between London and Paris, between Trafalgar Square and the Champs-Élysées, can be nothing short of a great Tour de France' (LeBlanc and Prudhomme, 2006).

As stated on the Tour de France official website, the Tour de France 2007 was intended to act as a showcase uniting 'history and emotion and, on the other, pragmatism and modernity' (LeBlanc and Prudhomme, 2006) but the decision to host the event in London, Kent and Canterbury was not completely straightforward. The associated fear of '7/7', security problems at Glasgow Airport, complaints about expenditure on festivals or the Olympics, media doping scandals dogging the sport and threatening spectator numbers meant that the judgement by Canterbury City Council (CCC) to pay £75,000 for the hosting fee and embark on the project was high risk. Planning for the Stage One Finish of The Tour de France involved solving problems as diverse as housing over 2000 support vehicles at the finish line; finding accommodation in the limited quality 4-star hotel stock for visitors, press and event organisers such as Transport for London and finding space for a French Market. An estimated 70,000 spectators (Kent Police figures) attended the event in a city with a population of 40,000 living within the city walls, in a highly sensitive to environment, including 1589 listed buildings and historic fabric further protected within a World Heritage Status and buffer. Spectators lined city walls protected by English Heritage and bends were configured in medieval city gateway roads for the race. So how was the Tour de France, a mega sporting event, planned and how did it impact on Canterbury's heritage environment and sense of place?

The Tour de France

The Tour de France is an annual bicycle race around France, now organised by the Amaury Sport Organization (ASO), which started in 1903 and has grown to become the largest annual international mega-event. In 2007 it involved 21 teams and 189 riders which tend to ride in a *peloton* formation, meaning that an end stage, especially on flat terrain, is characterised by a rapid passing, in seconds, of the majority of the riders after a long wait by spectators who have been holding a position or vantage

Figure 18.1: The end of the Peloton Courtesy of Martin Southam.

spot on the side of the road (Figure 18.1). One of the striking features of the event is the visual spectacle of the colourful blur of the rider's clothing that is covered with brands and sponsors and the sound and power of the *peloton*. The race is preceded by a *caravanne* of sponsors, similar to a carnival procession. The race can include stages in different countries such as Ireland and Germany. *Le Tour* is in some ways a traditional spectacle, with stages beginning and ending in historic towns and cities such as Amiens, Chatres, Marseilles, Macon, Tignes, Grenoble and Albi, making the end stage finish in Canterbury an obvious choice. The candidate towns take part in a selection process, like other bicycle races such as Il Giro d'Italia, the Tour acts as a catalyst for various towns and villages along the route to celebrate a festival.

The major motivations for participating in the event are the prestige and economic impact, including direct and indirect spend and press coverage leading to tourism and inward investment. For French cities *Le Tour* is also a reinforcement of local distinctiveness, a national ritual (Berridge, 2007) created by, celebrated and filleted in the press. 'The way in which *Le Tour* is presented by its media coverage as an exploration of France's historical, cultural and political heritage leaves those who follow it in little doubt as to the significance of castles, rivers, mountain passes and battle-fields' (Dauncey and Hare, 2003, p. 3). During filming the footage used does not depict the industrial towns and cities in the Alps and apart from including the Futuroscope theme park, the event is depicted as taking place within a natural idyllic environment of chateaux, Alpine landscapes, fields of sunflowers and medieval cities. *Le Tour* is a prime advertisement for the French tourist board, but transcends national identity, because although these landscapes are typically French, many European countries feature mountains or historic cities, therefore the setting of the riders' journey is a conscious creation of the edited past. The country, therefore, the cities on the route are treated as a 'stage' on which to mount performances (Richards, 2001).

These historical, quasi-mythical elements include the quest for a cup or trophy, involving individual tactics and shifting allegiances, the team logos or coats of arms, the emblematic jerseys redolent of knights and even, humorously, the name *Lance* Armstrong. (Lovell and Beedie, 2007). In recent years the doping scandals, new technologies and sponsorships have brought a contemporary edge to the sport and have also compromised the romantic nature to a certain extent due to sensationalism… 'the concept of "hero", as embodiment of valorized conduct in a distinct field of human endeavour such as the Tour, may have been attenuated permanently by a system of global forces surrounding this and perhaps similar international events' (Wieting, 2000, p. 361). There was still a sense of belief and absence of disillusionment in its nature in 2007, demonstrated by the volume of spectators on the streets, although the previous year's yellow jersey win was in dispute. The concept that 'in the Tour de France, sporting heroism can only truly be expressed in failure, since, almost by definition, winners are superhuman' (Wieting, 2000, p. 361) added to the drama narrative and concept of tragedy, making it a riveting spectacle.

Modern, technical elements layered with tradition, making the Tour de France a post-modern event (Dauncey and Hare, 2005), include cycling technology, athletic training, the *caravanne*, the sponsorship and, most explicitly, the media spectacle; '2965 hours of TV broadcast in 184 countries (1583 hours in Europe, 504 hours in America, 502 hours in Asia, 175 hours in Africa, 116 in the Middle east and 85 hours in the rest of the world)' (Desbordes, 2007). The technology used to film the race alters the perception of the event, which is often viewed by helicopter or from the back of a motorcycle camera which is 'in' the race. As LeBlanc commented 'Television magnifies the Tour' (LeBlanc in Dauncey and Hare, 2003) and creates an emotional landscape when riders are shown in close-up.

Tour Planning and Organisation in Canterbury

The decision by Canterbury to host the event was made in late 2005, with a decision to also host a stage of the Tour of Britain as an organisational practice run. The Tour de France would be the catalyst to create a city-wide event, designed to attract a variety of visitors and promote the city to the world's media. Although a typical English Heritage city, Canterbury prides itself on a globally recognised brand, an international character and proximity to Europe and is a strong participant in Interreg-funded projects. The Tour de France would therefore fit with an effort to capitalise on a 'glocal distinctiveness'. This was also reflected in the decision to allow the City Council's Tourism Unit to manage the event, as opposed to the cultural services, or sports development team.

Once the decision had been made to host the event, planning started. Intensive resources were required to stage the event, in particular specialist input during the preparation. The Tourism Manager, based in the Regeneration Unit, managed the project, with the backing of the Chief Executive and a two-year contract was created in 2006 for a Tour de France Project Manager. Groups were set up internally within the Council including a Members' working group, to inform members of progress, and win political support; an Officer Project Group included Highways representatives, the PR team, the Cultural Managers and the district Risk Manager and ensure that expertise was shared and creative ideas stimulated. The Support events were managed by the Cultural team and the Safety Group explicitly addressed risk management (Figure 18.2).

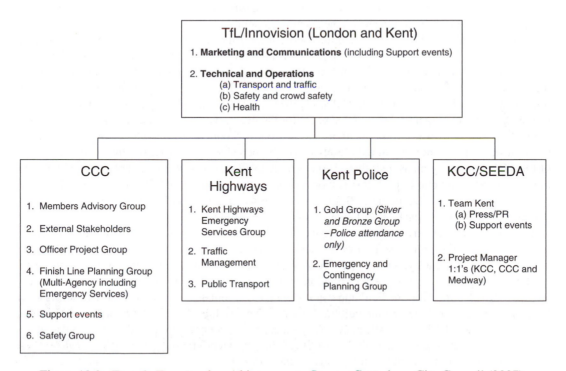

Figure 18.2: Tour de France sub-working groups. *Source*: Canterbury City Council (2007).

In addition to internal Council resources required for event planning, temporary workers were used on the day. Direct employment included 114 Canterbury City Council event staff and stewards were organised by Canterbury City Council which included 30 tourism staff worked on the day – 43 students from Canterbury College plus 14 Canterbury City Council staff (a mixture of Council Tourism Unit and Visitor Information Centre staff) plus 30 stewards from the Kent Volunteer service. Approximately 40–45 Kent County Council race route volunteers were organised by Kent County Council and Transport for London. For easy information management, the City was divided into nine tourist zones, each with a mobile stand distributing race information, with workers communicating via walkie-talkies. Three teams of researchers also interviewed the crowds investigating economic impacts, the event carbon footprint and spectators' perceptions of the event.

A mega-event coming to Canterbury created new partnerships, both internally and externally. To mirror Canterbury City Centre Co-ordination, an external Tour de France stakeholders group was implemented in 2006, intended to maximise the co-operation of stakeholders such as Stagecoach buses, Fenwick's department store, Whitefriars Shopping Centre and local cycling bodies, such as Spokes, meeting quarterly to discuss the preparation and serve as a vehicle for encouraging sponsorship opportunities, which resulted in Whitefriars erecting a big screen in the city centre. The following sponsors supported the 'Tour de Fun' events: Whitefriars, Barretts Garage, Abode, Berkeley Homes, Canterbury College and Seafrance and a total of £38,000 was raised in sponsorship to help cover the costs of the Tour de Fun programme. Canterbury already had strong links to French cities like Amiens and Rouen through Interreg projects such as Cathédrales en Lumière and links to organisations such as VisitLondon through the Kent Tourism Alliance. The new partnership with Transport for London was important, with the emphasis on preparing that London could cater for the 2012 Olympics, there was pressure to ensure the event ran smoothly.

Canterbury also worked closely with the wider Kent Tour de France team, particularly on areas where resources could be pooled and duplication avoided. One of these topic areas included a 'Good Living' Interreg bid in partnership with Nord Pas de Calais, which aimed to deliver a race economic impact report. These funds were then invested in a wider Transport for London regional economic impact study conducted by Sheffield Hallam University. The economic impact was a marketing tool, a significant factor in gaining political support for the event, which the Council estimated would be worth '£37 million' to the Kent economy (Kent County Council, 2007). The economic impact of the Tour de France is not monitored closely on the French side; 'paradoxically the economic impact of the TDF was rarely measured; there is one survey available … But it does not give real information about this economic impact; this is more a general report about the TV exposure and the media coverage of the TDF' (Desbordes, 2007). Cities such as Amiens who hosted an end stage in 2004 compiled a media press pack but not an economic impact study.

Due to the fact that heritage cities are prone to high numbers of day visitors and continually aspire to the staying market, plus the Tour de France was expected to attract a high number local fans as well as special interest cycling fans, a decision was made to mount cycling-themed events in the week preceding the race. These events took place in all spaces of the city at different times of the day and were branded the 'Tour de Fun' and were intended to stimulate a new sports-tourism visitor flow. 'The city becomes a stage and the cultural life and everyday life of the city are developed into one extended festival' (Richards, 2001, p. 60). A 'French style street ball' with food, music and an accordion band was planning for the night before Stage One, to extend the stay of visitors and also engender a sense of celebration, and 'communitas' in the host community, generating 'social leverage' for the event organisers (Chalip, 2007). Multiple city-wide events running under the cycling theme were supplemented by a 'Geants Parade', a French tradition, including French and local papier-mâché giant figures accompanied by marching school bands organised by a local arts company, Strange Cargo (Figure 18.3). The Geants were a key part of the Capital of Culture bid projects, a partnership project with France and the Geants parade took place before the race, culminating in a 'picnic' in a grassed-over piazza at the Whitefriars Shopping centre and adding a quirky, carnivalesque, ethnic feel to a day celebrating cycling and a strong element of 'glocal distinctiveness'. The Geants were then lined upon the city periphery to 'welcome' the riders. The events achieved the recommendations of the Yellow Book report to make the city a single cultural quarter for a day.

The heritage city is frequently highly prescriptive in its protection of the historic environment and its World Heritage Status also creates an added pressure. Although the Cathedral was not involved in the event, which fell outside the periphery of the World Heritage boundary area, the English Heritage protected Roman city walls ran as a perimeter to the race with spectators standing on the listed structure and on the land beneath the walls. The size of the event was daunting, and its transitory nature also makes it an appealing prospect for a conservation unit because it does not require fundamental changes to the fabric of the city. The inflatable podium and grandstand seats are magically all assembled and dissembled in 24 hours.

The Tour de France Stage One route stretched across Kent and a striking feature was its 'qualitative and quantitative uniqueness' (Dauncey and Hare, 2003). Altogether, 2900 metre of Heavy duty barrier, 6768 metre of light duty barrier, 182 traffic signs, 400 advance warning sins, 290 cones, 108 straw bales and 44 metre red/white plastic barriers were required. Held on the same weekend as Live Earth, *Le Tour*'s sustainable transport message was implicit in the cycling but contradicted by

Figure 18.3: Geants Parade Courtesy of Jane Lovell.

the size of the motorised caravan and numbers of support vehicles. As a result of the ASO's support vehicle requirements, car parking was much reduced in Canterbury, with parking reserved for team vehicles and a car park used as a French Market. Littering was controlled using bags hung from barriers. Waste management was addressed by the use of portaloos; over 80 were installed at key sites for the event, including disabled toilets. One of the unexpected features of the Tour de France is its direct sustainability. The Tour de France is a road race, so streets and city were closed and aside from the tour vehicles and riders they were largely empty. Although the caravanne was extensive and motorised, the impact of pollution was reduced by the event which severely restricted the usual Sunday traffic and in fact spectators expressed pleasure at being able to walk in what was normally a busy road, although more local residents had heard about the road closures than the event, prior to the race and the inconvenience of road closures were a feature of event anticipatory anxiety (Canterbury Christ Church University, 2007). The previous week, a London to Canterbury mass participation cycle ride brought an estimated 5000 riders to the city using the Tour de France route and had caused far more serious congestion problems. On the day, reclaiming the streets and city as a pedestrian zone was appreciated by the crowds as a benefit.

Event Impact

'Winner Robbie McEwen said he had never seen crowds like those in Kent' (Kent County Council, 2007). An estimated 4 million people attended the event in Kent and 50,000 in Canterbury (Canterbury City Council, 2007). Despite these figures, the new visitor flow seemed to work effectively, primarily due to the labour-intensive and detailed event organisation. At the post-event Stakeholder's Meeting the footfall in the Whitefriars shopping centre was reported to be up on the whole during the Sunday of the event. Trade was down, but some city centre businesses were not unhappy with the result. Individual Stakeholders, for example a motor dealership, subsequently reported that they had had the best two weekends of the year although some restaurants had mixed reviews, possibly because of the nature of the event, with spectators guarding their places for several hours at the race track barriers. A gradual build-up of people took place, followed by a U-turn when people watched the race and then many people returned to the city. Fenwicks Department store reported a peak of activity between 1 and 2 p.m. and then a lull, followed by another peak after the race had passed at 4 p.m. Like local residents they could appreciate the wider prestige and exposure of hosting the event (Bull and Lovell, 2007) and specifically, for Canterbury to be featured in French, American newspapers and as a race backdrop, on television. In the context of a 2007 summer of poor weather, terrorism, floods and foot and mouth crises, this was positive news coverage. The summer ball was attended by an estimated 1000 people and stimulated the evening economy, with an audience of families and the older generation and a further 500 people attended a classical concert held the previous week. The 'Geants Parade' also catered to families. Trains and buses were much busier than normal, 52% of spectators walked to the event and 15% used the train (Canterbury City Council, 2007) with a double bus service laid on. Only 200 people used the cycle facility at Whitefriars Shopping Centre. The overall visitor feedback from surveys conducted prior to the race and on the day of the race (Canterbury Christ Church University, 2007) was positive. Although the race was brief, the sense of 'communitas' (Chalip, 2007) and festival atmosphere may have mitigated host tension and only very few people commented that they found themselves 'stranded' by road barriers (Canterbury City Council, 2007). In London the temporary bridges were so popular that they were used in preference to the normal underpasses. Of 20 emails received by Canterbury City Council during the week following the event, 19 were positive and 1 negative. The positive host response to the event may have been created by the intensive operational planning by Canterbury City Council and its partners.

Sense of Place

'Festivals and events provide authenticity and uniqueness, especially with events based on inherent indigenous values; convenient hospitality and affordability; theming and symbols for participants and spectators' (Derrett, 2004 in Yeoman et al., 2004). This aspect of event authenticity, whether it is in the ceremony (ritual is inherent to *Le Tour*), the jerseys, the presentations, or a detail, for example, the French advertisers in the *caravanne*, which reinforce the impact for the spectator. This detail can be consciously cultivated by organisers, for example in the case of Canterbury's Stage One finish; policemen donned their old-style helmets for the occasion. The sense of place was established and reinforced by marketing design; over 52,000 pieces of literature were produced by Canterbury City Council to promote the event and a comprehensive press campaign in local papers, radio and TV stations combated the anticipatory anxiety of residents. Hallmark events, such as the Ludlow Food Festival and the Edinburgh Fringe reinforce place identity and a mega, multi-venue event such as the Tour de France can also be place specific. Over 200 banners promoting Canterbury were displayed around the city on the day, totalling more than 650 metre in length, meaning the message 'Canterbury Inspirational' was transmitted around the world. The striking element of the Tour de France is its international flavour and *Le Tour* stage finish in Canterbury was primarily an Anglo-Franco display. British cyclists and national landmarks were strongly featured in the press, but the multi-cultural aspects of the events were further emphasised by details such as French flags and French markets, creating an experiential element. Although this seems incongruous, some of the locally distinctive characteristics of Canterbury's are its proximity to the continent and the presence of international tourists in the city. When Canterbury was being judged for European Capital of culture status the judges commented on the variety of languages spoken on the streets. The city is, therefore, 'glocally distinctive'.

The sense of tradition is also mixed paradoxically with a sense of modernity and commercialism. *Le Tour* riders are in effect billboards advertising their various team sponsors on their racing skins, lending a global branded feel to the event. This gives the event and the city an odd relationship to both space and time, combining a post-modern event with a post-modern historic city. Although many elements of the Tour de France, for example the finish line paraphernalia, are similar throughout the race, whether taking place in Germany or France, there was little sense of 'placelessness' about the Canterbury end stage, which panoptically viewed from helicopters showed the city walls clearly juxtaposed with constant shots of the metonymic cathedral.

Conclusion

The 'post-modern historic city' and post-modern mega-event worked together when Stage One of the Tour de France came to Canterbury, augmenting and complementing the heritage sense of place in a traditionally contemporary, distinctive and appropriate way. Labour-intensive planning and implementation enabled event organisers to manage the typical heritage city and mega-event visitor management problems, using the city as a 'stage' with the majority of public space utilised. There is a political will to capitalise on the Tour de France success by staging further cycling specific events such as a grand prix, or a mix of sporting and other cultural elements. The opportunity to host a mega-event may never recur and the legacy strategy in terms of further events has not yet been established, although discussed by the Members', Officers' Project Group and External Stakeholders. As a pilot for the Olympics, operationally, although a key lesson on the demand on resources (after the race, the local Press used Freedom of Information to obtain figures spent on *Le Tour* by Kent County Council and Medway Council) the Tour de France 'success' may further reinforce Canterbury's festivalisation intention and aim to become a 'festival city'. It is doubtful, however, whether the chance to host an event on this scale will ever recur in Canterbury, but the relationship between the heritage city and the mega-event have been established by the Tour de France in 2007.

References

Ashworth, G. J. and Tunbridge, J. E. (1990) *The Tourist Historic City*. Belhaven Press: London and New York.

Bowdin, M. et al. (2006) *Events Management* (2nd edn), London: Elsevier.

Boyd, S. and Timothy, D. (2003) *Heritage Tourism*. London: Prentice Hall.

Berridge, G. (2006) *Events Design and Experience* Oxford: Butterworth-Heinemann.

Breakell, M. and Human, B. (1999) Practical Guidance for Tourism Management in Historic Towns: Making the Connections. *Conference Proceedings*, EHTF, Oxford Brookes University, Oxford, England.

Bull, C. J. and Lovell, J. (2007) The impact of hosting major sporting events on local residents: An analysis of the views and perceptions of Canterbury residents in relation to the Tour de France 2007. *Journal of Sport and Tourism*, 12(3–4), 229–248.

Canterbury Christ Church University and Canterbury City council (2007) Tour de France Residents' Survey.

Canterbury City Council (2004) *Local Attractions Data Table* Canterbury: Canterbury City Council.

Canterbury City Council (2007) Kent Police figures for the Tour de France, bus and train figures, attractions figures, Cambridge Model figures courtesy of Canterbury City Council Tourism development Fact Sheet (2004).

Chalip, L. (2006) Toward social leverages of sport events, *Journal of Sport and Tourism*, 11(2), 1–19.

Dauncey, H. & Hare, G. (2005) *The Tour de France 1903–2003: A Century of Sporting Structures, Meanings and Values*. London: Routledge.

Desbordes, M. (2007) *International Journal of Sport Management and Marketing* 2, (5–6) 526–540.

Getz, D. (2005) *Festivals, Special Events and Tourism*. New York: Van Nostrand.

Grant, M., Human, B. and le Pelley, B. (1999) Making the connections – Joined up thinking in action. Tourism Intelligence Papers. *Insights*, London: ETC, July, A20–23.

Harvey, D. (1989) *Condition of Postmodernity*, Oxford: Blackwell.

Kent County Council (2007) *Tour de France* Kent: Kent County Council. Available from http://www.kent.gov. uk/leisure-and-culture/sports/tour-de-france [Accessed 10:50 12/8/07].

Laws, E. and le Pelley, B. (2000) Managing complexity and change in tourism: The case of a historic city. *International Journal of Tourism Research*, 2, 229–246.

LeBlanc and Prudhomme, (2006) *Le Tour 2007* [Online] France: Amaury Sport Organisation. Available From: http://www.letour.fr/2007/TDF/presentation/us/edito.html [Accessed 8:00 8/7/2008]

Livingston, K. (2006) *Grand Start 2007* [Online] France: Amaury Sport Organisation. Available From: http://www.letour.com/2007/TDF/COURSE/us/grand_depart_2007.html [Accessed 8:00 9/7/2008].

Lovell, J. and Beedie, C. (2007) Personal Contact 2 August.

Lovell, J. and Stuart-Hoyle, M. (2006) Liberating the heritage city. In Smith, M. and Robinson, M. (eds.), *Cultural Tourism in a Changing World: Politics, Participation and (Re)presentation*. Clevedon: Channel View Publications.

Picard, D. and Robinson, M. (2006) *Festivals, Tourism and Social Change: Remaking Worlds*. Clevedon: Channel View Publications.

Richards, G. (ed.) (2001) *Cultural Attractions and European Tourism*. Wallingford: CABI.

Russo, A. (2002) The 'Vicious Circle' of Tourism Development in Heritage Cities. *Annals of Tourism Research* 29(1), 165–182.

Shone, A. and Parry, B. (2004) *Successful Events Management: A Practical Handbook* (2nd edn), London: Continuum, Thomson.

Snaith, T. and Haley, A. (1999) Residents' Opinions of Tourism Development in the Historic City of York, England. *Tourism Management* 20(6), 595–603.

Stevenson, D. (2003) *Cities and Urban Culture*. Maidenhead: Open University Press.

Stuart-Hoyle, M. and Lovell, J (2006) Liberating the Heritage City in *Cultural Tourism in a Changing World* (2006) Smith, M. and Robinson, M. (eds) Channel View: Clevedon, England.

Swarbrooke, J. (2002) Heritage Tourism in the UK – A Glance at Things to Come. Future for... *Insights* London: ETC, May, D35–48.

Wieting, S. (2000) Twilight of the hero in the Tour de France. *International Review for the Sociology of Sport*, 35(3), 348–363.

Yellow Book (2005) *Canterbury City of Imagination*. Canterbury: Canterbury City Council.

Yeoman, M. et al. (2004) *Festival and Events Management, An International Arts and Culture Perspective*. Oxford. Elsevier Butterworth Heinemann.

Chapter 19

Towards Safer Special Events: A Structured Approach to Counter the Terrorism Threat

Alexandros Paraskevas

Introduction

Connollystraße 31, Munich. On the doorway of the building there is a stone tablet with the inscription: 'The team of the state of Israel lived in this building during the XX Olympic Summer Games from 21 VIII to 5 IX 1972', and continues 'On 5 September, the following died a violent death', listing 11 athletes' names. Visitors and passers-by are encouraged to 'honour their memory'. The 5 of September 1972 may not be commemorated as much as the 11th of the same month 29 years later but it certainly started a new era for international terrorism: the era of targeting civilian special events.

   Several factors contributed to this change but the one cited the most is media coverage (see e.g. Jenkins, 1988, 2001). Alexander and Gleason (1981, p. 8) state that 'public perceptions of the level of terrorism in the world appear to be determined not by the level of violence, but rather by the quality of the incidents, the location, and the degree of media coverage'. Zedalis (2004) in her work on female suicide bombers contends that the media provides both an advertising and recruitment tool for terrorist groups. In a frightfully realistic analysis, Wilkinson (1990) argues that the saturation of the media with images of terrorist atrocity has raised the bar on the level of destruction that will attract headline attention. Moreover, he notes a shift from the politically minded terrorist to the vengeful and hard-line fanatic, concluding that civilian soft targets involve lower risk to terrorists. These gruesome observations are amply supported by terrorist attacks over the past years in sporting events (e.g. the Centennial Park bombing during the Atlanta Olympics, USA, 1996), cultural events (the Yosakoi-Soran festival bombing in Sapporo, Japan, 2000), theatrical events (e.g. the Dubrovka theatre siege in Moscow, Russia, 2002), rock concerts (the suicide bombings at the Krylya rock festival outside Moscow, Russia, 2003), amusement park shows (the Lumbini Amusement Park bombing in Hyderabad, India, 2007), conferences (the Intercontinental Hotel bombing in Athens on the eve of the Economist conference, Greece, 1999) or even wedding dinners (the Radisson SAS Hotel suicide bombing in Amman, Jordan, 2005). The common denominator for all these attacks was the

International Perspectives of Festivals and Events
Copyright © 2009 by Elsevier Ltd.
All rights of reproduction in any form reserved.
ISBN: 978-0-08-045100-8

purpose to inflict massive and indiscriminate civilian casualties, maximise the psychological impact of the attack and garner international media attention.

In spite of special events' high risk to become terrorist targets, the relevant literature is scant and normally addresses more general security and safety issues from a risk management perspective (e.g. Berlonghi, 1990; Bowdin et al., 2006; Tarlow, 2002) or from an impact on attendees perspective (e.g. Boger et al., 2005; Taylor and Toohey, 2006; Toohey et al., 2003). This chapter will first explore the nature of the events industry and the reasons why it attracts terrorist groups in conjunction with terrorist motivations and purpose and then propose a structured approach to counter-terrorism planning to be used as a guide by event planners and other event stakeholders.

Why Can a Special Event Become a Terrorist Target?

The Events Management literature defines special events as 'one-time or infrequently occurring events outside the normal programme or activities of the sponsoring or organising body' (Getz, 1994, p. 4). Under this term, Goldblatt (2005) classifies special events in:

- *Civic events* that can be centennials, sesquicentennials and bicentennials of cities and towns or celebrations rooted in long-standing religious, cultural and ritual traditions.
- *Expositions/exhibitions and trade shows*, which are events allowing retailers meet wholesalers or suppliers to introduce their goods and services to buyers.
- *Fairs and festivals*, which are public community events symbolised by a kaleidoscope of experiences comprised of performances, arts and crafts demonstrations and other media that bring meaning to the lives of participants and spectators.
- *Hallmark events*, also known as 'mega-events', which are a one-time or recurring events of major proportions, such as the Summer or Winter Olympic Games, the National Football League Super Bowl or other event projects of similar size, scale, scope and budget.
- *Meetings and conventions/conferences.*
- *Retail events*, which are events combining a live event with advertising, publicity and sales promotions.
- *Social life-cycle events*, such as weddings, anniversaries, funerals and reunions.
- *Sports events*, single or multiple games/matches (tournaments) combined with activities (such as pre-game giveaways, post-game fireworks, musical shows and trivia contests) that attract, capture and motivate spectators, regardless of the game's outcome, to keep supporting their favourite team.

These special events potentially carry with them great economic, social and political symbolism and consequently become for terrorists 'too valuable to be left unexploited' (Sönmez et al., 1999, p. 5). Terrorist attacks targeting such events generate media attention, inflict massive casualties, maximise economic impact and build coalition support for their cause. Thus, all the above types of events could be considered potential strategic terrorist targets and go through a rigorous evaluation towards this end. Looking, therefore, at special events from a counter-terrorism perspective, the definition of a special event could be modified to:

> A significant domestic or international event, occurrence, circumstance, contest, activity, or meeting, which by virtue of its profile and/or status represents an attractive target for terrorist attack.
>
> (McGee, p. 18).

In order to view a special event from a terrorist perspective, one needs to understand why this event is likely to become a terrorist target and this requires a broad understanding of what terrorism is and what are the motives of a terrorist.

Terrorism as a concept has for long been the subject of academic debate and often controversial, especially with regards to who is a terrorist and who is a freedom fighter, what acts and behaviours – depending on their legality and morality – can be labelled as terrorist and how state and non-state terrorism can be distinguished (see e.g. Chomsky, 2001; Lizardo and Bergesen, 2003; Schweitzer, 2002). In one of the first detailed analysis of the term, Schmid and Jongman (1988) list no less than 109 different definitions of terrorism with five common elements emerging with greater than 40% mentioning frequency: violence or force (83.5%); political (65%); fear or terror (51%); threat (47%) and psychological effects and anticipated reactions (41.5%). These common elements have led more recent scholars towards a kind of consensus on the definition of terrorism. For example, Ruby (2002, p. 10–11) isolates five defining criteria: motivation for the terrorist act (political or other), target towards which it is directed (non-combatants), actors (sub-national groups or clandestine agents), objective (creation of a fearful state of mind) and intended audience (larger than the immediate victims). Enders and Sandler (2002) use the very same criteria when they offer the following definition:

> Terrorism is the premeditated use or threat of use of extranormal violence or brutality by subnational groups to obtain a political, religious, or ideological objective through intimidation of a huge audience, usually not directly involved with the policy making that the terrorists seek to influence.

> Enders and Sandler (2002, p. 145–146).

A special event, whether it is a World Cup or a rock concert, lends itself for the use or threat of use of extranormal violence based on political, social or religious motives, as the resulting violence is clearly different from crime, personal vengeance or the act of someone mentally deranged. Although terrorist actions may seem irrational or delusional to the wider society, terrorists in fact act rationally, and there is no evidence to indicate that they are mentally ill/disordered or otherwise psychologically abnormal. Their carefully planned and executed actions are not typical of mentally disordered persons (Sageman, 2004). Zinaida Aliyeva and Zalikhan Elikhadzhiyeva have been recorded in the history as 'shahidkas', the Russian female derivative of the Arab word 'shahid' which is equivalent to 'martyr'. They both blew themselves up on 5 July 2003 at the Krylya rock festival in the north-western outskirts of Moscow killing 20 and injuring at least 60 bystanders. A crowd of around 40,000 people were attending this festival. Their plan was to enter separately the main festival area and detonate their 'shahid' belts, each containing the equivalent of one pound of TNT stuffed with screws and nails, to cause maximum casualties. They approached the crowded entrance of the Vuishevii Market next to the Tushino airfield (where the festival was taking place). Zinaida bought a ticket at a nearby clothes market and was pushing her way through the entrance queue when police officers, screening concert goers with a portable metal detector, spotted her and tried to lead her away. When she realised she had been caught, she detonated her belt. However, only a third of the explosives detonated, killing only herself and injuring three people. Zalikhan, who still was in the ticket queue, 100 metres away, remained there for about 15 minutes and when the crowd was substantial again she exploded her own belt killing 15 bystanders and injuring more than 60. Terrorists are motivated by their own personal agendas which may stem from completely different political, religious and psychosocial experiences such as strongly perceived oppression, humiliation or persecution, an extraordinary need for collective vengeance or a drive for expression of intrinsic aggressiveness (Victoroff, 2005). They rationalise their atrocities on moral ground as they believe that their actions are defensive, they are saving themselves from the great evil and they are compelled to commit their violence (Goertzel, 2002). Zinaida fitted perfectly the profile of the classic Chechen 'black widow' seeking to avenge the killing of her husband by Russian troops whereas Zalikhan was just a village girl who broke the moral rules of her strict religious community by running away with her stepbrother and was looking for her family's forgiveness (Paton-Walsh, 2003; Saradzhyan, 2004).

The crowd that a special event gathers allows also the attack to be directed towards non-combatants or civilians and is 'random,' so that everyone feels at risk. On 9 November 2005, three hotels (Radisson SAS, Hyatt and Days Inn) in Amman were attacked by suicide bombers killing 60 people and injuring about 115 others. More than half of those killed in the attacks were Jordanians. Six Iraqis, two Bahrainis and one Saudi Arabian also were among the dead. The deadliest of the three attacks was in the Radisson SAS hotel where two suicide bombers – a husband and a wife team – entered the Philadelphia Ballroom, where a Jordanian-Palestinian wedding reception with more than 250 guests was taking place. They were both appropriately dressed for the wedding but in the crucial moment the female suicide bomber, Sajida al-Rishawi, was unable to detonate her vest. Her husband Ali al-Shamari, pushed her out of the ballroom and jumped onto a dining room table detonating his two vests, one with ball bearings and the other with 22 pounds of the explosive RDX. Amongst the 38 people killed in the explosion, were the fathers of the bride and groom. Sajida, who was arrested later, was identified as the sister of three Iraqi men who were killed by US forces, one of whom allegedly was Al-Zarqawi's lieutenant (Eddy, 2005; Macintyre, 2005). The terrorist act itself intended to punish the Westerns and the 'corrupted' Muslims all over the world, not the victims themselves. An Al-Qaeda manifesto issued after the attack characterised the targeted hotels as a 'secure place for the filthy Israeli and Western tourists to spread corruption and adultery at the expense and suffering of the Muslims in these countries' (Fox News, 2005). It is a common practice for terrorists to absolve themselves from blame because they are performing a violent act for a superior cause and often under the auspices of a God (Piven, 2002). In order to explain to the Muslim world why these 'holy warriors' targeted hotels in an Arab capital resulting to the death of 57 Muslims, Al-Qaeda claimed that they have 'struck only after becoming confident that they are centres for launching war on Islam and supporting the Crusaders' presence in Iraq and the Arab peninsula and the presence of the Jews on the land of Palestine' (Fox News, 2005).

A special event can become a potential terrorist target for other reasons too. Tarlow (2002) notes that special events require a constant flow of attendees making it more difficult to identify any perpetrators among delegates, attendees, staff and volunteers. On the eve of the '3rd Economist Roundtable with the Government of Greece' conference, an annual event attended by Greek and foreign prominent personalities in politics and finance that was to be held in the Athens Intercontinental hotel (April 1999), a bomb exploded in the hotel killing 1 woman and injuring 1 man. 'Revolutionary Nuclei', the terrorist group that planted the bomb, had given warning about the bomb 30 minutes before the explosion (BBC News, 1999). The perpetrators allegedly entered the hotel premises dressed as gardening staff and planted the bomb in a flower pot next to a window. Tarlow (2002) also argues that special events are often organised close to major transportation centres, which will probably be disrupted by an attack thus causing even more panic (maximisation of psychological impact). So far, there are no examples of attacks to events taking place in such locations but there is a history of attacks targeting public transport systems (e.g. the sarin gas attacks carried out by the Aum Shinrikyo in the Tokyo subway system in March 1995, the bomb attacks in the Moscow Metro in

February 2004, the Madrid trains in March 2004, the London's underground and bus system in July 2005 and the suburban railway of Mumbai in July 2006), which makes such events even more vulnerable. Moreover, the event industry is so closely linked to other sectors of tourism such as restaurants, hotels and entertainment that a potential attack will cause widespread damage (maximisation of economic impact). A look at the impact of the 9/11 attacks on the United States and global tourism industry alone is enough to support Tarlow's views.

Counter-Terrorism Planning: A Strategic Approach

Although terrorism is unpredictable and depends on the smallest whim of individuals or loosely strung groups, special event planners need to take a strategic approach in ensuring the safety of all people that are part of the event, either attending or working for it, against a terrorist attack. They also have to convince insurers that they have taken all reasonable precautions against terrorists, in order to obtain a cancellation insurance policy. For example, AXA Colonia withdrew its cancellation insurance coverage of the 2002 FIFA World Cup due to huge losses imposed by the World Trade Centre attack and for two weeks the world was left in suspense about whether the World Cup was to happen at all (Croft and Hunt, 2001). The new insurers, National Indemnity, made sure that sufficient counter-terrorism measures were planned before offering a comprehensive cancellation insurance contract.

As every special event is different from another, planners can not assume a position of 'one recipe against a terrorist attack'. Rather, they need to go through the motions of developing counter-terrorist (CT) plans and measures for every new special event they are planning considering a multiplicity of factors and weighing these factors in light of the event's current circumstances as well as its past history. Figure 19.1 offers a structured approach that will help event professionals achieve this task.

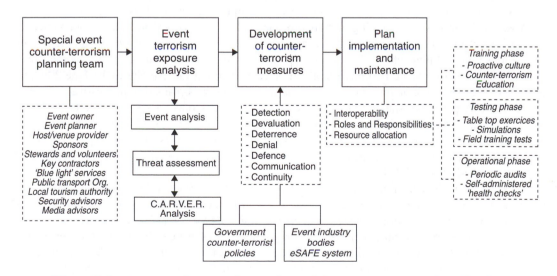

Figure 19.1: A structured approach towards special event counter-terrorism planning.

The Counter-Terrorism Planning Team

The complexity of the task dictates that CT plans are developed in coordination with all the special event stakeholders as different stakeholders will have different contributions in the various parts of the planning. These stakeholders will be:

> Groups or individuals who are affected or could be affected by an event's existence. Primary stakeholders are those individuals or groups without whose support the event would cease to exist. Secondary stakeholders are those groups or individuals who although are not directly involved in the event can seriously impede the event's success.
>
> Reid and Arcodia (2002, p. 492).

The primary stakeholders of a special event would be the *event owner* (private or public governing body of the event), the *event planner* (organisation in charge to plan and deliver the event) and the *host* (venue provider or country/city authorities hosting the event). The boundaries between these three types of stakeholders are often blurred as more often than not; the event owner is also the planner and/or the host. These stakeholders are also the primary decision-makers about every aspect of the event as they are the main budget holders for it. Their sensitivity and commitment towards CT measures will greatly influence the planning process and the decisions made by the group. Increasing importance as primary stakeholders have also the *sponsors* of the event (depending on their level of sponsorship) as the success of the event largely affects their return on sponsorship investment. Sponsors may act as a pressure group in taking extra CT measures for an event and in most cases require the existence of an event cancellation insurance contract prior to engaging in any sponsorship.

Other primary event stakeholders are the *stewards and volunteers*. One or more representatives from these stakeholder groups should be asked to participate in the CT planning team, as their vigilance and cooperation will be crucial for the successful implementation of measures. In the case of the Yosakoi-Soran Festival bombing, in Sapporo, Japan, it was the complete lack of communication between event planners and volunteers that resulted in the serious injury of one volunteer and the less serious injury of nine others. The Yosakoi-Soran Festival, which is held every June, attracts more than 40,000 participants and two million attendees each year. On the evening of 10 June 2000, the organisers received an anonymous email warning that a bomb was planted at the festival site. Half-trained security personnel started searching the vast area of the Odori Park (where the festival takes place) without alerting the hundreds of volunteers working for the festival. The bomb, consisting of a paper bag packed with gunpowder and nails, was detonated in the hands of an unsuspected 19-year-old male festival volunteer, Tomohiro Yasuda, who tried to move a paper cup that had been placed on an ash tray stand (Anon., 2000).

Secondary stakeholder groups that should also be included in the CT planning team would normally be *key event contractors*, the *'blue light' services* (police, fire and emergency services) and representatives from the *public transport organisations* and *the local tourism authority*.

The presence of one or more *security advisors* in this team is critical. People with expert knowledge and access to sensitive intelligence can make all the difference in the CT planning of a special event. For example, the organising committee of the Athens 2004 Olympics, although it had its special Olympic Games Security Division, invited and received advice in a regular basis from the

Olympics Advisory Group, a seven-nation (USA, Israel, UK, France, Spain, Germany and Australia) intelligence task force with extensive expertise in security planning of large sport events (Maditinos et al., 2006).

A recent development in terms of expert security and safety knowledge and advice is the eSAFE online system, developed by the National Laboratory for Tourism and eCommerce at Temple University (Philadelphia, USA), which offers to events professionals a common platform in which they can search, share, renew and reuse one another's knowledge and expertise to promote and facilitate safer and more secure event planning. The eSAFE system consists of three major components: (a) the Knowledge Base – a comprehensive warehouse of general security/safety knowledge for event planners consisting of expert publications; (b) the eSAFE Advisor – a guide that helps event planners narrow down their searches on particular security/safety aspects relevant to their event and (c) the ExpertNet which allows the user to connect with a community network of experts who are qualified event professionals and individuals who are recognised as experts in security/safety issues (Hu et al., 2006).

Media advisors would also be significant contributors especially in the planning of a communication strategy with regards to the planning teams' activities and decisions. Providing the media with carefully selected information about a special event's CT measures sends to terrorist groups a strong signal that the chances of success are slim (Kam, 1988, p. 233) and can, therefore, be a serious deterrent of terrorist attacks.

Terrorism Exposure Analysis

The first task of the CT planning team will be to assess the special event's exposure to a terrorist attack. There are many factors that will influence the team's evaluation of the event, starting with the type and size of the event itself, the possible threats to the event, that is the form that a terrorist attack could take in the event, its criticality as an event and its vulnerability to specific forms of terrorist attack. In order to address this task the team needs to go through three main steps: event analysis, threat assessment and criticality/vulnerability assessment.

In order to conduct an *event analysis*, the team needs to collect and share information about the particular features of the special event, so that a clear picture of how the event will be run and what are the security challenges that will be faced before, during and after the event's completion. This is the step where the team will appreciate the level of resources that are needed for the event's CT security. The features that normally shape the CT strategy for a special event are:

1. *Event size and venue*: The size and relative geographical dispersion of an event is an important consideration when determining resource requirements. Stadia and arenas will have different CT requirements from a theatre or a convention centre and from open spaces where festivals are taking place. The venue itself may be an attractive stage for a terrorist group to make its statement.
2. *Duration*: Events that last longer will have higher resource requirements than those who last one or half a day.
3. *Location and politics*: The state of political affairs at the location where the event will be organised, the current domestic and global terrorist activity levels, previous acts of terrorism in the region, threats or activities associated with the event or similar events need to be considered in order to realistically assess the danger of a terrorist attack.

4. *Attendance*: Events with high attendance, usually in confined spaces, are more likely to become targets of terrorists due to the increased number of casualties that could be inflicted. Such events provide an inviting target for various weapons of mass destruction.
5. *Dignitaries*: Special events normally draw government officials and celebrities from around the world. These people attract terrorist groups because of who they are, what they represent or simply because they are famous.
6. *Significance*: Several special events have a historical, religious, political or other symbolic significance attached to them, which increases their exposure to potential terrorist attack.
7. *Media coverage*: The greater the national or international significance of the event, the higher its media coverage will be. Terrorists are attracted by live media coverage as it represents an excellent opportunity to make their statement to a wide audience.

The next step at this juncture is an assessment about whether a range of terrorist threats pose a risk to the special event. This *threat assessment* will incorporate the knowledge gathered in the previous step into an understanding of the who, what, where, when and how of terrorist groups that may threaten the special event. In order for the CT planning team to evaluate the extent of terrorist threat posed to the special event they will then need to consider whether there are terrorist groups that would be attracted by the event and are able to gain access to it. These terrorist groups' capability to carry out an attack as well as their mode of operation (MO) have also to be taken into consideration.

Special events have been targeted with various terrorist modes of operation (MOs). In the 1972 Munich Olympics attack, the terrorists used *automatic weapons and grenades*. This MO has been replaced mainly by bombs that cause indiscriminate casualties. *Improvised explosive devices* (IEDs) such as the nail bomb in Sapporo and the vests suicide bombings in Moscow and Amman described above are the most common methods for terrorists to attack special events. Another method that is quite commonly employed to attack buildings, such as hotels and possibly convention centres or other closed special event venues (no incident of such an attack reported yet), is the use of large trucks or cars as *vehicle-borne improvised explosive devices* (VBIEDs or 'car bombs'). Examples of such types of attacks are the JW Marriott Hotel bombing, in Jakarta, Indonesia (5 August 2003) that killed 12 people and injured over 150 and the even more destructive Taba Hilton bombing, in the Sinai peninsula, Egypt (7 October 2004) where a truck driven into the hotel lobby exploded, causing the collapse of 10 floors of the hotel and leaving 31 people dead and 159 injured. *Fire bombs* are more popular with eco-terrorists and animal rights activists and usually aim at asset destruction rather than casualties. From 1998 to 2001, terrorists (allegedly members of the Earth Liberation Front) launched a series of attacks on tree farms and botanical research centres in Oregon and Washington, using fire bombs out of gasoline, road flares, batteries and digital timers (Taylor, 2006). The attack in the main terminal building at Glasgow Airport in June 2007 can be considered as a combination of the above MOs. Special events can also be used by terrorists for *hostage-taking* as exemplified by the Dubrovka Theatre siege in Moscow in October 2002, when 40 Chechen terrorists fully armed and with explosives strapped to their bodies took the 800–900 audience and cast of the Nord–Ost musical as hostages and threatened to kill them all unless Russian forces withdrew from Chechnya. The siege ended two days later when the Russian special forces (OSNAZ) stormed the theatre, having pumped a paralysing gas into the building's ventilation system. All the terrorists were shot dead and at least 129 hostages died – most of them from the effects of the gas, which hospitals couldn't treat because its composition was not classified (Dunlop, 2006). In October 2006, a threat of a plot to detonate seven 'dirty bombs' outside NFL stadiums – including venues located in Miami, New York, Atlanta, Houston, Oakland and Seattle – was deemed by the FBI as not credible. The threats have been posted on a website called 'The Friend Society' in a post called 'New Attacks on America: Be Afraid' and were later proved to be a hoax. (CNN, 2006) However, the threat of a terrorist attack with use of *radiological dispersal devices* (RDDs, the technical term for 'dirty bombs') is always existent. In November 1995, Chechen militants planted, but did not detonate, an RDD in Moscow's Izmailovo Park. The bomb consisted of dynamite and caesium-137 removed from a cancer treatment equipment. Reporters were tipped-off by the terrorists themselves about its location and it was defused (Vladykin, 2006). This incident illustrated that the possibility of such an attack is more than just theoretical. RDDs are combining radioactive materials with explosives in a bomb that aims more at creating panic and fear, disrupt economic and social activity of the affected area (as it may be contaminated for a long for months or even years) and long term rather than immediate casualties (Medalia, 2004).

After considering all these factors, the CT planning team will be able to assess the overall criticality of the event as well as its vulnerability to the threats identified above. This assessment will 'not only [be] used to determine what dangers to prepare for and how to meet them, but also to prioritize preparedness efforts' (Sauter and Carafano, 2005, p. 338). A systematic approach to this assessment can be through the use of C.A.R.V.E.R., a military targeting methodology developed by the US Special Forces for rating the relative desirability of potential targets (from the attacker's perspective) and for properly allocating attack or defence resources (Masse et al., 2007). The *C.A.R.V.E.R. analysis* criteria of criticality, accessibility, recuperability, vulnerability, effect and recognisability provide a framework for the special event evaluation as potential terrorist groups' targets.

The *criticality* of a special event can be assessed by considering its importance relative to other special events, the group of people potentially at risk and its political, economic and socio-cultural significance. A scale from 1 to 5 (raging from negligible to extreme) can be used to measure this criterion. A rating of 1 can be assigned to an event of a local or regional nature, a rating of 3 to the Super Bowl and a rating of 5 to International Monetary Fund/World Bank meetings or the Olympic Games.

The *accessibility* of a special event is rated by considering the ease with which the event can be reached, either physically or by stand-off fire. An event is deemed highly accessible when a perpetrator can physically infiltrate the perimeter of the event, or if the event can be attacked by direct or indirect methods. Factors that need to be taken into account in this criterion are the ease of infiltration/exfiltration, the perpetrators survival potential, the security situation en route to and at the event venue and the need for barrier penetration at the event venue. The possible use of stand-off weapons such as VBIEDs should also be considered when evaluating accessibility. The rating scale here can be: (1) very difficult to gain access; (2) difficult to gain access; (3) accessible; (4) easily accessible outside/internal security strong; (5) easily accessible/internal security weak.

Recuperability is an important criterion in the case of special events in closed venues such as convention centres, stadia and arenas, theatres or hotels. It is important to estimate how long it will take the host to repair, replace or bypass the damage inflicted by a terrorist attack. Recuperability will vary depending on the age and architectural complexity of the venue and with its redundant capabilities of space usage. The rating scale for this criterion can range from (1) easily replaced in a short period of time to (5) extremely difficult to replace.

The *vulnerability* of a special event and the venue in which it is taking place depends on the means (both organic personnel and material) and expertise the terrorists need to have to carry out the attack. This criterion is strongly correlated with weaknesses in physical structures, personnel protection systems, processes or other areas that may be exploited by terrorists. This assessment is crucial for the development of the CT measures needed to prevent or mitigate a terrorist attack. The rating scale for this criterion can range from (1) very low vulnerability to (5) very high vulnerability.

The *effect* of a possible attack considers not only public reaction in the vicinity of the special event venue, but also the domestic and international reaction as well. The rating scale for this criterion can range from (1) unfavourable social impact to (5) favourable social impact.

The criterion of *recognisability* refers to the degree to which an event has an 'icon status' for the wider society. Eric Robert Rudolph, for example, chose the 1996 Olympics in Atlanta and the Centennial Park in particular as the target in order to 'confound, anger and embarrass the Washington government in the eyes of the world for its abominable sanctioning of abortion on demand' (Copeland, 2005).

By performing the event analysis, the terrorist threat analysis and following the C.A.R.V.E.R. methodology the CT planning team can effectively identify the event's exposure levels to a terrorist attack and consequently develop appropriate CT measures for the event.

Development of Counter-Terrorism Measures

The measures to be developed must draw on the policy-making, risk, safety, security, intelligence and counter-terrorism expertise of the CT planning team and should aim at both prevention and mitigation of a terrorist attack targeting the special event. These measures should not only conform to the central government's (e.g. Department of Homeland Security) generic security and CT guidelines but also take into consideration the particular characteristics of the event as well as the results of its exposure to terrorist attack analysis. These measures may be physical, technological or operational but they will all aim to satisfy the 4D2C (devalue, deter, deny, defend, communicate, continue) principle of counter-terrorism planning (Grosskopf, 2004, Paraskevas and Arendell, 2007).

To *devalue* the special event is to lessen its significance and make it a less interesting target for terrorists. This can be achieved by making every possible effort to conceal vulnerable functions that may have emerged during the C.A.R.V.E.R. analysis, eliminating the use of hazardous materials and minimising to the best possible degree large assemblies of people in unprotected areas (e.g. queue management).

To *deter* a terrorist attack is to create a perception of unacceptable risk to those planning a terrorism attack, by increased security personnel and target hardening strategies (e.g. visible security presence, un-patterned security sweeps, use of technology for access control, surveillance, lighting and communications).

To *deny* is to prevent the access of both perpetrators and their resources to destinations, attractions and specific destination target assets. Physical measures such as landscape barriers, shapes and spatial arrangements that create controlled access and enhance visibility of potential intruders, stricter identity control of contactors and volunteers, attendee behavioural profiling, continuous monitoring of parking and peripheral areas and use of Automatic Number Plate Recognition (ANPR) can be quite effective towards this end.

To *defend* the special event is to take all those strategic and tactical/operational measures that should be in place to protect the participants of an event, in case that the means to devalue, deter and deny a terrorist attack fail to absolve the threat. Crowd control and evacuation plans, emergency services ingress and egress, specific situation handling contingencies (hostage situation, VBIED attack, suicide bombing, armed attack, etc.) fall into this group of measures.

Communicate stands for all types of CT-related communication, both internal (between all the event stakeholders) and external (media markets and other event organisers). As mentioned earlier in this chapter, carefully selected information on security measures and levels should be regular in order to reinforce the notion a more proactive stance of CT preparation and prevention. A number of communication programmes, such as a dedicated webpage in the event owner's website, e-newsletters, local newspaper articles and flyers, will raise awareness among stakeholders and the wider community.

Finally, to *continue* means to have in place all those plans and measures that will ensure that all event stakeholders are able to cope with an incident or attack and return to normality as soon as possible. The speedy resumption of the event's planned activities and the safety of participants and staff should be central in these measures. Event planners should make sure to extend their business continuity measures throughout their supply chains to ensure continuity of the event in case of any disruption (terrorism-related or not).

Plan Implementation and Maintenance

The implementation of the CT measures that were decided in the previous stages will largely depend on how committed are the various stakeholders to the special event security and safety. This commitment will primarily influence the resource allocation for the security of the event: Greece, for example, spent US\$1.2 billion (3 times more than Sydney 2000) for the Athens 2004 Olympics and Beijing is more likely to top this amount for the 2008 Olympics (Lei et al., 2005). The budget is usually managed by the event owner and allocated based on the event's criticality and identified vulnerabilities. Another important factor is the event stakeholders' interoperability, that is, their ability to be flexible in their cooperation and to speak the 'same language' across the board. Normally, as the CT measures and plans are crafted by all event stakeholders they will usually be acceptable by all parties involved and it will be more probable for them to adhere to their implementation throughout the event. The CT planning team will have to define clear roles and responsibilities for the various stakeholders. The plan implementation can be divided into three distinct phases: training, testing and operational.

In the training phase, implementation to successfully embed a proactive culture at all levels of the event stakeholders and in their day-to-day 'business as usual' ethos. The role of event staff (stewards) and volunteers in the successful implementation of CT plans is of paramount importance here and the main responsibility for educating them and raising CT awareness lies not only with the event planner but also with the rest of the event stakeholders. McGee (2006) emphasises the 'train-the-trainer' concept which advocates expert training of the planner's staff, will then transfer this training to the host organisation and the volunteers. He argues that this training phase should take place quite a lot of time prior to the event to allow more emphasis on stakeholder CT exercises that are very important in testing both event-specific CT knowledge and capabilities.

The testing phase, involves exercises that can be conducted in a variety of formats and that will assist with focusing on specific areas of preparedness and response. These exercises will enable the CT planning team to assess its ability to coordinate the response to a terrorist attack, verify critical security-related operational and technological functionality across the event venue, exercise communication and interoperability skills, increase staff's awareness of the CT plan and engage all involved stakeholders in a competence and capability self-assessment. Exercises may range from a table top exercise to a simulation or a full-scale field training exercise in coordination with the local authorities and the emergency services.

- The *table top exercise* (TTX) allows the event stakeholders to meet in one location and openly discuss the variables and options available in response to a number of different scenarios. Often, when the CT planning team is not as confined to only primary stakeholders and advisors, a TTX is the first opportunity for them to meet with the secondary stakeholders (key event contractors, police, fire and emergency services, representatives from the public transport organisations and the local tourism authority), to discuss a coordinated response to a terrorist attack and compare approaches, operating procedures and tactics.
- A *terrorist attack simulation* (TAS) provides an opportunity for the event team (owner, planner, host, staff and volunteers) to practice the execution of the CT activities focusing on one or more aspects of the plan. The TAS can combine both a simulation and an actual execution of the CT plan activities and can reveal valuable information about the performance of the various teams involved as well as any weaknesses and gaps in the tested aspects of the CT plan. In the aftermath of 9/11 and the war in Afghanistan, for example, Japan as a co-host of the 2002 Football World Cup carried out 15 TAS around the 10 cities. Most of these simulations took place in football stadiums, trains, event halls and other public facilities and involved mainly CBRN (Chemical, Biological, Radiological, Nuclear) terrorist attacks where the key players involved had to find, verify and decontaminate agents. Other roles involved coordination to cordon, rescue and bring victims to relevant medical facilities (Abhayaratne and Ackerman, 2004). Similar exercises were undertaken in the nine German states hosting the 2006 Football World Cup, undergoing however heavy criticisms from disaster management experts, such as Professor Wolf Dombrowsky of the University of Kiel, for not including all event stakeholders and the wider public, noting that entire French villages underwent such simulations before the 1998 World Cup (MSNBC, 2006).
- The *field training exercise* (FTX) activates all the components of the CT plan (what Dombrowsky suggested above) and it is the best means to evaluate CT plans prior to the event. Unlike the TAS, this exercise is larger in scope with a scenario that will closely portray a terrorist attack and will involve all event stakeholders performing actual operations and activities as specified in the CT plan (first responders, medical facilities testing mass casualty contingencies, expertise testing in handling a suicide bombing, a VBIED or a 'dirty bomb', etc.). The FTX validates all aspects of CT response and requires a significant commitment by the participating event stakeholders to adequately test their relevant capabilities.

The operational phase is the final phase of the CT plan implementation and covers the period immediately prior to and during the actual event. McGee (2006) argues that success during this phase depends largely upon solid relationships and mutual trust developed during the training and exercise phases between the various event stakeholders. Periodic checks and self-administered 'health checks' will ensure the appropriate implementation of the CT measures agreed.

Conclusion

As discussed earlier in this chapter, special events have all the features that make them ideal targets for people who seek to take advantage of others for political and other ideological ends, inflict maximum damage and promote their cause. The events industry exists to facilitate people celebrate all aspects of life, spiritual, material, social, cultural or, in one sentence, what Sofield and Li (1998) say when they talk about the 800-year-old Chrysanthemum Festival in China: '…[to express] both thanks for past prosperity and hopes for future wealth' (p. 277). For this celebration of life itself, people gather in crowds in open-air (parades, fairs and festivals) or closed venues (sports arenas, university or college campuses, corporate facilities, office complexes, art galleries, music halls and theatres) exposing themselves and the event organisers to risk. Event professionals become increasingly aware of this fact and engage in a wide range of risk management activities, which lead to measures that ensure the security and safety for event participants and staff. However, for the foreseeable future, the threat of a terrorist attack during a special event will always be there no matter what the level of preparedness from the side of the event stakeholders is.

This chapter presented a framework for special event counter-terrorism planning which offers event planners a structured approach to undertaking this task. A joint intelligence process from all event stakeholders is the foundation of this framework. However, a note of caution is needed here as all threat assessments and event criticality/vulnerability evaluations will always be highly subjective, assume intimate knowledge and understanding of terrorist groups and an abundance of accurate information about the event, the venues and the potential perpetrators. More often than not, these conditions are not entirely fulfilled and the results of the whole process will be far from being perfect. Nevertheless, the industry experience of counter-terrorism planning is continually growing with the help of governmental and non-governmental experts and wider industry initiatives such as the eSAFE system are positive steps towards ensuring events that are safe for both attendees and organisers.

References

Abhayaratne, P. and Ackerman, G. (2004) Manned gaming and simulation relating to terrorism and weapons of mass destruction: A review of the literature, The WMD Terrorism Research Project, Chemical and Biological Weapons Non-proliferation Program (CBWNP), Center for Non-proliferation Studies, Monterey Institute of International Studies, CA, online: http://www.dtra.mil/documents/asco/publications/MannedGamingWCover Summary.pdf, accessed 28 June 2007.

Alexander, Y. and Gleason, J. M. (eds.) (1981) *Behavioral and Quantitative Perspectives on Terrorism*. New York: Pergamon Press.

Anon. (2000) Police examine nail-bombing site. *The Japan Times*, Tuesday 13 June, online: http://search.japantimes.co.jp/member/nn20000613a7.html, accessed 15 June 2007.

BBC News (1999) Bomb rips through Greek hotel. *News. BBC. co.uk*, Wednesday, April 28, online: http://news.bbc.co.uk/2/hi/europe/330024.stm, accessed 17 June 2007.

Berlonghi, A. (1990) *Special Events Risk Management Manual: The Definitive Text in Safety, Security and Risk Management for Events*. Dara Point, CA: Berlonghi Publishing.

Boger, C. A., Varghese, N. and Rittapirom, S. (2005) The impact of the September 11 attacks on airline arrivals and conventions in nine major U.S. cities. *Journal of Convention and Event Tourism*, 7(2), 21–41.

Bowdin, G., Allen, J., O'Toole, W., Harris, R. and McDonnel, I. (2006) *Events Management* (2nd edn). Oxford: Butterworth-Heinemann.

Chomsky, N. (2001) U.S. – A leading terrorist state. *Monthly Review*, 53, 10–19.

CNN (2006) Feds: Threat against NFL stadiums not credible. *CNN.com*, Thursday 19 October, online: http://www.cnn.com/2006/US/10/18/football.threats/index.html, accessed 17 June 2007.

Copeland, L. (2005) Olympics bomber apologizes, but not to all victims. *USA Today*, Monday 22 August, online: http://www.usatoday.com/news/nation/2005-8-2-rudolph-sentencing_x.htm, accessed 15 March 2007.

Croft, J. and Hunt, B. (2001) AXA terminates insurance for 2002 World Cup. *Financial Times*, Friday 12 October, online: http://www2.assinews.it:443/rassegna/articoli/arc/ft131001axa.html, accessed 15 June 2007.

Dunlop, J. B. (2006) *The 2002 Dubrovka and 2004 Beslan Hostage Crises: A Critique of Russian Counterterrorism*. Stuttgart: ibidem-Verlag.

Eddy, C. (2005) *Analysis: Amman, Jordan, Suicide Bomb Attacks at Three Hotels*. Manhattan, NY: Center for Policing Terrorism, online: http://www.cpt-mi.org/pdf_secure.php?pdffilename = JordanHotelBombings2005, accessed 22 June 2007.

Enders, W. and Sandler, T. (2002) Patterns of transnational terrorism, 1970–1999: Alternative time-series estimates. *International Studies Quarterly*, 46, 145–165.

Fox News (2005) Al Qaeda Addresses Muslim Deaths. *FOXNews.com*, Thursday 10 November, online: http://www.foxnews.com/story/0,2933,175235,00.html, accessed 14 March 2007.

Getz, D. (1994) Event tourism: Evaluating the impacts. In Ritchie, J. R. B. and Goeldner, C. R. (eds.), *Travel, Tourism, and Hospitality Research: A Handbook for Managers and Researchers* (2nd edn). New York: Wiley, pp. 437–450.

Goldblatt, J. (2005) *Special Events: Event Leadership for a New World* (4th edn). New York: Wiley.

Goertzel, T. G. (2002) Terrorist beliefs and terrorist lives. In Stout, C. E. (ed.), *The Psychology of Terrorism: Theoretical Understandings and Perspectives*, I. Westport, CT: Praeger, pp. 97–111.

Grosskopf, K. R. (2004) *Strategies to Devalue, Deter, Deny and Defend (D4) Terrorist Targets: A Study of Physical, Psychological and Operation Methods to Protect Buildings and Critical Infrastructure*. University of Pittsburgh: Center for National Preparedness.

Hu, C., Racherla, P. and Singh, N. (2006) Developing a knowledge-based system using domain-specific ontologies and experts: The eSAFE case study for the event management. In Hitz, M., Sigala, M. and Murphy, J. (eds.), *Information and Communication Technologies in Tourism: Proceedings of the ENTER 2006 International Conference in Lausanne*. Switzerland, Vienna: Springer, pp. 273–284.

Jenkins, B. M. (1988) Future trends in international terrorism. In Slater, R. O. and Stohl, M. (eds.), *Current Perspectives on International Terrorism*. London: Macmillan, pp. 246–266.

Jenkins, B. M. (2001) Terrorism and beyond: A 21st century perspective. *Studies in Conflict and Terrorism*, 24, 321–327.

Kam, E. (1988) *Surprise Attack: The Victim's Perspective*. Cambridge, MA: Harvard University Press.

Lei, L., Zhou, R. and Jing, L. (2005) Firms eye 2008 Olympic security budget. *China Daily*, Thursday 12 May, online: http://www.ebeijing.gov.cn/News/LocalNews/t20050512_234591.htm, accessed 22 April 2007.

Lizardo, O. and Bergesen, A. J. (2003) Types of terrorism by world-system location. *Humboldt Journal of Social Relations*, 27, 162–192.

Macintyre, D. (2005) Failed bomber tells of attack on hotel in televised confession. *The Independent*, Monday 14 November, online: http://news.independent.co.uk/world/middle_east/article326901.ece, accessed 14 March 2007.

Maditinos, Z. J., Vassiliadis, C. and Charlebois, S. (2006) Mega Events: Challenges for Contingency Planning, Opportunities for Tourist Promotion. Paper presented in the International Conference of Trends, Impacts and Policies on Tourism Development, Hellenic Open University, Heraklion, Crete, Greece 15–18 June, online: http://tourism-conference.eap.gr/pdf%20files/Maditinos,%20Z.J.,%20Vassiliadis,%20C.%20&%20Charlebois,%20S.pdf, accessed 18 May 2007.

Masse, T., O'Neil, S. and Rollins, J. (2007) *The Department of Homeland Security's Risks Assessment Methodology Evolution, Issues, and Options*. Washington, DC: Congressional Research Service, Library of Congress, online: http://www.fas.org/sgp/crs/homesec/RL33858.pdf, accessed 8 July 2007.

McGee, J. A. (January 2006) International special events. *The FBI Law Enforcement Bulletin*, 10–18.

Medalia, J. (2004) Terrorist 'Dirty Bombs': A Brief Primer. Congressional Research Staff Report for Congress. Order Code RS21528 , April 1, online: http://www.fas.org/spp/starwars/crs/RS21528.pdf, accessed 23 May 2007.

MSNBC (2006) Germany not ready for terror, expert says. *msnbc.com*, Tuesday 4 April, online: http://www.msnbc.msn.com/id/12152310/

Paraskevas, A. and Arendell, B. (2007) A strategic framework for terrorism prevention and mitigation in tourism destinations. *Tourism Management*, 28, 1560–1573.

Paton-Walsh, N. (2003) The day suicide bombers came to a Moscow rock concert-and left 20 dead. *The Observer*, Sunday 6 July, online: http://observer.guardian.co.uk/international/story/0,6903,992421,00.html, accessed 22 April 2007.

Piven, J. S. (2002) On the psychosis (religion) of terrorists. In Stout, C. E. (ed.), *The Psychology of Terrorism: Theoretical Understandings and Perspectives*, III. Westport, CT: Praeger, pp. 120–147.

Reid, S. and Arcodia, C. (2002) Understanding the role of the stakeholder in event management. In Jago, L., Deery, M., Harris, R., Hede, A. and Allen, J. (eds.), *Conference Proceedings of Events and Place Making*. Sydney: UTS Australian Centre for Event Management, pp. 470–515.

Ruby, C. L. (2002) The definition of terrorism. *Analyses of Social Issues and Public Policy*, 2(1), 9–14.

Saradzhyan, S. (2004) Summer suicide bombers were society outcasts. *The St. Petersburg Times*, Tuesday 10 February, online: http://www.sptimes.ru/index.php?action_id = 2&story_id = 12249, accessed 22 April 2007.

Sageman, M. (2004) *Understanding Terror Networks*. Philadelphia: University of Pennsylvania Press.

Sauter, M. A. and Carafano, J. J. (2005) *Homeland Security: A Complete Guide to Understanding, Preventing, and Surviving Terrorism*. New York, NY: McGraw Hill.

Schmid, A. P. and Jongman, A. J. (1988) *Political Terrorism: A New Guide to Actors, Authors, Concepts, Data Bases, Theories and Literature* (revised edn). New Brunswick, NJ: Transaction Books.

Schweitzer, G. E. (2002) *A Faceless Enemy: The Origins of Modern Terrorism*. New York: Perseus.

Sofield, T. H. B. and Li, F. M. S. (1998) Historical methodology and sustainability: An 800-year-old festival from China. *Journal of Sustainable Tourism*, 6(4), 267–292.

Sönmez, S. F., Apostolopoulos, Y. and Tarlow, P. (1999) Tourism in crisis: Managing the effects of terrorism. *Journal of Travel Research*, 38(1), 13–18.

Tarlow, P. (2002) *Event Risk Management and Safety*. New York: Wiley.

Taylor, J.M. (2006) Six suspects arrested for string of eco-terrorist attacks. *Environment News*, Wednesday 1 February 1, online: http://www.heartland.org/Article.cfm?artId = 18443, accessed 27 July 2007.

Taylor, T. and Toohey, K. (2006) Impacts of terrorism-related safety and security measures at a major sport event. *Event Management*, 9(4), 199–209.

Toohey, K., Taylor, T. and Lee, C.-K. (2003) The FIFA World Cup 2002: The effects of terrorism on sport tourists. *Journal of Sport and Tourism*, 8(3), 186–196.

Victoroff, J. (2005) The mind of the terrorist: A review and critique of psychological approaches. *Journal of Conflict Resolution*, 49(1), 3–42.

Vladykin, O. (October 2006) A terrorist's dream: Are the world's radioactive materials safely stored? *The Moscow News*, 48, online: http://english.mn.ru/english/issue.php?2006-48-10, accessed 12 May 2007.

Wilkinson, P. (1990) Terrorist targets and tactics: New risks to world order. *Conflict Studies*, 236, 7.

Zedalis, D. D. (2004) *Female Suicide Bombers*. Honolulu, HA: University Press of the Pacific.

Index